Time for a Visible Hand

The Initiative For Policy Dialogue Series

The Initiative for Policy Dialogue (IPD) brings together the top voices in development to address some of the most pressing and controversial debates in economic policy today. The IPD book series approaches topics such as capital market liberalization, macroeconomics, environmental economics, and trade policy from a balanced perspective, presenting alternatives, and analyzing their consequences on the basis of the best available research. Written in a language accessible to policymakers and civil society, this series will rekindle the debate on economic policy and facilitate a more democratic discussion of development around the world.

OTHER TITLES PUBLISHED BY OXFORD UNIVERSITY PRESS
IN THIS SERIES

Fair Trade for All
Joseph E. Stiglitz and Andrew Charlton

Economic Development and Environmental Sustainability
Ramón López and Michael A. Toman

Stability with Growth
Joseph E. Stiglitz, José Antonio Ocampo, Shari Spiegel,
Ricardo Ffrench-Davis, and Deepak Nayyar

The Washington Consensus Reconsidered
Narcis Serra and Joseph E. Stiglitz

Capital Market Liberalization and Development
José Antonio Ocampo and Joseph E. Stiglitz

Industrial Policy and Development
Mario Cimoli, Giovanni Dosi and Joseph E. Stiglitz

Time for a Visible Hand

Lessons from the 2008 World Financial Crisis

Edited by
Stephany Griffith-Jones, José Antonio Ocampo,
and Joseph E. Stiglitz

OXFORD
UNIVERSITY PRESS

OXFORD

UNIVERSITY PRESS

Great Clarendon Street, Oxford OX2 6DP

Oxford University Press is a department of the University of Oxford.
It furthers the University's objective of excellence in research, scholarship,
and education by publishing worldwide in

Oxford New York

Auckland Cape Town Dar es Salaam Hong Kong Karachi
Kuala Lumpur Madrid Melbourne Mexico City Nairobi
New Delhi Shanghai Taipei Toronto

With offices in

Argentina Austria Brazil Chile Czech Republic France Greece
Guatemala Hungary Italy Japan Poland Portugal Singapore
South Korea Switzerland Thailand Turkey Ukraine Vietnam

Oxford is a registered trade mark of Oxford University Press
in the UK and in certain other countries

Published in the United States
by Oxford University Press Inc., New York

© Oxford University Press 2010

The moral rights of the authors have been asserted
Database right Oxford University Press (maker)

First published 2010

British Library Cataloguing in Publication Data

Data available

Library of Congress Cataloging in Publication Data

Data available

Typeset by SPI Publisher Services, Pondicherry, India
Printed in Great Britain
on acid-free paper by
Clays Ltd., St Ives Plc

ISBN 978–0–19–957880–1 (Hbk)
    978–0–19–957881–8 (Pbk)

1 3 5 7 9 10 8 6 4 2

Acknowledgments

The book is the outcome of the research of a task force on Financial Market Regulation of the Initiative for Policy Dialogue (IPD) at Columbia University, directed by Stephany Griffith-Jones, José Antonio Ocampo, and Joseph Stiglitz. IPD is a global network of over 250 economists, researchers, and practitioners committed to furthering understanding of the development process. We would like to thank all task force members, whose participation in provocative dialogues and debates on financial market regulation informed the content of this book.

We gratefully acknowledge the contributions of the authors. In addition, we acknowledge the dedication of IDP staff members Sarah Green and Farah Siddique, who helped organize task force meetings and coordinated the various stages of production of the book. Our thanks also to former staff member Ariel Schwartz and IPD interns Alexander Berenbeim, Sarah Bishop, Vitaly Bord, John Conway Boyd, Eduardo Gonzalez, Kevin E. Jason, Emily-Anne Patt, and Kohei Yoshida.

We thank our editor Sarah Caro and the staff of Oxford University Press for bringing this book into publication.

We are most grateful to the Brooks World Poverty Institute and the Ford Foundation for funding the meeting of the IPD Task Force on Financial Market Regulation, out of which this book was conceived. Finally, we acknowledge the John D. and Catherine T. MacArthur Foundation, the Rockefeller Brothers Fund, and GTZ for their generous support of IPD's work.

Contents

List of Figures

List of Tables

Contributors

Yilmaz Akyüz was the Director of the Division on Globalization and Development Strategies at the United Nations Conference on Trade and Development (UNCTAD) until his retirement in August 2003. He was the principal author and head of the team preparing the Trade and Development Report, and UNCTAD coordinator of research support to developing countries (the Group-of-24) in the IMF and the World Bank on International Monetary and Financial Issues. He is now Special Economic Advisor to South Centre, an Intergovernmental Think Tank of the Developing Countries, based in Geneva.

Gerard Caprio is Professor of Economics at Williams College and Chair of the Center for Development Economics there. From 1998 until January 2006, he was the Director for Policy in the World Bank's Financial Sector Vice Presidency. He served as Head of the financial sector research team in the Bank's Development Research Group from 1995–2003, and previously was the Lead Financial Economist there.

Fernando J. Cardim de Carvalho is a professor of economics at the Institute of Economics at the Federal University of Rio de Janeiro. A former chairman of the National Association of Graduate Schools of Economics of Brazil, he has done consulting work for, among others, the National Development Bank of Brazil, the National Association of Financial Institutions of Brazil (ANDIMA), CEPAL, G-24 and NGOs like Ibase (Brazil), Action Aid USA and WEED (World Economy, Ecology and Development—Germany).

Jane D'Arista is an economic analyst with the Financial Markets Center. She has written on the history of US monetary policy and financial regulation, international and domestic monetary systems and capital flows to emerging economies. She has served as a staff economist for the US Congress and lectured in graduate programs at Boston University School of Law, the University of Massachusetts at Amherst, the University of Utah and the New School University.

Roberto Frenkel is Principal Research Associate at CEDES and Professor at the University of Buenos Aires. Presently he is also Director of the Graduate Program on Capital Markets (University of Buenos Aires) and teaches graduate courses at the Di Tella and FLACSO—San Andrés Universities in Argentina and University of Pavia in Italy.

Charles Goodhart, CBE, FBA is a member of the Financial Markets Group at the London School of Economics, having previously (1987–2005) been its Deputy Director. Until his retirement in 2002, he had been the Norman Sosnow Professor of Banking and Finance at LSE since 1985. Before then, he had worked at the Bank of England for seventeen years as a monetary adviser, becoming a chief adviser in 1980. In 1997 he was appointed one of the outside independent members of the Bank of England's new Monetary Policy Committee until May 2000.

Bruce Greenwald currently serves as the Robert Heilbrunn Professor of Asset Management and Finance at Columbia University's Graduate School of Business. He is an authority on value investing with additional expertise in productivity and the economics of information. In addition, he consults world-wide on a variety of issues concerning capital markets, business strategy, corporate finance and labor performance. Prior to Columbia, Professor Greenwald taught as a professor at the Harvard Business School and Wesleyan University.

Stephany Griffith-Jones is Financial Markets Director at the Initiative for Policy Dialogue at Columbia University, and was Professorial Fellow at the Institute of Development Studies. She has published widely on the international financial system and its reform.

Jan Kregel is a senior scholar and Director of the Monetary Policy and Financial Structure program at the Levy Economics Institute of Bard College, and currently holds the position of Distinguished Research Professor at the Center for Full Employment and Price Stability, University of Missouri—Kansas City and Professor of Development Finance at the Tallinn University of Technology, Estonia. He was formerly Chief of the Policy Analysis and Development Branch of the United Nations Financing for Development Office and Deputy Secretary of the UN Committee of Experts on International Cooperation in Tax Matters.

Perry G. Mehrling is Professor of Economics at Barnard College, Columbia University where he has taught since 1987. His research interests lie in the monetary and financial dimensions of economics, a field he approaches from a variety of methodological angles. His most recent book is Fischer Black and the Revolutionary Idea of Finance (Wiley 2005).

José Antonio Ocampo is Professor at Columbia University, teaching in its School of International and Public Affairs, and a Fellow of its Committee on Global Thought. He is a member of the UN Commission of Experts on Reforms of the International Monetary and Financial System. He is former Under-Secretary-General of the United Nations for Economic and Social Affairs, former Executive Secretary of the UN Economic Commission for Latin America and the Caribbean, and former Minister of Finance, Agriculture, and Planning of Colombia.

Avinash Persaud's career spans finance, academia and public-policy in London and New York. He is currently Chairman of Intelligence Capital, a financial consultancy and a member of the board of three investment boutiques. Previously, he was Managing Director, State Street Corporation; Global Head, currency and commodity research, J. P. Morgan; and Director, fixed income research, UBS.

Martin Rapetti is a research associate at the Centro de Estudios de Estado y Sociedad (CEDES), Buenos Aires and a PhD candidate at the University of Massachusetts, Amherst. He is interested in macroeconomics, development, finance and Latin American economics.

Y. V. Reddy served for five years as the Governor of Reserve Bank of India and retired on September 5, 2008. He is currently Emeritus Professor in University of Hyderabad. Prior to being the Governor, he was Executive Director at the International Monetary Fund since August 2002. Prior to this, he was Deputy Governor, Reserve Bank of India. Formerly, he was Secretary, Ministry of Finance, and Additional Secretary, Ministry of Commerce in the Government of India. He served Government of Andhra Pradesh, India in several capacities. He was also advisor in World Bank. He was recently elected as Honorary Fellow of the London School of Economics and Political Science.

Joseph E. Stiglitz is University Professor at Columbia University, teaching in its economics department, its business school, and its School of International and Public Affairs and chairman of its Committee on Global Thought. He chaired the UN Commission of Experts on Reforms of the International Monetary and Financial System, created in the aftermath of the crisis by the President of the General Assembly. He is former chief economist and senior vice-president of the World Bank and Chairman of President Clinton's Council of Economic Advisors. He was awarded Nobel Memorial Prize in Economics in 2001.

Philip Turner has been at the Bank for International Settlements (BIS) since 1989. He is at present Head of Secretariat Group in the Monetary and Economic Department, responsible for economics papers produced for central bank meetings at the BIS. His main area of research interest in an earlier position at the BIS was financial stability in emerging markets and he has written on banking systems and on bank restructuring in the developing world. Between 1976 and 1989, he held various positions up to Head of Division in the Economics Department of the Organisation of Economic Co-operation and Development (OECD) in Paris. He holds a PhD from Harvard University.

Marion Williams is Governor of the Central Bank of Barbados, a position which she has held since 1999. She is a fellow of the Institute of Bankers (FCIB) of the UK, and a certified management accountant (CMA). She was the first President and a founding member of the Barbados Institute of Banking and Finance. She is a former chairman of the Steering Committee of the Caribbean Regional Technical Assistance Centre (CARTAC) and Chairman of the Executive Committee of the Caribbean Centre for Monetary Studies (CCMS). She received a national honor of Gold Crown of Merit by the Government of Barbados in 2006.

Acronyms

ABS	asset-backed securities
ACT	Association of Corporate Treasurers
ADB	Asian Development Bank
AFL-CIO	American Federation of Labor and Congress of Industrial Organizations
AFTE	Association Française des Trésoriers d'Entreprise
AIG	American Insurance Group
APEC	Asia-Pacific Economic Cooperation
ASBA	Association of Supervisors of Banks of the Americas
BCBS	Basel Committee on Banking Supervision
BFS	Board for Financial Supervision
BIS	Bank of International Settlements
bp	basis points
BoP	balance of payments
CDO	Collateralized Debt Obligations
CDS	credit default swap
CESR	Committee on European Securities Regulation
CGFS	Committee on the Global Financial System
CIC	China Investment Corporation
CPSS	Committee on Payments and Settlement Systems
CRAs	credit ratings agencies
CRAAC	Credit Rating Agency Assessment Center
CRD	Capital Requirements Directive
ECB	European Central Bank
EMBI	Emerging Markets Bond Index
EME	emerging market economies
ERISA	Employee Retirement Income Security Act
FASB	Financial Accounting Standards Board
FATF	Financial Action Task Force
FD	fiscal deficit
FDI	foreign direct investment

FDIC	Federal Deposit Insurance Corporation
Fed	Federal Reserve
FHA	Federal Housing Administration
forex	foreign exchange
FSA	Financial Services Authority
FSAP	Financial Sector Assessment Program
FSF	Financial Stability Forum
FSI	Financial Stability Institute
GRF	Global Reserve Fund
GSE	government-sponsored enterprise
HIPC	Heavily Indebted Poor Countries
HLCCM	High Level Committee on Capital and Financial Markets
HLI	highly leveraged institutions
IAIS	International Association of Insurance Supervisors
IASB	International Accounting Standards Board
ICT	Information and Communication Technologies
IFRS	International Financial Reporting Standards
IIF	Institute for International Finance
IMF	International Monetary Fund
IOSCO	International Organization of Securities Commissions
IRB	Internal Ratings Based
LIBOR	London Inter-Bank Offer Rate
LOLR	lender of last resort
LTCM	Long-Term Capital Management
MBS	mortgage-backed securities
NASDAQ	National Association of Securities Dealers Automated Quotations
NBFC	non-banking financial company
NDR	aggregate demand for addition to reserves
NFS	net foreign surplus
NGS	net government savings
NIE	newly industrialized economy
NPS	net private savings
NRSROs	nationally recognized statistical rating organizations
OECD	Organisation for Economic Co-operation and Development
OFI	other financial institutions
OIS	overnight indexed swaps

Acronyms

OTC	over the counter
PD	probability of default
PDCF	primary dealer credit facility
QDII	qualified domestic institutional investor
QFII	qualified foreign institutional investor
RBI	Reserve Bank of India
RER	real exchange rates
RMBS	Residential Mortgage Backed Securities
ROA	return on assets
ROSC	Report on Observance of Standards and Codes
SDRs	Special Drawing Rights
SEC	Securities and Exchange Commission
SIV	structured investment vehicle
SLF	short-term facility
SPE	special purpose entity
SRO	self-regulating organization
SWF	Sovereign Wealth Funds
TAF	Term Auction Facility
TALF	Term Asset-backed Securities Loan Facility
TARP	Troubled Assets Relief Program
TSLF	Term Security Lending Facility
UNCTAD	United Nations Conference on Trade and Development

1

Introduction

Stephany Griffith-Jones, José Antonio Ocampo, and Joseph E. Stiglitz

The world financial meltdown of 2008 has shattered into pieces the sophisticated but conceptually hollow premise on which the framework of self-regulating markets had been built. The dominance of this conceptual apparatus in recent decades has left, as its legacy, the worst global financial crisis since the Great Crash of 1929, the worst recession since the Second World War and a collapse of international trade. As a result, the world is also experiencing a mounting social crisis, reflected in particular in escalating unemployment and underemployment, and significant reductions in the value of pension funds. The developing world, which had been experiencing in recent years one of its best growth records in history, has also been dragged into the crisis.

Financial crises are not new, and the growing financial market liberalization since the 1970s has led to a good number of them. The United States itself has experienced three of them: the banking crisis generated by excessive lending to Latin America (usually not recognized as a US banking crisis, as it was Latin America that at the end paid a heavy price—a "lost decade" of development), the savings and loan crisis of the late 1980s, and the 2008 financial crisis. It has also recorded major stock market crashes, such as Black Monday in October 1987 and the collapse of Information and Communication Technologies (ICT) stocks in the early 2000s. Many industrial countries have also undergone financial crises in recent decades—Japan being the most noteworthy case— and, of course, the developing world has experienced an unfortunate record number of them. However, the depth of the 2008 crisis and its worldwide systemic implications are unique and present major policy and conceptual challenges.

This book aims to look at these challenges, with a particular emphasis on policy implication. It is the outcome of a seminar organized in July 2008 by the Initiative for Policy Dialogue of Columbia University and the Brooks World Poverty Institute of the University of Manchester, and part of a research project supported by the Ford Foundation. At the time of the Manchester seminar, the crisis was well underway, but the financial meltdown that followed the collapse of Lehman Brothers in mid-September 2008 had not taken place, nor had the government and central bank activism in industrial countries that subsequently followed. At that point, some, including many in the US Administration, thought that the world had "turned a corner." But we were convinced even then that matters were likely to get worse, and that we should begin thinking more deeply about the causes of the crisis, what should be done in response, and what to do to prevent a recurrence. The papers prepared for the initial conference have been significantly updated to reflect the events and policy decisions between the time of the conference and March 2009, when the manuscript was sent to the publisher.

The book is divided into four parts. The first part looks at the causes, magnitude, and broad policy implications of the US financial crisis. It underscores both the distinctive aspects of the current crisis, as well as the "universal constants" behind all crises that have also been reflected in the current one. It also explores whether the current attempt at re-regulating finance (the third in the US since the late nineteenth century) will be more capable of providing durable financial stability. A final chapter in this section explores the macroeconomic response to the crisis, as well as the management of foreclosures and the financial rescue packages.

The second section focuses on regulatory reforms, both national and international. After looking at the broad principles that should underlie a new and more effective system of financial regulation, different authors look in detail at the mechanisms of massive expansion of central bank liquidity, the broad principles for an effective financial regulation, specific key aspects of regulation relating to rating agencies and credit default swaps, and appropriate institutional frameworks.

The third section focuses on developing economies, in a sense, the innocent victims of the current turmoil. It first looks at the management of capital flows in Asia and afterwards at the lessons that can be drawn from the experience of a highly successful country, India. It then explores recent changes in the global financial system and their effects on developing countries, through both the capacity to maintain competitive exchange rates and the accumulation of international reserves as a preventive device.

The final section explores broader issues of international monetary reform, with particular emphasis and specific proposals on the reform of the global reserve system. Two parallel chapters propose an entirely new system that would overcome the problems of the current dollar-based system by creating a global reserve currency. It is an old idea—Keynes proposed a global reserve system some seventy-five years ago—but as the March 2009 Report of the UN General Assembly Commission on Reforms of the International Monetary and Financial System has underscored, it is an idea whose time has come.

Our book thus attempts to draw on our analysis of the 2008 crisis to make a fairly comprehensive and ambitious set of policy proposals in the fields of national and global regulation, national macroeconomic management, and reform of the world monetary system. At the time of sending the book to press, debates on national and global policy responses were quite active, including on the initiatives launched by the Group of Twenty (G-20) during their April 2009 London meeting. Some interesting initiatives have been put forth, such as the renewed issuance of Special Drawing Rights (SDRs), and steps towards better international regulation, with emphasis on both more comprehensive regulation and the adoption of the principle of counter-cyclicality. However, many concerns remained as to the adequacy of the fiscal stimulus throughout the world and the unsettled position of banks in industrial countries, but particularly in the US. We hope this book will contribute to the ongoing dialogue on a better design of policies that will replace the ones that have failed in the past.

The crisis in the United States

As highlighted by Stiglitz in Chapter 2, the global financial crisis is distinctive in its origins, its magnitude, and its consequences. Stiglitz examines the failures that led to the crisis and, in particular, the important role played by information and incentives problems. On the basis of this diagnosis, the author provides recommendations on how to reform financial regulation to prevent future crises.

The crisis provides a wonderful case study in the economics of information. Stiglitz illustrates how the models—those used explicitly by or implicit in the mind of both regulators and market participants—ignored the imperfections and asymmetries of information. Since incentives mattered, distorted incentives at both the individual and organizational level led to distorted behavior. These distorted incentives included executive compensation systems in banks, conflicts of interest in rating agencies, problems caused by the repeal of Glass-Steagall, moral hazard, the use of complexity to reduce competition and increase profit margins, as well as moral hazard problems created by securitization. While financial markets have changed markedly since the Great Depression, some of the underlying problems giving rise to crises remain the same—most notably excessive leverage.

On the basis of this diagnosis of what went wrong, Stiglitz suggests some regulatory reforms that will reduce the frequency and depth of such occurrences in the future. Regulatory reform is, however, not just a matter for the long term. This crisis is a crisis in confidence, and it is hard to restore confidence in the financial system if the incentives and constraints—which led to such disastrous outcomes—are not changed. The author lays out the principles of a good regulatory system. It should improve incentives for market actors and regulators, have better and more transparent accounting frameworks, and provide for adequate, counter-cyclical capital requirements. Stiglitz also calls for institutional innovations, such as a financial products safety commission—to ensure the safety, efficacy, and appropriate use of new financial products—and a financial markets stability commission, to oversee the overall stability of financial markets—ideas that have since come to become widely accepted.

Chapter 3 by Caprio argues that many of the features of the crisis are disturbingly familiar: they reflect "universal constants" of financial market behavior, particularly incentive systems that are conducive to excessive risk-taking and lax oversight by markets and supervisors alike. In the author's view, one of the major mistakes that authorities made was putting their faith in a static set of rules, ignoring the dynamics of the regulatory game—that is, the fact that any static set of rules will end up inducing innovations designed to evade the same rules.

According to Caprio, the goal of regulation should be a financial system that takes prudent risks in supplying a large volume of useful financial services efficiently, to the broadest part of society, and with the least corruption. A dynamic system has to have as many participants as possible, with the incentives to uncover new forms of risk-taking that would then compel supervisors to act. The supervisors' main job should be to require far greater information disclosure to the public and verify that it is not false or misleading. More comprehensive disclosure allows society to monitor supervisors and hold them accountable.

A critical ingredient in regulation is how firms compensate risk takers. The supervisory agency could give lower scores to firms that award more generous current compensation and high scores to those with a greater percentage deferred far out into the future. Regulation can also improve incentives by exposing to the legal system those who take excessive risk managing other people's money. Money managers should be asked to exercise the highest degree of fiduciary responsibility in line with their published objectives, and could face lawsuits for improper conduct, subject to the interpretation of the courts. The same legal liability that money managers face should be extended to those who rate firms, so raters should be compelled to publish more information about their ratings, and courts need to hold the principals of these firms liable for their pronouncements.

Chapter 4 by Kregel notes that the United States financial system is currently undergoing its third episode of major financial turmoil and response in the form of financial re-regulation. The first was the creation of the national bank system in the 1860s, the second was the New Deal legislation of the 1930s, and the third is that currently under way. The first two episodes produced similar responses and similar financial structures, and laid the basis for subsequent crises. Given the similarity of the present crisis with the two previous experiences, there is, therefore, the risk that the solutions introduced will in fact lay the groundwork for the next crisis.

Kregel emphasizes the fact that financial innovations have not only led to the co-mingling of commercial and investment banking, but also to a series of new institutions (hedge and private equity funds) that have taken on both traditional investment as well as commercial banking functions, but without the regulation of either. Some of the major implications of this are that there is no longer any precise relation between financial institutions and functions, and that regulated banks no longer are the primary source of system liquidity, and thus are no longer the major transmission mechanism of monetary policy. This implies that any attempt to re-regulate the US financial system must start from a decision to either re-impose this identity between institutions and functions, or to shift to a system based on functional regulation.

One way to see this is that the United States is facing its third try at deciding between a segmented or a unified banking system. Many European countries have had the latter for many years without the same experience of financial crisis. What have they done that is different? Germany provides a good example: it rejected separation of commercial and investment banks after its 1930s banking crisis and maintained universal banking. Regulators operate a system in which the bank's balance sheet is effectively split into short-term commercial banking activities requiring short-term maturity matching, and capital market activities requiring long-term maturity matching. This is the equivalent of extending commercial bank regulation to investment banks, yet recognizing that the regulations must differ. Interesting lessons can be applied to US regulation, recognizing, however, that these requirements have not sufficed to protect all German banks in the current crisis.

Entering into a more detailed analysis of policy responses, Stiglitz lays out in Chapter 5 four of the key aspects: monetary and fiscal policy, reducing the mortgage foreclosures, and financial sector restructuring. Keynes long ago recognized that monetary policy is typically ineffective in a downturn. He likened it to "pushing on a string." Interest rate reductions prevented a meltdown of the financial markets but were unable to reignite the economy. The burden must therefore shift to fiscal policy.

Given that the deficit soared since the early 2000s, it is especially important, in the author's view, that fiscal policy aim at as big a "bang for the buck" as possible. Increasing unemployment benefits rank high in this criterion; tax cuts rank low, other than for low income individuals. Noting that the US has one of the worst unemployment insurance systems among industrialized countries, strengthening it should be an important component of any American stimulus, not just because it is the right thing to do but because money received by the unemployed would be spent immediately and so would help the economy. A second criterion is that the money should create an asset, to offset the increased debt associated with the stimulus package. A third criterion is that any spending should be consistent with the country's long-term vision. Federal government support of research and development (R&D) to reduce its dependence on oil is an example of what should be included. Assisting the states and localities to make up for the shortfall in revenues and helping them address the striking inadequacies in infrastructure is another example. These investments, as well as those in education, would stimulate the economy in the short run and promote growth in the long run, far more than tax rebates would.

A major challenge is how to save the homes of the hundreds of thousands of those who otherwise would lose their homes, and not bail out the lenders. A novel proposal is a "Homeowners' Chapter 11"—a speedy restructuring of liabilities of poorer homeowners, modeled on the kind of relief for corporations that cannot meet their debt obligations.

Stiglitz argues that the downturn will be longer and deeper because of the failure of the Bush Administration to design a quick and effective response. In his view, the Obama Administration finally came up with a stimulus package that might work—but it was too little, and also had design problems. It came up with a mortgage restructuring program—but it too was too little, and not designed to address one of the key problems—that of mortgages that were underwater. But its real failure was its incapacity to come up with an effective program to restart lending. It focused on the past, dealing with the "legacy" assets, rather than looking forward. It may work, but as this book goes to press, it looks increasingly unlikely that this gamble will pay off—and the costs to the taxpayer will be high.

Reforming financial regulation

The second part of the book focuses on a detailed analysis of regulatory reform. In the first chapter of this section, Chapter 6, Turner examines the principles underlying central bank liquidity actions taken during the financial crisis. The toolkit of central banks has expanded dramatically. The author then poses some fundamental questions. Which measures should remain permanently in place? How could some of the dangers in this expansion of the role of central banks in markets be addressed?

A bigger toolkit always seems better, provided those using its potentially dangerous tools are fully cognizant of the attendant risks. Only central banks can provide the assurances of liquidity often needed in a financial crisis. In the extreme conditions prevailing in the latter part of 2008, it was natural that fighting the crisis received priority. Before this crisis, nobody expected the scale of operations central banks would be drawn into—and many of these operations will at some point have to be unwound. A lot of these measures, however, will probably be permanent. Turner suggests three areas where the changes decided on during this crisis are likely to endure: increased term financing, wider deposit arrangements at the central bank, and better cross border provisions of liquidity.

One danger, according to the author, is that highly visible central bank operations can distract attention from fundamental credit problems. Public confidence in banks holding large volumes of bad assets can be restored only by some form of government guarantee or by the government taking such assets off banks' balance sheets. It took the virtual seizure of credit markets in September 2008 to convince most governments of the need for an overall strategy to address this issue.

The international dimension of central bank policies has become essential because the largest banks are active in many jurisdictions. Recent central bank swap arrangements to address foreign currency funding difficulties were a very concrete manifestation of international central bank cooperation and, according to Turner, should endure.

D'Arista and Griffith-Jones emphasize, in Chapter 7, the seeming contradiction that the more liberalized the financial system is, the greater the need for more effective regulation, to avoid massive and costly crises. The chapter develops the two basic principles on which such future financial regulation should be based.

The first principle is counter-cyclicality. It aims to correct the main manifestation of market failures in banking and financial markets: their boom–bust nature. The key idea is that (forward-looking) provisions and/or capital required should increase as risks are incurred, that is when loans grow more, and fall when loans expand less. The application of this principle in Spain and Portugal shows that it is possible to design simple rules to make it effective.

The second principle is comprehensiveness. For regulation to be efficient, the domain of the regulator should be the same as that of the market that is regulated. In the United States, commercial banks represented before the crisis less than 25 per cent of total financial assets; furthermore, only a part of commercial banking activity was properly regulated, with off-balance sheet activities largely excluded. A system of regulation that focused only on parts of the banking industry and that regulated neither the rest of the banking system nor much of the rest of the financial system clearly did not work. The application of the principle of comprehensiveness thus requires that minimum liquidity and solvency requirements be established in an equivalent way for all financial activities, instruments, and actors.

Finally, D'Arista and Griffith-Jones agree with other authors in this volume that flawed incentives played a critical role in the crisis, and they propose modifying incentives for bankers and fund managers so these are compatible with more long-term horizons for risk-taking. This would break the current link to short-term profits, which encourages excessive short-term risk-taking and boom–bust behavior of financial markets. An easy solution would provide that any bonus would be accumulated in an escrow account. This could be cashed only after a period equivalent to an average full cycle of economic activity has taken place.

Persaud provides in Chapter 8 complementary analysis on the design of banking regulation and supervision in the light of the credit crisis. In the author's view, two fundamental flaws in financial regulation led to the biggest crisis of modern times. The first was to put market evaluations of risk at the heart of financial regulation, through external ratings and risk measures derived from market prices. The essential problem is that market prices may improperly evaluate risk in the presence of market failures. The second flaw was to assume that common standards, such as value-accounting and risk measures, are good and that diversity is bad, thus underestimating the advantages different players have to assume different risks.

Persaud proposes a model of banking regulation based on three pillars. The first will replace the notion of "risk sensitivity" with the concept of risk capacity, based on mark-to-funding. Independently of legal distinctions, regulation would focus, on one hand, on a capacity of different agents to absorb risks, and, on the other, on systemic risks. Those institutions with short-term funding, which have little capacity to hold market and liquidity risk, would be subject to a capital adequacy regime, based on short-term measures of value and risk, mark-to-market accounting, and high standards of transparency. This would be pro-cyclical, but it would be addressed explicitly by a counter-cyclical second pillar. Those institutions with long-term funding liquidity (like a traditional pension fund or endowment fund) would be exempt from the capital adequacy regime, but would adhere to a new "solvency regime" that allows institutions to use long-term measures of valuation and risk in determining and reporting their solvency. The quid pro quo of not being required to follow mark-to-market price and value systems is greater disclosure.

The second pillar of regulation would entail putting the credit cycle back at the heart of the capital adequacy regime rather than as an afterthought. Capital adequacy requirements should rise and fall with the overall growth in bank assets, with clear rules formulated perhaps in conjunction with the monetary authorities. Like several other authors in this volume, Persaud believes that this reform is essential.

The third pillar would be about maximizing transparency where it will benefit investor protection, with the constraint of not reducing heterogeneity in the behavior of all market participants. Indeed, the whole regulatory framework should seek to support the natural diversity in the financial system and should draw on the systemically beneficial role of risk absorbers—those that have a capacity to diversify risks across time.

Credit Rating Agencies (CRAs) have been regarded as one of the villains of the current financial crisis. Certainly they failed to predict the general downturn in US housing prices, but so did almost everyone else. Their high ratings allowed pension funds and others to provide money to the mortgage markets, through triple-A rated securities consisting of pieces of subprime mortgages. Not surprisingly, there have been calls for better regulated rating agencies.

Chapter 9 by Goodhart examines how, if at all, credit rating agencies should be regulated. The author argues that most proposed regulation of

CRAs is either useless or likely to be counterproductive. The CRAs were dragged into the broader regulatory framework (for example, Basel II) against their wishes and, perhaps, as the US Securities and Exchange Commission has suggested, they should now be removed from this role. Since CRAs are essentially forecasters, the author proposes a small, independent (but publicly funded) Credit Rating Agency Assessment Centre (CRAAC), paid by the industry, to provide a public evaluation of all the CRA forecasts.

More specifically, Goodhart suggests that all CRAs should be required to provide confidential details of their ratings in a numerically quantified format to the proposed CRAAC. This Centre would maintain *ex post* accountability of CRAs by comparing forecasts with outcomes and publish reports on comparative accuracy. CRA forecasts should have two numerical dimensions: central tendency, and a measure of uncertainty (forecast confidence), the latter perhaps being supported by a modest pre-commitment penalty. Conflicts of interest are an important concern. This can be handled by appropriate adjustment of the payment mechanism and by requiring all products to be rated by two or more CRAs.

One of the ways in which this crisis is different from all previous crises is the role played by new instruments, illustrated so forcefully by the bail-out of the American Insurance Group (AIG). AIG had provided credit default swaps (CDS) to many other financial institutions, and if AIG failed, there was a worry of a bankruptcy cascade, as those to whom it had provided "insurance" might also fail.

Based on the importance of CDS, Mehrling argues in Chapter 10 that the current crisis is best seen as the first test of the new system of structured finance. That test has revealed the crucial role played by credit insurance of various kinds, including CDS, for supporting both valuation and liquidity of even the top tranches of structured finance products. The various government interventions in 2008 amount, in his view, to the public sector going into the credit insurance business in response to the crisis—by either writing credit insurance or taking over insurance contracts written by others. The author calls this the "Paulson-Bernanke CDS put." In his view, a basic lesson of the crisis is that the government must be in the credit insurance business in normal times as well.

The problem with this form of intervention is that it is both too broad and too narrow, and both too temporary and too permanent. It is too broad insofar as it provides a floor under the value of portfolios containing a very wide range of securities, and too narrow insofar as it is focused on portfolios held by particular market participants rather than on the markets themselves. It is too temporary insofar as it envisions no continuing support for markets, and too permanent in that it envisions long-term government exposure to the referenced assets.

The underlying problem according to Mehrling is that the Fed is operating on the securities themselves, rather than on the relevant swap—no doubt as a result of the fear of supporting swaps that do not arise from any real funding operation. The author argues that there needs to be a recognition that swaps are here to stay and need their own discount facility. The key element of such a facility would be recognizing that the risk in the triple-A tranches of credit and their derivatives is not diversifiable: it is systemic risk. It follows that government involvement in credit insurance should focus here. It may be desirable to have a standing facility, with a rather wide bid-ask spread, thus making sure that insurance does not get too cheap, therefore facilitating an unsustainable credit expansion, but also that is does not get too expensive, therefore sparking a spiral in the other direction. The model, obviously, is the standing facility through which modern central banks provide liquidity to the money market.

The final chapter in this section, Chapter 11, by Williams, attempts to analyze the national and international financial governance systems, their strengths and weaknesses. A number of issues are explored and a number of recommendations made. The author does not call for a total revamp of the financial governance structure, but rather for a number of improvements, among them some dealing with the issue of legitimacy. It is also important, since some of these issues had been identified prior to the current difficulties, to ensure that systems and regulated entities accelerate their responses to the recommendations already available.

In particular, Williams emphasizes that serious institutional gaps have emerged, with no international financial institution having a clear mandate to require remedial regulatory measures when risks arise, especially from large countries like the United States. She argues for creating a multi-purpose regulatory oversight body. This could be based on the Financial Stability Forum (FSF), but it would require global representation and clear authority. A key issue would be defining a body that could develop how FSF recommendations would be implemented, with the Bank for International Settlements (BIS) being a good candidate once its membership is broadened. In contrast, she argues that, although the IMF may be well positioned to evaluate the feedback effects between financial system behavior and the macroeconomy, it is not clear that it is best positioned to set regulatory criteria. At a national level, Williams emphasizes the need for adequate regulatory mandates and information to provide policy-makers with enough tools to ensure financial stability, given increased inter-connection and internationalization of financial markets.

Developing country perspectives

Focusing in the next part on the crisis and developing countries, the first chapter, Chapter 12 by Akyüz, deals with the management of capital flows and financial vulnerability in Asia. There is a growing consensus that vulnerability of emerging markets to financial contagion and shocks depends largely on how capital inflows are managed, since options are limited during sudden stops and reversals. Vulnerabilities associated with surges in capital flows lie in four areas:

(i) currency and maturity mismatches in private balance sheets, especially of financial institutions; (ii) credit, asset and investment bubbles; (iii) unsustainable currency appreciations and external deficits; and (iv) reliance on help and policy advice from the IMF rather than self-insurance against sudden stops and reversals of capital flows. Crisis prevention should thus aim to prevent fragility in private balance sheets and external payments, to check financial and investment bubbles, and to build adequate self-insurance against reversal of capital inflows.

After a brief interruption, capital flows to emerging markets recovered strongly from the early 2000s, with Asia being among the main recipients. Asian policy-makers did not generally opt for tighter restrictions over capital inflows. In fact, Asian capital accounts are invariably more open today than they were during the 1997 crisis. Rather than applying tighter counter-cyclical restrictions over capital inflows, most countries in the region chose to relax restrictions over resident outflows and to absorb excess supply of foreign exchange by intervention and reserve accumulation. In this way, most of them successfully avoided unsustainable currency appreciations and accumulated substantial amounts of international reserves.

However, the Asian emerging market economies are now much more closely integrated into the international financial system than they were in the run-up to the 1997 crisis. Foreign presence in Asian markets has increased, as well as portfolio investment abroad by residents. This has resulted in greater fragility of the domestic financial system by contributing to asset, credit, and investment bubbles, and increased the susceptibility of the Asian economies to shocks and contagion from the current global financial turmoil. The combination of asset deflation with sharp drops in exports and consequent retrenchment in investment can no doubt wreak havoc in the real economy. This explains why the slump in industrial production in Asia during the 2008 crisis has been more significant and more rapid than in 1997–8.

Therefore, in Akyüz's view, Asia may have learned some of the wrong lessons from the last crisis. It improved domestic regulation and transparency, strengthened external payments, and accumulated large reserves. But its greater integration into the global financial system has meant that Asia has been exposed to greater risk, with little direct gain from access to more capital. More importantly, Asia allowed itself to be more integrated into the global financial system, without putting into place counter-cyclical regulatory mechanisms that would have provided protection against the vicissitudes of global financial markets. In a sense, policies pursued over the past decade made Asia's financial markets less vulnerable to the problems that afflicted the region a decade ago, but perhaps more vulnerable to the kind of shock that confronted the global economy in 2008.

Given his experience as Governor of the Reserve Bank of India, Reddy provides a practitioner's perspective in Chapter 13. The author highlights several broad issues which need to be kept in view while considering changes in the regulatory structures of developing economies. During a crisis, whatever has to be done must be done promptly, comprehensively, and effectively to bring stability. But in rewriting regulatory structures, some broader issues need to be considered. Most developing economies recognize the continuing need for reforms in their financial sectors. However, the crisis of 2008 raises doubts as to the efficacy of known and existing models of financial sectors in the advanced economies, particularly the Anglo-Saxon model. Thus, in the future, reforms in the financial sector may have to be cognizant of the evolving understanding of the subject, and hence gradualism commends itself.

In light of the recent experience with what may be termed as "excessive financialization of economies," the author poses several questions. Should there be a review of the sequencing and pacing of reforms in the financial sector relative to the fiscal and the real sectors in developing economies? In view of the observed volatility in capital flows and of commodity prices, how should the policies relating to the financial sector in developing economies provide cushions against such shocks? Reddy argues that the case for harmonized counter-cyclical policies (monetary, fiscal, and regulatory) in developing economies is stronger than for other countries due to the greater weight that needs to be accorded to stability. Specifically, he argues for measures such as those taken by the Reserve Bank of India to limit asset bubbles, via requiring banks to increase risk weights, make additional provisions, and impose quantitative limits on lending. This protected banks against a serious downturn in asset prices.

India also has developed institutional innovation by, for example, establishing a very effective Board for Financial Supervision within the Central Bank. Besides senior Central Bank officials, it has a number of eminent individuals, including some from civil society and the corporate sector.

Reddy also claims that financial inclusion should be at the center of any financial policy. This means ensuring access to all the relevant financial services to all sections of the population, but this should not be equated with aggressive lending or simple provision of micro-credit with profit-motive driving the process. In fact, experience with the 2008 crisis shows that those banks with significant retail base tended to be more resilient.

The remaining two chapters of this section also represent a bridge to some of the issues dealt with in the last part of the book. Frenkel and Rapetti argue in Chapter 14 that in the 2000s the emerging market economies found a new way to participate in the global financial markets. In their view, one of the most important aspects was the stronger emphasis on the relationship between foreign saving, reserve accumulation, and the effect of competitive real exchange rates (RER) on economic growth. The authors find major theoretical explanations and empirical support for the RER–growth link.

The current global financial and economic crisis has brought back the discussion about international financial architecture. The emerging debate has so far focused on the degree of regulation of global financial markets and potential reforms of multilateral financial institutions. These initiatives share the spirit of the proposals of the late 1990s and early 2000s, which were developed as a result of the crises in emerging markets economies. The proposals called for building institutions capable of preventing, managing, and compensating for the instability of the system. This agenda is still valid today. However, it should be broadened to take into account the lessons from the period 2002–8.

One important lesson underlines the key role of markets for developing countries' exports. The experience of financial globalization tells us that capital inflows and external savings are by no means substitutes for growth-cum-exports. Therefore, together with institutional reforms aimed at stabilizing the workings of the global financial system, developing countries should also call for a deeper reform, intended to consolidate the positive features of the 2002–8 configuration. For instance, they should pursue an international agreement on RER and exchange rate regimes that would lead to high growth rates.

One objection to the proposal of targeting competitive RER, current account surplus, and foreign exchange reserves accumulation is that it implies a fallacy of composition. Certainly, this kind of strategy cannot be followed by all countries at the same time. However, Frenkel and Rapetti simply interpret empirical evidence as suggesting that developed countries can best contribute to poor countries' development by providing markets for their (infant) products, instead of providing savings. A situation like this would certainly call for international coordination, in order to reach an agreement on RER levels among developing and developed countries, and avoid fallacy of composition effects.

Chapter 15 by Carvalho explores, in turn, the accumulation of international reserves as a defensive strategy, as well as the reasons and limitations of their "self-insurance" function. Conceptually, countries demand reserves of foreign currencies for a similar set of reasons to those which explain why individuals demand liquidity. However, while individuals hold liquid assets primarily to effect transactions, countries do it mostly for precautionary reasons. Again, as in the case of individuals, the stronger the demand for money, the harder it is to obtain liquidity in public sources and money markets.

The experience of emerging countries with balance of payments crises in the 1990s taught them that liquidity can be impossible to obtain during a crisis. The most important source, loans from the IMF, comes with a heavy price tag in the form of policy conditionalities. Therefore, in the 2000s, many emerging countries accumulated reserves as a precaution against new balance of payments crises. However, countries that accumulate reserves out of capital inflows are in a much more fragile position than those which obtain current account surpluses. In fact, countries suffering current account deficits become more and more vulnerable to changes in market sentiment and capital flow reversals. Besides, even when reserve accumulation is successful at making a country more secure, it may be deleterious to the international economy since money holding is fundamentally deflationary.

In conclusion, the chapter notes that international liquidity provision remains as important now as it was in the recent past. Carvalho argues that the best alternative would clearly be an international monetary system where a new international currency could be created according to global liquidity needs, as well as for emergency liquidity facilities to protect countries from adverse temporary external shocks. Both were features of the original Keynes plan at Bretton Woods. At a national level, Carvalho argues that, if the world monetary system is not appropriately reformed, the main alternative to reserve accumulation is capital controls.

Reforming the global monetary system

The final section of the book includes two parallel contributions on the reform of the international monetary system, particularly the global reserve system.

In the first of these chapters, Chapter 16, Ocampo argues that the current global reserve system exhibits three fundamental flaws. First, it shows the deflationary bias typical of any system in which all the burden of adjustment falls on deficit countries (the anti-Keynesian bias). Second, it is inherently unstable due to two distinct features: the use of a national currency as the major reserve asset (the Triffin dilemma) and the high demand for "self-protection" that developing countries face (the inequity-instability link). The latter is related, in turn, to the mix of highly pro-cyclical capital flows and the absence of adequate supply of "collective insurance" to manage balance of payments crises, which generate a high demand for foreign exchange reserves by developing countries. This implies, third, that the system is inequitable (the inequity bias), and that such inequities have grown as developing countries have accumulated large quantities of foreign exchange reserves.

In his view, the major deficiencies in the current system can only be solved through an overhaul of the global reserve system. The most viable is completing the transition that was launched in the 1960s with the creation of Special Drawing Rights (SDRs). This implies putting a truly global fiduciary currency at the center of the system, thus completing a trend towards fiduciary currencies that has characterized the transformation of national monetary systems over the past century.

Given the pro-cyclicality of finance towards developing countries, and the high demand for foreign exchange reserves that it generates, this has to be accompanied by reforms aimed at guaranteeing that SDR allocations are used to at least partly correct these problems, through either one or a mix of a series of alternatives. One would be tying the counter-cyclical issues of SDRs with IMF financing during crises, thus improving the provision of collective insurance.

This means that SDRs that are not used by countries should be kept as deposits in (or lent to) the IMF, so that they can be used by the institution to lend to countries in need. More ambitious alternatives would include an asymmetric issuance of SDRs, which would imply that all or a larger proportion of allocations be given to countries that have the highest demand for reserves—that is, developing countries—or designing other development links in SDR allocations—for instance, allowing the IMF to buy bonds from multilateral development banks. A final alternative is to encourage the creation of regional reserve arrangements among developing countries that provide complementary forms of collective insurance.

In the parallel chapter, Chapter 17, Greenwald and Stiglitz argue that an ideal system of international payments should be characterized by stability and balance: stability in exchange rates and the absence of sudden crises, and balance in the sense that individual national economies should suffer neither from deflationary effects of chronic external deficits nor the distorting consequences of chronic external surpluses. Both requirements are essential to the efficient international movement of goods and resources. Yet neither requirement appears to have been met by the current dollar-based reserve currency system. Recurrent crises in Asia, Latin America, and Eastern Europe, and chronic and growing US payments deficits (with their associated deflationary impact) are longstanding characteristics of the current system.

Looking at the global reserve system from the perspective of a global general equilibrium, Greenwald and Stiglitz argue that the increase in the demand for reserves—understandable from the perspective of self-insurance, as discussed in the chapters by Carvalho and Ocampo—leads to a deficiency in global aggregate demand. However, if some countries run surpluses, others must run trade deficits. This has been offset in recent years by the US spending beyond its means; in a sense the US became the consumer of last resort—but also the deficit of last resort. This system is fundamentally unsustainable.

The authors debunk the twin deficit theory of US trade deficits—that fiscal deficits are associated with trade deficits—by showing that the US ran trade deficits both when it had fiscal surpluses and when it had fiscal deficits. They then argue that, if anything, trade deficits may *cause* fiscal deficits; the deficiency in aggregate demand caused by imports in excess of exports "forces" governments concerned about maintaining full employment to run fiscal deficits. In this sense, the demand for reserves by developing countries generates an insufficiency of world aggregate demand that must be filled by a US trade deficit.

The authors argue that, without reform, these problems will continue to plague the global economy. The current move towards a two (or three) currency reserve system could be even more unstable than the dollar reserve system, which they suggest is already fraying. However, a simple set of institutional reforms which bear a striking similarity to those which Keynes cited in connection with the failure of the pre-Bretton Woods system would go a long way toward alleviating these difficulties. They show how such a system could be designed not only to reduce incentives for countries to accumulate reserves but also to provide finance for needed global public goods. The global system would be stable, more likely to remain near full employment, and more equitable.

Part I

The Crisis in the United States

2

The Financial Crisis of 2007–8 and its Macroeconomic Consequences[1]

Joseph E. Stiglitz[2]

The United States and Europe are now in the midst of a significant economic slowdown. It is imperative that we understand what has led to the problem, critical if we are to devise appropriate policy responses—including designing regulatory frameworks that make the recurrence of another such crisis less likely. The cumulative loss in output—the gap between what output would have been had there not been a crisis, and what is actually produced—will almost surely amount to in excess of several trillion dollars before the economy recovers.[3]

The analysis here is motivated in part by observations of a large number of banking crises, especially in developing countries. In many ways, this financial crisis has similarities to those earlier crises, though certain aspects of the resolution are markedly different. In my book *Roaring Nineties*, I provide an interpretation of the market scandals of the late 1990s and early years of this century. Here, I want to provide a similar interpretation of the 2007–8 crisis, a critique of the policy responses undertaken so far, and a set of proposals for the way forward. In my earlier work, I argued that information and incentive problems played important roles in the financial market scandals of the late 1990s. In this chapter, I want to show that they also have played an important role in the financial crisis of 2007–8.

Financial markets are supposed to allocate capital and manage risk. They did neither well. Products were created which were so complicated that not even those that created them fully understood their risk implications; risk has been amplified, not managed. Meanwhile, products that should have been created—to help ordinary citizens manage the important risks, which they confront—were not.

No one can claim that financial markets did a stellar job in allocating resources in the late 1990s—97 per cent of the investments in fiber optics took years to see any light. But at least that mistake had an unintended benefit: as the costs of interconnections were driven down, India and China became more integrated into the global economy. This time, there were some short-term benefits from the excess investments in real estate: some Americans enjoyed the pleasures of home ownership and lived in a bigger home than they otherwise would have—for a few months. But at what a cost to themselves and the world economy! Millions will lose their homes, and with that, their life savings. Meanwhile, as families are being forced out of their homes, the homes get trashed and gutted; in some communities, government has finally stepped in—to remove the remains. In others, the blight spreads, and so even those who have been model citizens, borrowing prudently and maintaining their homes, find market values depreciating beyond their worst nightmares.

US banks mismanaged risk on a colossal scale, with global consequences, and meanwhile, those running these institutions have walked away with billions of dollars in compensation. By some estimates, approximately 40 per cent of corporate profits in recent years have accrued to the financial sector. It has played an important role in providing finance to the truly innovative parts of the US economy, through venture capital firms, and these have been well rewarded for their services. But this is only a small part of the US financial system. From a systemic perspective, there appears to be a mismatch between social and private returns—and unless social and private returns are closely aligned, the market system cannot work well.

This chapter provides an analysis of *some* of the sources of the problem, and it provides a set of proposals for the design of a new regulatory framework, which will make the recurrence of such problems less likely in the future. A companion chapter (Chapter 5, Responding to the Crisis) provides a critique of current policy responses and suggestions for what *should* be done.

The source of the problem

Many factors contributed to the current problem, including lax regulations and a flood of liquidity. We can push the analysis back, asking why the excess liquidity and lax regulations? What were the political and economic forces leading to each? Elsewhere, I have explained, for instance, how growing inequality, a tax cut for upper income Americans, global imbalances, and rising oil prices contributed to what would have been—in the absence of loose monetary policy and lax regulation—an insufficiency of aggregate demand, in spite of large fiscal deficits. I explain too the role played by monetary policies, which focused excessively on inflation and paid insufficient attention to the stability of financial markets; these policies were often justified by simplistic economic theories.[4]

Here, I focus more narrowly on how particular deficiencies in the regulatory framework contributed to the housing bubble, focusing in particular on the *supply side,* the behavior of lenders. There were other regulatory failures, which contributed on the demand side—the failure, for instance, to restrict predatory lending.

Some of the same factors that had contributed to the earlier problems were at play here. There were incentives for providing misleading information and conflicts of interest. Two additional elements were present: incentives for excessive risk-taking and fraudulent behavior (a problem that played an important role in the savings and loans, S&L, debacle).[5] Perhaps more important though than these perverse incentives was a failure in modeling: a failure to understand the economics of securitization and the nature of systemic risk, and to correctly estimate small probability events.[6]

Incentive problems

EXECUTIVE COMPENSATION SYSTEMS

Executive compensation schemes (combined with accounting regulations) encouraged the provision of misleading information. Executives that are paid with stock options have an incentive to increase the market value of shares, and this may be more easily done by increasing reported income than by increasing true profits. Though the Sarbanes-Oxley Act of 2002 fixed some of the problems that were uncovered in the Enron and related scandals, it did nothing about stock options. With stock options not being expensed, shareholders often were not fully apprised of their cost. This provides strong incentives to pay exorbitant compensation through stock options.[7] But worse than this dissembling, the use of stock options encourages managers to try to increase *reported* income—so stock prices rise, and with the rise in stock prices, so too does managers' compensation; this in turn can lead them to employ bad accounting practices.

In addition, stock options—where executives only participate in the gains, but not the losses—and even more so, analogous bonus schemes prevalent in financial markets, provide strong incentives for excessive risk-taking. By undertaking high-risk ventures, they might garner more profits in the short term, thereby increasing compensation; but subsequent losses are borne by others. In a sense, these incentives were designed to encourage risk-taking. The problem is that they encouraged *excessive* risk-taking because of the mismatch between private returns and social returns.

Accounting frameworks exacerbated these problems. Banks could record profits today (and executives enjoy compensation related to those profits), but the potential liabilities were placed off the balance sheet.

INCENTIVES FOR ACCOUNTING FIRMS

The Enron/WorldCom scandal brought to the fore long recognized incentive problems with accounting (auditing) firms, and some clear conflicts of interest. Hired by the CEOs, and with much of their pay related to consulting services, auditors had an incentive to please the CEOs—to improve accounts that overstated profits, which led to higher share value and greater CEO compensation. Sarbanes-Oxley took important steps to improve matters—the accounting firms were limited in providing non-accounting services, and they were hired by the audit committees of corporate boards. Yet, few thought that this would fully resolve the problems. Boards, including audit committees, are still often beholden to the CEO, and typically see the world through lens provided by the CEO. Accounting firms still have an incentive to please the CEO and the companies that hire them. This may provide part of the reason that the accounting firms did not do the job that one might have hoped in exposing off-balance sheet risks.

SECURITIZATION

Recent years have seen increasing reliance on markets, including securitization, and a decreasing reliance on banks for the provision of credit. Much of the attention has focused on the greater ability of markets to diversify risk. Markets, by underestimating the extent to which these risks were correlated, overestimated the risk diversification benefits. Meanwhile, markets ignored three other problems.

As early as the 1990s (Stiglitz, 1992), I questioned this move to securitization. Securitization creates new information asymmetries—banks have an incentive to make sure that those to whom they issue mortgages can repay them, and to monitor behavior to make sure that they do (or that the probability that they do is high). Under securitization, the originator only has an incentive to produce pieces of paper that it can pass off to others.[8]

The securitization actually created a *series* of new problems in information asymmetries: the mortgages were bought by investment banks and repackaged, with parts sold off to other investment banks and to pension funds and others; and parts retained on their own balance sheet. In retrospect, it was clear that not even those creating the products were fully aware of the risks. But the complexity of the products made it increasingly difficult for those at each successive stage of the processing and reprocessing to evaluate what was going on.

Securitization poses two further problems. It may make renegotiation more difficult when problems arise. It is impossible to anticipate fully all contingencies and to specify what is to be done in each in the loan contract. When the borrower cannot meet his repayments, it may be mutually beneficial to renegotiate—the costs are lower than default (foreclosure on a mortgage). Yet such renegotiation may be more difficult under securitization, when there are many creditors whose interests and beliefs differ. Some may believe that by bargaining hard, they can get more on average, even if it means that some of the loans will fall into default. This is especially the case when those who assume the risk do not fully trust those who manage the loan to act in their behalf; they may worry that their incentives (related to management fees) are not fully in accord with the creditors', and so may impose restrictions on renegotiations. Moreover, the banks may have a richer "information" context with which to evaluate the problems; they can more easily ascertain whether the default is a "strategic default" (where the borrower is simply trying to have his debt burden reduced), and whether a loan restructuring—deferring repayments—will allow the borrower eventually to repay, or whether it will simply mean that the cumulative loss will be greater. Especially in the litigious US context, renegotiation has proven difficult, because any creditor has an incentive to sue those responsible for renegotiating saying they could have done a better job.[9] This problem should have been anticipated: it was far harder to renegotiate the securitized debt in the 1997–8 crisis than to renegotiate the bank debt in the Latin American debt crisis of the 1980s.

The second is that the new securities that were created were highly nontransparent. Indeed, their complexity may have been one of the reasons that they were so "successful." In the East Asia crisis, there was a great deal of criticism of the countries of East Asia for their lack of transparency. But it was precisely this lack of transparency that had, in some sense, attracted investors to these countries. They believed that they had "differential information" which would allow them to get above normal (risk adjusted) returns. In addition, it was the complexity of the product that helped generate the "supernormal" returns. Participants in New York's financial markets put their trust in the reputations of these premier financial institutions and the rating agencies. They have reason to be disappointed.[10]

RATING AGENCY INCENTIVES

The rating agencies had been widely berated for their failures in the 1997 global financial crisis. They had underrated the risks in East Asia; but as the risks became so large that they could no longer be ignored, their sudden downgrading of these assets forced them to be sold by pension funds and other fiduciaries. They had clearly contributed to financial market instability.[11] It seemed strange, given this record, that Basel II put such stress on rating agencies.[12] The rating agencies again failed.[13] They played a critical role: their *financial alchemy*—converting C-rated sub-prime mortgages into A-rated securities safe enough to be held by pension funds—ensured a continuing flow of funds into these mortgages. Not unlike medieval alchemists who believed there was money to be made by converting base metals like lead into gold, there was plenty of money to be made—and shared by all involved in the process—in the conversion of these assets.

Part of the problem is again flawed incentives: Rating agencies—paid by those who they were rating—had an incentive to give them "good grades"[14] and to believe in the ability of the investment banks to successfully engage in financial alchemy.

NEW CONFLICTS OF INTEREST AND A NEW CULTURE: REPEAL OF GLASS-STEAGALL

During the discussion of the repeal of the Glass-Steagall Act, critics had worried about conflicts of interest which might open up as a result of the breaking down of the barriers between investment and commercial banks. Advocates had said, "Trust us." Besides, they said, we will construct Chinese walls to make sure that there are not abuses. Critics were (as it turned out, rightly so) skeptical and raised the question: if effective Chinese walls were constructed, where were the economies of scope that provided the rationale for the mergers? (See Stiglitz, 2003.)

That the elimination of the barriers between investment and commercial banking provided more scope for conflicts of interest was amply demonstrated by the Enron/WorldCom scandals, e.g. the commercial division lending to firms for which the investment division had issued IPO's, in order to make them seem more "viable."[15]

Was it just an accident that so many problems in the financial system surfaced so soon after the repeal of Glass-Steagall in 1999? These conflicts of interests may have not been at the center of the problem, but they clearly played a role—so too in the 2007–8 crisis. Indeed, the closer interplay between investment banks and commercial banks almost surely contributed to the necessity of the Fed bail-out of Bear Stearns. It was not just a few investors' wealth that was at stake should Bear Stearns fail, but the entire financial system.

There have been other effects of the integration of investment and commercial banks that almost surely played a role in the debacle. The culture of conservatism that had traditionally dominated commercial banking came into clash with the speculative drive of the investment banks, and it was the latter culture that dominated.[16]

THE BERNANKE-GREENSPAN PUT AND MORAL HAZARD

Economists have long been aware of the distorted incentives that bail-outs provide. If a bank gambles (e.g. by making risky loans) and wins, the shareholders keep the gains. If a bank gambles and loses, there is a limit to the losses. The government picks up the pieces.[17] That is one of the reasons for the need for close supervision of banks; just like a company providing fire insurance needs to make sure that those insured have sprinklers, to reduce the extent of losses, so too the government, which either implicitly or explicitly is providing insurance, needs to make sure that banks are not engaging in excessive risk-taking.

Allowing the banks to grow in size and to become so interdependent exacerbated the risk of being "too big to fail," and therefore the risk of bail-out. The repeated bail-outs—including of a hedge fund, LTCM (Long-Term Capital

Management)[18]—made it clear that the United States would not let one of its major financial institutions fail.

The Fed has now extended the coverage of bail-outs ("lender of last resort") to investment banks, exacerbating all the problems to which we have already called attention.

Though the adverse incentive effects of bail-outs are clear, it is not always so clear who benefits from them.[19] The question is, what would have happened were there not a bail-out? Who is better off? Who is worse off? Clearly, taxpayers are worse off: at the very least, they have assumed risks that would otherwise have been borne by others. The full answer depends in part, of course, on the terms of the bail-out. For instance, in the discussion below of the bail-out of Bear Stearns, those who would have lost money if Bear Stearns had gone under are better off. Bear Sterns' shareholders are better off than they would have been had it gone under. Those who had "bet" on Bear Stearns going under are worse off. Part of the reason that it is difficult to get a fully satisfactory answer to this question is that there is uncertainty about what would have happened if there had not been a bail-out. If it would have led to a cascade of other failures, then all of those who otherwise would have gone under have benefited.[20]

CREATING A CREDIT FREEZE

Even before September 15, 2008, and the real freezing of credit markets following the bankruptcy of Lehman Brothers, it was apparent that credit markets were not functioning properly. The reason for the malfunctioning was transparently the lack of transparency: they were so non-transparent that when problems began to surface, no bank knew what its own balance sheet looked like, let alone that of a bank to which it might lend.

There is a striking similarity between what happened after Lehman Brothers was allowed to go bankrupt and the outcome of IMF (International Monetary Fund) and US Treasury policies in Indonesia's banking crisis of 1997. At that point, sixteen banks were shut down; the IMF made it clear that others would follow, that it would not disclose which banks would close, and that there would be at most limited deposit insurance. What followed was a panic, as funds fled the private banks.

This time, it was already evident that many banks were in serious difficulties. The presumption was that the government would bail out at least the larger banks. By allowing Lehman Brothers to go into bankruptcy, the Treasury and Fed were, in effect, saying: "Other banks will be allowed to fail; we will not tell you which we will allow to fail and which we will not. But we will not provide any guarantees." What followed was a predictable panic.

Problems were made worse by large counterparty risks, with huge outstanding positions. Again, the analogy to 1997 is instructive. Some Korean banks believed that they had purchased insurance against exchange rate changes, but they had failed to assess counterparty risk. In the complex web of interdependence, a failure of one institution could lead to a failure of others. One could not tell who was or was not financially viable, because one could not assess which "insurance" policies would or would not pay off.[21]

TRANSPARENCY AND COMPLEXITY

Much attention has been centered on the lack of transparency of financial markets. However, it is not just the lack of transparency that is key, but also the complexity of the products created: even if the terms of the contracts were fully disclosed, it would be difficult to assess fully their import.

It should be clear that there are strong incentives for complexity (and lack of transparency). The more transparent and standardized markets are, the more competitive, and profit margins are lower. Lack of transparency and high levels of complexity were thus a central part of the business model of US financial institutions.

At the same time, it should be clear that increasing transparency (improved information) will not necessarily lead to greater market stability (see Furman and Stiglitz, 1998). More deeply, the forces that have given rise to the current crisis will not be resolved simply by increasing transparency. The incentives that gave rise to lack of transparency (see Edlin and Stiglitz, 1995) and increased complexity would still be at play. Deeper reforms are required.[22]

INCENTIVES—AND OPPORTUNITIES—FOR FRAUD

It should have been obvious to almost anyone involved—from those originating the mortgages, to those repackaging and securitizing them, to the rating agencies, and to the regulators—that there was something very wrong going on. Some of the mortgages required no documentation and no down payments. With some of the appraisal companies owned by the mortgage originating companies, there were clear conflicts of interest. A structure was in place for fraudulent behavior—for loans greater than the value of the house—and it is clear that such fraudulent behavior did occur.[23] Incentives matter, and if there are perverse incentives, there are perverse outcomes.

Both the regulators and those buying these securities should have been suspect: a 100 per cent non-recourse mortgage is an option—if the price of the house goes up, the owner keeps the difference, if it goes down, he walks away. Providing such mortgages is equivalent to giving away money. But banks are not traditionally in the business of giving away money, especially to poor people. How can one make money by giving away money? The answer was simple: they were in the business of creating pieces of paper that they could pass on to others. As the expression goes, a fool is born every moment, enough to create a market: especially when these fools are aided and abetted by wise men, with strong reputations, rating agencies, and long established investment banks.

Not all of the mortgages provided, in effect, 100 per cent financing.[24] This provided another incentive for bad behavior. Much has been written in recent years about the amount of money that lies at the bottom of the pyramid, and US financial institutions were determined to extract as much of that money out as fast as they could. Many put their life savings into the purchase of their homes—money that in effect went to pay commissions to the mortgage brokers and others who benefited from the housing boom so long as people continued to finance and refinance their homes. They walked away with their commissions, no matter what happened to housing prices; the poor were left to bear the risk.

Many recognized that there was predatory lending going on. Not surprisingly, the predation was especially strong among those who were financially not well educated. There were attempts to stop this predatory behavior, but lobbyists for those who were doing well by exploiting these groups prevailed.

WHAT WAS GOING ON? REGULATORY AND ACCOUNTING ARBITRAGE? MISPRICING RISK AND EXCESSIVE LEVERAGE?

Incentives clearly played an important role in the debacle. But even with (conventionally defined) well designed incentives, problems may have occurred, because social and private returns differed. There were opportunities for regulatory arbitrage. If, for instance, one could somehow convert the C-rated sub-prime mortgages into A-rated securities, then one could open up a huge potential demand from fiduciaries that could not otherwise have purchased these assets. The gains from regulatory arbitrage were large, ample enough to pay everyone along the production chain, from the rating agencies (that gave their seal of approval), to the investment banks (who did the repackaging), to the mortgage brokers (who manufactured the pieces of paper to be repackaged).

Accounting anomalies (especially with stock options) provide further opportunities for "arbitrage," such as booking profits on repackaging, while retaining some of the unsold assets and the implicit risks off-balance sheet.

Some of what was going on was a new version of an old game: leverage. With high leverage, one can make large profits on a limited amount of capital—if things turn out right. The new instruments allowed, in effect, very high leverage, in a non-transparent way. There were points of high leverage throughout the financial system, from the homeowners with low down payment homes upwards. But one of the insights of modern finance theory (from Modigliani-Miller onwards) is that there is no money to be made in leveraging in a well-functioning financial market. The risk increases with the leverage, and if markets are pricing assets correctly, there is nothing to be gained in risk adjusted returns.

To put it another way: trading in securities markets is (approximately) a zero sum game. The profits of the winners are matched by the losses of the losers. There are social returns only to the extent that there is finely honed matching of risks; the scale and nature of the transactions suggests that *that* was not what was going on. Rather, there seems to have been massive deception and self-deception that somehow something real was going on, generating enormous net real value.

Modeling Problems

Still, many of the mistakes of the financial markets (including the banks and rating agencies) are attributable not to bad incentives, but to bad models—mistakes in modeling that were and should have been obvious before the collapse (bad incentives may well have encouraged them to adopt faulty models). They failed to understand the perverse, predictable, and predicted consequences of the incentive structures that they had created (described above).

FAILING TO UNDERSTAND DIVERSIFICATION

Market participants (including banks and rating agencies) systematically ignored (or underestimated the importance of) systemic risk. They thought that securities consisting of a large number of mortgages would have a small probability of losing more than, say, 10 per cent of their market value. Based on recent history, what was the probability of large numbers going into default at the same time?

They failed to realize that diversification has only limited value when risks are correlated; a fall in the price of housing, a rise in the interest rate, and an economic downturn all could give rise to correlated risk—an increase in the default rate. The 2007–8 sub-prime mortgage crisis was not the first time that financial markets seemed to have underestimated both systemic risk and unlikely events. Once in a century problems seemed to be happening every ten years.

These failures were multiplied with default insurance. If the products being insured had correlated risks, then the net worth of the insurance companies would be insufficient to make good on their promises. We have seen this play out: as the insurance companies have lost their ratings, the products that they insured have lost their ratings, in a cascading of down-grading.[25]

FAILING TO UNDERSTAND SYSTEMIC RISK—A CRITICAL FAILURE OF THE BASEL II FRAMEWORK

Basel II required banks to manage their own risks—as if that is what they would not have done on their own. It presumed that the regulators could monitor complicated risk management systems of banks, and that the rating agencies could assess risk. It is now clear that banks did not know how to manage risks and that the rating agencies did not know how to assess risk (or did not have the incentives to do it well).

But there was a more fundamental flaw with the Basel II framework. Banks obviously *should* have incentives to manage their risks. Regulators needed to focus on those areas where individual private risk management might not accord with managing social or societal risks well.

One obvious example is provided by what happened (and what had happened earlier, in 1987): if all banks are using similar risk management systems, they may all try to sell certain assets in particular contingencies, in which case they can't; prices fall in ways that were not anticipated. Using similar risk management systems can give rise to correlated risks, with far larger than normal price movements.[26]

Banks have been criticized for using the same (or similar) models.[27] That is not really the key issue: indeed, if they are all using the right model, based on rational expectations, then they would have to be using the same model.[28] The problem was that they were all using similar wrong models. They were using models that were not consistent with rational expectations; they were all using models that were such that, if they all used that model, the outcome could not have been consistent with the models themselves.

There was a role for the regulator: at the very least, it could have checked the consistency of the models. Each firm may have been unwilling to share its model with other firms—they presumably believed that their ability to manage risk well may have given them a competitive advantage over other banks. But they can be required to share their model with the regulator, who can assess the systemic implications and the consistency of the models with systemic behavior.

More generally, it was a major failing of Basel II not to recognize that there are systemic externalities—presumably one of the reasons for regulation in the first place.

DETECTING PONZI SCHEMES

In this crisis, as in many earlier crises, a little thought about the economic situation should have revealed that what was going on was not sustainable. Understanding why this is the case may be as much a matter of social psychology as of economics. Market participants reinforce each other's beliefs about the "correctness" of their views. But certain short sighted and dysfunctional aspects of markets may play a role. For instance, those who did not engage in the "game" would not have had as high returns on their equity—and stock prices would have suffered. Even without distorted incentives, a bank that resisted the conventional wisdom would have been the subject of a take-over move.

Behind the scenes, somewhat obfuscated by the financial market "innovations," were two classic problems: excessive leverage (typically in a non-transparent form) and a pyramid scheme. Everything might have worked well if home prices had continued to rise. Those who borrowed beyond their ability to pay would have made sufficiently large capital gains that they could have repaid what was owed. Those who lent without due diligence would have done just as well as those who had.

With many loans having in effect negative amortization, the borrowers owed more at the end of the period than at the beginning. Some expressed concern about what would happen when they had to pay the full interest due (as in most of the loans, after an initial period of "teaser rates"). They were told not to worry: they would easily refinance the loan. They would then even be able to spend some of the capital gains, through mortgage equity withdrawals.

But it should have been obvious that it was unlikely that prices could have continued to rise, even without an increase in the interest rate. Real incomes of most Americans have been declining. Yet median house prices (even adjusting for overall inflation) were increasing, and dramatically so. There was an obvious limit to the amount that can be paid for housing. Anybody looking carefully at housing prices saw that what was going on was not sustainable. How could prices (adjusted for overall inflation) continue to rise, as real incomes of most Americans, and especially those at the bottom, continued to fall? Everyone in the system should have realized that they were engaged in a classical pyramid scheme.

INTELLECTUAL INCOHERENCE

It should have been obvious that there was something wrong with the reasoning underlying much of what was going on in the financial markets. The failures to recognize the problems make it difficult to reconcile behavior with any notion of market rationality.

Those creating the new products argued that the new financial instruments were fundamentally changing the structure of the economy—it was these fundamental changes which presumably justified their huge compensation. But at the same time, they were using data from before the introduction of these new instruments to estimate the parameters of their models, including the likelihood of default. If it were true that they had opened up a new era, surely these parameters would have changed.

How could they not have recognized that securitization had altered incentives? How could they not have responded by tightening monitoring? How could they not have recognized that there was something peculiar about the non-recourse mortgages that were being issued? How could they not have recognized the perverse incentives to which the short sighted and asymmetric compensation systems (where executives shared in the gains but not the losses) were giving rise? Some academics did raise questions about each of these aspects of the market, but "the market" studiously ignored these warnings.

There were other examples of intellectual incoherence. One of the reasons for the drying up of interbank credit flows was the large derivative positions. The banks had failed to net out these positions. When asked why, the response was that it was "easier" to undo a derivative position by creating a new offsetting position. The two were equivalent, so long as there was no bankruptcy, and no one could imagine the bankruptcy of one of the major banks. Counterparty risk was assumed away.

Yet, among the fastest growing parts of the derivative market were credit default swaps—bets on whether one of the major banks would go bankrupt. Surely, they must have recognized the enormous mess that would have been created by the default of a major bank, and that failing to net out positions was giving rise to enormous systemic risk.[29]

Perhaps most significantly, many in the financial market argued that financial markets were relatively efficient, believed in the Modigliani-Miller theorem, understood that there was no such thing as a free lunch, and yet were still unfazed by the huge returns accruing to the financial sector. These were presumably the just rewards for increasing the ability of the economy to allocate resources and manage risks; and yet where were the corresponding improvements in the *real economy*? The only thing that could be pointed to was the unsustainable increase in investment in sub-prime housing.

The failure of the financial system to perform its essential functions: what were they doing? Regulatory arbitrage?

In short, it is hard to reconcile what happened in that episode (as in the earlier ones) with any model of "rational" behavior. But whether rational or irrational, failures in financial markets in the late 1990s and in 2007–8 have highlighted the importance of information imperfections. In each instance, the results were clear: the financial system failed to perform the functions which it is supposed to perform, allocating capital efficiently and managing risk. In the late 1990s, there was massive excessive investment, say, in fiber optics; in the first decade of this century, there was massive excessive investment in housing. And while new products were created to facilitate the management of risk, they actually created risk.

While they were creating risks with their new products, they were not creating the products that would help manage the socially important risks that needed to be managed. They were (for the most part) not creating risk products that were tailored to the needs of those that needed to have risk managed (their failure to manage their own risks suggests that they might not have had the competence to do so, even if they had wanted to). In many cases, funds would buy the new derivative products as part of portfolios. Sub-prime mortgages and other assets were being sliced and diced, and then recombined, and the result-ing products would then be mixed with other similarly artificially constructed products—and no one could easily ascertain the risk properties of the resulting portfolio. As I suggest below, they were not really managing risk; they were engaged in regulatory arbitrage.

There were real social needs for risk management, evidenced by the fact that millions of Americans may lose their homes.[30] The new mortgages increased the risk borne by poor homeowners of interest rate fluctuations and credit market conditions. This was especially true of those mortgages with reset provisions or balloon payments, which were often sold on the presumption that the individuals could refinance their mortgages. There are alternative mortgages that would have shifted more of the risk to the market or made it easier for individuals to manage these risks (e.g. mortgages with variable matu-rities but fixed payments).

One hypothesis about what was really going on—beyond a fancier and harder to detect pyramid scheme, or the newest form of accounting deception, to replace those that had been exposed in the Enron/WorldCom scandals—is that this was a fancy version of regulatory arbitrage. The problem facing finan-cial markets was how to place the high risk sub-prime mortgages that were being created into sources of funding, many of which were highly regulated (such as pension funds). These are regulated for a good reason: these institu-tions are fiduciaries, entrusted to make sure that funds are available for the purposes intended, including financing individuals' retirement. They are, ac-cordingly, not allowed to speculate on highly risky securities. The bonds they invest in must have a high rating. These regulations give rise to the demand for financial alchemy. If poorly rated sub-prime mortgages could somehow be converted into an asset with a high enough rating to be placed in pension funds and other fiduciaries, there was money to be made: if these assets could yield a slightly higher return than other comparably rated bonds, then there was an insatiable demand. The difference between the return on the low rated sub-prime mortgage and the AAA products created by financial alchemy provided billions of dollars to be divided among all those participating in the scam—from those originating the mortgages (both the companies and those who worked for them), to those who did the repackaging, to the rating agencies.

Someone, everyone had forgotten the oldest of economic adages: there is no such thing as a free lunch. Evidently, in their minds, money had been left on the table for decades, and only the power of modern finance had found it. Where were the billions of dollars of true welfare gains that corresponded to the billions of dollars of apparent profits, bonuses, and commissions coming from? Never mind, if no one could find a good answer.

There was, of course, a simple answer, provided by the capital gains-based pyramid scheme—some were cashing in on the gains, leaving the future losses to others. At the same time, it became clear that financial prowess had not only created new vehicles for what might be called systemic deception, but had also exposed a deeper problem within the capitalist system. It was difficult at best to tell who was managing assets well and who was taking a long run gamble that would pay off well to the fund manager but likely at the expense of those whose funds he was managing. One could create assets that had a low probability of a large loss. Assume, by way of example, that an asset had a 95 per cent probability of a return that was above normal by 1 per cent—in conventional terms, "almost certain"—but a 5 per cent probability of a loss of x per cent. If $x > 20$ per cent, the expected return to this risk asset is actually less than a safe asset. But on average, it will take twenty years before finding out the value of x. It will be twenty years before one finds out whether the 1 per cent excess return is enough to compensate for the loss. But, of course, the hedge fund managers are not paid on the basis of twenty-year performances; they walk away with the positive returns, regardless of the loss that occurs in that twentieth year.

Preventing future crises: reforming financial regulation

As we have repeatedly emphasized, there is a compelling argument for regulation: the actions within the financial sector have effects on *others*, and government (partly as a result of this) will have to bear the costs of mistakes. Government, as *insurer of last resort,* must do what it can to lower the probability of the (implicitly or explicitly) insured against event occurring.[31]

It is clear, for all the best intentions, that regulations imposed in the past have not worked, and as we think of new regulatory systems, we have to think of the reasons for the failure of past systems. At least three factors play a role: (a) recent beliefs—grounded neither in economic theory nor in historical experience—in self-regulation (that market discipline ensures that only the best survive) has resulted in deregulation; (b) regulatory capture—the regulatory mechanism has been captured by those that it is supposed to regulate, especially common in the international context; and (c) a lack of understanding of finance and accounting has led to regulatory frameworks that are open to regulatory arbitrage and manipulation. In addition, there is always a lack of balance: there is no comparison between the compensation of the regulators and those they are supposed to be regulating. This may contribute to regulatory capture, but it should be clear—it does not make regulation infeasible. We have a tax system which collects taxes, even though those paid to avoid taxes are paid far more than the tax collectors. But an understanding of this imbalance has implications for the design of the regulatory system.

There are two more challenges facing the design of the regulatory system. We want to encourage innovation, and we want to promote macro-stability. We have noted earlier how some regulations, for instance, may act as automatic destabilizers.

Finally, in our world of globalization, each country worries about competition. There is a worry this will generate a race to the bottom. I believe that good regulation is, or can be, a competitive advantage. Singapore has attracted funds because those putting money into that country have some confidence that its banks are viable. But just as actions of banks have externalities, so too do regulatory frameworks, and it would be best if there were coordinated actions in adopting good regulatory frameworks. But if this is not achieved, I argue in the final subsection, Europe and the United States have sufficient economic influence to ensure the adoption of good regulatory frameworks within their borders.

In the paragraphs below, I describe certain key aspects of the regulatory framework that I think may not have received sufficient attention: (a) regulators should focus more on improving incentives; (b) we need to pay more attention to accounting frameworks; and (c) we need some new regulatory frameworks that look more carefully at both the risk properties of particular financial assets and the characteristics of the overall financial system.

Improving incentives

There have been problems in market incentives and regulatory incentives that almost surely played an important role in each of the problems detailed above. For markets to work well, private incentives have to be aligned with social objectives. This has not been the case. Here are a set of reforms that would at least improve the alignment of incentives.

IMPROVED INCENTIVES IN SECURITIZATION

One of the problems with securitization is that mortgage originators did not hold the mortgages and so had less incentive to ensure that the borrower had the ability to repay. Their incentives were directed at *persuading* the buyer of the mortgages that they had the ability to pay. *Requiring that mortgage originators retain a fraction of the risk of the loans that they originate would encourage greater care in lending.*

IMPROVED INCENTIVES IN RATING AGENCIES

This is one of the two incentive issues that have been widely discussed: with rating agencies being paid by those putting together the complex products, they have an incentive to please those who are paying them. The problems are analogous to those confronting the accounting firms, which Sarbanes-Oxley attempted to address. The fix here is not so easy. There are large numbers of buyers of securities, and it is not obvious how to design a system in which the buyers of the securities pay the cost. The problems are related to fundamental problems in the supply of information; it is one of the reasons that in some key areas (like food safety) we do not rely on private certification. There is at least an overlay of government oversight. This is part of the motivation for the financial products safety commission discussed below.

IMPROVED INCENTIVES IN HEDGE FUNDS AND FINANCIAL MANAGERS

Part of the problems in recent years in financial markets may be related to the incentive structures facing hedge fund managers, and financial managers more generally. These are incentive structures designed to enhance risk-taking. The question is, are they encouraging excessive risk-taking, partly at the expense of the public? The incentive structures encourage gambling. Financial managers can do well for themselves if they make large amounts one year, even if such amounts are offset by equal losses the next. The former results in large bonuses; the latter has no penalty.

It is when the hedge funds interact with regulated financial entities, like banks and fiduciaries, that the problems become particularly acute. Government has imposed regulations on these financial entities for good reason— concern about systemic risk and the protection of the savings of retirees. It is not the intent of government to give opportunities for those in the financial markets to make money through regulatory arbitrage or by taking advantage of implicit or explicit government insurance (bail-outs). But the current system gives them ample opportunity to do so. Accordingly, the incentive pay structures of those hedge funds or financial entities that either receive funds from or provide products to these regulated financial institutions should be regulated. The incentive pay structures within the regulated financial institutions (banks, fiduciaries) should similarly be regulated.

At a minimum, bonuses must be based not on performance in any single year but on performance over a much longer time period; at least a substantial part of the bonus paid in any one year should be held in escrow, to be offset against losses attributable to the investments made in subsequent years.

Critics will worry about the excessive obtrusiveness into the market economy. Is there not a risk that such regulation interferes with innovation—including innovation in incentive structures? There are two answers to such concerns. First, in those parts of the financial system where there is not an overriding public interest, there is still scope for such innovation for testing out new incentive schemes and evaluating them. Second, and more to the point, there are real questions about the nature of the innovations in compensation schemes in recent years. Greater reliance on stock options, *at least for firms that are not cash constrained,* seems more driven by a concern towards deceiving shareholders than to increasing managerial efficiency. The resistance of corporations to having the value of stock options disclosed in ways that share-holders can understand is certainly suggestive. A closer look at executive compensation suggests that there is in fact little relationship between pay and long-term performance—in bad years (when the stock does not do well), executives find alternative ways of receiving their compensation. Moreover, there are better ways of providing compensation that provide higher powered incentives with less risk to managers and with tax benefits (see Stiglitz, 2003).

IMPROVED INCENTIVES FOR REGULATORS

The full regulatory authority of the regulators (e.g. of the Fed) was not used to prevent the current problems. It was only after the crisis that the Fed adopted regulations—a classic case of closing the barn door after the horses are out. There is a large literature on regulatory capture; self-regulation typically does not suffice, partly because of incentives (those in the financial markets were making good money; no one wants to be a party pooper), partly because of mind-set (those within the industry are less likely to see a bubble than disinterested third parties).

Those entrusted with regulating the industry have to identify with those who are most likely to lose in the event of a malfunction of the market, not with those who are winning as a result of the malfunction of the market. At the very least, there is a need for greater balance.

In many industries, expertise resides mainly in those in the industry, and this poses a particular problem in the design of regulatory authorities. There are today, however, large numbers of highly qualified individuals who understand financial markets (especially in academia) who could play a more active role in regulation. One would still have to take precautions, e.g. against revolving doors.

CONFLICTS OF INTEREST

Conflicts of interest give rise to distorted incentives. There are several potential conflicts of interest that have surfaced; at this juncture, it is important to ascertain what role they played. Those involved in the mortgage business (at any point in the supply chain) should not have a financial interest in firms that appraise property values. The problems are obvious.

Similarly, for a financial firm to buy "insurance" for its mortgages (bonds) from a company in which it owns a large stake vitiates the purpose of insurance. It is not insurance, but self-insurance. It does not transfer the risk, even if it helps improve "ratings." But if it does help improve ratings, it is almost surely partially due to failures in the rating methodologies.

At the time Glass-Steagall was repealed, there were worries about a variety of forms of conflicts of interest. In the years since, it appears that some of those worries, at least in some instances, were justified. While there may be no appetite for reinstating restrictions, more thought should be given to regulations, with penalties for those that disregard them, that might address some of the problems that have appeared.

Information, accounting and capital adequacy frameworks

Much recent discussion has focused on increased transparency and more extensive disclosure. It has become increasingly clear that disclosure requirements by themselves will not suffice and that the manner in which information is disclosed makes a difference. The latter point was highlighted by the controversy over disclosure of stock options and the requirement that they be "expensed." Many firms that made extensive use of stock options did not object to disclosing that information in footnotes, presumably because they understood that such disclosures would have few consequences; they objected strenuously to even conservative approaches to accounting for these stock options because it would reveal the extent to which ownership claims were being diluted.[32]

Accounting is important, because it provides frameworks in which information is presented. On the basis of that information, taxes are levied, firms make decisions—for example, about which activities to expand and which to contract—and investment gets allocated. Flawed and distorted information leads to flawed and distorted decisions. The problem, repeatedly noted, is that there are incentives to provide flawed and distorted information. Firms have an incentive to provide too low an estimate of profits for tax purposes and too high an estimate to persuade investors to invest more in their company. These countervailing incentives often act as a check against each other.

In recent years, innovations in accounting (not all of positive value) have enabled some firms to maintain, in effect, multiple books—presenting one set of numbers to tax authorities, and another set of numbers to investors. But just as they learned how better to deceive tax authorities (by and large, viewed as a legitimate activity), they learned how better to deceive investors. Making matters worse, distorted compensation systems—including stock options—provided even stronger incentives for providing distorted information.[33]

The Enron/WorldCom scandals of the early years of this decade exposed some of these accounting problems. Not enough attention has been paid to the failure of the accounting frameworks in the current context. They signaled huge profits in 2003–6, but did not signal the offsetting even larger losses that have now been exposed. This should not have happened; what it signals is, I think, that something is wrong with the accounting frameworks.

Bad accounting frameworks not only do not provide accurate information; they also lead to distorted behavior. Not marking to market, for instance, provides an incentive for excessive risk-taking: one can sell off assets that have gained in value, recording a profit, and hold on to assets that have decreased in value (keeping them at book value.)

But we are beginning to discover some consequences of (poorly designed) mark to market systems. Banks are now marking to market their liabilities. As their default probability increases, the value of their bonds decreases, and so their balance sheet improves. Bonds, of course, may have covenants that they cannot be bought back at below par—without such covenants, borrowers would have an incentive to announce bad news, to depress the value of their debt, so they could buy it back at below par. Never mind that the fall in the price of bonds indicates that the firm is going to face higher borrowing costs in the future—it is signaling worse future prospects for firms. Under current US rules, the firm can record an improvement in its position.

In the current crisis, off-balance sheet assets were obviously incorrectly priced. Banks could book some of the profits they made in "repackaging" sub-prime mortgages, even though they retained residual risk in these off-balance sheet mispriced assets. It is not clear to what extent these accounting problems simply misled those looking at the banks and to what extent these provided the underlying motivation for the transactions. In any case, it is clear that accounting failures provided scope for the problems that have been uncovered.

While the problems of not marking to market have long been understood, the recent crisis has exposed some of the problems of using marking to market for capital adequacy (highlighting problems that critics actually raised before mark to market was imposed): market prices might *overshoot,* with the decline in market prices exceeding the "true" decrease in value, forcing the bank to unnecessarily raise more capital and/or cut back on lending. The cutback in lending would, in turn, lead to further weakening in the economy (it is, perhaps, ironic, that from the champions of markets comes an argument based on market failure). Marking to market may thus exacerbate the automatic pro-cyclical effects of capital adequacy standards.

Given the long standing tendency of financial markets to over expand in booms, there is a need for counter-cyclical controls. One form is cyclically adjusted capital adequacy standards. In the most recent crisis, a simpler set of controls might have sufficed. As the bubble progressed, while the probability of a decline in price increased, the loan-to-value ratios increased. Requiring larger down payments (and assigning disproportionately higher risk to higher loan-to-value mortgages) almost surely would have dampened the bubble.

Designing better provisioning requirements (and adjusting these to the changing circumstances) might both have dampened the fluctuation and ensured that the consequences of the breaking of the bubble were less. While Greenspan often said that one cannot predict with certainty when there is a bubble, as home prices increased (relative to incomes), the likelihood that prices would fall (by any given amount) was increased, and there should, accordingly, have been larger provisions.

By the same token, there are other indications of impending problems, and these ought to be incorporated in provisioning requirement and capital adequacy standards. Research suggests that there may be some simple indications of problems. Had these been employed, red flags would have been raised about some of the potential problems. As a World Bank study—headed by Amar Bhattacharya, carried out before the 1997 crisis—indicated,[34] a strong indicator of a looming problem, for instance, is rapidly expanding credit (in the aggregate, or in particular institutions). The capacity of institutions to expand rapidly and their ability to make sound judgments about credit worthiness is limited. Problems in lending typically do not show up until two or three years after the rapid expansion has begun, so that in such situations the ratio of non-performing loans provides a poor indicator. There is seldom an economic transformation that would warrant this kind of rapid credit expansion. One of the recommendations of the World Bank study was the imposition of "speed bumps," for instance requiring higher than normal risk adjustments in capital adequacy standards and greater provisioning for such rapid credit expansions.[35]

New regulatory frameworks

Improvements in incentives and accounting frameworks will help, but they will not suffice. Financial markets have been plagued with manias and bubbles that inevitably burst. One can never be sure that one is in a bubble until after it bursts—but as prices soar beyond historical ranges, the probability that one is in such a bubble increases. For all the sophistication of modern risk management techniques, they have done little to affect the occurrence of these bubbles; perhaps as we learn how to manage risk better, we take more risks, and the new financial innovations have facilitated the ability to take on these additional risks (some argue that the use of modern risk management actually makes crises more frequent). In the case of many of the new financial products, it was difficult to ascertain what was their *economic* function, i.e. they were not really tailoring risk products to meet the particular risk profile of particular investors. Were the assets that were stripped apart reassembled in ways that contributed to a lack of transparency? It is clear that no one really understood fully the risk characteristics. These products, rather than helping individuals manage risks, made it more difficult.

FINANCIAL PRODUCTS SAFETY COMMISSION

Financial markets have innovated, but these innovations have resulted in hundreds of thousands of loans that go beyond individuals' ability to pay. Even many of those that are making their payments are facing hardship, anxiety, and stress. Clearly, the financial sector has not done a good job at analyzing the consequences of the products that they produce. Defective products can clearly have disastrous effects both on those who buy them and on the economy.

In the current instance, those evaluating risk have made a number of systematic mistakes which we have already called attention to.[36]

Earlier, I explained the problem of having private sector certification. A financial products safety commission could help fill in the gap, particularly in relationship to products being produced and invested in by regulated entities. Each product would have to have a stated objective (e.g. in what ways was it helping manage and mitigate risk; what was the risk profile for whom the product was intended). Its risk characteristics would be identified, using conservative models which paid due attention to the failures previously noted. The *Financial Products Safety Commission* would evaluate whether products provided significant risk mitigation benefits of the kind purported by the product. There would be a presumption that there "is no free lunch," i.e. that higher returns could only be obtained at the expense of greater risk, and a strong presumption against complex products, the full import of which are hard to analyze.

The Financial Products Safety Commission would establish transparency standards that all those dealing with regulated financial entities would have to satisfy (including hedge funds and sovereign wealth funds). It would have the power to ban certain products from the balance sheets of these regulated entities (just as there are currently restrictions on the assets that they can hold).[37]

Critics will worry that the Commission will inhibit innovation. As in our earlier discussion of compensation, there are two responses. First, there can still be unrestricted innovation in the unregulated parts of the financial system. Products can be tried out there. They can be evaluated: who is buying them? Do they really understand the risks? Is it meeting some real risk need? Second, we have seen that most of the innovation in recent years—while highly privately profitable—has had questionable social benefits; with the subsequent market turmoil to which these instruments have given rise, the net social return is almost surely negative. Indeed, from a theoretical perspective, it should have been obviously so: much of the finance literature is premised on the assumption of "spanning," that there is (close to) a full set of securities in the market for addressing most of the relevant risks. It is this assumption that allows the easy pricing of derivatives and other new securities. If that is the case, then the only value of new products is the lowering of transactions costs from "prepackaging" certain risk products—and with relatively efficient capital markets the benefits of pre-packaging are likely to be small. Moreover, when a truly innovative product with social value is created, at most the cost would be a slight delay in its introduction; the social cost of that is likely to be small, in comparison with the costs of the kind of crisis we are now facing. Furthermore, restricting unproductive innovation may finally induce financial markets to direct their attention to providing risk products that are needed to help ordinary individuals manage their wealth, products such as inflation adjusted bonds and GDP bonds. Ironically, financial markets resisted the introduction of these innovative products.[38]

The Financial Products Safety Commission, working together with the Financial Systems Stability Commission, would have the responsibility for identifying gaps in the current financial system—risks that are not being handled well (such as risks previously discussed with current mortgages) or groups that do not have access to credit—and help design new products that would address these needs. We should remember that the government and government created institutions have traditionally played an important role in key financial innovations—a much greater role than market advocates typically recognize.[39] There is no reason to believe that they could not play as important a role in the future as they have in the past.

These reforms are particularly important given the scope for regulatory arbitrage that has been exposed in the recent crisis. Sub-prime mortgages were transformed, as if by financial alchemy, into AAA assets, so that they could be placed in fiduciaries who otherwise would not have been allowed to hold these risky products. Limitations in our accounting system similarly provide scope for "accounting arbitrage." We understand better now some of the *wrong* motivations for the production of new financial products.

REGULATORY INSTRUMENTS AND THE FINANCIAL MARKETS STABILITY COMMISSION

Not all the regulatory instruments that could have been used have been used to control the bubbles that have imposed such costs on the economy. For instance, increasing collateral requirements (margin requirements, down payments) was a natural instrument to have employed, both in the stock bubble of the 1990s and the housing bubble of today. The problem, noted earlier, is that the Fed (partly out of ideology) has been reluctant to use these instruments.

In the current regulatory framework, the focus is mostly on individual institutions (is a particular bank "safe and sound"). Little attention is placed on the *overall* framework. Financial markets have become increasingly interrelated. One cannot look at the system focusing on banking alone or on securities markets alone. There is a need for a Commission that looks at the financial markets overall and assesses whether the various regulatory agencies are doing what they should be doing to maintain financial market stability. The Financial Systems Stability Commission would for instance have the responsibility for ensuring that there is not excessive *systemic* leverage. It would look at systemic properties, e.g. how the entire system responds to shocks, looking for policies and institutions that would diminish rather than amplify the effects of any shock. (It would, accordingly, work to ensure that there are not built-in automatic destabilizers, such as those associated with inappropriately designed capital adequacy standards.)

This Commission, like the Financial Products Safety Commission, should not be dominated by those from the financial markets, but should rather be more broadly representative with, for example, economists who take a broader systemic view, and reflect the concerns and views of main street and labor as well as financial markets.

We noted earlier that regulatory authorities need to pay increased attention to indications of crises (problems of "vulnerability").[40] Earlier, we noted one of the factors is rapid expansion of credit. Rapid expansions of credit into new markets (like the sub-prime market) should be the subject of increased regulatory scrutiny. To be sure, we should encourage financial innovation—making credit available to those who previously did not have access can be a valuable social contribution. But sometimes (perhaps often) there was a good reason that credit was not made available—there was a high risk of non-repayment. There is a need for balance and caution—encouragement for the creation of new products, but also an awareness of the potential risks.

BOUNDARIES OF REGULATION

Government has a legitimate argument for imposing regulations on entities that threaten the stability of the financial system. There has long been a view that investment banks do not need to be regulated, because their owners, and not the public, bear the risk if they make bad investments. The government financed bail-out of Bear Stearns has laid to rest such claims. The rationale for the government bail-out (as for the government orchestrated bail-out of LTCM) was that there would be systemic consequences if a failure occurred. This means that any entities that are closely interlinked with those parts of the financial system over which government has regulatory responsibility (banks, pension funds, other fiduciaries, etc) need to be regulated. The extent and nature of the regulation should presumably depend on the nature of the systemic risks which problems in each entity (or from correlated behavior in a group of firms) might pose.

Thus, one might argue that gambling between consenting adults should be allowed: only those party to the gamble are at risk. On this reasoning, hedge funds that do not sell financial products to or receive loans from banks or other regulated entities should have at most limited regulations, e.g. certain behaviors might be proscribed. Hedge funds (or similar entities) wishing, however, to sell financial products to or receive loans from banks would have to register as "qualified financial entities," and be subject to more extensive regulation, including regulations concerning disclosure and incentives.

INTERNATIONAL PERSPECTIVES

Each country, in designing its own regulatory framework, has a tendency to focus on impacts within its own country. Just as each bank ignores the externalities to which its actions give rise, so too is true for individual countries. For instance, some countries have expanded their banking system by *regulatory competition*, including weakening regulations designed to ensure compliance with the tax code. There is a worry, noted earlier, that regulatory competition will result in a race to the bottom.

The first best solution would entail coordination in the design of good regulatory standards. The limitations of Basel II have already been mentioned. If appropriate regulatory standards are not established, then it will be necessary for each country to design its own regulations to protect itself. It cannot rely on regulations of others. European banks' losses from sub-prime mortgages now appear to be greater even than those of US banks.

It would be easy to enforce good standards, especially on those countries that have become noted for their role in evading regulations and taxes. There is little reason that so much financial activity occurs in many of these off-shore centers, except to avoid taxes and regulatory oversight; but this undermines the integrity of the global financial system. These off-shore centers survive only because we allow them, and there is no reason that this should continue. The US, for instance, has already shown that it can enforce its standards concerning financial relations with terrorist groups. It could do so as well with those who are engaged more broadly in tax evasion, money laundering, or other such anti-social activities (the recent response of Germany and others to the tax evasion disclosures out of Lichtenstein highlight that much more can be done than has been done in the past). Similarly, restricting regulated American or European financial entities in their dealings with financial institutions and other entities in jurisdictions that have failed to comply with OECD (Organisation for Economic Co-operation and Development) transparency standards or other regulatory standards that US or Europe might agree upon, and which did not cooperate in providing records of accounts to tax authorities in the United States, would shortly either put these "rogue" financial institutions out of business—or force them to change their behavior.

Concluding comments

The United States—and much of the rest of the world—is experiencing a major problem in its financial system, a financial crisis which has evolved into the most serious global economic downturn since the Great Depression. As we have noted, this is at least the third major problem involving US financial institutions in the last quarter century. Not only were they not the font of wisdom in the management of risk that they purported to be, but they did not even understand well the products that they were creating. There will be many innocent victims of these failures—the consequences are not limited to the institutions themselves. Taxpayers as a whole are now bearing risks as a result of the financial systems' failure to manage its risks.

Doctors learn a great deal from pathologies. So too, economists should learn from the failures of the economic system. We have attempted to provide a broad, theory-based diagnosis of what went wrong and, on the basis of that diagnosis, to prescribe remedies—short-term remedies that will minimize the depth and duration of the downturn, and long-term regulatory reforms that will reduce the frequency and depth of such occurrences in the future. We have looked for reforms that are consistent with other goals, such as promoting innovation, stabilizing the economy, and maintaining some semblance of equity. Realism requires a recognition that even with our most valiant efforts, there will be crises in the future. If we succeed in reducing the riskiness of the system, it will encourage market participants to take more risk. Whatever regulatory system we devise, there will be those who will try to find weaknesses and exploit those weaknesses for their own gain, even if it imposes costs on others—and those in the financial markets will continue to use their financial clout to induce the political processes to make "reforms" (as arguably they did in the repeal of Glass-Steagall) that enhance their profits, at the expense of the well-being of society more generally.

The entire episode exemplifies many of the principles elucidated by the economics of information—yet many of the models explicitly or implicitly in the mind of both regulators and market participants ignored the imperfections and asymmetries of information, to which actions within the financial markets were contributing. Incentives matter, but distorted incentives lead to distorted behavior. Incentives at both the individual and organizational level were distorted. Some of the recent actions taken to address the current problems have the potential of exacerbating these distortions in the future.

The crisis will affect the ongoing debates about the design of economic systems. There will be fewer supporters of unfettered markets. It is clear that markets have not worked precisely in the way that its advocates believed they would. Indeed, today some who said they recognized the high risk associated with high leverage argue they had no choice: their stocks would have been severely punished if they had run against the current, and indeed they may not have survived. The arguments presented earlier make clear how difficult it is to ascertain whether above normal returns are a result of excessive gambling—with a price to be paid in the future—or a result of differential returns to rare insights into the economy. And inevitably, reward structures are more sympathetic to those who failed when everyone else failed in a similar way. This encourages the kind of herd behavior, an example of which we have just seen (see Nalebuff and Stiglitz, 1983).

These are the deeper issues raised by this crisis. But whatever one's views about these broader issues, there is a growing consensus on the need for reforms in the financial sector. It is ironic that while, supposedly, market institutions have improved and our understanding of economics has increased, financial crises have become no less frequent—and in some respects have become even worse. If confidence in our financial system is to be restored, there needs to be reason to believe that constraints and incentives have been altered in fundamental ways. If we are to make crises less frequent and less severe in the future, we have to think more deeply about the causes of the crises, the pervasive market failures which give rise to them. We have to design regulatory frameworks that address these underlying problems. This chapter has attempted to outline what that entails.

Notes

1. Paper prepared for a meeting on Financial Regulation sponsored by the Initiative for Policy Dialogue and Brooks World Poverty Institute, Manchester, July, 2008. The author is indebted to Stephany Griffith-Jones for helpful comments. Financial support from the Ford, Mott, and Rockefeller Brothers Foundations is gratefully acknowledged. Since the paper was originally written, the financial meltdown has in fact turned much worse. I have revised the paper to take into account some aspects of the subsequent events.
2. Columbia University and Brooks World Poverty Institute, Manchester.
3. Potential growth is usually estimated at between 3.0 and 3.5 per cent. In the fourth quarter of 2007, growth was 0.6 per cent, and in the first quarter of 2008 it was 0.7 percent. Consensus forecasts for the remainder of 2008 and into 2009 suggest *at best* anemic growth.
4. For an alternative perspective, see Greenwald and Stiglitz (2003).
5. Cf. the discussion in the context of the S&L crisis of Akerlof and Romer (1993). The S&L crisis and the Enron (and similar) scandals made clear that the incentives which led to excessive risk-taking were closely related to those that led to fraudulent behavior. In the current crisis, charges of fraud have been brought, for instance, against UBS and some of its traders for promoting securities that they knew were riskier than they disclosed—much akin to the now famous discrepancies in analysts' statements to each other and to their clients in the dot-com bubble. Though such prosecutions may be helpful, it should be clear that they will not resolve the problems. It will only lead to more careful framing of claims about the attributes of different assets.
6. See Taleb (2007).
7. Such problems are, of course, a reflection of deeper problems in corporate governance, which arise from the separation of ownership and control, to which Berle and Means (1932) called attention. I helped provide modern information theoretic foundations for these issues (Stiglitz, 1985). A large subsequent literature has verified empirically the importance of these concerns. Later, I make reference to the literature showing that observed stock option schemes, for the most part, cannot be viewed as part of an optimal compensation scheme.
8. This does not fully explain the market failures, because markets should have anticipated these problems and taken off-setting measures. They did not, and indeed, modelers used default data from periods prior to securitization to estimate default rates.

9. One of the proposals for helping address the foreclosure problem is to make it more difficult to sue.

10. Some argue that the conversion from partnerships to corporations by some of the leading investment banks may have provided incentives to "cash in" on their reputation.

11. See Ferri et al. (1999).

12. Though this is no longer the case in the Internal Ratings Based approach adopted by the US.

13. See the excellent chapter in this book by Goodhart on how to improve their behavior.

14. One might argue that this would have been offset by their desire to maintain their reputation. The short-term focus that follows from the market imperfections meant that the concern for loss of reputation may not have been given the weight that it otherwise would. Moreover, when all are engaging in similar practices, there is little risk: where else can they turn? In effect, they are rewarded, and punished, on the basis of relative performance. (See Nalebuff and Stiglitz, 1983a, b.)

15. These and related conflicts of interest played a role in some of the worst scandals in the late 1990s, for instance in the allocation of underpriced shares in IPOs to CEOs.

16. Further problems may have been raised by differences in accounting practices and regulations between commercial and investment banks, especially with respect to marking to market. Financial Accounting Standard No 115 offers three alternative ways to account for debt and equity securities depending on the intent for holding them. Choosing among these alternatives becomes less clear, and gaming the system becomes easier, when a bank acts as both a commercial and an investment bank. The full text of FAS 115 may be obtained from <http://www.fasb.org/pdf/fas115.pdf>.

17. This gives rise to convex pay-offs, which in turn give rise to excessive risk-taking. The problems arise whenever there is limited liability. Due diligence on the part of those providing capital to the enterprise is supposed to provide at least some check against abuses. Here, deposit insurance reduces, if it does not eliminate, the extent of the check. Those who provide capital to the bank can ignore the risks. This has led some to criticize deposit insurance. As the Bear Stearns and LTCM bail-outs illustrate, governments will bail out any financial institution whose bankruptcy can give rise to a systemic risk. The major players are simply too large to fail, and they, and those who provide them credit, know it. As Jerry Caprio once put it, there are two kinds of countries, those that have deposit insurance and know it, and those who have deposit insurance and don't know it. Moreover, monitoring banks to ensure that they are in a position to repay their deposits is a public good; it is inefficient to rely on each depositor to do its own monitoring. The credit rating agencies' recent performance makes clear the difficulties of relying on the private sector for the risk assessment. There are simply too many conflicts of interest. See also Stiglitz (1993).

18. This was a publicly orchestrated but privately financed bail-out, but the argument for government intervention was that if even one large institution of this kind failed, it could bring down the entire financial system.

19. This point was made forcefully in the IMF bail-outs in the late 1990s: it was clear that while the bail-outs were typically described as bail-outs of the country, they were more accurately described as bail-outs for the lenders. The former was, of course, the view taken by the Treasury (whose interests, not coincidentally, may have been closely

aligned with the Wall Street beneficiaries). I was on the Council of Economic Advisers at the time of the bail-out; we were not totally persuaded.

20. In the Mexican bail-out, critics suggest that the main beneficiaries were Wall Street investors who held the bonds. There is little evidence that the bail-out played an important role in Mexico's recovery. Indeed, it may have hindered the adjustment. See Lederman et al. (2001, 2003).

21. See, for instance, Greenwald and Stiglitz (2003), Delli Gatti et al. (2006) and Battistona et al. (2007).

22. That there are deeper market failures should be evident from the Fundamental Theorems of Welfare Economics, which argue that when markets work well, all the relevant information is conveyed by price signals. For a critique of these perspectives, see Stiglitz (1994) and Greenwald and Stiglitz (2003).

23. This was especially true given the incentive structures. For instance, mortgage brokers originating the mortgages were paid a commission. They faced no penalties in the event of a foreclosure. They had an incentive to oversell, to explain how the markets were going up and would continue to go up, how the more one borrowed the more one made, how there would be no problem in obtaining additional finance when interest rates increased under the reset provisions. In some cases, they may have been deliberately misleading those who they were trying to persuade to borrow; in other cases, they had deceived themselves. The situation was conducive to corruption: enough money to be split among the brokers, the appraisers, and the borrowers that all could gain from deception. In some cases, there were overt conflicts of interest—where mortgage originators had financial stakes in the appraisers.

24. Some of the mortgages did not initially provide 100 per cent financing, but since the initial payments were less than the full interest that should have been due, they represented negative amortization, and the amount owed became greater than the value of the house.

25. The problems are multiplied further with credit default swaps, which can either be viewed as forms of insurance or bets, amplifying systemic problems.

26. See Persaud (2000) and Goodhart and Persaud (2008b).

27. Persaud (2000) has argued persuasively for the advantages of maintaining heterogeneity of views.

28. Of course, those with different assets and liabilities will face different risks, and the "models" may accordingly pay more attention to the relevant risks.

29. They were caught in part by their own business model, in which they made money through complexity (product differentiation.) This makes netting out more difficult.

30. The fact that developing countries continue to bear the brunt of exchange rate and interest rate fluctuations is another example of the financial markets' failure to transfer risk from those less able to bear it to those more able to do so. See Stiglitz (2006), especially chapter 8, "The Burden of Debt".

31. There are other aspects of regulation in the financial (and other) sectors, which we have discussed elsewhere: ensuring competition and consumer (borrower, investor) protection and ensuring access to credit for underserved groups.

32. I have discussed the issue of disclosure requirements more extensively elsewhere. See Stiglitz (2009).

33. One can design incentive systems with less risk and better incentives than traditional stock options. Indeed, these result in corporate executives bearing risks of random stock market fluctuations, unrelated to their activities (including changes in interest rates). In practice, however, stock options have served more as an excuse for high corporate compensation; when shares have fallen, the executives have found other ways of receiving compensation, so that the relation between corporate performance and compensation is relatively weak. See Stiglitz (2003).
34. See World Bank (2007).
35. A proposal along these lines has been put forward by Goodhart and Persaud (2008a). They focus on the growth of individual bank assets. Attention should also be directed at high growth rates of particular assets, e.g. home mortgages.
36. To recap: (a) They have underestimated the importance of correlated risks; (b) they failed to recognize that securitization increased the problems of information asymmetries, affecting incentives of those originating loans; and (c) they failed to take account of systemic risks and fat tails.
37. Alternatively, it could impose restrictions, limiting purchases to a certain fraction of their portfolios—given the risk that can be hidden inside these products, any purchases should be viewed with care.
38. I saw this first hand when, as a member of the Council of Economic Advisers, I pushed for the introduction of inflation adjusted government bonds. The resistance appeared related to the fact that such bonds have low turnover—i.e. generate less profits for Wall Street. Similarly, when Argentina tried to introduce GDP bonds as part of its debt restructuring (something I had strongly supported), there was great resistance from financial markets.
39. There is a long list: mortgages that are widely available, securitization of mortgages, student loans, small business loans.
40. In the aftermath of the East Asia crisis, a literature developed trying to identify the factors that made a country more vulnerable. See Furman and Stiglitz (1998) and the studies cited there. Interestingly, I suspect in terms of the factors identified there, it should have been apparent that the US was highly vulnerable.

References

Akerlof, G. A. and Romer, P. M. (1993) 'Looting: The Economic Underworld of Bankruptcy for Profit.' *Brookings Papers on Economic Activity*, 1993(2), pp. 1–60.

Battistona, S., Delli Gatti, D., Gallegati, M., Greenwald, B., and Stiglitz, J. E. (2007) 'Credit Chains and Bankruptcy Propagation in Production Networks.' *Journal of Economic Dynamics and Control*, 31(6), pp. 2061–84.

Berle, A. and Means, G. (1932) *The Modern Corporation and Private Property*.

Delli Gatti, D., Gallegati, M., Greenwald, B., Russo, A., and Stiglitz, J. E. (2006) 'Business Fluctuations in a Credit-Network Economy.' *Physica A*, 370, pp. 68–74.

Edlin, A. and Stiglitz, J. E., (1995) 'Discouraging Rivals: Managerial Rent-Seeking and Economic Inefficiencies.' *American Economic Review*, 85(5), December, pp. 1301–12.

Ferri, G., Liu, L.-G., and Stiglitz J. E. (1999) 'The Procyclical Role of Rating Agencies: Evidence from the East Asian Crisis.' *Economic Notes*, 28(3), pp. 335–55.

Furman, J. and Stiglitz, J. E. (1998) 'Economic Crises: Evidence and Insights from East Asia.' *Brookings Papers on Economic Activity*, (2), pp. 1–114.

Goodhart, C. A. E. and Persaud, A. (2008a) 'A Party Pooper's Guide to Financial Stability.' *Financial Times*, June 5.

—— (2008b) 'How to Avoid the Next Crash.' *Financial Times*, January 30.

Greenwald, B. and Stiglitz, J. E. (2003) *Towards a New Paradigm for Monetary Policy*. London: Cambridge University Press.

Lederman, D., Menéndez, A. M., Perry, G., and Stiglitz, J. E. (2001) 'Mexico—Five Years After the Crisis.' *Annual Bank Conference on Development Economics 2000*. Washington, DC: World Bank, pp. 263–82.

—— (2003) 'Mexican Investment After the Tequila Crisis: Basic Economics, "Confidence" Effect or Market Imperfection?' *Journal of International Money and Finance*, 22, pp. 131–51.

Nalebuff, B. and Stiglitz, J. E. (1983a) 'Information, Competition and Markets.' *American Economic Review*, 73(2), May, pp. 278–84.

—— —— (1983b) 'Prizes and Incentives: Toward a General Theory of Compensation and Competition.' *Bell Journal*, 14(1), Spring, pp. 21–43.

Persaud, A. (2000) 'Sending the Herd off the Cliff Edge.' *World Economics*, 1(4), pp. 15–26.

Stiglitz, J. E. (1985) 'Credit Markets and the Control of Capital.' *Journal of Money, Banking, and Credit*, 17(2), May, pp. 133–52.

—— (1992) 'Banks versus Markets as Mechanisms for Allocating and Coordinating Investment.' In J. A. Roumasset and S. Barr (eds.), *The Economics of Cooperation: East Asian Development and the Case for Pro-Market Intervention*. Boulder: Westview Press, pp. 15–38.

—— (1993) 'The Role of the State in Financial Markets.' *Proceeding of the World Bank Conference on Development Economics 1993*, Washington, DC: World Bank, pp. 41–6.

—— (1994) *Whither Socialism?* Cambridge, Mass.: MIT Press.

—— (2003) *Roaring Nineties*. New York: WW Norton.

—— (2006) *Making Globalization Work*. New York: WW Norton.

—— (2009) 'Regulation and the Theory of Market and Government Failure'. In D. Moss and J. Cisternino (eds.) *New Perspectives on Regulation*. Cambridge, MA: The Tobin Project.

Taleb, N. (2007) *The Black Swan: The Impact of the Highly Improbable*. New York: Random House.

World Bank (1997) *Private Capital Flows to Developing Countries: The Road to Financial Integration*. World Bank Policy Research Report. Washington, DC: World Bank.

3

Sub-Prime Finance: Yes, We are Still in Kansas[1]

Gerard Caprio, Jr.[2]

Introduction

Financial crises, which seemed like such a 1990s thing, are back. After two decades with an estimated 130 crises worldwide during the 1980s and 1990s, many had concluded prematurely that the period of calm in most financial markets since 1998 meant that the financial system had evolved to such an extent that crises were an unfortunate experience of the past, except for a few of the usual suspects like Argentina. The end of financial history had arrived, we were told. Especially in advanced economies, new financial instruments were efficiently slicing and dicing risk, parceling it out to those who could bear it best. So prevalent was this view that in a paper on banking crises for the *Oxford Handbook of Banking* (Caprio and Honohan, 2009) on which work commenced in the spring of 2007, comments on the outline advised of the need for a section on the "end of crises." Fortunately the paper was not due until late 2007, so the comments on the need for such a section rapidly were muted.

Far from ending, financial history has been doing a great job of hitting us over the head to remind us that the basic forces that motivate human behavior in financial markets are alive and well. As Talleyrand said, "History teaches nothing, but punishes those who fail to learn its lessons." As this chapter goes to press, punishments are being meted out in large doses, and the pain looks set to continue. In this brief chapter, I would like to first review some of the "universal constants" of financial market behavior, or at least the constants when incentives systems are conducive to absurd risk-taking, and there is very lax oversight by markets and supervisors alike. Then in the final section I will discuss the necessary elements of a policy response. To be clear up front, while eliminating financial crises would be easy, I do not think that societies would like to live in such a state. The Barcelonan authorities in 1390 finally had enough of bankers gambling with other people's money, and beheaded a banker outside his bank (Kohn, 2008). This policy response was reported to have been quite effective, killing off not just a risk-taking banker but also any financial risk-taking, and economic growth as well. Most countries today are at a far different extreme—rather than flirting with excessive liability in finance, some financial sector participants enjoy a generous safety net while societies permit staggering levels of compensation to those whose risk-taking leads to the impoverishment of employees and shareholders of financial firms as well as innocent bystanders.[3] Political economy forces predominate in financial sector regulation—"them that's got the gold make the rules." Or at least that is how financial sector regulation has often played out in history, and empirically, Barth, Caprio, and Levine (2006) document the importance of politics in regulatory choices. With staggering losses in the current crisis, it will be interesting to see if this time is any different; as of early 2009, taxpayers look to be bearing a heavy burden.

Déjà vu all over again

It was not so long ago that a crisis was brought on by investors hungry for yield, who decided in large numbers to put a significant amount of their resources into a surefire investment. The firm benefiting from their enthusiasm was the world leader in its field, and best of all, the key players there had done it before, making huge sums of money in the process. They had the best talent that one could gather, led not only by those with great success in the private sector but blessed by great political connections as well. Notwithstanding some early successes, they finally failed miserably, as a series of events, which the public was told could not have been anticipated, occurred. Perhaps most embarrassingly of all, for the fiercely independent entrepreneurs, government intervention (though not a "bail-out") was necessary by US authorities—the government that most urges private sector solutions on others.

Some hearing this might assume that the above description refers to the 2008 failure of Bear Stearns, perhaps even more recall the Long-Term Capital Management (LTCM) affair, but instead, the case in question was the sorry saga in the late nineteenth century of the Panama Canal (McCullough, 1977). Ferdinand De Lesseps represented the combination of Meriwether, Mullins, and Merton, the protagonists of the LTCM drama. He began his career as a diplomat, and then achieved world renown by building the Suez Canal. Surely he was the best at canal building, so he could safely be entrusted with the savings of so many French families—it is estimated that one family in ten lost its life savings in the resulting fiasco, as its shares fell to zero, and its debt paid but a few centimes per franc.

While De Lesseps did know canal building, it turns out that building canals through sand and in a dry climate, is entirely different than building them

51

through rocky soil with tenacious tree roots and tropical diseases that killed 25,000 workers. The photo of the broken and abandoned machines resembles one from another instance when local conditions were ignored—the Kongwa Groundnut scheme in Tanganyika in the late 1940s.[4] Interestingly, in Panama, the job that the French private corporation was unable to do was completed by a US public sector organization, the US Army. The Army succeeded where a private group did not in part because like many bureaucracies, it had a hard time making decisions, and put two people in control, one of whom was an Army doctor who insisted on not doing anything until they could discover why so many workers were dying. As a result, in addition to building the Panama Canal, they also were the first to note the role of mosquitoes in spreading yellow fever, and to figure out strategies to cope with it.

So why is this case relevant? The rush to invest one's money in "sure things" that will pay a high return seems to be a decidedly human characteristic, even when one realizes that it is a high-risk venture. Consider the statements of two prominent bankers almost 300 years apart in time, John Martin and Chuck Prince:

When the rest of the world are mad, we must imitate them in some measure. (John Martin, Martin's Bank, 1720)

When the music stops, in terms of liquidity, things will be complicated. But as long as the music is playing, you've got to get up and dance. We're still dancing. (Chuck Prince, ex-CEO, Citibank, July 2007)

Both bankers understood that they were taking risks—Martin in particular had studiously kept his bank out of the South Sea Bubble until just before the end. Many others bought in just before the peak, and then liquidated, as did Isaac Newton—selling his investment early on in South Sea Company shares and then buying back in, and thereby losing a fortune at the end. Both Martin and Newton seem to have been unable to resist the prospect of riches. As Charles Kindleberger (1989) put it, "There is nothing so disturbing to one's well-being and judgment as to see a friend get rich." Some eternal truths about humans' ability to assess risk and make financial decisions seem evident, and increasingly are confirmed by behavioral and even neuroeconomics, the latter showing that it is the pleasure centers of the brain, rather than its logical parts, that are heavily engaged in these decisions. Individuals are not fully rational in assessing risk, but rather are subject to framing—as Kahneman and Tversky (1979) showed—and exhibit myopia, a particular type of framing in which the recent past frames many decisions.

The general lessons adduced from previous crises depend on the degree of specificity of the observer. While some adhere to a Tolstoy-like view of crises "every happy family is the same, every unhappy family is unhappy in its own way," there are in fact a number of common features to crises. To be sure, it is true that no crisis in history had the plethora of new financial products or the volume of derivative instruments that, at the least, contributed to the ability of market participants to disguise what was occurring in the 2008 crisis. However, the incentive to disguise risk-taking is hardly new.

In many respects, the 2008 crisis is very familiar. Residential and/or commercial real estate booms have been prominent features of crises around the world, notably in Japan (1990s), Malaysia (mid-1980s), Mexico (1994), and Sweden (1991–4), even when overall macro stability seemed assured. High leverage ratios, also a part of the recent crisis, were featured in East Asia in the late 1990s, particularly in Korea. Indeed, Hy Minsky noted that macro-stability contributes to financial instability—prosperity encourages private market participants to increase their borrowing. More generally, economic booms and increasing asset prices have been noted as antecedents of financial crises for as long as modern banking has existed. Asset price boom in equities and property might some day be found to increase the brain's production of some narcotic-like drug, because in most booms, the actors seem to believe that "this time, it is different," or in other words, some exogenous shifts mean that said prices will continue to rise, as seen in each of the above real estate booms, the 1970s oil price bubble, the emerging market lending binge of the 1970s and early 1980s, and the tech boom. In each case, as with the recent real estate boom, those who pointed out the possibility of a bubble were told "Sovereign debt does not default," or "housing prices might slow, but never decline," notwithstanding historical evidence very much to the contrary.

In addition to what Keynes might have described as animal spirits gone berserk, several factors seem to be at work. First, whenever a block of investors or more, usually financial intermediaries such as banks, reallocate their portfolio in a given direction, although individually they have no influence on asset prices, as a group their shift tends to increase prices of the favored assets, which then produce additional portfolio adjustment in the same direction, etc. Although the timing of the portfolio shift might merely be a random event, often there is some economic change that drives it, one common example being financial liberalization. A decline in interest rates on low risk assets often sets in motion a particular portfolio change, namely encouraging investors to venture further out on the risk frontier in search of yield. When real riskless rates are near zero or negative, the temptation to search for yield can become irresistible, and investors' simultaneous moves make it seem as though the shift is low risk, for returns in the favored object of speculation inevitably rise as the herd piles into it. We have seen this movie play out before, in each of the aforementioned booms.

Second, regulatory change often plays a part as well. As countries deregulated their financial systems, they not only removed controls on interest rates and the powers or activities permitted to intermediaries, but often gave them more freedom to reallocate their portfolio, reducing in the process pre-existing requirements to hold high reserves, meet liquidity requirements, invest in government bonds, or direct credit in line with government goals. For example, the gradual deregulation in Malaysia in the early 1970s led banks to buy less of what they already held—directed loans and highly liquid claims—and to invest more in property and buildings, which were only a few percentage points of the banking system's portfolio. Every year, real estate and commercial property prices rose, and every year the banks decided that in this "new world" it was sensible to invest still more in this area, with the result that in some years over 50 per cent of new lending went into it. The boom in prices collapsed in the mid-1980s, no doubt as the limits to this reallocation became evident.

Texas banks in the 1970s were hardly much more diversified, investing in stuff in the ground (oil), the ground (property), and stuff built on top of the ground (commercial real estate). No doubt it came as an unprecedented shock when oil prices finally went down, so too did land prices, commercial real estate, and of course the banks. Similarly, as the 2008 crisis was beginning, hedge fund managers, in their letters to clients, were saying that events that were truly impossible to anticipate led to their losses and in some cases closure. The claim in effect was that the event was a "black swan," an event that is not anticipated at least until one example is encountered (Taleb, 2007). To be sure, people are not good at anticipating black swan events—unprecedented or exceptionally rare occurrences, such as the discovery of black swans in Australia, which forced the revision of European belief as to the color of swans. However, the housing bubble, the decline in lending standards, and the financial alchemy of recent years—notably the ability to create AAA-rated securities from those BBB-rated and below—were evident for all to observe, and similar waves of excessive risk-taking have been all too common throughout history. Rather than a black swan, the 2008 crisis seems all too familiar. Behavioral finance also notes that investors often interpret increases in the prices of the assets that they have purchased as evidence of their own acumen, and declines as reflecting events that were impossible to anticipate.

Third, crises have been common before central banks existed to regulate the flow of credit, and before they adopted the position as lender of last resort (LOLR). But after the rise of the LOLR, and with the spread of deposit insurance (roughly 85 countries having adopted it since the 1970s), crises have become much more expensive in their fiscal cost (Caprio, Demirguc-Kunt, and Kane, 2008, and sources cited there). Fourth, new financial instruments, introduced as part of technological progress, deregulation, or advances in finance, often precipitate financial crises, as they lead to new risks or old risks in a new guise. Bankers expanding into new, exotic foreign markets forget that they suffer the greatest information asymmetries vis-à-vis the locals, and often are forced to retrench after serious losses. Securitization not only encouraged home ownership for those who could sensibly afford it, but also for those who could not. Loan sales, which many of us were taught did not happen due to adverse selection, occurred in large volumes thanks to this advance.

The unfortunate casualty in this crisis was information: if banks could move assets and activities off their balance sheets to opaque entities, few thought of the consequences when the banks needed to be able to demonstrate their solvency and could not. Tools to encourage borrowing to buy assets are always justified to help a broader array of people participate in financial markets, but the same tools can be used for greater leverage and of course to generate commissions for some. While some innovations are driven by the demands of the non-financial sector—swaps are a splendid way to lower financing costs and meet the risk preferences of companies—they are also regularly motivated by the desire to exploit the government's safety net or the wish to avoid regulation (see Caprio, Demirguc-Kunt, and Kane, 2008).

Another common feature of financial crises is that actors in the sector will attempt to weaken bonding (the incentives that encourage behavior more in line with the long- term interests of the firm) and accountability. One mechanism is through the payment of lavish compensation for high current returns, allowing risks to be understated (see Barings in the 1990s, UBS and Bear Stearns more recently). Yet, *whenever* compensation in financial services advances significantly, one should always suspect that excessive risks are being taken. That these risks have moved off an intermediary's balance sheet does not mean that they have departed the planet. With little disclosure, supervisors' and market participants' investigation often stopped at the balance sheet of the intermediary. In the past, how to deal with excessive risk-taking was understood: bank officers used to have to post bonds, out of which losses could be deducted, and their bonuses were deferred until they retired, so they could not profit quickly from taking large risks. If the bank failed as a result of their behavior, their deferred compensation was lost. More recently, enormous compensation induced great risk-taking, and left us with some institutions that incurred enormous risk, and understood what they were doing, and others that were also taking great risk, but did not understand it at the time.

Banks and ratings agencies applied seemingly sophisticated models with patently myopic assumptions—ignoring the correlation across adjustable rate mortgages when interest rates rose and housing prices decelerated, let alone declined. When judgments seem to be beyond belief in their shortsightedness, one should look elsewhere for answers. In this case, incentives were encouraging originators, packagers, raters, etc., to get on board and not raise questions.

And here is a key point surely worth emphasis: in addition to the scandalous incentives in the financial services industry—money flowing into intermediaries and ratings agencies and out to their principals in astonishing amounts—there was the scandal in supervision. Where were the canaries in the coal mine? Clearly in this latest crisis, evidence of market failure and government failure has been in ample supply. The critical supervisory failure in my view is that supervisors, as sanctioned by Basel (not surprising, as supervisors have dominated that discussion), have focused on the disclosure of information to supervisors and not to the public. Given the information problem in finance, this is the wrong orientation. Supervision should want as many informed observers as possible so that they can learn from the market and concentrate their ever scarce resources where most needed. What did supervisors know, and when did they know it? Did they not understand that risks were not being fully removed from banks' balance sheets? Did they think that housing prices were going to rise without limit? Unfortunately it is difficult to hold supervisors accountable, as society does not have the information, or the mechanisms, to answer these questions.

The regulatory community is often late to detect problems. This is due to skill gaps—the private sector can draw the best talent, or at least those who have succeeded in technical training, by virtue of high compensation levels—and because official supervisors either can be restrained directly or indirectly by politicians, or face unfavorable incentives, such as that of covering up problems that emerge on their watch.

Finally, all of these historical lessons occur against the backdrop of the fragile nature of fractional reserve banking. Banks are highly leveraged, opaque, engage in maturity transformation, offer demandable, short-term debt, and have assets denominated in fiat currency (Caprio and Honohan, 2009). Summarized in this fashion, perhaps the surprise is not that crises occur, but that there are not more of them. While all of these factors were at work in the latest crisis, perhaps the most notable was the degree of opacity, which surprised many. Lulled by the favorable credit ratings that many securitized products received, investors failed to do due diligence on their purchases, and officials sanctioned their lack of effort through various regulations that require the purchase of highly rated paper, and by giving a "seal of approval" to Nationally Recognized Statistical Rating Organizations to perform such ratings (Caprio, Demirguc-Kunt and Kane, 2008, and articles cited there by Sylla and Partnoy). Although this particular feature of the crisis is new, the phenomenon of investors thinking that their assets were much safer than was realized *ex post* is familiar. In times past, they were assured by bankers and stockbrokers of the safety of their portfolio, whereas this time the bankers and securitizers paid the ratings organizations quite well to obtain such encouragement.

Policy fixes: something old, something new

The key lessons of history, summarized in the second section, offer an agenda for policy reform. It is assumed that the goal of regulation is not to have the safest possible financial system, because while a very safe system would be possible, the cost would be too high—as noted earlier in the example of fourteenth century Barcelona (Kohn, 2008). Rather, the goal should be a financial system that takes *prudent* risks in supplying a large volume of useful financial services efficiently, to the broadest part of society, and with the least corruption. In other words, societies value an array of goals: financial sector development, the cost of producing those services, the stability of the system, access to these services, and limited corruption in the sector.

The lessons of history reviewed above then suggest the need to rethink the approach to regulation and supervision in the wake of the crisis and especially to take account of the dynamics of the regulatory game. In other words, as we have just seen, any static set of rules will end up inducing innovations that help evade the same rules. Ed Kane (2000) and Joseph Stiglitz (2001) have written on this issue at length, the point being that a fixed set of rules in financial regulation is about as useful as a Maginot line. Yet many are proposing a new fixed line every day (e.g. slightly adjust the Basel II accord, abandon or adopt more fully mark to market accounting, etc.), and only a few, such as Brunnermeier et al. (2009), who recommend automatically varying capital with the cycle, take account of the dynamic game nature of the problem. Yet static approaches must fail. Thus, the 1988 Basel Accord introduced the notion of arbitrary risk weights for different asset classes. The ensuing boom in securitization might have partly been in response to other factors but surely was an attempt by banks to shed assets with higher risk weights so as to economize on their cost of capital.

Many government officials seemed to take securitization as a sign of strength, noting that banks were passing on risks to those who could bear them best. At the same time, compensation levels had exploded in the financial services industry, a sure sign that excessive risks were being taken. Nonetheless, supervisors stuck to their approach to risk-based supervision, only adding further complications to the planned approach in Basel II. Supervisors instead should have been trying to reduce the growing opacity of the industry and uncover the sources of increased risk.

A dynamic system has to have as many participants as possible with the incentives to uncover new forms of taking risk wherever it is going on in the sector, and compel supervisors to act on the basis of the signals provided. A top priority for reform then should be revising the approach to the incentives of supervisors, and indeed what we ask of supervision. The cornerstone of prudential supervision has been the information that banks have to disclose to supervisors. Unfortunately a good part of the information conveyed to supervisors does not get disclosed to markets, which not only limits market discipline but reduces society's ability to hold officials accountable. At times, of course, officials inevitably will have their hands tied by the political process, such as when lobbying by Fannie and Freddie resulted in a "regulation-lite" model. So in addition to ending the static nature of supervision is the need to revamp the job description. Rather than having the focus of supervisory efforts be to get banks to reveal information to officials, who then would interpret it or conceal it, supervisors' main job should be that of requiring far greater

57

information disclosure to the public and of verifying that information, meting out significant penalties when it is false or misleading.

It would even be timely to debate whether supervisors should be allowed to keep any information confidential that is pertinent to the health of individual institutions. Although the disclosure of significantly negative information could lead to a run on a bank, allowing information to remain confidential until it threatens the financial system risks far larger damage and compels most governments to extend safety net support. If supervisors have any private information, they might not act on it, yet the public will never know. And if it is so difficult to deduce the risk positions of financial intermediaries, then it would seem useful to have as many "watchful eyes" on their activities as possible. Some in the supervisory community view this recommendation as reducing the importance of their function. In fact, although it would permit more active monitoring by markets, especially those with a pecuniary interest, it would both be making supervision more practical—giving supervisors a task that could be accomplished—and more likely to help improve the safety and soundness of banking. Most importantly, more complete disclosure allows society to monitor supervisors and hold them accountable, and would make it easier to reward and punish supervisors with the granting of large, deferred bonuses (pensions) and their forfeiture in cases of costly supervisory negligence.

Second, it is clear that market participants need incentives to use information. If all participants are credibly insured, then they will not have the incentive to use the information. So some creditors need to be credibly uninsured, so that they have the incentive to monitor intermediaries. A long-standing proposal to require that banks issue subordinated debt in lumpy amounts (for example, creating creditors with much at stake) and at regular intervals, is a sensible way to do this. More recent proposals to have banks buy insurance or credit default swaps (Evanoff and Wall, 2000; Caprio, Demirguc-Kunt and Kane, 2008; Kashyap, Rajan and Stein, 2008) share the same strategy, as the creditors or insurance providers would be exposed to a downside when banks fail without the ability, which shareholders enjoy, to profit from increases in their risk-taking.[5]

Banks oppose this strategy because they view it as being costly for them and their managers. Consider the reaction of subordinated debt holders or insurance providers to a significant rise in compensation in a bank. Given their financial interest, they would press banks for more information to be sure that risk was not on the rise, and if unable to so convince themselves, they would sell the debt or demand an increased premium, limiting banks' ability to continue the practice. Subordinated debt acts to complement bank supervision. Since these creditors face no upside to risk-taking and are the first, after equity holders, to sustain a loss, they are highly motivated to monitor the institutions whose debt they hold. Since this "run" would be highly visible, it would force supervisors to concentrate their resources where needed, and could allow them to close banks while net worth is still positive.

Even though creditors might be wary of intermediaries paying substantial compensation levels, there is a long history—including the Panama Canal episode—of investors and creditors being too trusting. Also, as has been seen in recent years, the market seems to have a difficult time limiting compensation where information on risk positions is imperfect. Thus it is possible, and worth discussion, that authorities might need to help the industry in this regard. The least interventionist step would be to require significantly more disclosure about the level of, and even more importantly the mechanism for decisions on, total compensation in financial intermediaries. This would have to be enforced for any intermediary, hedge funds included, above a certain size, because even hedge funds, once sufficiently large, can pose systemic risk. Further along on the interventionist path is to consider having supervisory ratings—such as the CAMELS[6] ratings—as a function of compensation. In fact, one can argue that in assessing management and risk management systems, the most important ingredient is how firms compensate risk takers. So the supervisory agency could give lower scores to firms that award more generous current compensation and high scores to those with a greater percentage deferred far out into the future. The latter would help management avoid paying out high compensation to those whose decisions led the firm's portfolio to "blow up" after their compensation was already paid out.

Regulation also can improve incentives by exposing to the legal system those who manage other people's money. The requirement that various intermediaries only hold highly rated paper allowed those managers to hold securities that they should have known were risky; in effect, it protected managers from being accountable. Instead, the requirement for money managers should be that they exercise the highest degree of fiduciary responsibility in line with their published objectives. Money managers then could face lawsuits for improper conduct, subject to the interpretation of the courts after listening to other financial experts.

Additionally, the government should de-license ratings firms, that is return to the pre-1975 era when there were no Nationally Recognized Statistical Ratings Organizations. Instead of licensing, governments can look to ways to encourage the quality and availability of financial sector information, such as by subsidizing entry into the ratings business. The same legal liability that money managers face should be extended to those who rate firms, so raters should be compelled to publish more information about their ratings, and courts need to hold the principals of these firms liable for their pronouncements.

These recommendations contain elements of what used to help limit risk-taking in finance, as well as distinctly new features for the regulatory landscape. Providing supervisors with both carrots and sticks, and ensuring that they and managers of financial intermediaries have incentives compatible with society's goals for the financial sector are not new ideas. For example, the idea of bonuses for supervisors is an old idea that dates back to at least the early nineteenth century in the case of the Suffolk Banking system. Having bank officers post large bonds dates back to the origin of modern banking. So while the precise ways in which risk-taking bank officers have been robbing shareholders, sometimes creditors, and of late taxpayers are novel, the principle most certainly is not. Getting the government out of the business of certifying rating agencies is very much a return to the status quo ante. Greater disclosure of information, including of compensation, is new, and is a response to the complexity of modern finance and runaway compensation levels. Whereas in the past some weight could be put on a reputation mechanism, the value of reputation derives in large part from how it helps the bearer earn compensation in the future. When intermediaries pay out what used to be regarded as a multi-generational fortune in a single year, the return to maintaining one's reputation shrinks markedly.

It is clear that political economy considerations drive financial sector regulatory choice. Barth, Caprio, and Levine (2006) showed that the private interest view does a better job in explaining regulatory choices than that based on the public interest. However, the current crisis, by fundamentally shaking up the financial services industry, at least in the United States and United Kingdom, offers a greater opportunity to reshape the rules of the game in finance than at any time since the 1930s. That regulatory effort attempted to confine risk-taking and greatly limited what the sector could do. The globalization of financial services makes it difficult to impose draconian restrictions, and suggests instead that the attention of reformers be concentrated on incentives and information. In 2009, with the new US administration, we shall see if the crisis was sufficiently large to provoke the needed reforms. The crisis has revealed that the financial system "is still in Kansas," meaning that many of the forces shaping finance and leading to unwise risk-taking continue to rule. The regulatory debate promises to show whether we are ready to leave Kansas yet, or not.

Notes

1. Paper presented at the Financial Markets Task Force Meeting, Manchester, July 1–2, 2008. The author thanks Stephany Griffith-Jones, Joseph Stiglitz, and task force participants for their comments but retains all responsibility for any errors and omissions.
2. Williams College.
3. I presented this paper a few months after the failure/bailout of Bear Stearns (the shareholders took a loss, but creditors were made whole) and finalized it the weekend of the government takeover of Fannie Mae and Freddie Mac.
4. The soil in the Kongwa was perhaps even less friendly to clearing than that in Panama. One observer, quoted at <http://www.sjsu.edu/faculty/watkins/groundnt.htm> put it this way: "In patches the thickets of scrub are impenetrable. A rhinoceros can force a way through, a snake can wiggle through: but no size or shape of animal in between."

5. What needs further debate is the role of regulation in the subordinated debt and/or insurance market. For example, does the government need to qualify the writers of credit default swaps on banks or assure the existence of the resources to cover the contract? (Also the Mehrling point, whether private insurance against systemic risk makes sense?)
6. CAMELS ratings are used to classify US banks. The following are considered when assigning the rating: capital adequacy (C), asset quality (A), management (M), earnings (E), liquidity (L) and sensitivity to market risk (S).

References

Barth, J. R., Caprio, G. and Levine, R. (2006) *Rethinking Bank Regulation: Till Angels Govern.* Cambridge: Cambridge University Press.

Brunnermeier, M., Crockett, A., Goodhart, C., Persuad, A., and Shin, H. (2009) 'The Fundamental Principles of Financial Regulation.' *Geneva Reports on the World Economy*, 11.

Caprio, G. and Honohan, P. (2009) 'Banking Crises.' Forthcoming in Allan Berger, Philip Molyneux, and John Wilson (eds.), *The Oxford Handbook of Banking*. Oxford: Oxford University Press.

Caprio, G., Demirguc-Kunt, A. and Kane, E. J. (2008) 'The 2007 Meltdown in Structured Securitization: Searching for Lessons not Scapegoats.' Paper presented at World Bank Conference on Risk Management (October).

Evanoff, D. and Wall, L. (2000) 'Subordinated Debt and Bank Capital Reform.' Federal Reserve Bank of Atlanta Working Paper 2000-24 (November).

Kahneman, D. and Tversky, A. (1979) 'Prospect Theory: An Analysis of Decisions Under Risk.' *Econometrica*, 47, pp. 313–27.

Kane, E. J. (2000) 'The Dialectical Role of Information and Disinformation in Regulation-Induced Banking Crises.' *Pacific Basin Finance Journal*, 8, pp. 285–308.

Kashyap, A., Raghuram R. and Stein, J. (2008) 'Rethinking Capital Regulation.' Paper prepared for the 2008 Federal Reserve Bank of Kansas City Symposium on 'Maintaining Stability in a Changing Financial System.'

Kindleberger, C. P. (1989) *Manias, Panics, and Crashes: A History of Financial Crises*. New York: Basic Books.

Kohn, M. (2008) 'The Origins of Western Economic Success: Commerce, Finance, and Government in Preindustrial Europe.' Manuscript in progress <http://www.dartmouth.edu/mkohn/orgins.html>.

McCullough, D. (1977) *The Path Between the Seas: The Creation of the Panama Canal, 1870–1914.* New York: Simon and Schuster.

Taleb, N. (2007) *The Black Swan: The Impact of the Highly Improbable.* New York: Random House.

Stiglitz, J. E. (2001) 'Principles of Financial Regulation: A Dynamic Portfolio Approach.' *World Bank Research Observer*, 16(1), pp. 1–18.

4

Background Considerations to a Re-Regulation of the US Financial System: Third Time a Charm? Or Strike Three?

Jan Kregel

Introduction

In the aftermath of the subprime mortgage crisis, the Federal Reserve converted section 13, paragraph c of the March 21, 1933, Amendment to the Glass-Steagall Act[1] into a permanent feature of its lender of last resort function through the discounting of the mortgage assets of investment banks and other capital market institutions such as primary and broker dealers. This has brought forth suggestions that the same prudential regulations that are applied to deposit takers be extended to investment banks and broker/dealers, while leaving the 1999 Gramm-Bliley-Leach Financial Services Modernization Act unchanged. The former US Treasury Secretary, Henry Paulson, had also recommended consolidation and extension of the writ of certain regulatory agencies. However, the history of financial regulation in the United States suggests that this would simply be a repeat of the reactions, by legislators and regulators, to two previous financial crises, neither of which proved durable or capable of providing financial stability.

Prudential regulation[2]

Prudential regulation in the United States initially concentrated on ensuring the redemption value of private bankers' circulating promissory notes. The failure to reconfirm the second Bank of the United States as the national bank of the United States in 1832, and the introduction of the Independent Treasury

62

System based on payments by the Federal government in gold, relinquished the means of payment function to private sector financial institutions that could only be created under state charter and regulation.

This ushered in the period of free banking which lasted from the final demise of the Second Bank of the United States in 1836 to the issue of the first Federal circulating medium—the now famous "Greenback"—issued by the Union government to provide finance for the Civil War. When this limited issue proved insufficient for its war financing needs, the Union government introduced in 1863 the National Banking System, and created the Office of the Comptroller of the Currency (OCC) to supervise the issue of national bank notes by the federally chartered national banks.

In the free banking period between 1836 and 1863, the means of payment was comprised of private bankers' notes, in general backed by reserve holdings of the relevant state government securities or by specie. The new national system required reserve holding of Federal government debt for the issue of national bank notes by nationally chartered banks. However, the market value of these securities varied with changes in interest rates and other factors, which meant that the actual coverage represented by reserves held against national bank notes varied pro-cyclically because the securities were usually valued at par in both systems.

In order to ensure dominance of national notes, a tax was placed on state bank notes. To defend their position, state chartered private banks replaced their note issue with deposits subject to check. This extended the need for prudential regulation to bank deposits as well as national bank notes. Since the deposit banks were state banks, they were regulated by state governments. This created an initial dichotomy in US bank regulation, with the state regulators, responsible for prudential regulation of deposit taking by state banks and the OCC for national banks, issuing national bank notes.

Preventing the Money Trust from using other people's (deposit) money

The financial system in the United States before the creation of the Federal Reserve, according to Louis Brandeis, was one in which "the four distinct functions of banks (commercial banking, trust and insurance, corporate underwriting, and brokering) each essential to business, and each exercised originally, by a distinct set of men, became united in the investment banker" (Brandeis, 1914, pp. 5–6).

He noted that such a system would not be conducive to competition:

Can there be real bargaining where the same man is on both sides of the trade? The investment banker, through his controlling influence on the Board of Directors, decides that the corporation shall issue and sell securities, decides the price at which it shall sell them, and decides that it shall sell the securities to himself. (Brandeis, 1914, p.11)

He also noted that the large profits that resulted from concentration "led to a revolutionary change in the conduct of our leading banking institutions," in which banks sought to become investment bankers, leading to their "departure from the legitimate sphere of the banking business, which is the making of temporary loans to business concerns" (Brandeis, 1914, p. 26). However, the main criticism was that the control of bank deposits—other people's money—was the source of this power of concentration and of the exorbitant profits of investment banks.

Brandeis' observation concerning the move in the early 1900s to concentration of banking activities in large multi-function investment banks must be seen in the context of the fact that national banks had initially been allowed to engage fully in capital market activities. However, after a challenge by the Comptroller of the right of the large New York banks to operate in securities, by 1908 national banks were regulated to only commercial banking activities. National banks thus faced an increasing competitive disadvantage relative to state chartered banks which were usually allowed to operate without restriction in securities markets. To protect their profitability, national bankers created state chartered security affiliates that were outside the writ of the Comptroller. The first such affiliate was formed under state charter by First National City Bank in 1911.

Separation of commercial and investment banks

The regulatory response to the federal investigations of the "money trust" produced central bank and securities regulations by state governments in the form of "blue sky" laws. The existence of legal limitations on the maximum issue of greenbacks, and subsequently of national bank notes, meant that the supply of currency was limited, independently of the needs of trade, and there was no means of increasing the supply of notes to meet the frequent loss of confidence in deposits of state banks. In 1875, the limitation on the note issue was eliminated, but this still did not provide a sufficiently elastic supply of currency. This, together with popular reaction against the money trust, led to the creation of the Federal Reserve System, composed of twelve District Federal Reserve Banks that could issue Federal Reserve notes. These notes had to be backed 40 per cent in gold and 60 per cent in discounts on private commercial loans.

The elasticity of the note issue was thus resolved by adopting the real bills doctrine, which restored the role of the bank—as a deposit taker and lender of short-term funds for commercial purposes—as the central institution in the system. This finally made the note issue unique and unified, but retained the diverse quality of deposits issued by individual state and national banks. As a result, the main task of prudential supervision was to insure the maintenance of convertibility of private bank deposits into Federal Reserve notes.

Profitability and investment activities

It was the 1927 Pepper-McFadden Act that finally clarified the range of activities permitted to national banks. In this period, as in the days of the money trust, national banks that were limited to commercial banking activities suffered from falling profitability. The continued expansion of free banking in many states led to widespread overbanking. At the same time, the 1920s stock market boom brought with it the possibility of national banks' commercial clients funding their short-term financing needs through longer-term capital market issues.

Even before the 1929 stock market crash, analysts were predicting the demise of the commercial banks as bank loans extended by national banks continued to decline. Lauchlin Currie, an adviser to the Federal Reserve and the Treasury in the 1930s (Currie, 1931, pp. 701–2), notes that over the period 1922–8 there was a tendency for larger, successful firms to reduce their bank borrowing, due to "a realization of the dangers inherent in loans of any description and particularly bank loans" (Currie, 1931, p. 708). Whether Currie was right in identifying the cause of the decline in business lending or whether it was simply the fact that firms were encouraged by the banks directing them to their securities affiliates—since the stock market boom made it much cheaper to raise funds as the Fed was putting pressure on interest rates—the end result was a decline in the quality and liquidity of "commercial" bank assets.

The solution to the commercial banks' dire need for additional sources of revenue was provided by the McFadden Act, which allowed national banks to "buy and sell without recourse marketable obligations in the form of bonds, notes or debentures, commonly known as investment securities... This did not include the power to buy and sell stocks" (Valentine, 1951, p. 400).

Despite the expansion in activities that the Act provided, national banks went further and side-stepped national regulation of their activities by organizing independent securities affiliates with state charters.

Generally speaking it may be said that by 1929 in the field of long-term financing the commercial banks and their affiliates occupied a position comparable to that of private investment bankers from the standpoint of physical facilities, capital employed, and the volume of securities underwritten and distributed. (Valentine, 1951, p. 401)

While, the money trust was not reconstructed, the combination of functions in a single institution, deplored by Brandeis, had been reconstituted.

New Deal legislation

After the 1929 stock market collapse, conditions facing commercial banks deteriorated rapidly. Currie was led to the conclusion that commercial banks "belong to a past era." He supported this position by pointing out that banking statistics for December 31, 1932, indicated that 65 per cent of banks' lending was against security and bonds, and only 8 per cent could be considered as commercial loans. He "sought to explain the decline in bank loans as due to a recognition of the extent to which loans intensify the dangers of a drastic decline in net earnings and of insolvency should gross earnings decline" (Currie, 1934, p. 41).

Currie concludes,

If economic progress continues to be associated with the increasing importance of larger corporations having access to the stock and bond markets, there is a strong probability that the commercial loan will continue to decline in the future. The decline in the commercial loan, in other words, appears to be intimately related to the changing structure of business which is bringing about a change in the methods of financing of business. (Currie, 1934, p. 41)

He suggests that banks will be left with savings deposits as a source of funding individual lending, while other institutions should be expected to emerge to meet any lending demand beyond the ability of these banks (Currie, 1934, p. 152).

However, the bank holiday in 1933 and the depression produced a stronger regulatory response in the form of the 1933 Glass-Steagall Act. While the major objective of the Act may be seen as the prudential regulation of banks to ensure the value of public deposits in terms of Federal Reserve notes, it did this by restoring the separation of commercial and investment banking, limiting the activities of deposit-taking commercial banks to short-term commercial lending. It thus followed Brandeis' recommendation of establishing a direct correspondence between the definition of a regulated institution and its function in providing deposits, excluding investment banks from this activity.

The legislation clearly recognized that, just as in the era of the money trust, the difficulties had been caused by the declining profitability of commercial banks. Thus, effective regulation had to be compatible with a restoration of the profitability of commercial banks. Indeed, the Federal Advisory Council had indicated that the return to the "real bills" doctrine in commercial banking would require the sale of bank portfolios, and thus reduce earnings and create a further downward pressure on asset prices in already depressed conditions.

At the time of the new regulations, roughly half of national bank earnings were generated by capital market activities. It sought to substitute for these now forbidden sources of earnings by providing a monopoly on deposits and limiting over-banking through the FDIC deposit insurance, and limiting the costs of deposit funds through Regulation Q (the prohibition against payment of interest on demand deposits). It would thus seem that it was clear in the minds of the authors of the Emergency Banking Act that prudential regulation had to be framed so as to ensure the profitability of the financial institutions. These concerns substituted the role of bank reserves as the major prudential policy tool.

National "blue sky" laws

The second objective of the New Deal legislation was to protect individuals from the fraud and malfeasance that had been identified with the activities of the state regulated securities affiliates of national banks. The regulation of the activities of firms in capital markets thus followed a similar logic to the Banking Act. Under the New Deal securities laws, all other financial firms, such as investment banks and securities firms, were defined as firms engaged in those activities that are excluded from commercial banks—namely securities. Indeed, these investment banks were included in Glass-Steagall 1933 only as an after-thought, because, although their primary activities were as underwriters and capital market intermediaries, they used little capital. However, they did hold substantial amounts of corporate client money on deposit, largely from the proceeds of underwriting for large commercial clients, rather than the general public. Thus, legislative consistency required that they should be treated just as other deposit takers. But this would have prevented them from operating their core business of underwriting and intermediation. Many investment banks thus chose to cease taking deposits, limiting the financing of their activities to borrowing in private capital markets or using partner's capital.

In contrast to commercial banks, regulation of these "excluded" financial institutions was undertaken in an entirely different way, through the creation of the US Securities and Exchange Commission (SEC). Rather than being based on the definition of the type of institution, as in the 1933 Act, regulation of non-deposit takers followed the tradition of the blue sky laws. Regulatory authority was based on the assets dealt in by the financial institution: i.e., as being engaged in the business of effecting transactions in securities for the account of others, or engaged in the business of buying and selling securities for their own benefit. Regulatory authority was thus based on the definition of the product—the type of security, independently of the organization—or on the definition of the firm as a broker, or a dealer, underwriter or primary investor. All institutions undertaking such activities were classified by exclusion as investment banks. This is because the New Deal legislators were more concerned with protecting the individuals investing in securities than in reg-ulating the activities of the firms that traded and sold securities. The major organizing principle of the SEC was thus "sunshine"—providing transparency, rather than providing prudential regulation through capital or loan-loss re-serves.

Institutional and functional regulation

Thus, the regulatory regime that emerged from the New Deal legislation was not based on a reasoned analysis of the advantages of product-based or function-based regulation versus institution-based regulation. Although it did create an identity between a functional regulatory authority based on financial products or services (deposit taking, real bills lending), and an institutional regulatory authority based on the definition of the institution (commercial banks versus investment banks and securities firms), this was primarily due to restored historical preference of regulators for "real bills" based banking.

As a result of the New Deal legislation, the US emerged from the war with a dual (State-Federal bank charters and regulation), segmented (commercial and investment banks), unit banking (branching restrictions determined by state law) system. From the regulatory point of view, the situation was complicated by the existence of national banks, supervised by the OCC, as distinct from state chartered banks, regulated by state banking commissions, and the regulations of the Fed, which depended on regulatory authority to ensure implementation of monetary policy.

The exceptional regulation of thrift institutions maintained this approach by creating a set of institutions with a specific function—the provision of home mortgage financing through the Federal Home Loan Bank and the Federal Housing Administration (FHA), and the government sponsored enterprises.

As a result of these historical preferences, there was no recognition of any need to make a distinction between functional and institutional regulation in the New Deal system, since they were identical. However, this identity quickly broke down as the protections given to commercial banks were subject to two sorts of competitive pressures: on the one hand, from the increasing use of prudential regulations for monetary policy purposes, and, on the other, from other institutions that did not face similar prudential regulation. This happened as commercial banks lost deposits as thrifts, and brokerage houses competed for private household deposits, and Treasury bills became more attractive to businesses, for the purposes of management of liquidity, than regulated deposits.

This third repetition of a decline in the profitability of commercial banks did not mean that households and corporations were being deprived of the functions and services traditionally offered by commercial banks, simply that these same functions were being satisfied by other financial institutions, such as thrifts and commercial paper offered by investment banks, usually at a lower cost and with greater efficiency. Other examples include credit card companies, which provide a form of payments service; money market mutual funds, which offer a low-risk savings and transaction vehicle for businesses and consumers; and commercial paper which is a substitute (often a low-cost one) for commercial loans.

This intrusion into the activities of commercial banks and the negative impact on profitability eventually led to regulatory responses to restore the competitiveness of commercial banks by expanding the kinds of capital market services that they could offer. There were a number of important steps in this process, such as the move to eliminate Regulation Q interest rate controls and the creation of exemptions for one-bank holding companies. Since the decline in the profitability of commercial banks was linked to the one-sided nature of Glass-Steagall regulation, recovery in profitability was linked to reducing those regulations, usually without recognition that this meant that the identity between institution and function was being eliminated.

Bank holding companies could thus be created with affiliates that were able to offer consumer finance and mortgage services. Restrictions on branching and deposit interest rates were reduced or eliminated completely. However, since deregulation also increased competition, it also led to a reduction in bank profits in some activities. Indeed, one of the original objectives of Regulation Q was to eliminate competition for deposits and to restrict the deposit activities of investment banks to protect commercial banks from competition for their core source of funding.

Nonetheless, deregulation has given banks a freer hand to respond to non-bank competitors' attempted inroads into their markets. In some instances, regulations produced the opportunity for non-bank firms to profit from providing substitutes to the activities of commercial banks. Money market mutual funds are an example. By using the flexibility provided by the Bank Holding Company Act, by developing sophisticated liability management techniques, by major expansions abroad, and by creative and innovative adaptations of "conventional" banking services, banks have expanded into additional activities that have generated alternative sources of income.

Data reported by Gerald Corrigan (1982) show that the return on assets (ROA) for regulated banks increased until 1973, but then declined, even though it was substantially higher in 1981 than in 1956. The significance in the shift away from traditional commercial banking—represented by taking deposits and lending to commercial borrowers for the short term, and producing income from the positive net interest—may be seen in the decline of this source of income relative to income from fees and commissions. Between 1956 and 1981, the fee income of insured commercial banks rose from 11.3 per cent of operating income net of interest expense to 19.5 per cent. This trend is also reflected in the rise in return on equity which reached a peak in 1981.

At the same time, there were changes in the environment facing investment banks, such as the 1975 May Day elimination of fixed brokerage commissions, and the introduction of shelf registration that both played a role in increasing competition among investment banks and in inducing them to seek alternative forms of income generating activity. An example was the bundling of deposit accounts, credit cards, and consumer lending along with brokerage accounts by retail brokers such as Merrill Lynch. Finally, the rise of financial engineering, and the rapid increase of computational power that produced the "unbundling" of the various characteristics of fixed income assets also played an important role in generating competition between investment and commercial banks.

In this period, official attempts to save the Savings and Loan Banks from competition from both commercial banks and investment banks brokers/dealers through measures to increase thifts' profitability, to allow them to "grow" out of the crisis produced by deregulation, bankrupted the whole industry and lay the ground for the origination and securitization of mortgages by investment banks.

Thus the 1980s and 1990s saw a repetition of the two prior experiences of falling commercial bank profitability. As in the previous cases, it produced the same solution in the form of the 1999 Financial Modernization Act. The Act again restored the combination of commercial and investment banking, as well as the two principles of bank regulation of financial functions, and resulted in the creation of areas without appropriate regulation, which were exposed in the subprime crisis of 2007. However, financial innovation has not only led to the grouping of commercial and investment banking, but also to a series of new capital market institutions. In particular, hedge funds and private equity funds have taken on both traditional investment banking functions as well as commercial banking functions, but without the regulation of either.

The result of this process is that, in contrast to Glass-Steagall, there is no longer any precise relation between financial institutions and functions. This implies that any attempt to re-regulate the US financial system must start from a decision to either reimpose this identity between institutions and functions, or to shift to a system based on functional regulation. Thus, the first decision that has to be taken in the process of re-regulation is whether it should be based on institutions or on functions or products.

One of the major implications of the financial innovation that was produced by deregulation is the unbundling of risks in financial products. This has multiplied the number and kinds of products, and allowed the creation of new financial institutions without preserving the one on one correspondence between institutions and functions. Transactions accounts are offered by brokers/dealers, following a principle first used by J.P. Morgan in keeping deposit accounts for the financial market activities of its clients. But while J.P. Morgan dealt with corporations, the extension of retail brokerage accounts has turned these into the equivalent of retail deposit accounts. So the question arises: should they be regulated as equivalent to deposits, or should they be part of the regulation of brokers/dealers? From this point of view, it would be a mistake to extend prudential regulations, which were originally designed to ensure the payments system based on private bank deposits, to financial institutions that do not provide those functions.

Deposits and liquidity

The second implication of the breakdown of the identity between institutions and function that accompanied the process of financial innovation is that regulated banks no longer are the primary source of system liquidity, and thus are no longer the major transmission mechanism of monetary policy. The basic role of insured commercial banks in providing liquidity comes from their ability to issue insured deposits that are guaranteed to be equivalent in value to Federal Reserve notes. The liquidity of assets, and thus their value, is created by the willingness of banks to accept them as collateral against loans that take the form of the creation of a deposit. However, in the present system, the creation of liquidity comes primarily from the existence of organized derivative markets in which positions in assets can be acquired against the posting of margin that is only a small percentage of the position exposure, or in which assets can be underwritten and sold in capital markets. Thus a "margin" multiplier has replaced the "deposit" multiplier as the basic source of liquidity in the system.

Since it is now possible to have increasing liquidity without any direct impact on bank assets and liabilities, prudential regulation thus no longer has a direct impact on system liquidity. The traditional transmission mechanism for monetary policy has also been eliminated. This point has been made by Martin Mayer in his recent book on the Fed (Mayer, 2001). Any justification for applying prudential regulation to non-deposit taking banks thus cannot rest on defending the value of deposits, but on the control of liquidity and the effectiveness of monetary policy.

Evaluating the product

Any shift towards regulation of products or functions must carefully evaluate the products that are the sources of financial instability. For example, the junk bond crisis was not initially due to the existence of non-investment grade bonds. The existence of the distinction between investment grade and non-investment grade assets creates an imbalance in favor of the former, and against the latter. This would naturally lead to non-investment grade bonds having lower than equilibrium prices, and thus excess risk adjusted rates of return. Michael Milkin had simply sought to arbitrage the mispricing created by an arbitrary non-market distinction. His problems started when he began to manufacture non-investment grade securities.

A similar process was involved with subprime loans. The existence of a barrier between conforming and non-conforming loans that qualified for support from the government sponsored entities created a similar excess return for subprime and Alt-A loans that financial institutions sought to arbitrage, just as Milkin had before. However, difficulties arose in both markets when assets started to be manufactured that could take advantage of the arbitrage—Milkin's creation of new, manufactured junk—and the origination of income statement subprime loans, which no longer carried the excess returns that had been the initial justification of the market.

Junk bonds and securitized mortgage lending had existed for years without creating difficulties. Thus, the subprime collapse should not be an excuse to eliminate asset securitization, or even mortgage securitization. Securitization was not the problem; the problem was in the process of creation of the assets that were securitized, and their distribution across the institutional investor base.

Product regulation

In the current context, it would seem that there is a clear benefit to pursuing product rather than institutional regulation. Nevertheless, one should also reflect on the objective of prudential regulation. If it is only to provide a secure payments system and a secure vehicle for private savings, the solution is simple. The government or the Federal Reserve can provide a secure payments system—indeed many countries once had such systems in the form of postal savings systems. This would satisfy the traditional objective of prudential regulation of providing a secure payment system. This is not really different from the traditional proposals for 100 per cent reserve banking made by Hayek and others in Chicago in the 1930s, and renewed in the discussions over bank reform after the real estate crisis at the end of the 1980s. The implication is that this would leave the rest of the financial system largely unregulated for prudential purposes.

The alternative[3]

The United States is therefore facing its third try at deciding between a segmented or a unified banking system. Many European countries have had the latter for many years without the same experience of financial crisis. What have they done that is different? Germany provides a good example. Germany rejected a separation of commercial and investment banks after its 1930s banking crisis and maintained universal banking. In Germany, regulators operate a system in which the bank's balance sheet is effectively split into short-term commercial banking activities requiring maturity matching, and capital market activities requiring long-term maturity matching. This is equivalent to extending commercial bank regulation to investment banks, yet recognizing that the regulations must differ.

The German Bank Law, which rules today, is thus a direct descendant of the Law introduced in 1934. It is based on the indirect approach to the problem of bank stability and the protection of depositors via the "Principles Concerning the Capital Resources and Liquidity of Credit Institutions." The most basic of these is Principle II, the "liquidity principle," which limits long-term assets to long-term liabilities. Long-term funding is defined as the sum of the bank's own equity, the bank's sale of bonds, other long-term borrowing by the bank, 60 per cent of savings deposits and 10 per cent of current accounts, and time deposits held by non-financial entities.

In addition, Principle III limits the bank's portfolio of loans, advances, discounted bills, quoted shares, and liabilities of other credit institutions to a maximum of 60 per cent of the sum of its current and time deposit liabilities to non-financial entities, 35 per cent of its current and time deposit liabilities to financial entities, 20 per cent of its savings deposit liabilities, 35 per cent of its borrowing with a maturity from one month to four years, and 80 per cent of the bank's issue of acceptances, notes, bills drawn on itself and international letters of credit.

Principle I sets capital adequacy rules which require a bank's capital (including reserves and retained earnings) to be a minimum of 1/18 (a little over 5.5 per cent) of total lending to firms and individuals, plus its book credits and non-controlling equity interests. Since the 1974 Herstatt Bank crisis (which was the result of speculative foreign exchange trading), there have been additional regulations limiting open foreign exchange positions to 30 per cent of capital plus reserves and retained earnings.

Until the Herstatt crisis, Germany had no depositor insurance. In 1974, the Bundesbank set up the Liquidity-syndicate Bank, which accepts bills drawn by banks facing liquidity shortages and which can be discounted at the Bundesbank. In 1976, the banks themselves created a private "deposit insurance fund" which reimburses individual depositors for up to 30 per cent of the bank's most recently published net worth statement. Membership of banks in both institutions is voluntary.

The basic framework has been extended to adapt to financial innovations. In 1990, Principle I was extended to include capital requirements to risk-adjusted off-balance sheet exposures for financial swaps, forward contracts and option rights. In addition, Principle Ia limits a bank's outstanding acceptances, promissory notes, and bills drawn on debtors to a maximum of 1.5 times its own capital, calculated and reported on a daily basis. In 1990, Principle Ia "was amended more substantially to limit all 'price risks,'—including in particular those arising from off-balance sheet financial instruments—to 60 [per cent] of a bank's liable capital" (Deutsche Bundesbank, 1990, p. 39). Within this 60 per cent limit, there are individually binding class limits of 30 per cent for foreign currency and precious metal risks, 20 per cent for interest rate risks from interest rate forward contracts and options, and 10 per cent of other forwards and options on shares and index-linked contracts. These limits were reduced to 21, 14, and 7 per cent respectively, from January 1, 1993, onwards, when the Fourth Amendment to the Act introduced the new European Union Banking Directives.

In addition, new financial products have made it necessary for Principle I to be:

extended to constitute a general counterparty risk principle going beyond mere credit risk. Principle Ia...provide(s) a general set of rules aimed at containing...the price risks involved in certain types of transactions which are particularly risk-prone because they require little or no capital input (leverage effect).

Furthermore, there are regulations on the size of loans: single loans cannot exceed 75 per cent (reduced to 50 per cent in 1985) of the bank's own capital; and all large loans cannot exceed eight times the loan capital. These large loans, defined as those which exceed 15 per cent of bank capital, have to be reported without delay to the Bundesbank, and all loans above a certain minimum (which has been changed over time) also have to be reported.

The main duty of the recording center is to ascertain the overall indebtedness of borrowers who have obtained credits of or exceeding DM 1 million from two or more institutions, and to inform the lending institutions regarding the amount of their borrowers' total credit indebtedness and the number of lenders. (Bundesbank, 1962, p. 95)

In addition, the Supervisory Agency may inspect banks' asset portfolios and make recommendations based on them.

During the discussions over the 1999 Financial Modernization Act, the German system was reviewed but rejected in favor of the bank holding company model. Given the disappointing performance of that model, perhaps it is time to return to a discussion of universal banks—not as a banking model, but as a model for regulation.

Notes

1. The first Glass-Steagall Act of 1932 (not the better known second or Emergency Banking Act), added paragraph 3 to Section 13 of the Federal Reserve Act, and opened the discount window to non-banks in unusual and exigent circumstances. The FDIC Improvement Act of 1991 amended the paragraph to allow the Fed to lend directly to non-bank firms in times of emergency. It is not clear why the Fed could not have lent directly to Bear Stearns, rather than indirectly through J.P. Morgan Chase.
2. Material in this section and the following draws on Kregel (1996, 1997).
3. Material in this section draws on Kregel (1992, 1995).

References

Brandeis, L. (1914) *Other People's Money and How the Bankers Use It.* Bedford: St. Martin's.
Corrigan, E. G. (1982) 'Are Banks Special?' *Annual Report*, Appendix, Federal Reserve Bank of Minneapolis.
Currie, L. (1931) 'The Decline of the Commercial Loan.' *Quarterly Journal of Economics*, 45(4), pp. 698–709.

—— (1934) *The Supply and Control of Money in the United States*. Cambridge: Harvard University Press.

Deutsche Bundesbank (1962) 'The New Banking Law and the Deutsche Bundesbank's Cooperation in Bank Supervision.' *Annual Report*, pp. 94–110.

—— (1990) 'The new Principles I and Ia Concerning the Capital of Banks.' *Monthly Report*, August, p. 36 ff.

Kregel, J. A. (1992) 'Universal Banking, US Banking Reform and Financial Competition in the EEC.' *Banca Nazionale del Lavoro Quarterly Review*, 182, pp. 231–54.

—— (1995) 'Market Form and Financial Performance.' *Economic Notes*, 24(3), pp. 485–504.

—— (1996) *Origini e sviluppi dei mercati finanziari*. Arezzo: Banca popolare dell"Etruria e del Lazio / studi e ricerche.

—— (1997) *The Past and Future of Banks*. Ente Einaudi: Rome.

Mayer, M. (2001) *The Fed: The Inside Story of How the World's Most Powerful Financial Institution Drives the Markets*. New York: Free Press.

Valentine, R. W. (1951) 'Investment Banking – History and Regulation.' In Herbert V. Prochnow (ed.), *American Financial Institutions*. New York: Prentice Hall.

5

Responding to the Crisis[1]

Joseph E. Stiglitz[2]

The financial crisis that began in August 2007 turned into a recession in late 2008 and is now well on its way to being the longest and deepest downturn since the Great Depression. There is a growing consensus that at certain critical times it has not been well managed. This chapter deals with four critical problems: (a) monetary stimulation; (b) fiscal policy; (c) handling the foreclosure problem; and (d) rescuing failing financial institutions.

It was written in August 2008, before the Lehmann Brothers bankruptcy, before the massive bank bail-out, and before Obama's stimulus package and his foreclosure program. As this chapter goes to press, much has changed—but, remarkably, much has stayed the same. I have added a brief "April 2009" postscript to three of the sections.

Monetary policy

Much of modern economic policy discussions begin with the premise that monetary policy should bear the brunt of the responsibility for stabilization. Fiscal policy, it has been argued, moves too slowly. By the time that a tax cut or stimulus package is enacted and implemented, the economy is likely to have turned around.

But under current circumstances, monetary stimulus is likely to be ineffective for several reasons, and even if it were effective, it is not obvious that it is desirable. Over recent years, monetary policy has worked mainly by encouraging a housing bubble, which has sustained a consumption boom. If monetary policy works through the same channels, it is not clear that that is desirable—it will simply prolong the adjustment period. No one wants to recreate another housing bubble.

Moreover, monetary policy typically works by encouraging banks to lend more and to lower interest rates. Banks are not going to be willing and able to lend, given the impairment to their balance sheets and the uncertainties which they face—including uncertainties concerning their balance sheets. Moreover, with prospects of a continued decline in real estate, it is not clear that households either will be willing to take more money out of their housing in mortgage equity withdrawals.

Keynes long ago recognized that monetary policy is typically ineffective in a downturn. He likened it to pushing on a string. So far, interest rate reductions have had two effects: (a) they may have contributed to a weaker dollar, thus helping export US problems to other countries—from a global perspective, this is simply a new version of a "beggar thy neighbor" policy; and (b) their actions may have prevented a meltdown of the financial markets—but at an unnecessarily high cost. Preventing a meltdown is not the same as reigniting the economy.

Today, monetary policy faces two further challenges: increased liquidity in US (or European) markets does not necessarily translate into lower real interest rates—especially lower real medium- or long-term interest rates—if there is a belief that the lower interest rate will lead to higher inflation. As interest rates were raised by the Fed in the period after 2003, it had less of an adverse effect than some had expected, because medium- and longer term interest rates did not increase in tandem. Today, we face the possibility that something similar will happen: as interest rates are again lowered, medium- and long-term interest rates may not fall. They may even increase.

Second, increased liquidity in US (or European) markets does not necessarily translate into increased investment expenditures in the US (or Europe). The liquidity that is provided to financial markets can be spent wherever investors believe the returns are highest. There are worries that the increased liquidity in Western financial markets will show up as increased demand for real estate assets in China and elsewhere in Asia.

Even Fed Chairman Ben Bernanke seems to have given up on the notion that monetary policy can rekindle the economy. The burden must shift to fiscal policy. Unfortunately, there has been little attention paid to basic economic principles in the design of the stimulus package.

April 2009 postscript

The defining event in financial markets occurred a little over a month after our conference. The Fed and Treasury let Lehman Brothers go bankrupt on September 15 with little thought given to the ramifications, including to money market funds. Rumors had been flying about the potential demise of Lehman Brothers at least since the fall of Bear Stearns. The Fed and Treasury seemed to believe that markets should have prepared themselves for a collapse but, remarkably, they did not check on whether they had. They had not. With the failure of Lehman Brothers, a key money market fund "broke the buck"—i.e. was unable to pay back fully those who had deposited their money with the fund. For a while, it suspended payment. Panic broke out in the markets. Shortly thereafter, AIG (American International Group) faced default before it was rescued. It was clear that the Fed and Treasury were veering from one strategy to another, without a clear set of principles. No one could ascertain who would be bailed out or under what terms. While there were vague references to bailing out systemically important institutions, some suspected having political connections was more relevant than systemic importance. The AIG money, for instance, was passed onto "counterparties" to which AIG had sold derivatives. While the government initially hid where the money went, when it was eventually disclosed, it turned out that the biggest recipients were foreign banks—if they had been systemically important, and at risk, presumably their governments would have bailed them out. Goldman Sachs was the largest American recipient, but it had claimed that it would have easily survived an AIG bankruptcy. With Paulson having come from Goldman Sachs, and with its CEO reportedly having been in on the meetings discussing the AIG bail-out, this seemed to confirm the political connections theory. At this point, some $200 billion has gone to AIG. In the final quarter of 2008, credit markets and lending seemed to tighten greatly, contributing to the downturn.

In the ensuing months, the Fed pushed interest rates effectively down to zero to little effect. Lending did not pick up. The concerns that I expressed, that lowering the Treasury bill rate would not translate into greater availability of credit at lower lending rates, have proven to be the case. We have had a new version of a liquidity trap of the kind that Greenwald and Stiglitz (2003) pointed out. Banks' willingness and ability to lend, and the terms at which they lend, do not just depend on the Treasury bill rate or the monetary base. If their equity base is eroded, if they face high uncertainty in the value of their portfolio, and if lending becomes highly risky, then credit availability may be restricted, and the spread between the Treasury bill rate and the lending rate may increase.

What no one could have anticipated in August 2008 was the Fed's willingness to move from being the lender of last resort to the lender of first resort as credit markets froze. It more than tripled its balance sheet, taking onto its balance sheet assets that central banks normally shun. It also began to undertake other measures, trying to change the term structure of interest rates—with some success. Lower long-term interest rates would, it hoped, help revive the real estate market.

Together with the US Treasury and other government agencies, the Fed also took actions to shore up the banking system, including extending guarantees to depositors. These too helped prevent the collapse of the banking system but did not restart lending, and they may have contributed to another problem: with deposits in US banks guaranteed, some foreigners may have shifted their money to the United States. The dollar strengthened (at least for a while), hurting exports, which were already suffering as the US downturn became a global recession.

Fiscal stimulus

The United States needs a stimulus, but it needs to be well designed and quick-acting (and if current trends continue, the same will be true for Europe). Any stimulus will add to the deficit, and with the deficit soaring since 2002, it is especially important to have as big a bang for the buck as possible. The stimulus should address long-term problems—and at the very least, it should not make them worse. If money is spent to create an asset, the nation's balance sheet may not be worsened—it may even be strengthened, as the increased liability from more government borrowing is matched by an asset.

Automatic stabilizers—programs that lead to increased spending if and only if the economy goes into a downturn—are able to dose out the right medicine as the economy needs it. The US has one of the worst unemployment insurance systems among advanced industrialized countries. It should begin by strengthening it, not just because it is the right thing to do but because money received by the unemployed would be spent immediately and so help the economy. Unemployment insurance has the biggest bang for the buck.

Unfortunately, states and localities are already beginning to feel the pinch—and will do so even more as property values fall.[3] Typically, they cut back spending in tandem with the decrease in revenues (most states are required to have balanced budgets and are loath to raise taxes in the midst of a recession). This acts as an automatic destabilizer. The federal government needs to provide some assistance to the states and localities to prevent this from happening and, even better, to help them address the striking inadequacies in infrastructure. New Orleans levees and Minneapolis bridges are the tip of an iceberg: we as a country have underinvested in infrastructure. Spending on infrastructure would promote growth in the long run and strengthen the economy in the short run.

The Bush Administration had long taken the view that tax cuts (especially permanent tax cuts for the rich) are the solution to every problem. This is wrong. The problem with tax cuts in general is that they perpetuate the excessive consumption that has marked the US economy. However, middle and lower income Americans have been suffering throughout the 2000s—median income is lower today than it was in 2000. A tax rebate targeted only at lower and middle income households makes sense, especially since it would be fast acting.

There is some reason to be worried that the bang for the buck from tax rebates may be less than in previous occasions, because of the high level of indebtedness and the growing awareness of difficulties in obtaining credit going forward. Many Americans can be expected to use some or all of their tax rebates to pay off some of their debts. There would be real benefits for their sense of security; and the financial system may benefit from a lower rate of defaults, but the stimulus to the economy, in terms of increased expenditures, may be less.[4]

It would be nice, of course, if we could stimulate investment in plants and equipment, not just in more housing. But the standard ways of doing this are largely gifts to corporations for investment that they would otherwise have done—the bang for the buck is remarkably small. It is possible to craft a more effective investment stimulus, a marginal investment tax credit, but in the past, the corporate sector has shown little interest in such measures. It is the gift they want, not the stimulus.

US infrastructure, and public investment more generally, has been starved for a long time. The United States should be engaged in R&D to reduce its dependency on oil and should be investing more in public transportation. These investments would bring triple dividends, not just the ordinary direct economic returns, but would make us more energy secure and, by reducing the demand for oil, could help drive down the price of oil. Not a single one of the world's top ten airports lies in the United States. Studies show that the returns to public investment in R&D are extraordinarily high. These public investments would be complementary to private investments, and by increasing the returns to the private sector, would actually encourage investment there.

Other forms of public investment, such as in education, would stimulate the economy in the short run—far more than tax rebates would—and promote growth in the long run (again, far more than tax rebates.)

In 2001, the Bush Administration used the impending recession as an excuse for the tax cuts for upper income Americans—the very group that had done so well over the preceding quarter century. The cuts were not designed to stimulate the economy, and they did so only to a limited extent. Many of the country's current woes can be traced to that decision. To keep the economy going, the Fed was forced to lower interest rates in an unprecedented way and to look the other way as the US engaged in reckless lending. The economy was sustained—on borrowed money—but it was unsustainable. The example, unfortunately, was copied by other countries, and now the problems at the bottom are worse, especially with rising food and energy prices.

We have described what a good stimulus program should focus on: (a) maximizing the bang for the buck—the largest stimulant per dollar of deficit; (b) addressing the country's long run problems; (c) being fast acting; and (d) creating an asset to offset the liability of new debt.

This time the US, and other countries that face a slowdown, need a stimulus that stimulates. We know how to design a stimulus that works and will help address some of the United States' glaring problems, many of which (including the disparity between the rich and the poor) have only grown worse.

April 2009 postscript

In February 2009, the Obama Administration succeeded in getting a $787 billion stimulus bill passed without the support of any Republicans in the House and with the vote of three Republican Senators. By then, the downturn was worsening, and it seemed clear that the stimulus would not be sufficient. Moreover, it was not as well designed as hoped—partly in the vain attempt to get more Republican support. About a third of the stimulus was in the form of household tax cuts, and with stock markets crashing and home prices falling, it seemed increasingly likely that much of the money from the tax cuts would be saved (or spent to repay debt), rather than used to stimulate the economy.

Much of the tax cut was back loaded—only about a quarter of the spending would occur in 2009—and the cutbacks in state and local spending were worse than I feared. California alone had cutbacks of $40 billion. So much, if not most, of the 2009 stimulus at the federal level would be offset by a negative stimulus at the state and local level. The worry was that the stimulus would not work, not because Keynesian economics was wrong but because there was no real stimulus. Some stimulus would be provided by the looming federal deficit, expected in 2009 to exceed 10 per cent of GDP. That in turn would be offset by the reductions in exports, the cutbacks in investment, growing unemployment, and large increases in household savings. Most forecasters are now predicting a bleak year, even with the stimulus.

The foreclosure problem

Given that the problem in the financial sector originated with foreclosures, one might have thought that that problem would be the first to be addressed. However, it has not been, and the number of anticipated foreclosures has been mounting. What once seemed like high estimates—that a quarter of all homes would be underwater, with the value of the mortgage exceeding the value of the house—now seem conservative.[5] Not all of these will default. Yet, unless something is done about the foreclosure problem, more mortgages will go into default, with follow-on consequences for the financial sector.

Dealing with the current foreclosure problem: a Homeowner's Chapter 11

There are a number of easy ways of dealing with the foreclosure problem—such as bailing out the lenders at the same time as writing down the loans—which, in the absence of budget constraints and worries about future moral hazard would make everyone (other than the ordinary taxpayer) happy. Individuals could stay in their homes, and lenders would avoid taking a hit to their balance sheets. Knowing that the government is taking this risk off balance sheets would contribute to alleviating the credit crunch.

The challenge is how to save the homes of the hundreds of thousands of those who otherwise would lose their homes and not bail out the lenders, who should be made to bear the consequences of their failures to assess risk.

One answer is a "Homeowners' Chapter 11"—a speedy restructuring of liabilities of poorer homeowners, modeled on the kind of relief that we provide for corporations who cannot meet their debt obligations. Chapter 11 is premised on the idea that keeping a firm going is critical for the firms' workers and other stakeholders. The firm's management can propose a corporate reorganization which the courts review. If found acceptable, there is a quick discharge of debt—the corporation is given a fresh start. The Homeowners' Chapter 11 is premised on the idea that no one gains from forcing a homeowner out of his home. There are large transaction costs associated with foreclosure. The house is often trashed, and surrounding houses decrease in value—making further foreclosures more likely.

This relief should be available for households with income below a critical threshold ($150,000) and with non-household, non-retirement wealth below some critical threshold (perhaps dependent on age). The house would be appraised, and the individual's debt would be written down to, say, 90 per cent of the level of that appraisal (reflecting the fact that were the lender to have to proceed with foreclosure, there would be substantial transaction costs). The borrower could then get an FHA (Federal Housing Administration) loan as described in the next section.

Banks have resisted this proposal, because it would force them to recognize a loss. They would rather hold on to the mortgage, hoping against hope that something will happen to revive housing prices. Government bail-outs have exacerbated the problem—the government has become an implicit (in the case of Citibank, explicit) insurer of large losses, while the banks will reap all the gains if real estate prices revive.

Treasury has resisted this proposal because if banks had to recognize the losses, more money would have to be put into the banks. It too has been hoping that something will happen to avoid having to put more money into the banks.

Some have opposed this, suggesting it would be a windfall gain to those who purchased a home on speculation around an increase in house prices. The criticism is a little odd, since in fact everyone in the market was speculating on an increase in real estate prices. We have been willing, nonetheless, to bail out the banks. But there is an easy way around this problem, one which would make the Homeowners' Chapter 11 more fully analogous to corporate chapter 11: a large fraction of the capital gain upon sale of the home would go to the lender. In effect, there would be a debt-to-equity swap. Those who bought a house mainly to speculate on the capital gain would find such a deal unattractive. It acts as a *self-selection* device.

Low interest loans

A second important initiative to make home ownership more affordable is to provide lower interest rates. One way of doing that is for the government to extend the benefits of its low cost access to fund homeowners. The government has, in effect, been doing that with its bail-out of Bear Stearns. But why should it do that just for banks? The government can borrow at a very low interest rate, lend it to homeowners at a rate slightly higher, and actually make a profit. The fiscal position of the United States can be improved at the same time that the foreclosure rate can be reduced.

Banks have resisted this initiative as well, and again, for an obvious reason: they don't want competition from the government, even if they have proven to have done so poorly at credit assessment and mortgage design to have put at risk the entire economy.

Expanded homeownership initiatives

Advocates of the reckless sub-prime mortgages argued that these financial innovations would enable large numbers of Americans to become homeowners for the first time. They did become homeowners—but for a very short time and at a very high cost. The fraction of Americans that will be homeowners at the end of this episode is likely to be lower than at the beginning. The objective of expanding homeownership is, I believe, a worthy one, but clearly the market route has not worked well—except for the mortgage brokers and investment banks that profited from them.

Many conservatives have blamed the home ownership initiatives for the crisis. But that is wrong. No government official encouraged the banks to lend to individuals beyond their ability to repay. The lenders were supposed to do appropriate credit assessment. They failed—partly because of the flawed incentive structures noted in the previous chapter. Moreover, the worst practices did not occur in government housing programs (Fannie Mae and Freddie Mac.) The private sector showed that it did not need any government assistance to engage in bad lending practices. Indeed, many in the mortgage industry resisted laws that would have restricted the predatory lending practices that played a major role in the crisis.

The underlying problem is simple to state: median household income has been falling and house prices rising. This means that housing is becoming less and less affordable to more and more Americans. There are no easy fixes to the declining incomes—other than shifting the burden of taxation away from these individuals and towards those who have been doing well. Nor is there any way—short of public housing programs—that we can quickly reduce housing prices (the current market correction is likely to make housing more affordable).

At the current time, there is an argument for helping lower and middle income Americans *temporarily* with their housing costs (over the longer run, there is a question about whether it is appropriate to distort the allocation of resources to housing). Note that the US (and many other countries) does this with upper income individuals—tax deductibility of mortgages and property taxes means than the government pays a large fraction of the carrying costs. But ironically, it does not do that with those who need the help the most.

A simple remedy is converting the current mortgage and property tax deduction into a flat rate cashable tax credit; the reduction in the subsidy to upper income Americans could help pay for the subsidy for poorer Americans. Even better would be a progressive subsidy, with a higher rate for the poor than the rich. A 25 per cent tax credit would increase the affordability of housing for many Americans. A complementary initiative is to provide low interest loans along the lines discussed in the previous subsection.

New mortgages

Ironically, the financial sector, for all of its claims at innovation, has not innovated in ways which are directed at shifting risk from poor Americans to those who are more able to bear the risk. For instance, even if mortgages have variable rates, poor Americans struggling to make ends meet need to know what their monthly payments are going to be. One can have fixed payments, even with variable rate mortgages, if one lets the maturity of the mortgage be variable. Danish mortgage markets have provided an alternative which has worked well for that country for more than two centuries.

The government has repeatedly had to take the initiative in innovating financial products (like making mortgages widely available) that meet the needs of ordinary citizens. When they are proven, the private sector often steps in. This may be another instance where government will have to take the initiative because of the failure of the private sector to do what it should.

Preventing foreclosures

There is little, at this juncture, that government can do to prevent large numbers of mortgages from going "underwater," i.e. the mortgage will exceed the value of the property. But not all properties that are underwater will go into foreclosure. In a world with full rationality and perfect pricing, clearly individuals who see that the value of the house is less than the value of the mortgage should default: they can buy another (or the same) house at the lower price, and will be better off at least by the amount that the house is underwater. But individuals care about their reputation, and many will be reluctant to go into foreclosure. That is why the kinds of programs described in the previous section may help: if they can stay in their homes and meet their mortgage payments, they will try to do so.

There are other proposals that affect incentives to default. One proposal (due to Martin Feldstein) would exchange, say, 20 per cent of the individual's current mortgage for a lower interest rate government loan (the government could pass on the advantage of its lower borrowing rate, so that the program would not cost the government anything). But the government loan would *not* be a non-recourse loan, so that even if the individual defaulted on his house, he would still be obliged to repay. There would then be little incentive to default. Individuals would only default when the price of the house was lower than the non-recourse debt, and for that to happen would require a very large fall in real estate prices.

One interesting aspect of the proposal is that it implicitly recognizes a market failure in financial markets—that the government has an advantage, both in raising funds (because of the almost zero probability of default) and in collecting. These have provided part of the rationale for government student loan programs and government mortgages; yet the political right has often insisted that the government not engage in these financial activities.

Beyond that, this proposal would, in effect, be giving a large gift to lenders— in effect, homeowners would be asked to give up their option in return for a lower interest rate. Most likely, financially unsophisticated borrowers would not understand the market value of the option and would only see the reduced payments. In a sense, the government would be duplicitous, unless it informed them of the value of the option.

However, a slight modification of this proposal would reduce the likelihood of foreclosure at the same time that it would not be giving such an unwarranted transfer to lenders. The government could act as an intermediary, allowing lenders to buy back the option at a fair market value (thereby reducing the uncertainty which they and markets face), and encouraging households to: (a) use (most of) the proceeds to buy down the value of the outstanding mortgage; and (b) convert another 10 per cent to 20 per cent of the mortgage into a recourse loan with interest at the government interest rate (plus an appropriate transactions cost). Lenders participating in this program would, of course, have to waive any pre-payment penalties.

April 2009 postscript

I had watched with amazement as the crisis worsened, and President Bush refused to do anything about the underlying problem, the mortgages. Providing $700 billion to the banks without doing anything about the mortgages was akin to a mass blood transfusion to a patient suffering from internal hemorrhaging.

President Obama finally came forward with a proposal to deal with the foreclosure problem in February 2009. It was an important step in the right direction—but not enough to likely prevent large numbers of foreclosures still occurring. There were limited mortgage restructurings for those who went through bankruptcy proceedings. Ironically, prior law made it more difficult to restructure a mortgage on a primary residence than on a yacht. Many individuals will, however, resist going through bankruptcy, with all that that entails. The Homeowners' Chapter 11 was intended to facilitate the process and give homeowners better terms.

With the government takeover of Fannie Mae and Freddie Mac, it is easier for government to restructure many mortgages. It also provided access to lower interest rates. But the private sector still seems reluctant to renegotiate many mortgages and has been successful in restricting the scope of government low-interest loans. The Obama plan provided some (very limited) incentives for banks to restructure certain mortgages. The major objection to the Obama initiative is that the restructurings involve temporarily lower interest rates, not lower principle—yet the underlying problem is that the price of the house is less than the value of the mortgage. With prices lower than mortgages, incentives to default are strong, and the evidence is clear that those with mortgages underwater are more likely to default. Yet not only was the principle not written down, no direct incentives (e.g. of the kind discussed above) were put in place aimed at reducing foreclosures. The first is explicable partly because the renegotiation of principle would force the recognition by the banks of their losses, and as we have noted, the banks are going to great lengths to avoid that—supported by Treasury.

In the beginning of April, 2009, the Financial Accounting Standards Board took an action which weakened further incentives to renegotiate mortgages. It gave banks greater latitude not to write down the value of impaired mortgages. This meant that the cost of renegotiating mortgages effectively went up—because renegotiation would entail recognizing losses, which in turn would entail finding new funds for recapitalization. This compounded problems from the flawed bank restructuring, described in the next section. Part of that program entailed government guarantees on losses. With such guarantees, there were strong incentives for delay, for any gain would accrue to the holder of the mortgage, while most of the losses from delay would accrue to the government.

Financial rescue

Given the magnitude of defaults on the sub-prime mortgages, it is not surprising that these problems became translated into problems elsewhere in the system. Given the lack of transparency in the banks—who had moved so much of their risk taking off balance sheet—it is especially not a surprise that there was a "run" on a bank, with market participants pulling their money out (not rolling over loans). Even if they would have eventually fully recovered their assets, the risk of having their money tied up for an extended period of litigation, at a time when credit was tight, was simply not worth the slightly higher returns that they might receive.

Greenwald and Stiglitz (2003) and Battiston et al. (2007) have emphasized the importance of credit interlinkages and how defaults in one part of the system can lead to defaults elsewhere. It is easy to construct models of bankruptcy avalanches. The fear was that a default by Bear Stearns would lead to a series of other defaults and a run on other banks. Indeed, even after Bear Stearns was bailed out (through a Fed financed acquisition by J.P. Morgan) the fear of further defaults was so great that the Fed extended its lender of last resort facility to investment banks. Even most critics of the Fed agreed that, at that point, it had no choice. It may have failed in providing an adequate regulatory structure; it almost surely failed in acting too late. But given the risks at that moment, a bail-out seemed inevitable.

The criticism is addressed towards the form of the bail-out, which entailed potentially huge transfers of wealth to J.P. Morgan and large transfers to Bear Stearns shareholders, while taxpayers were put at risk for large amounts without any compensation. If taken as a precedent, it expanded the scope of moral hazard, rewarding those who had engaged in excessively risky behavior and had been already richly compensated. The defense that something had to be done quickly was hardly a defense: that there were potential problems had long been recognized, and it is hard to believe that contingency plans had not been thought through. Wall Street wanted a bail-out, and Wall Street got a bail-out, perhaps not as extensive as it had hoped, but still on terms that were unconscionable, in a manner that was not transparent and that seemingly paid little attention to the large distributions of wealth that were generated. Conflicts of interest (bordering on corruption) abounded.[6] The bail-out took the form of a non-recourse loan from the Fed to J.P. Morgan to acquire Bear Stearns (originally for $236 million, upped to $1.2 billion). The Fed gave $30 billion to J.P. Morgan and got what was supposed to be an equivalent amount in collateral consisting of a melange of assets, including sub-prime mortgages. No one is sure how they were priced. If the value of the assets falls below $29 billion, J.P. Morgan absorbs the first billion of losses, but taxpayers are at risk for the remainder (and obviously, for the first billion, if J.P. Morgan itself were to go bankrupt).

Non-recourse loans are, in effect, put options. If the value of the collateral goes below $29 billion, J.P. Morgan has little incentive to pay back the loan. In discussing the risk, attention has focused on the probability of default, particularly important because no one is sure how they were priced in the first place, i.e. what probability of default was built into the pricing. But there is a second problem: interest rate risk. If interest rates rise, then the value of the assets declines. Some of these assets are 30-year mortgages, meaning that they are highly sensitive to long-term interest rates. Providing a non-recourse loan even if the assets are currently correctly priced is like giving away an option—an option with a very high value.

Particularly irksome was that the government stood to lose large amounts of money (both on the credit risk and the interest rate risk), but there was no upside potential. Meanwhile, Bear Stearns shareholders walked away with $1.2 billion, less than they would have liked, but still more than they should have, especially given their failure to manage risk appropriately.

There were many ways that the taxpayers could have been protected and at least received some compensation. For instance, shareholder value could have been put into escrow, until it was clear that taxpayers' money was not at risk. The first $1.2 billion of losses would be paid either by J.P. Morgan or by shareholders. J.P. Morgan could have been asked to pay a risk premium up front and to pay the market value of the implicit put. If the collateral turned out to be more valuable than the value assigned to it, the government could have demanded a fraction of the excess.

Bailing out Bear Stearns also entailed large redistributions. Many had bet on Bear Stearns going into bankruptcy (in credit default swaps). Those that had bought insurance against this risk (bet that it would happen) were deprived of money that they otherwise would have received; those that provided the insurance received a windfall gain. This market is itself not very transparent, but allegedly among those who received large windfall gains were the big investment banks—including J.P. Morgan. In defense of the bail-out, one could argue that the risk of a bail-out should have been priced into the insurance in the first place. Still, the fact that J.P. Morgan was, in part, being bailed out should have played into the terms at which the bail-out occurred.

The events subsequent to the bail-out evidenced many of the potential conflicts of interest. The CEO of Bear Stearns was hired by J.P. Morgan, at handsome compensation. Clearly, a promise (pay-off) of this kind could interfere with his ability to negotiate in the best interests of the shareholders. Shareholders had to vote on the acquisition. But it is easy to show that those who had sold insurance against the risk of Bear Stearns going bankrupt had an incentive to buy shares, to ensure that the acquisition went through, even if shareholders as a whole might have thereby been disadvantaged.[7]

The bail-out orchestrated by the regulators illustrates a problem common to discretionary regulatory policy, an issue that arose in the bail-out of Long-Term Capital Management (LTCM) a decade earlier, where no public money was involved. The regulator has a variety of carrots and sticks for inducing cooperation. Lack of cooperation can induce tighter scrutiny; fuller cooperation can buy regulatory forbearance, now or in the future. In the case of LTCM, banks were induced to contribute funds to bail out the hedge fund benefiting, not necessarily incidentally, many of the corporate executives of the same banks who were contributing money (another instance of the complex web of conflicts of interest). Was participation in the bail-out in the best interests of the shareholders? The New York Fed believed it was in the interests of the system as a whole. Whether the individual banks agreed, and whether it was in the best interests of the individual participating bank, is another matter.

In the case at hand, this combined with lack of transparency to leave a high level of uncertainty: it does not appear that J.P. Morgan got a bad deal; on the contrary. But was it because it outsmarted the Fed? Because there were relatively few institutions able and willing to take over Bear Stearns, and the Fed wanted, at any cost, to avoid a collapse, given the exigencies of the moment, it could drive a hard bargain.

There were several alternative courses. One which the UK eventually took (though the delay in doing so may have cost it a great deal) is nationalization. Whether the legal framework would have allowed the US to do this may not be clear; but it was not clear whether the Bear Stearns bail-out was legal.

It is curious that it has become acceptable for a foreign government, or, equivalently, a fund owned by a foreign government, to bail out (or take over) a failing bank (as happened in the case of Merrill Lynch and Citibank), but there is still a reluctance to allow one's own government to do so. The standard rationale against governments running/nationalizing banks is ideological: governments shouldn't do it; the private sector is better at running banks and other such enterprises than the public sector. But the private sector has, in these instances, demonstrated its incompetence. The public purse is at risk. The government has a large stake in how the resolution is managed. Indeed, with implicit or explicit deposit insurance, it has more at stake than anyone else does. Yet it is difficult to provide incentives for any private firms that are compatible with the interests of the state. It is far better to have the government manage the resolution. In the case of Bear Stearns, the public interest was even more complicated. There was a public interest in maintaining the integrity of the financial system. There were no formal liabilities, as in the case of deposit insurance. What was required may not have been clear. In the event, there was a huge transfer of wealth to J.P. Morgan to ensure that this was done.

(There is a rationale for encouraging foreign government bail-outs: the arm's length bargaining ensures that the foreign government is not likely to be engaged in hidden transfers of wealth, as may have happened in the Bear Stearns bail-out and as has happened in bail-outs in many countries. On the other side, one of the concerns of government ownership of banks is that resources get directed according to political, not economic, objectives. This should presumably be more acceptable if it is one's own government's political agenda. However, as I have explained elsewhere,[8] if there are concerns about resources being used in ways that go counter to public interest, it is a sign of an inadequate regulatory framework—the problems could arise as well with domestic private ownership.)

There were still other alternatives: the government could have lent to Bear Stearns directly. This would have been more transparent. And it would have been easier to design a system of allowing the government to participate in the upside potential, as the government did when it helped engineer Chrysler's bail-out. Still a third alternative, more akin to the Chrysler bail-out, would be providing a public guarantee to private funds, though—other than ideology—it is not clear why this is preferable to the direct provision of government funds.

Again, in the instance, it may not have been consistent with the legal framework, though the Fed's announcement that, going forward, it stood willing to lend to other investment banks suggested that it believed that it did have regulatory authority. The issue here is the design of the appropriate framework: it would seem desirable to give government the right to lend, in return for taking a share of the potential gain or at sufficiently high interest rates to compensate for the risk that the collateral was less than the value assigned.[9,10]

Ownership is often defined as the residual claimant on the returns to an asset and residual control. Current banking frameworks leave the government as the residual holder of negative claims and, in effect, with considerable residual control rights—when things turn out badly, but not when they turn out well. They can run things once the patient gets to the hospital, but they pick up the hospital bills and can do little (or at least not enough) to prevent the accidents that lead to hospitalization.[11] This seems neither efficient nor equitable; in many countries, such policies have resulted in huge transfers of resources from the public to the private sector (e.g. in Mexico's banking crisis).

*Further comments on equity injections, capital adequacy
standards, and forbearance*

Typically, financial injections into the banking system occur before the actual meltdown, while the bank is viable but has failed to meet its regulatory capital adequacy standards. Banks facing such a situation can be forced to comply. Again, typically, when banks face a problem of inadequate capital in an economic downturn, they have found it difficult to raise the required capital. Part of the reason is (as here) the uncertainty concerning the value of the assets and liabilities—made even worse here because of the lack of transparency in off balance sheet accounting and the complexity of products. Part of the reason is that in downturns, uncertainty is heightened and there is a general scarcity of liquid funds for the bail-out.

In early 2008, it appeared that the current instance may be an exception or it may be a harbinger of a new world. The world was awash with liquidity—in fact excess liquidity was often blamed for the problems. In several instances, sovereign wealth funds came to the rescue. In today's world of globalization, it appeared that banks could turn to the global financial market. Funds may be scarce in the United States, but there is a whole world to turn to outside the United States. There may be another factor at play: the banks being bailed out are controlled by their managers. Their interests may not fully coincide with those of their shareholders. The managers may have been more willing to give up a greater share in the ownership of the bank to save the institution. On the other hand, the sovereign wealth funds may have been more willing to pay more than a typical risk averse buyer, focused on the actuarial value of the assets and their risk, to obtain a large share in these iconic assets.

But by late 2008, these hopes of a new world of global finance coming to the rescue seemed a dream of a distant past. The sovereign wealth funds which had invested in the US, and especially in its banks, had been badly burned. They had learned how non-transparent the institutions were and how great the uncertainty about the true state of their balance sheet. Besides, the downturn had turned global, and many of the countries with liquid funds began to focus more on problems within their own region.

In the 1997 East Asian financial crisis, the International Monetary Fund (IMF) strongly urged government regulators to strictly enforce capital adequacy standards. I argued that such a policy could be counterproductive; if the banks couldn't raise additional capital, it would force a contraction of their loan portfolio, further deepening the economic downturns, and possibly even worsening balance sheets, contributing to a downward spiral. The IMF policy of no-forbearance was, in effect, instituting an automatic destabilizer into the economy.

One of the challenges in designing a regulatory regime based on capital adequacy standards is how to prevent this destabilizing behavior. One proposal is to introduce counter-cyclical standards, i.e. that automatically loosen the standards when the economy is weak and tighten them when the economy is strong. This proposal is discussed in the previous chapter and elsewhere in this book.[12]

Some urged government capital injections, since with these capital adequacy standards could be met, and a few countries took this course. Capital adequacy standards are supposed to serve two functions: they ensure that the bank has enough capital at risk that it does not take on excessive risk; and they provide a buffer, so that the government does not have to put up as much money should things turn out badly. When the government puts up money to meet capital adequacy standards, it is doing little to protect taxpayers' money: if it puts the money in the form of equity, its money is now at risk even if the bank survives but simply gets a low return. But more important is the fact that incentives are little affected: controlling shareholders care about their wealth, not the wealth of the government; what they have at risk is unchanged. Indeed, it can be shown that under some circumstances, incentives are adversely affected. The existence of capital adequacy standards lowers the franchise value of a firm (it is a constraint imposed on the firm, and therefore has to lower owners' expected discounted (utility of) future income), and dilutes existing shareholders' claims on future franchise value. As a result, the bank may even engage in more risky behavior—at the expense of taxpayers (see Murdock and Stiglitz, 1993; Helmann et al., 1997, 1998, 2000, 2002).

Restricting hidden bail-outs

Increasingly, there are concerns that the Fed currently is too centered on bailing out ailing banks and financial institutions (and possibly even those losing money on the stock market) and less with maintaining the real strength of the economy.

This perspective was put forward by Princeton economics professor Uwe Reinhardt in a letter to the *Financial Times* (February 21, p. 10):

You report that the Federal Reserve has quietly lent US banks "on relatively attractive terms" some $50bn to ease the credit crunch now befalling main street American business... Would it not have been more efficient for the Fed to have lent the $50bn directly to main street business, on similarly subsidized terms, in place of feeding horses that may or may not feed the birds? After all, unlike most solid real businesses, banks worldwide have amply demonstrated their inability to fully understand and value the assets—often just casino-like bets—into which they place the enormous sums entrusted to them ... I realize, of course, that the Fed's lending directly to Main Street would immediately be decried as "socialism" in our financial press. Miraculously, when the Fed bails out inept private banks on sub-sidized terms it is called "prudence" rather than socialism. That may fool seasoned adults, but not any straight-thinking freshman in economics.

The fact is that when the Fed buys mortgages and other assets that are not widely traded, there is a risk that it will be overpaying—the lack of transpar-ency should itself be a concern in a democratic society. It is understandable why the Fed wanted to do something about the freezing of credit markets; it is understandable that those in the affected institutions wanted a bail-out. However, it was incumbent on the Fed to do so in ways which did not put at risk taxpayers' money,[13] and which did not reward the financial institutions for their behavior. The fact is that the financial markets created these non-transparent hard-to-price financial instruments; they should now bear the consequences. If the Fed has used only a small fraction of the financial ingenuity that went into the creation of the mess, it could have protected American taxpayers against the risks; it could, for instance, have insisted that the banks from which it bought these mortgage backed instruments provide insurance that, should the value of these instruments decline, e.g. as a result of an increase in default rates, the banks would make the Fed whole. One could only surmise that it deliberately decided not to protect American taxpayers and that it may have done so because what was desired was a bail-out.

Congress should consider passing legislation to ensure that when the Fed engages in such risky transactions, American taxpayers are protected, and that whatever it does should be done more transparently. Similar legislation should be undertaken in other countries.

In the transition from Communism to the market economy, it became clear how government's control of the banking system (either directly through ownership of banks, or indirectly, through the granting of bank licenses and regulatory supervision) affected the wealth distribution: those, and only those, who had access to capital could buy the assets, typically at far below prices that represented fair market value. The question today is whether central bank liquidity is doing something similar, though admittedly on a far less grand scale. If the central bank lends money to Bank A, and Bank A lends money to Hedge Fund Alpha, and Hedge Fund Alpha uses some of the money to buy shares in Bank B, and at the same time, the central bank lends money to Bank B, and Bank B lends money to Hedge Fund Beta, and Hedge Fund Beta uses some of the money to buy shares in Bank A, we can recapitalize both Bank A and Bank B. It is a private sector recapitalization—of course all funded by the government, but with a set of smoke and mirrors so confusing that no one (outside a few skeptic economists—and who pays attention to them anyway?) can figure out what is going on. The wonderful thing about this charade is that it perpetuates the longstanding dogma: privatize assets while socializing risk. If the banks do well, the hedge funds walk off with the profits; if the banks do poorly, the taxpayers pick up the pieces.

Is this really what is happening? In a sense, one can't really answer that question: funds are fungible. We don't have a clear view of what would have happened but for the extra liquidity provided to the banking system. What is clear is that the extra liquidity makes the recapitalization of the banking system easier.

April 2009 postscript

The weaknesses in the US banking system turned out to be far worse than most imagined, even in August 2008. Then, it was clear that there were massive losses on sub-prime mortgages. It was clear too that problems would be spreading to other mortgages, and to other forms of credit. It was clear too that the losses that had been taken were far smaller than the total losses. There were a lot of losses somewhere in the system, some in US banks, some outside.

The Bush Administration finally realized that something had to be done and asked for a blank check of $700 billion with no Congressional oversight or judicial review. Congress eventually gave Treasury close to a blank check but insisted on some oversight. Treasury and Fed continued to vacillate in their views about what to do. First, they argued for a "cash for trash" proposal, entailing the government buying off the "toxic assets." They were eventually persuaded that such a proposal would not work—the process of buying them off separately would be too slow. They then tried direct "equity injections," giving the banks money in return for preferred shares and some warrants, to give at least some upside sharing of potential gains. The terms that the US government got, however, in these deals were very bad. The Congressional Oversight Panel estimated that *at the time* the value of the shares and warrants was about two-thirds of the value of the money given to the banks. When the program (called TARP, Troubled Asset Relief Program) was initiated, there was much talk that the government would not only get its money back but also make a profit. A few months later, the Congressional Budget Office estimated that the government would get back less than 50 per cent of what it gave the banks. Clearly, prospects of recovering the money with adequate compensation for risk and the time value of money were nil.

While it was clear that TARP would lead to substantial increases in the government's national debt, the hope was that it would lead to more lending. It did not. The new Obama Administration's economic team, dominated by those who had advocated policies that had led to the mess and/or regulators who had failed to do an adequate job of oversight and were seen to be too close to the failing banks, continued the policy of shoveling out money to the banks. The new deals that it struck with the banks were even worse for the taxpayer. Some of them, entailing underwriting losses, distorted incentives.

In late March 2009, they came up with a new program, a public private partnership, where the government provided or guaranteed most of the funds, thereby absorbing most of the losses, but the private sector shared in 50 per cent of the gains as the partnerships bought off assets from the banks. The Administration sold it as using the private sector to help "discover" the true value of the assets, but the structure of the partnership meant that the private sector was only finding the value of the upside potential of the assets; the value of the option, with the government absorbing most of the losses, was obviously much greater than the value of the asset. The gains to the banks were at the expense of the taxpayers. It was a costly redistribution of the banks, one which at the same time distorted incentives.

If the program worked, it would only be at a very high cost to the nation's debt and at an unnecessarily high cost. Even with such massive redistributions, there was concern that the program might not work, partly because the banks were allowed to keep the toxic ("impaired") mortgages on their books at over-inflated prices. Even if they could sell them at prices that were greatly in excess of their true value, the best prices they could get for them might be considerably less than the value on their books, and that would force them to recognize the losses, which in turn would force them to raise more capital.

There was an alternative—the usual bank "bankruptcy" procedure, entailing temporary nationalization, with the government honoring obligations to insured depositors but with shareholders and unsecured creditors facing losses. Obviously, the shareholders of those banks likely to go under and their friends did not take warmly to this proposal. They preferred the Bush–Obama plan of continued bail-outs, with government getting little in return—little in the way of finance, little in the way of control. Yet with banks having misused so much of the money they received—to continue to pay dividends or to pay outsized bonuses seemingly for record losses—as this book goes to press, it is not clear whether this will be politically feasible. It is certainly not economically desirable. The normal procedures of financial reorganization would be far preferable to this form of ersatz capitalism (or corporate welfarism) of socializing losses while privatizing profits. We were, in effect, confusing the issue of bailing out banks with the issue of bailing out bankers and their shareholders.

The bank rescue plan is the weakest part of the response of the new Administration to the crisis. The prospect of lending being resuscitated remains weak, while the prospect of large burdens on the government remains high. Even if banks' ability to lend is restored, their willingness to do so may not be. Resuscitating the banks may be necessary for the economic recovery, but it is not sufficient.

Concluding comments

The financial crisis in the United States has grown into a global economic crisis, the worst since the Great Depression. As this book goes to press, it is not clear how deep the downturn will get, how long it will last, or how robust the recovery will be. The US recovery will, almost surely, depend in part in what happens elsewhere in the world. Nevertheless, what seems clear at this juncture is that the downturn will be longer and deeper because of the failure of the Bush Administration to design an effective response. It refused to do anything about the mortgages. When it came to a stimulus, it went back to its time-worn view that a tax cut was the appropriate medicine for any economy's ills. When it came to the ailing banks, it veered erratically from one course of action (or inaction) to another.

The new Administration finally came up with a stimulus package that might work—but it was too little and not well designed. It came up with a mortgage restructuring program—but it too was too little, and not designed to address one of the key problems, that of mortgages that were underwater. Its real failure was coming up with an effective program to restart lending. It focused on the past, dealing with the "legacy" assets, rather than looking forward. It was too influenced by the interests, concerns, and perspectives of the banks. It took a calculated risk: perhaps a policy that pleased the banks would manage to get us over the crisis, smoothly, without generating too much resentment from the rest of society and at not too great of a cost to the taxpayer. It may work, but as this book goes to press, it looks increasingly unlikely that the gamble will pay off. The cost to the taxpayer is high, public resentment is mounting, and it's not working. It is, of course, not too late for the new Administration to change course.

This is, in part, a crisis in confidence—confidence in our financial system has eroded. But if it appears that our financial system has managed to capture the government for its own interests, then confidence in our government will be equally eroded.

Notes

1. Paper prepared for a meeting on Financial Regulation sponsored by the Initiative for Policy Dialogue and Brooks World Poverty Institute, Manchester, July, 2008. The author is indebted to Stephany Griffith-Jones for helpful comments. Financial support from the Ford, Mott, and Rockefeller Brothers Foundations is gratefully acknowledged. Since the paper was originally written, the financial meltdown has in fact turned much worse. I have revised the paper to take into account some aspects of the subsequent events.
2. Columbia University and Brooks World Poverty Institute, Manchester.
3. A similar dynamic occurred in the 2001 downturn.
4. There should be something done about foreclosures—along the lines discussed in the previous section. But not too much should be spent on this. A big fund would almost surely wind up being a bail-out fund for investors, and they are not the ones who need help from taxpayers.
5. Estimates from First American CoreLogic for December 2008 put the ratio of houses with negative equity at 20 per cent of all mortgages. Since then house prices have continued to fall. Applying the scenarios for future home price declines from the bank stress tests, the total proportion of negative equity mortgages could hit anywhere from 41–55 per cent.
6. Similar concerns of corporate corruption had been noted in the publicly orchestrated but privately financed LTCM bail-out. Shareholder money was being used to in part bail out personal investments by corporate officials.
7. Assume, for instance, that if the company had gone into bankruptcy, it would have been worth $400 million and (in the original offer) shareholders only got $250 million. But bankruptcy might have exposed the providers of insurance to an additional risk of $200 million. They gain more in *not paying out on their insurance* more than they lose in market value. They would vote for the acquisition, even if it was not in the interests of the shareholders as a whole. As Stiglitz (1972) and Grossman and Hart (1980) point out, the equilibrium may not be consistent with shareholder value maximization. A small shareholder who believes that the acquisition will go through (that those who will vote for acquisition are in a majority) will not pay more than $2.50 a share, if there were a million shares. But, say, a bank (or even better, a consortium of banks) that had large outstanding liabilities if Bear Stearns goes bankrupt would be willing to pay more than $2.50 a share to obtain controlling interest to ensure that the acquisition did go through. Of course, minority shareholders—that are not at risk if Bear Stearns goes bankrupt—are left short changed.
8. See Stiglitz (2009).
9. It is curious that those who believe in free markets are not only willing to accept a government financed bail-out but demand it; while they argue for the virtues of market determined prices, in these circumstances, they seem to suggest that market prices undervalue assets.
10. Stiglitz and Weiss (1981) explain why charging an interest rate high enough to compensate for the risk may have adverse incentive effects, so that more complicated financial instruments—or even nationalization—may be required.

11. In Orszag and Stiglitz (2002), we explain the need for better regulation (accident prevention) in those instances (such as here) where, it is argued, that when an accident occurs, there must be government action.

12. Another proposal is to use discretion. Most countries engage in discretion. Hopefully, the central bank can distinguish among the circumstances in which banks find themselves: is it an isolated bank that is facing a problem, in which case forbearance should not be engaged in; or is it systemic risk? (Of course, the government has to be careful—it can unwittingly encourage correlated behavior, which can increase systemic risk.) One of the criticisms of the IMF and the US Treasury in the East Asia crisis was their failure to recognize the possible desirability of discretionary forbearance. They worried that it would give rise to moral hazard—concerns that were evidently muted in the Bear Stearns bail-out.

    In addition, the objective function of the IMF and the individual countries may have differed markedly. The former may have been concerned with consequences for the *global* financial system; the latter focused more narrowly on consequences for the national financial system and economy.

13. Profits of the Fed are turned over to the Treasury, so that any losses have a direct impact on the Treasury.

References

Battiston, S., Delli Gatti, D., Gallegati, M., Greenwald, B., and Stiglitz, J. E. (2007) 'Credit Chains and Bankruptcy Propagation in Production Networks.' *Journal of Economic Dynamics and Control*, 31(6), pp. 2061–84.

Greenwald, B. and Stiglitz, J. E. (2003) 'Macroeconomic Fluctuations in an Economy of Phelps-Winter Markets.' In Philippe Aghion, Roman Frydman, Joseph Stiglitz, and Michael Woodford (eds.), *Knowledge, Information, and Expectations in Modern Macroeconomics: In Honor of Edmund S. Phelps*. Princeton, NJ: Princeton University Press, pp. 123–36.

Grossman, S. J. and Hart, O. D. (1980) 'Takeover Bids, the Free-Rider Problem, and the Theory of the Corporation.' *Bell Journal of Economics*, 11(1), pp. 42–64.

Helmann, T., Murdock, K., and Stiglitz, J. E. (1997) 'Financial Restraint: Toward a New Paradigm.' In M. Aoki, H. Kim, and M. Okuna-Fujiwara (eds.), *The Role of Government in East Asian Economic Development*. Oxford: Clarendon Press, pp. 163–207.

—— (1998) 'Financial Restraint and the Market Enhancing View.' In Y. Hayami and M. Aoki (eds.), *The Institutional Foundations of East Asian Economic Development*. London: Macmillan, pp. 255–84.

—— (2000) 'Liberalization, Moral Hazard in Banking and Prudential Regulation: Are Capital Requirements Enough?' *American Economic Review*, 90(1), pp. 147–65.

—— (2002) 'Franchise Value and the Dynamics of Financial Liberalization.' In A. Meyendorff and A. Thakor (eds.), *Designing Financial Systems in Transition Economies: Strategies for Reform in Central and Eastern Europe*. Cambridge, Mass.: MIT Press, pp. 111–27.

Murdock, K. and Stiglitz, J. E. (1993) 'The Effect of Financial Repression in an Economy with Positive Real Interest Rates: Theory and Evidence.' Mimeo, August.

Orszag, P. and Stiglitz, J. E. (2002) 'Optimal Fire Departments: Evaluating Public Policy in the Face of Externalities.' The Brookings Institution, January 4 <http://www.brookings.edu/views/papers/orszag/20020104.htm>.

Stiglitz, J. E. (1972) 'Some Aspects of the Pure Theory of Corporate Finance: Bankruptcies and Take-Overs.' *Bell Journal of Economics*, 3(2), pp. 458–82.

—— (2009) 'Regulation and the Theory of Market and Government Failure.' In D. Moss and J. Cisternino (eds), *New Perspectives on Regulation*. Cambridge, Mass.: The Tobin Project.

—— and Weiss, A. (1981) 'Credit Rationing in Markets with Imperfect Information.' *American Economic Review*, 71(3), pp. 393–410.

Part II

Reforming Financial Regulation

6

Central Banks, Liquidity, and the Banking Crisis[1]

Philip Turner[2]

The origins of the "liquidity crisis"

One of the functions of financial intermediation is to liquefy illiquid investments. As Keynes put it in *The General Theory*:

> Of the maxims of orthodox finance none, surely, is more anti-social than the fetish of liquidity, the doctrine that it is a positive virtue on the part of investment institutions to concentrate their resources upon the holding of 'liquid' securities. It forgets that there is no such thing as liquidity of investment for the community as a whole ... Capital markets provide liquidity to make investments which are 'fixed' for the community more 'liquid' for the individual.

In drawing lessons from the liquidity aspects of the international banking crisis that broke in August 2007, the benefits that Keynes identified must be kept in mind. It is quite natural that financial innovation has steadily pushed this "liquification" function further in the decades that have followed Keynes remarks. In his day, only a limited range of debt instruments were traded in capital markets. Financial intermediation through banks largely took the form of non-traded and illiquid bank loans.

Since then, however, the balance sheets of banks have become more dependent on capital markets. On the liability side, banks have relied more on (typically short-term) funding in wholesale markets and less on retail deposits collected from households. Banks have become more dependent on continued access to wholesale markets and households have increasingly placed their savings in lucrative capital market products, rather than in bank deposits. On the asset side, bank loans have been increasingly securitized and sold to other banks and to non-bank investors.

This long-run process dramatically accelerated from around 2003. Major commercial banks attracted non-bank investors (and other banks) to their securitized products by providing back-up liquidity through various capital market structures. At the same time, investment banks greatly increased their leverage, both directly on their balance sheets and indirectly through their holdings of products that were themselves leveraged. All this widened the apparent scope of capital markets, as a greater range of loans were securitized, and in forms that were increasingly complex. Because of their vast range and complexity, such products—left to stand alone—were unlikely to have liquid markets. These markets could appear to be liquid only because of the demand of highly geared financial institutions.

The crisis that broke in August 2007 was the result of a reckless acceleration of this process. As so often in the history of banking crises, pressures first became widespread in the wholesale markets where banks borrowed and in the markets where banks sought to sell their assets. Banks became unable to borrow or to sell their stocks of securitized assets. Hence it was on the evaporation of liquidity that attention first focused. This was Phase 1 of the crisis (see the box, Four Phases of Crisis, p. 104).

But it soon became clear that liquidity strains were symptoms of the more fundamental question concerning the solvency of major financial institutions. The real issue was the scale of the failure of lending institutions to correctly assess and price credit risks across many business lines. Many firms had taken such risks because they assumed (or hoped) they had hedged their risks by contracts with monoline insurers by imaginative but fragile hedging strategies, by the use of credit default swaps (CDS), or by some other strategy (e.g. off balance sheet structures) which gave the impression that the risk had passed to someone else.

The crisis dashed these hopes. Hedges proved imperfect. And it was of course the concentration of credit default swaps with a few major counterparties that prompted much recent action by central banks. It was felt that large-scale failures on such CDS contracts would have damaged the functioning of the whole system.[3] The implications of credit derivative markets for public policy action in a crisis are a major topic in its own right.

Banks had also under priced the liquidity services they provided, and this was reflected in the extremely tight pricing of many hedging products. Additionally, many banks had relied too much on short-term funding and had not issued enough straight fixed-term debt. The liquidity guarantees banks provided were opaque (e.g. terms of support in case a supposedly independent structure failed) and were in any case of uncertain value as bank default risk rose. In the event, the supposed liquidity of many products proved quite illusory. The realization that some banks were holding large portfolios of poor credit risks made lenders less willing to lend to them.

Because the pricing links with deeper markets were approximate (and in some cases non-existent), the true value of the securitized assets was uncertain and leverage meant that estimated values turned out to be extremely sensitive to general market developments. Neither banks nor supervisors were aware of the size of aggregate exposures, which in any case was heavily dependent on prospective macroeconomic developments. The true scale of leverage was hidden and the ramifications of pervasive linkages between different market segments were underestimated. Losses from delinquencies on US sub-prime mortgages engendered skepticism about the whole model and prompted the realization that potential liquidity demands on (as well as write downs by) major banks would be huge. This spilt over to money markets but did not originate in them.

The roles of the central bank, the regulators, and the government

Given the path chosen by the financial industry in the major centers, it had been quite clear for many years that impossible-to-predict shocks could make it difficult for banks to sell assets and could put bank funding markets under exceptional strain. This could happen even if no major individual bank faced a solvency crisis. But nobody knew just when the break would come, and in the meantime banks found it profitable to push their securitization strategies to its limits. The sheer scale of the crash that followed came as a shock.

Among failures in policy framework that have been identified, three are of particular relevance for this chapter:

(1) The modalities of the emergency lending facilities of central banks.

(2) The management of liquidity risks by banks. In theory, it is the banks themselves that have prime responsibility for ensuring that they manage their own increased liquidity risk effectively. In practice, however, there is a collective action problem: an individual bank cannot reverse its positions if other banks also choose to do so at the same time. Because of this, there is a role for regulating the liquidity management of banks.

(3) Government support for weak banks. Once public confidence in banks is severely eroded, only the government has the capacity to reassure depositors and other creditors. But it takes time for governments to recognize that weak commercial banks need to be recapitalized and to build political support for aiding the banks. During the immediate aftermath of most banking crises, therefore, governments are tempted to expect too much of central banks.

This chapter will focus primarily on (1) because central bank liquidity policies create moral hazard risks. (2) is also discussed below.

FOUR STAGES OF CRISIS

This crisis is still unfolding at the time of writing (March 2009). But four main phases can be discerned. In Phase 1, from around July to December 2007, the focus was on the liquidity of interbank markets, as well as on uncertainties about the valuation of securitized products held by banks and on the assets involuntarily assumed onto bank balance sheets of assets. A plausible case could be made that, in such circumstances, aggressive lending by central banks could—without generalized government involvement—help restore liquidity in interbank markets and provide time for valuation uncertainties to be resolved.

In Phase 2, which began in early 2008, doubts increased about the survival of firms at the centre of the global financial system—given the increasing prospect of a recession, fears of a credit crunch and a fuller realization of the sheer size of losses facing some major banks. This culminated in the collapse of Bear Stearns, and prompted the government to broker a takeover in March 2008. This provided only a short respite for other major banks and investment grade companies. During this phase it became clear that only government action to capitalize or guarantee banks could avert a deepening crisis. But most governments at first took only piecemeal measures dictated by events. Central banks in effect had to step into this policy vacuum even though it was no longer plausible that central bank lending could by itself prevent a collapse.

The bankruptcy of Lehman Brothers in September 2008 marked the beginning of Phase 3. Global credit markets virtually froze. The governments of major countries committed themselves to use public funds and state guarantees to keep their banks afloat. But markets did not improve partly because of the deepening recession, partly because markets did not find government commitments fully credible.

Phase 4 marked the difficult process of restoring confidence in the solvency of major financial institutions.

Emergency liquidity assistance by central banks

The issue of emergency liquidity assistance had been repeatedly discussed in general terms within the Committee on the Global Financial System (CGFS), a committee of senior central bankers that meets regularly at the Bank for International Settlements (BIS), but central banks did not work out in advance what specific measures they might take to address a liquidity crisis. Banks should manage their own risks and not count on the central bank to rescue them. Public debate about the lender of last resort (LOLR) function of central banks was therefore avoided. The European Central Bank's (ECB) Statute, for instance, does not explicitly consider its LOLR role.[4]

So, in the end, central banks had to work out pragmatically which steps to take as events unfolded from August 2007. The terms on which they provided liquidity (in terms of collateral, counterparties, maturity of operations and currency composition) widened more radically than scarcely anyone would have imagined before August 2007. Central banks contemplated, with

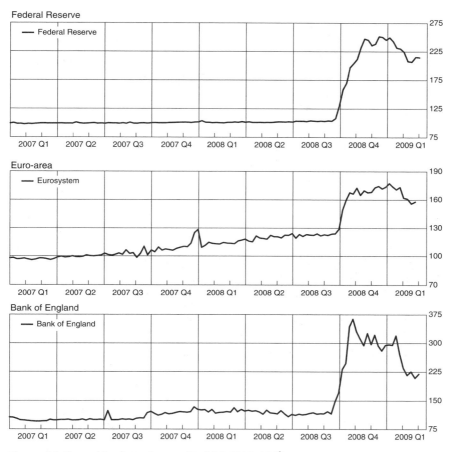

Figure 6.1 Central bank total assets (End Q2 2007=100[1])

Note: An increase in total assets does not necessarily imply a corresponding increase in reserves supplies to domestic banks.

[1] At the end of February 2009, assets of the Federal Reserve were about $1,950 billion, of the ECB about 1,850 billion and of the Bank of England about £180 billion.

Sources: Bank of England; European Central Bank; Federal Reserve.

government, even more far-reaching measures as the crisis deepened with major firms on the brink of failure.

During the first phases of this crisis (up to the bankruptcy of Lehman Brothers), however, total central bank balance sheets generally did not rise dramatically (Figure 6.1).[5]

Press headlines of massive injections of central bank liquidity therefore tended to give the wrong impression: the subsequent re-absorption of liquidity as central

105

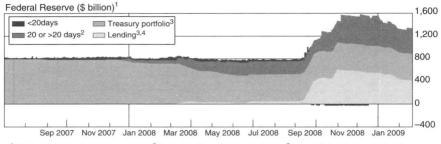

Federal Reserve ($ billion)[1]

^{1} Original maturity in business days. ^{2} Including Term auction facilities. ^{3} Linear interpolation of weekly observations. ^{4}Primary discount credit, primary dealer credit facility, Maiden Lane (Bear Stearns), AIG, commercial paper and money market mutual fund support measures.

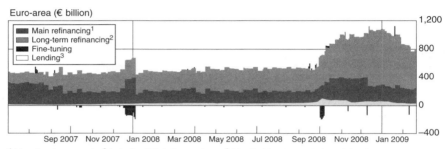

Euro-area (€ billion)

^{1} Maturity of one week. ^{2} Including US dollar auctions. ^{3} Marginal lending and other claims in euro on euro area credit institutions; linear interpolation of weekly observations.

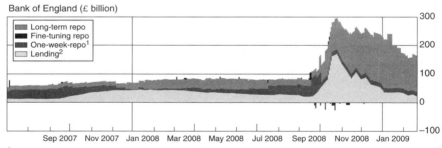

Bank of England (£ billion)

^{1} The decline in one-week repos starting in September 2007 offsets an increase in reserves being supplied by drawings under the support facility provided to Northern Rock. ^{2} Includes US dollar lending and lending to UK deposit protection.

Figure 6.2 Open market operations and lending: amounts outstanding

Sources: Bank of England; European Central Bank; Federal Reserve.

banks strove to maintain their desired monetary stance and to limit lending was not properly understood. But central bank measures did lead to radical change in the composition of central bank balance sheets: the average maturity of central bank loans lengthened (Figure 6.2) and the nature of the collateral changed.

Despite the radical scale and nature of central bank operations, the functioning of inter-bank money markets remained impaired. Although central banks managed to keep overnight rates close to their policy targets for most of this time, the spread between overnight rates and the corresponding three-month LIBOR quotations has remained wide (Figure 6.3).

LIBOR reflects the average of expected overnight rates over the maturity quoted plus a term premium plus a credit premium (because deposits by one major bank with another were typically unsecured). While banks were willing to quote rates when polled by those computing daily LIBOR averages, there was very little actual dealing beyond very short maturities between banks.

With the bankruptcy of Lehman Brothers, credit markets froze and interbank markets (i.e. in the sense of transactions between private institutions) virtually

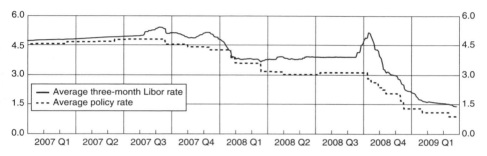

Figure 6.3 Interbank and policy interest rates (%)[1]

[1] Weighted average of the Euro-area, the UK and the US, based on 2005 GDP and PPP exchange rates.

Sources: Bank of England; Bloomberg; Datastream; European Central Bank; Federal Reserve; International Monetary Fund.

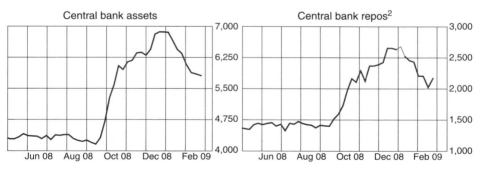

Figure 6.4 Central bank assets and repos ($ billions)[1]

[1] Total of Federal Reserve, ECB, Bank of Japan, and Bank of England weekly data.
[2] Including also US dollar repos for central banks other than the Federal Reserve.

107

disappeared. Central banks were forced to be the counterparty even for non-banks on an extremely wide range of transactions ("market maker of first resort"). In addition to increased lending via the discount window and its primary dealer credit facility, the Federal Reserve provided indirect lending to money market funds and purchased commercial paper through special purpose vehicles. At the same time, many commercial banks deposited their surplus funds at the end of the day with the central bank rather than risk placement with another commercial bank: central bank liabilities and assets rose dramatically as central banks virtually replaced the normal interbank market. The combined assets of the Federal Reserve, the ECB, Bank of Japan and the Bank of England rose from just over \$4 trillion in August 2008 to over \$6 trillion by late October (Figure 6.4).

Recommendations of the CGFS

A Committee on the Global Financial System (CGFS) Study Group, working closely with the BIS Markets Committee, analyzed money market developments and central bank liquidity actions during the early phases of this crisis (CGFS, 2008). Those responsible at major central banks for market operations took part in this Study Group so the report provides a unique insight into the operations conducted by central banks over the period from mid-2007 to June 2008.[6]

The debate about how central banks can be more effective in their actions is still very much alive and many issues remain to be resolved. Nevertheless, there was a consensus in the Study Group on seven recommendations that entailed a significant widening of central bank actions. These are summarized briefly:

(1) The operational framework should be capable of achieving the desired policy target even when faced with large and unpredictable shifts in the aggregate demand for reserves. The Study Group found that the measures required to stabilize overnight rates in extreme cases of market turbulence could even require central banks to replace the interbank market for overnight funds. This is not desirable in normal conditions: allowing interbank markets to distribute reserves has the benefit of encouraging banks to manage their own liquidity and making them test their names by seeking to borrow from peers.

(2) In order to counter a misdistribution of reserves across banks, central banks may need to conduct operations with an extensive set of counterparties and against a broad range of collateral.

(3) When some key financial markets become impaired, central banks should be prepared to expand their intermediation activities and, if needed, take steps that go beyond adjusting the aggregate supply of distribution of reserves. For instance, central banks could increase the maturities of their provision of term funds when term interbank money markets become impaired. Alternatively, they could add to their lists of eligible collateral some illiquid assets.

(4) Global channels for distributing liquidity across borders may become impaired in times of financial turmoil [and] central banks should strengthen their capacity to counter problems in international distribution of liquidity (e.g. by establishing swap lines among themselves or accepting denominated assets or obligations booked abroad as collateral in their operations).

(5) Misinformation and misinterpretation of central bank actions are more likely and costly in times of stress. During such periods, central banks should enhance their communication with participants and the media.

(6) Central banks should reduce the stigma associated with a bank's use of central bank lending facilities. Standing loan facilities are important central bank instruments for providing liquidity insurance to banks. However, the effectiveness of such facilities is undermined if banks worry that their use could send a negative signal about their health (the so-called stigma problem). Stigma tends to be greater in stressed times (because such borrowing can signal to others that the borrower is in difficulty).

(7) The expectation that central banks will act to attenuate market malfunctioning may create moral hazard by weakening market participants' incentives to manage liquidity prudently. Central banks should carefully weigh the expected benefits of actions to re-establish liquidity against their potential costs and, where necessary, introduce or support safeguards against the distortion of incentives.

The major widening of the scope of central bank liquidity provision to banks took place almost by accident in response to an unexpectedly severe crisis. The measures taken were designed under intense time pressures. Several steps are explicitly temporary expedients, often designed as stopgaps until government measures could be put in place. A number of emergency facilities are likely to terminate in their present form. Some of the measures of indefinite duration will be reversed. As the financial crisis deepened and as policy rates moved closer to zero (thus limiting further cuts—a "conventional" policy instrument), central banks also contemplated actions that went well beyond liquidity provision to banks, taking policy into "non-conventional" territory. This could include central bank purchases of government bonds and of private sector debt instruments.

Nevertheless, in reviewing central bank liquidity actions, it is important to think beyond the present crisis. Some of the recent extensions of scope are likely to become permanent features of central bank tools for liquidity provision.

Weighing the drawbacks

Any assessment of the desirability of various liquidity policies must begin with a consideration of possible downsides. What are the drawbacks of such radical extension of the scope of central bank liquidity provision? Six drawbacks are usually identified.

(i) *Contamination of monetary policy*

The argument here is that massive injections of central bank liquidity (perhaps accompanied by a temporary deviation of the central bank policy rate from target) can send a signal that monetary policy has been eased. The CGFS Study Group reports that central banks during the early phases of this crisis have in general successfully prevented liquidity operations from contaminating monetary policy in this way.

A major difficulty, however, is that the measurement of the stance of monetary policy in a financial crisis is itself more difficult than in normal times. First, there is a wider than usual gap between the overnight rate (normally the target for monetary policy)[7] and three-month money market rates (which usually determine rates paid by borrowers in the real economy). Second, banks may wish to restrict lending and so do not pass on reductions in their funding costs. Third, it is very difficult to assess how a banking crisis and a recession will affect inflation expectations. For instance, easing by the Federal Reserve between mid-2007 and mid-2008 appears very substantial when measured by the overnight rate deflated by headline inflation but much less so when the three-month LIBOR rate is deflated by "core" inflation (Figure 6.5).

In these circumstances, it may be better for central banks to tolerate some volatility in the overnight rate than to constrain liquidity operations. The possible drawback of contaminating monetary policy, therefore, is not overwhelming and could be met by clear communication to the market.

(ii) *The central bank taking the responsibilities of government*

This is a much more serious drawback because actions that put at risk taxpayers' money are the responsibility of the elected government accountable to parliament. Point (iv) below is one possible scenario—but there are many others. In addition, central banks will not usually be able to put at risk taxpayers' money from a foreign government! This fact will inevitably constrain central bank actions. Without good assurances from the foreign government, they will not want to take large exposures to a fragile foreign bank operating within their jurisdiction.[8]

There may, however, be ways of designing policies that combine government assumption of credit risk with central bank liquidity provision. The Federal Reserve's Term Asset-backed Securities Loan Facility (TALF), announced in November 2008, is one such hybrid. In effect, $20 billion of funds voted by Congress under TARP were leveraged to support non-recourse lending against $200 billion of AAA-rated asset-backed securities (ABS) backed by recent

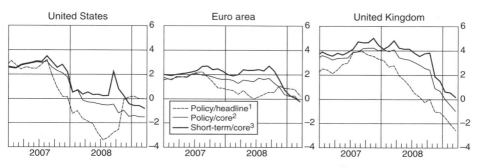

Figure 6.5 Measures of real interest rates (%)

[1] Nominal rate deflated by 12-month changes in consumer prices.

[2] Nominal policy rate deflated by 12-month changes in core consumer prices.

[3] Three-month money market rates deflated by 12-month changes in core consumer prices.

consumer and small business loans. The design of such hybrids should incorporate a prudent assessment of possible credit losses.

(iii) *Avoidance of credit losses*

The valuation of collateral taken is key. Taking illiquid paper as collateral presents a problem because such paper has no reliable market price. Hence the central bank will have to use other valuation methods, and will often rely on an estimate of the capitalization of cash flows. It will also have to decide on the appropriate "haircut" to apply. Such haircuts should reflect the uncertainty over valuations, the volatility of market value and the liquidity risk of the instrument.

(iv) *Inadvertent aid to a failing bank*

The longer the term of central bank lending is, the greater the risk that the central bank will find itself lending to a bank that fails. Extending liquidity assistance to a failing bank can give that bank's other short-term creditors (e.g. in wholesale markets) the opportunity to escape without suffering the losses they would bear if the bank were forced to halt operations. This may increase the eventual cost to the government. The central bank would then have to justify this to the government, and perhaps to parliament (see Chapter 5).

Aid to a subsidiary of a failing foreign bank could be even more difficult to explain to the government. Such lending could in effect provide cash that the subsidiary can move to its head office ahead of an impending bankruptcy. This means that the local creditors of the subsidiary will get less in subsequent (local) bankruptcy adjudications.

In both cases, the central bank may have protected itself by taking good collateral with a prudent haircut, but its actions may have harmed its fellow citizens.

(v) *Central bank replacing the market*

As Buiter (2008a, 2008b) has observed, central banks since the Second World War have moved away in their operations from purchasing or accepting as eligible collateral private sector securities. Instead, for such purposes they have increasingly used central government debt securities. One attraction in central banks accepting as collateral only such paper is that it has a large, liquid market. Hence, central bank operations have only limited effects on the market prices of such paper. Using large markets can allow central banks to avoid giving preferential treatment for certain private borrowers (Kohn, 2008). If central bank operations were to come to dominate small, illiquid markets, price discovery would on the contrary be impaired. Keeping markets alive wherever possible is important because markets can discipline behavior and send very useful signals or information about changing economic conditions.

An additional consideration is that central bank operations that deviate from market prices expose the central bank to adverse selection risks. One particular aspect of this is that illiquid collateral should be more heavily discounted than liquid collateral because this is what the market would do. If the central bank does not do this, then it will tend to replace the market for the more illiquid assets.[9] This does not mean that the central bank should necessarily alter these illiquidity discounts if market liquidity conditions deteriorate as a crisis deepens. Indeed increasing haircuts as the crisis worsens could defeat the very purpose of central bank action. Buiter (2008b) has made a good case for the central bank becoming in a crisis the market maker of last resort.

(vi) *Moral hazard*

Banks become too relaxed about making adequate provision for their own liquidity because they think they can rely on the central bank to rescue them. This requires consideration of:

(1) "Constructive ambiguity." On this argument, banks could be left unsure about whether and how liquidity assistance would be provided. This may argue in favor of central banks being sparing in the introduction and announcement of new semi-permanent arrangements. "Constructive ambiguity" have long been favorite words in the lexicon of central banks. But the recent crisis has strengthened a powerful counterargument: a well thought out framework announced in advance could create better incentives for banks than ad hoc and blanket measures decided upon in a crisis.

(2) Effective penalty pricing. There are several issues to consider. One difficulty lies in the reluctance for the central bank to risk being seen as signaling, by penalty pricing, a heightened risk of insolvency. A second is that the terms of liquidity support extended to a bank that has just taken over a failed bank may be more lenient—because moral hazard with respect to the new management is less. Nevertheless, it should be possible to incorporate into an announced liquidity facility definitions of schedules of access that imply progressively steeper charges as use of the facility rises.

(3) Greater regulation on (or supervisory guidance about) bank liquidity. Historically, central banks used to require banks to hold a proportion of their assets in liquid instruments (usually deposits with the central bank and government bonds). Variation of such ratios was also often a major instrument of monetary control. In most advanced economies, however, such ratios have fallen into disuse. International agreements about bank regulation have instead focused on bank capital requirements. The next section explores this issue further.

Central banks and the regulation of bank liquidity

Up until the late 1970s, central banks generally relied on simple mechanisms (such as aggregate liquidity ratios and the requirement to hold reserves) to regulate the liquidity of the balance sheets of their banks. In many emerging markets, such mechanisms are still in place—although many have scaled them back considerably to lower the costs of bank intermediation and give banks greater flexibility in managing their liquidity.[10] Nevertheless, simple rules or ratios did help the authorities in several major EMEs (emerging market economies) manage the severe liquidity shocks seen in September and October 2008. Brazil, China, and India, for instance, were able to release liquidity into interbank markets by lowering required reserves held at the central bank.

During the 1980s, however, the emphasis of regulators in developed markets shifted from simple rules and ratios to encouraging banks themselves to better manage their own maturity-related risks. The regulatory ratios that remained were very low and often did not bind. It became clear after the crisis had broken that many banks had not recognized the liquidity risks in complex products and off balance sheet items and had not considered the possibility that wholesale funding markets would dry up. This experience focused the attention of both banks and regulators on bank liquidity issues. The crisis also raised for supervisors and regulators the controversial issue of the self-sufficiency of affiliates of foreign banks in the liquidity of their balance sheets.[11]

A consultation paper published by the Basel Committee in September 2008 on liquidity risk management (see BCBS, 2008a) laid out some principles to guide both bankers and regulators. This is an authoritative attempt to draw practical lessons from the crisis for the management of liquidity by banks. But there should be no illusion that prudential regulation can provide a simple solution because liquidity risks are notoriously hard to model and to assess. At least three dimensions are important: maturity mismatches between assets and liabilities; the liquidity characteristics of securities held as assets; and the retail versus wholesale sources of funding. As Kohn (2008) has observed, prudential regulation

requires difficult and necessarily somewhat arbitrary judgments about the types of liquidity stress scenarios that institutions should plan to confront without access to central bank credit and, correspondingly, those scenarios in which institutions in sound financial condition can appropriately rely on central bank credit.

Is there some way of attenuating moral hazard by rewarding banks to hold more liquidity in normal times which can then give them greater or cheaper access to central bank liquidity in a crisis? Goodhart (2009) suggests a Preferential Access Scheme which would allow banks to "earn" cheaper access to central bank liquidity in times of stress. He envisages setting tranches for bank borrowing from the central bank for each bank individually, with the amount of each bank's access predefined according to a variable that would depend on some base of liquid assets, on the nature of liabilities (e.g. the retail deposit base) and on a "score" based on the overall liquidity of the bank in preceding periods. This could encourage banks to improve their liquidity position in order to access cheaper funding.

Others argue for simpler forms of minimum liquidity requirement even if such measures cannot be perfect. D'Arista and Griffith-Jones put forward a proposal in Chapter 7. Leijonhuvfud (2009) suggests that reserve requirements on banks should be increased. Goldstein (2008) argues for the development of a definition of (narrow) regulatory liquidity and a quantitative benchmark of it. In any event, designing a simple liquidity ratio is very difficult in the modern banking system. Not only do different banks have very different exposure to possible liquidity shocks, but the funding policies and asset holdings of various institutions are also very diverse.

National regulators are at present actively reviewing the regulation of liquidity. The UK Financial Services Authority (FSA) recently announced proposals for a new liquidity policy which would require banks to hold a higher amount and quality of liquid assets (FSA, 2008). It raised the possibility of banks in its jurisdiction being induced by such regulation to increase their holdings of government bonds to 6–10 per cent of their total assets (compared with an average of 5 per cent currently). As a minimum, such ratios should also be used as cross-checks by regulators: most regulators do indeed rely on various quantitative measures as useful complements. It would be very helpful to have a harmonized toolbox of metrics for regulators worldwide. Private sector counterparties dealing in opaque and complex firms have argued for publication of some benchmark measures.[12] Certainly, the liquidity policies of central banks could benefit from the wide acceptance of quantitative benchmarks for banks. While it will be challenging to secure international consensus on benchmarks which reflect the liquidity position of a variety of different banks, this is an effort worth pursuing.

What will remain permanent?

Some of the new measures triggered by this crisis are likely to represent a near-permanent broadening of central bank liquidity operations. In some sense, exceptional measures nearly always create the expectation that they would be repeated in similar circumstances. So it is probably not possible for central banks to return the position that existed before the crisis even if specific liquidity schemes are phased out. Nevertheless, some measures clearly suffer from the major drawbacks cited above, which would become more serious if they were to become permanent. While it is premature to draw any firm conclusions about any permanent changes to central bank operating frameworks, the issues involved merit debate.

Three permanent measures?

A case could be made that three measures could be considered a useful, permanent addition to tools of central bank liquidity policy—provided certain limits are kept in mind. These are:

Increased term financing

When term funding markets dried up, banks were forced to roll over term finance with overnight or very short duration borrowing. The volume of overnight liabilities thus snowballed. Such a shortening of liabilities made banks appear unnecessarily vulnerable. It also became clear as this crisis evolved that some part of the term premiums in interbank markets reflected liquidity pressures rather than worries about the creditworthiness of banks seeking term funding. Central bank provision of term finance (not just overnight funds) is clearly justified in such circumstances.[13]

As for pricing strategies, it may be important to limit the magnitude of any divergence in the three-month interbank rate from the policy rate because it is the three-month rate that is a key pricing benchmark for other lending. Secondly, loss of money market liquidity (or extreme day-to-day volatility in pricing) has more serious effects than a loss of liquidity in markets for longer-term instruments because large amounts become due each day (Kohn, 2008).

115

As part of its extraordinary policy of quantitative easing in the early 2000s, the Bank of Japan went from pushing the policy rate to virtually zero to doing the same in term markets. It succeeded in driving term rates to very little above zero—but only at the price of finding itself on one side of virtually all interbank transactions, facing difficulties in reviving a genuine interbank market when quantitative easing ended.

Normally, however, the central bank cannot realistically hope to replace the market in determining with precision the three-month rate. Nor will most central banks want to fix the three-month rate too precisely because such an attempt would be read by markets as indicating the future stance of monetary policy. For this reason, if central banks wish to indicate to the public their objective for a key money market rate (such as three-month LIBOR), they should do so as a range (as the Swiss National Bank does at present), or have a price schedule that rises as larger amounts are sought e.g. the Bank of England's new permanent "discount window facility."

Central banks to offer wider deposit arrangements for banks

At times of market stress, the central bank will find it very hard to assess how much liquidity the banking system needs. Central banks want to keep to a minimum the risk of undersupplying liquidity in their daily operations—which could dislocate the banking system or undermine confidence in banks. Hence the danger is that too much liquidity is supplied. Therefore, mechanisms need to be in place to limit any unintended downward pressure on overnight rates that could result from an accidental oversupply of liquidity. One simple way to put a floor under rates is for the central bank to pay banks an interest rate on excess reserves deposited by the banks with the central bank.

As a matter of general principle, it is desirable that central bank operations at the margin (and on both sides of the balance sheet) take place at rates that are related to market prices in order to minimize possible distortions. Several conflicting considerations will have to be balanced on the size of the spread between the policy rate and the rate of interest paid on commercial bank deposits at the central bank. On the one hand, a narrow spread will set a floor under overnight rates that is close to the policy rate. On the other hand, to encourage banks to place funds with each other (and not the central bank), the spread should be significant. If not, there will be a substantial expansion of central bank balance sheets. The central bank becomes the counterparty for most transactions. This is not desirable.

The crisis has also highlighted another aspect of central bank liabilities policies. As central banks lengthen the size and maturity of their lending operations (i.e. assets), they may need increased flexibility on the liability side—for example, by widening the range of deposit facilities offered or by floating central bank bills. The Bank of England, the Swedish Riksbank, and the Swiss National Bank started in October 2008 to issue one-week bills (mainly to the banks).

The ECB announced a similar scheme. The wider the range of deposit instruments or bills at the disposal of the central bank, the easier are "mopping up" operations. By December 2008, bank deposits with the ECB had reached 200 billion. To encourage banks to trade with each other, the ECB lowered the interest rate on deposits to restore the usual width in the corridor (i.e. between the standing lending facility and the deposit facility).

Better cross-border provision of liquidity

International banking business involves usually three central banks: the central bank where the bank conducts this business; the central bank where the bank is headquartered; and the central bank of the currency used. Which central bank should take responsibility for emergency liquidity has always been a thorny question. The 1983 Concordat on the roles of host and home supervisors was:

never intended to be an agreement about the provision of lender of last resort facilities to the international banking system . . . there is no automatic link between . . . responsibility for supervision and the assumption of a LOLR role. (Bank of England, 1981)

Indeed, this issue had been extensively discussed among central banks in the early 1970s. After the sharp increases in oil prices, it became likely that the oil exporters would deposit large surpluses with international banks in the highly liquid "Eurodollar" market.[14] Banks would re-lend at longer maturities. Hence international banks could, as a group, face a general liquidity problem if there was a significant withdrawal of short-term funds. What would such a liquidity crisis mean for the responsibility of central banks as lenders of last resort to the Eurodollar markets?

There was a worry that central banks would not be able to react quickly because of unresolved disagreements among them. Central banks at that time therefore examined whether it would be possible to reach some prior working agreement about the division of responsibilities among them. After much debate, the conclusion was that [with reference to the problem of the lender of last resort in the Euromarkets], "it would not be practical to lay down in advance detailed rules and procedures for the provision of temporary liquidity."[15]

Although this formal position has remained in place ever since, informal understandings among central banks have evolved. For instance, discussions among central banks in the preparations for Y2K confirmed the general presumption that the host country central bank would have the initial responsibility for providing liquidity support to a foreign bank. But it was also recognized that the home country central bank might become responsible very soon after such support became necessary.

Central Banks, Liquidity, and the Banking Crisis

The recent crisis has again demonstrated the importance of the cross-border dimension. To understand why, it is useful to review the currency funding strategies of banks before the crisis. During the period 2000–7, European banks in particular had taken advantage of extremely liquid currency swap markets to expand their US dollar assets by borrowing euros (or other currencies) while using swaps to hedge the resultant exchange rate exposures. This meant they were holding longer-term or comparatively illiquid dollar assets financed by short-term euro borrowings which had to be constantly rolled over. As long as these markets work smoothly with minimal spreads, such rolling over is not problematic. But during the recent turmoil, foreign exchange (forex) swap markets dried up because the underlying liquidity in national term interbank markets evaporated. This meant European banks were searching for dollars to roll over their positions.

To mitigate such a problem, cross-border swap operations between central banks can be particularly useful for both borrowing and lending central banks. Swap operations allow central banks which hold limited forex reserves to lend foreign currency on a large scale to their banks. Even central banks with large holdings of forex reserves are helped because the use of a swap allows them to avoid withdrawing local currency liquidity from the domestic financial system.[16] The central bank whose currency is in demand also benefits: a foreign bank which cannot liquefy its dollar assets in its own market would be forced to do in US markets—thus aggravating pressures there.

In this crisis, swap operations among the major central banks were used on a very large scale to very good effect. The initial step took place when the Federal Reserve's term auction facility (TAF) announcement in December 2007 was linked to a swap operation with the ECB and the Swiss National Bank. The central bank in the jurisdiction the borrowing bank is operating in assumes the credit risk (and manages collateral).

The failure of Lehman Brothers aggravated the global shortage of dollar funding. The three-month overnight spread for dollars rose by early October to 350 basis points—well above that of other international currencies (Figure 6.6).

The scale and scope of central bank swap lines therefore widened dramatically after September 2008—see Table 6.1. Four central banks then got unlimited access to dollar swaps with the Federal Reserve, allowing them to conduct what was termed "full-allotment US dollar operations at fixed rates." This meant that commercial banks could borrow as many dollars as they pleased and at a fixed rate. By end-October, outstanding usage of forex swap lines by the ECB, the Bank of England and the Swiss National Bank exceeded $300 billion. Inter-central bank swap lines of this magnitude are quite unprecedented. Towards the end of 2008, the three-month/overnight spreads for the international currencies had again converged, with the spread in both euros and dollars falling to around 100 basis points. While lower than at the worst of the crisis, this spread remains much above earlier historical norms.

118

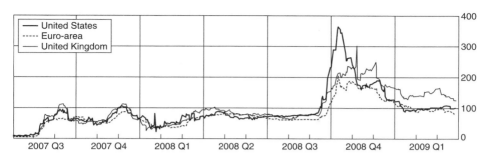

Figure 6.6 Three-month LIBOR–OIS spreads (basis points)
Source: Bloomberg.

Table 6.1 Federal Reserve provision of dollar funding under inter-central bank swap arrangements[1]

Partners	First announced	Max amount	Drawn	Supported operations[2]
Swiss National Bank	12.12.07	–	Yes	1M, 3M, 1W
European Central Bank	12.12.07	–	Yes	1M, 3M, 1W; and FX swaps
Bank of England	18.09.08	–	Yes	1M, 3M, 1W
Bank of Japan	18.09.08	–	Yes	1M, 3M
Bank of Canada	18.09.08	$30 bn		–
Reserve Bank of Australia	24.09.08	$30 bn	Yes	1M, 3M
Sveriges Riksbank	24.09.08	$30 bn	Yes	1M, 3M
Central banks of Brazil, Mexico, Singapore and South Korea,	29.10.08	$30 bn		–

[1] Information as at 21 November 2008.
[2] Repo or collateralized loans, unless otherwise indicated. 1M = one month; 3M = three month; 1W = one week.
Source: Ho and Michaud (2008).

Another possibility for enhanced cross-border cooperation is that major central banks could provide liquidity assistance against a common list of high-quality government bonds denominated in the major international currencies. The central banks of two European countries with large international banking activities (the Bank of England and the Swiss National Bank) routinely accept foreign collateral. The reluctance of other central banks to accept foreign collateral seems to have diverse roots: nervousness about undermining liquidity in their own government bond markets; greater familiarity in operations with local counterparties; and tradition.

119

One further issue deserves a mention. If central banks apply differing collateral terms, the international banks operating in various jurisdictions can be expected to arrange their business so that the central bank with the most lax collateral standards can be expected to end up holding the collateral of the lowest quality. This point is quite general: whenever central banks offer different conditions in their liquidity operations, they must expect to be "gamed" by international banks.

Caution about other measures

Central banks have a clear public policy role to do what is needed to keep markets operating during extreme periods of risk aversion and flight to liquidity. The financial crisis that began in August 2007 is clearly such a case, and central banks have responded accordingly.[17] Nevertheless, many of the recent extensions of central bank operations do have major disadvantages. Measures, therefore, should be designed so that they are used only in exceptional circumstances. Exceptional measures could include:

Willingness to accept illiquid paper as collateral

Banks will continue to hold good credit (i.e. with better lending standards than applied to US sub-prime mortgages) but illiquid assets. When markets as a whole have been hit by a flight to liquidity, the central bank may be the only institution in a position to accept such illiquid assets as collateral. Provided such assets are priced conservatively, the risks to the central bank can be limited. Accepting illiquid collateral makes it even more important for the central bank to be able to be sure that its counterparty is creditworthy.

In normal (i.e. non-crisis) circumstances, however, it is not the job of the central bank to liquefy any form of illiquid asset that banks choose to hold. It is possible that imposing very conservative valuation standards would make it unattractive for banks to use such facilities in normal times.

Adopt a wider range of counterparties

A similar argument applies to widening the list of counterparties. In normal conditions, liquidity provided to major commercial banks can be expected to spread almost automatically throughout the system so there is no need for the central bank to conduct operations with every bank. But in a crisis, the normal flow of funds through the financial system can become blocked. Hence the central bank may have to deal directly with many and more diverse financial institutions.

One reason for limiting the range of counterparties is the cost for the central bank in monitoring the viability of banks that are their counterparties. If the central bank has direct supervisory responsibilities for such banks, such monitoring will be required in any case. Broadening central bank lending to other financial institutions such as mutual funds, insurance companies and so on can be seen as desirable only as a short-term response to a crisis. One apparent justification of recent action—to prevent the seizure of credit derivative markets—raises the question of the need for alternative policies to ensure that the functioning of such markets is not held hostage to the survival of a few, highly leveraged firms.

Lending against assets with credit risk

The Federal Reserve's Term Security Lending Facility (TSLF, created in March 2008) and the Bank of England's Special Liquidity Scheme (in April 2008) broke new ground in that they were based not on central bank reserves operations but on swapping illiquid assets with credit risk (especially mortgage-related paper), such assets could not be used in normal market repo transactions. As the Bank of England statement made clear, this represents a quasi-fiscal operation for which the government takes responsibility.

Outright purchase of private sector assets

Assets that central banks have bought in recent months include private sector assets such as equities, commercial paper, corporate bonds and asset-backed securities. The outright purchase of assets by the central bank may have a significant impact on prices, particularly when markets are thin. There are two reasons why purchasing assets is a much more radical step than accepting such assets as collateral for loans. One is that with outright purchases the central bank assumes fully the market and credit risks of buying such assets (unless special structures are designed to transfer the risk to the government). Assessing credit risks is a major challenge for a central bank. In practice, they tend to rely on external credit ratings; while this could appear to create an objective process of risk limitation, any uncritical reliance on such ratings does have drawbacks.

Another concern is the exit strategy. While there is an automatic exit from lending on the repayment date, asset acquisitions reverse automatically only when the instrument matures.

Outright purchase of government bonds

The central bank purchase of long-term government debt matched by the issuance of short-term liabilities would tend to flatten the yield curve—because the private market is being asked to take less duration risks. But a policy can be only a temporary expedient because it entails the public sector assuming greater interest rate risk (and, for some countries, refinancing risk). In the short term, however, it can signal a policy intention to hold interest rates low for some time. In addition, interest rates on some loans and other debt contracts may be linked to the yields on certain benchmark maturities of government bonds. Such effects are likely to be transitory. A change in government debt issuance policy (such as reducing issuance of long-term bonds and increasing the issuance of short-term bills) would have a similar effect.

Conclusion

The financial crisis that started in August 2007 led to a quite unexpected expansion in the central bank's toolkit for conducting liquidity operations. A bigger toolkit always seems better, provided those using its potentially dangerous tools are fully cognizant of the attendant risks. Only central banks can provide the assurances of liquidity often needed in a financial crisis. In the extreme conditions prevailing in late 2008, it was natural that fighting the crisis received priority. Before the crisis, nobody expected the scale of operations central banks were drawn into. Many measures will probably be permanent. This chapter suggests three areas where changes decided on during this crisis are likely to endure: increased term financing; wider deposit arrangements at the central bank; and better cross-border provision of liquidity.

But many other operations will at some point have to be unwound. Many of the exceptional measures taken recently have significant adverse side-effects which are likely to be felt in an uncertain way at some point in the future. Reversing such exceptional policies in good time may not be easy, because the size and the timing of the impact of very large changes in central bank balance sheets on the real economy are not known with any precision. Central banks will be cautious about reversing these policies, particularly when the banks are still weak.

A final danger is that highly visible central bank operations can distract attention from fundamental credit problems that central banks cannot resolve. Public confidence in banks holding large volumes of bad assets can be restored only by some form of government guarantee or by the government taking such assets off bank balance sheets. It took the virtual seizure of credit markets in September 2008 to convince most governments and their legislatures of the need for an overall strategy to address this issue.

Notes

1. This chapter reflects my own views and not necessarily those of the BIS. I am very grateful for comments and suggestions from those involved in the work on a recent CGFS report—Dietrich Domanski, François-Louis Michaud, and Bill Nelson. Thanks to Stephen Cecchetti, Mary Craig, Charles Goodhart, Stephany Griffith-Jones, and Már

Gudmundsson for helpful comments. Thanks too to Gert Schnabel and Garry Tang for the graphs and Clare Batts for secretarial assistance.

2. Bank for International Settlements.
3. See Mehrling's chapter within this volume (Chapter 10); Mehrling argues that credit default swaps need their own discount facility. In Bagehot's day, he argues, a bank's acceptance of a bill of exchange made, given the central discount facility at the Bank of England, an illiquid asset liquid. He has argued in favor of an "official CDS backstop": by setting the prices of a few key insurance contracts, the government could give Bagehot's "lend freely but at a penalty rate" dictum a modern guise.
4. Good descriptions of the inherent difficulties of the LOLR role of central banks are Stevens (2008) and White (2008).
5. This graph does not include the extraordinary operations taken from March 2008 as several large firms faced failure. Such operations have clear fiscal dimensions under the Federal Reserve's TSLF and the Bank of England's SLS (see below). In September 2008, the US Treasury issued new bills to facilitate an increase in the size of the Federal Reserve's balance sheet in order to cope with a widening of the central bank's counterparties.
6. See also Cecchetti and Disyatat (2009) for a discussion of how the principles that should govern the lender of last resort function of central banks depend on the precise nature of the liquidity shortages.
7. One notable exception, however, is the Swiss National Bank, which has a target range for the three-month LIBOR rate for the Swiss franc rather than an overnight rate.
8. Buiter (2008) points out that the lender of last resort function in the Euro-area is assigned to the national central banks.
9. Chailloux et al. (2008) refers to Gresham's Law of Collateral: when central bank collateral policies differ from market conditions, banks will exploit the arbitrage possibilities thus created such that the average quality of collateral provided to the central bank will fall.
10. The construction of "maturity ladders"—of assets and liabilities—over selected maturity dates (next day, next week, etc.) was one simple tool which encouraged early action to close prospective liquidity gaps. See BIS (2000) and BCBS (1992) for discussions of various earlier approaches.
11. On this, the UK FSA (2008) noted that the default of an international financial firm can put the creditors and customers of its local affiliates at a disadvantage. It concluded that, "the starting point of our new liquidity regime is that a UK regulated firm or branch must be self-sufficient for liquidity purposes." Any waiver from this new regime would be subject to stringent criteria.
12. See Davies (2008). Several comments during the consultative period of the Basel Committee's *Principles for Sound Liquidity Risk Management and Supervision* made this point. For instance, the Institute of Chartered Accountants noted a need "…in the longer run … for some form of quantitative requirements, agreed with the regulator. It is undesirable for too great a range of regimes to persist across countries" (Basel Committee, 2008b).
13. CGFS (2008) notes banks eagerly took up offers of central bank term finance. The fact that auction stop-out ratios were high suggests that the banks' underlying funding needs were only partly met. See also Michaud and Upper (2008).

14. "Eurodollar" means dollars traded outside the US, and is not to be confused with the currency of the Euro-area.
15. Communiqué of G-10 Governors, September 10, 1974, BIS.
16. By contrast, selling forex reserves to the banks drains liquidity from the domestic banking system.
17. In addition, but not considered here, quantitative measures may be needed to effect further easing of monetary policy once nominal policy rates are close to zero.

References

Bank of England (1981) 'Developments in Cooperation Among Banking Supervisory Authorities.' *Bank of England Quarterly Bulletin*, 21 (June).
Bank for International Settlements (2000) 'Managing Foreign Debt and Liquidity Risks.' BIS Policy Papers No. 8 <http://www.bis.org/publ/plcy08.htm>.
Basel Committee on Banking Supervision (1992). 'A Framework for Measuring and Managing Liquidity' <http://www.bis.org/publ/bcbs10b.htm>.
—— (2008a). 'Principles for Sound Liquidity Risk Management and Supervision' <http://www.bis.org/publ/bcbs138.htm>.
—— (2008b). 'Comments Received on "Principles for Sound Liquidity Risk Management and Supervision"' <http://www.bis.org/publ/bcbs138/cacomments.htm>.
Buiter, W. H. (2008a) 'Can Central Banks Go Broke?' CEPR Policy Insight No. 24 (May).
—— (2008b) 'Central Banks and Financial Crises.' Paper presented at the Federal Reserve Bank of Kansas City's symposium on "Maintaining Stability in a Changing Financial System," at Jackson Hole, Wyoming (August).
Cecchetti, S. G. and Disyatat, P. (2009) 'Central Bank Tools and Liquidity Shortages' Federal Reserve Bank of New York Economic Policy Review <http://www.newyorkfed.org/research/conference/2009/cblt/CB_Tools_and_Liquidity_Shortages.pdf> accessed on June 18, 2009.
Chailloux, A., Gray, S., Klueh, U., Shimizu, S., and Stella, P. (2008) 'Central Bank Response to the 2007–08 Subprime Crisis: Experiences and Lessons Drawn.' IMF Working Paper 08/210.
Committee on the Global Financial System (2008) 'Central Bank Operations in Response to the Financial Turmoil.' CGFS Papers No. 31 <http://www.bis.org/publ/cgfs31.htm>.
Davies, R. (2008) 'Points of Principle.' *Risk* (August).
Financial Services Authority (2008) 'Strengthening Liquidity Standards.' Consultation Paper 08/22 (December).
Goldstein, M. (2008) 'Financial Regulation After the Subprime and Credit Crisis.' Peterson Institute for International Economics.
Goodhart, C. A. E. (2009) 'Liquidity and Money Market Operations.' In *The Regulatory Response to the Financial Crisis*. London: Edward Elgar.
Ho, C. and Michaud, F-L. (2008) 'Measures to Alleviate Foreign Currency Funding Shortages.' *BIS Quarterly Review* (December) <http://www.bis.org/publ/qtrpdf/r_qt0812y2.htm>.
Kohn, D. L. (2008) 'Money Markets and Financial Stability.' Presentation at the Federal Reserve Board of New York and Columbia Business School Conference on the role of money markets, May 28, 2008.

Leijonhuvfud, A. (2009) 'Two Systemic Problems.' CEPR Policy Insight No. 29. (January).

Mehrling, P. (2008) 'Credit Default Swaps: The Key to Financial Reform.'

Michaud, F-L. and Schnabel, G. (2008) 'Central Bank Balance Sheets,' *BIS Quarterly Review* (December).

—— and Upper, C. (2008) 'What Drives Interbank Rates? Evidence from the LIBOR Panel.' *BIS Quarterly Review* (March) <http://www.bis.org/publ/qtrpdf/r_qt0803f.pdf>.

Stevens, G. (2008) 'Liquidity and the Lender of Last Resort.' 7th Annual Sir Leslie Melville lecture, Reserve Bank of Australia (April).

White, B. (2008) 'Bagehot Revisited.' *Central Banking*, 19(1), August, pp. 68–71.

7

Agenda and Criteria for Financial Regulatory Reform

Jane D'Arista and Stephany Griffith-Jones[1]

> The more free-market oriented our economy, the greater its need for official financial supervision.
>
> Henry Kaufman, *Financial Times*, August 6, 2008

Introduction

The global financial crisis that started in mid-2007 follows many deep and costly financial crises within developing economies throughout the last twenty-five years. This more recent crisis, like previous ones, is the result of both: (i) inherent flaws in the way financial markets operate—such as their tendency toward boom-bust behavior; and (ii) insufficient, incomplete, and sometimes inappropriate regulation.

Financial crises tend to be very costly from a fiscal point of view (i.e. that of the taxpayer), from their impact on lost output and investment, and from their impact on people, many of whom are poor, innocent bystanders.

It is therefore urgent and important to reform financial regulation, so that financial crises are less likely to occur in the future. The new systems of financial regulation should attempt to deal with the old unresolved problem of inherent pro-cyclicality within banking and financial markets. They should also deal with new features such as the growing scale and complexity of the financial sector, the emergence of new and unregulated actors and instruments, as well as the increased globalization of financial markets. To do this adequately and to avoid regulatory arbitrage, regulation has to be comprehensive.

It is these two broad principles, *comprehensiveness* and *counter-cyclicality*, that will provide the framework for our proposals detailed below. It is encouraging that, at least rhetorically, G-20 leaders have expressed general commitment to these principles. However, what is crucial is the extent to which they will actually be implemented.

Comprehensiveness

With regard to comprehensiveness, in order for regulation to be efficient, it is essential that the domain of the regulator is the same as the domain of the market that is regulated. Furthermore, lender-of-last-resort type facilities provided by national central banks are increasingly being extended to new actors and instruments during the current turmoil. As a result, a corresponding expansion of regulation to actors and activities that have been, or are likely to be, bailed out is essential to avoid moral hazard. At the European level, the European Central Bank (ECB) has been acting quickly and significantly to provide liquidity, but the supervisory function has been lacking. The Financial Stability Forum (FSF, 2008) recommends going further via the establishment of swap lines among central banks to provide liquidity in different currencies during times of stress. While the internationalization of lender-of-last-resort facilities seems both inevitable and desirable, given European and globalized private financial players, it needs to be accompanied by a corresponding and considerable strengthening of the international dimension of financial regulation. If the latter is not done, moral hazard will significantly increase once again as financial activity and risk-taking will grow rapidly in areas where international regulatory gaps exist but there is implicit or explicit coverage by lender-of-last-resort facilities.

We will therefore propose comprehensive measures at two levels: *transparency* should be required of all actors and activities. This will entail both registration and disclosure of relevant variables for all financial institutions. This is a precondition for comprehensive regulation, but one that will also benefit other financial market participants and investors, as well as macroeconomic authorities.

There should be *comprehensive* and equivalent regulation to cover all entities that invest or lend on behalf of other people, and all activities which they undertake. As we discuss below, such regulation needs to be done in ways that protect both liquidity (which we propose could be done through liquidity requirements for individual institutions as well as required reserve holdings by all institutions with national or regional central banks), and solvency (which would be based on capital and would build upon, as well as improve, the existing Basel banking regulatory framework while widening its requirements to other financial institutions).

In fact, adequate liquidity and capital buffers are linked, as sufficient reserves—implying higher levels of liquidity in individual institutions and in the whole system—will alleviate the pressure on capital in times of stress.

Counter-cyclicality

A key market failure in the financial system is the pro-cyclical behavior of most financial actors, which leads to excessive risk-taking and financial activity in good times, followed by insufficient risk-taking and financial activity in bad times. As a consequence, a key principle and desirable feature for efficient regulation is that it is counter-cyclical to compensate for the inherent pro-cyclical behavior of capital and banking markets. The desirability of such an approach has been increasingly stressed by international institutions, such as the Bank for International Settlements (BIS, 2005a, 2008) and leading academics (Ocampo and Chiappe, 2001; Goodhart and Persaud, 2008). This implies varying regulatory requirements for reserves, loan to asset value ratios, capital, provisioning against losses, etc., according to the phase of the economic cycle; as discussed below, regulatory variables such as capital could thus be varied according to the growth of total assets, and/or the expansion of assets in particular sectors, for example loans for housing. As former BIS Chief Economist, William White (2007), pointed out, this would use "monetary and credit data as a basis for resisting financial excesses in general, rather than inflationary pressure in particular."

The following section briefly outlines the Federal Reserve's (Fed) policy failures and the evolution of the financial system (with an emphasis on US markets) and their link with the origins of the financial crisis. In the next section, we develop what we believe are the key principles and criteria for a financial regulation that minimizes systemic risk, and illustrate them with analysis of specific sectors (e.g. off-balance sheet transactions) and important issues (e.g. compensation schemes). The concluding section develops our main regulatory proposals for liquidity and solvency.

Deregulation, systemic change, and policy failures

After the eruption of the subprime mortgage crisis in the summer of 2007, criticisms of past and present policies of the Fed and other regulatory authorities became more frequent. In December 2007, the Fed's belated proposal for regulating all mortgage lenders suggested that it was engaged in the proverbial closing of the barn door after the horses were out. Why the Fed and other authorities had not thought such restrictions were needed earlier seemed evidence of their ideological commitment to deregulation rather than a pragmatic assessment of developments that could cause market disruption and systemic fragility.

In the case of the Fed, ideology shaped policy outcomes beyond its failure either to condemn or control poor lending practices and fraud. The Fed's monetary influence weakened as it gave priority to deregulation and innovation, and abandoned credit flows to the pro-cyclical pressures of market forces; monetary policy itself had lost its ability to stabilize financial markets and the economy. The Fed paid no attention to the fact that foreign capital inflows were driving up the supply of credit and also failed to notice the explosion of debt that unchecked credit expansion produced. Moreover, as debt soared, the Fed ignored the asset bubbles it fueled.

Also ignored were critical changes in the structure of financial markets that eroded the ability of regulatory authorities to monitor markets and supervise individual institutions and their increasingly diverse activities. Meanwhile, structural change also undermined the effectiveness of monetary tools used to transmit policy initiatives to the real economy and the Fed's ability to conduct counter-cyclical operations. As its bailout of Bear Stearns in March 2008 made clear, the Fed recognized that it was facing a systemic crisis but initially struggled to act systemically. Together with its failure to criticize and curb abusive lending practices, the Fed's passivity in responding to major changes in financial structure and regulation contributed to the prolonged and pervasive reach of the credit crunch that the subprime mortgage defaults unleashed.

The following discussion focuses on the policy failures of the Fed and other central banks, arguing that monetary authorities in advanced economies were complicit in creating the conditions that led to the crisis; the crisis could not have occurred in the absence of the excessive liquidity they created. While it is clear that the unprecedented escalation in leverage that increased the vulnerability of the financial system to a funding crisis was made possible by deregulation of many activities and products, this escalation also depended on the fuel supplied by loose monetary policy.

Our evaluation of the monetary factors that contributed to systemic weakness and crisis leads us to argue that reforms of financial regulation must include a reassessment of the relationship between the central bank, the financial system and the economy. In the recent, heady era of booms based on financial engineering, the impact of imbalances in credit flows on the real economy tended to be overlooked. In the process, central banks and financial institutions seemed to have forgotten that finance must serve real economic activity if its own soundness and stability is to survive.

Liquidity, credit growth, and asset bubbles

In the aftermath of the collapse of the major stock indices in 2000, the Fed began to flood US markets with excess liquidity. To address its concerns about the economy's sluggish response to the stimulus already provided and the potential for deflation, it maintained a nominal federal funds rate of 1 per cent from June 2003 through 2004 by generating a continuous stream of liquidity that pushed the real rate of interest into negative territory over the period. As investors' "search for yield" intensified in the low interest rate environment, the unprecedented increase in the availability of funding spurred escalating amounts of leveraged speculation in the form of carry trades, where the effect of borrowing short term at low rates is to drive down rates on the higher yielding, long-term assets in which the funds are invested. Excess liquidity was also reflected in narrowed risk premia and eased credit standards—developments mentioned by former Federal Reserve Chairman Alan Greenspan in his appearance before the Senate Banking Committee in February 2005, but without acknowledgment of their link to excess liquidity.

Before Greenspan's testimony, the June 2004 BIS Annual Report argued that there was in fact a direct link between accommodative monetary policies in the G-3 countries (the United States, the Euro-area and Japan) and mounting liquidity in global financial markets. The report pointed to quantitative measures such as the monetary base, broad money, and credit to the private sector—all of which had expanded rapidly since 1999 in a large group of countries—as clear evidence of exceptional liquidity growth. Moreover, in 2003 the BIS had specifically criticized the Fed for creating a situation in which a potential US downturn could become more severe due to the domestic debt build-up encouraged by monetary ease, and had published research establishing a link between asset bubbles and excessive credit growth. It had also warned about increasing speculation, pointing to a rising volume of leverage in domestic and international financial systems in 2002 that was fueling the credit expansion (BIS 2002, 2003, 2004; Borio and Lowe, 2002).

The Fed and other central banks ignored BIS warnings despite a major sell-off in bond markets in March 2005 that revealed an escalation in leverage and carry trade activities. They made no effort to address the troubling link between excess liquidity and debt-financed speculation or the even more problematic connection between liquidity and credit growth. Oblivious to the final link in that chain—the asset bubbles inflated by debt and lulled by stable indicators for wholesale and consumer prices—central banks took no action to deal with the inflation in asset prices.

Leveraged capital flows and credit expansion

Sizable, pro-cyclical capital flows over the past two decades have played an important role in weakening the impact of changes in policy rates on the availability of credit in financial markets. In the United States, for example, raising the short-term policy rate in 2004 failed to halt the decline in long-term interest rates or prevent the flood of new borrowing that followed in 2005 and 2006—a period of exceptionally large capital inflows. But the Fed's efforts to revive credit flows and economic activity by lowering interest rates in a downturn had also proved unreliable as a result of capital outflows during the recession in the early 1990s. At that time, relatively little of the Fed's ample infusion of liquidity was transmitted to the real economy. As interest rates fell, the search for higher yields by domestic and foreign holders of US assets had prompted outflows—mostly to Mexico—that prolonged the recession. Credit growth resumed when the Fed raised interest rates in March 1994 and US and foreign investors returned to US assets, leaving Mexico in crisis.

By the middle of the 1990s, the growth of cross-border carry trade strategies had further undermined the ability of the Fed and other central banks to expand or curtail the transmission of liquidity to their national markets.[2] These strategies, triggered by interest rate differentials on assets denominated in different currencies, increased the amount of leveraged speculation by financial institutions and fueled yet another set of asset bubbles to add to the string that began in Japan in the 1980s, moved through emerging markets in the 1990s and started to afflict the US and other advanced economies at the turn of the century. The pattern that has developed over the last two decades suggests that relying on changes in interest rates as the primary tool of monetary policy can set off pro-cyclical capital flows that tend to reverse the intended result of the action taken. As a result, monetary policy no longer reliably performs its counter-cyclical function and its attempts to do so by changing the policy rate may even exacerbate instability.

Throughout 2004 and 2005, for example, borrowing reached truly massive proportions both in the US and abroad. The Fed's measured increases in policy rates had no cooling effect on rising debt levels. In fact, they spurred foreign private inflows into dollar assets at home and abroad by encouraging carry trade strategies that borrowed low interest rate yen to purchase higher yielding dollar assets. Escalating speculation was reflected in record-breaking growth in borrowing in external banking markets, the great majority of which was channeled to financial institutions and used for position-taking by commercial and investment banks and hedge funds (BIS, 2005b, 2006).

With capital flows into the US in 2005 rising to twice the amount needed to finance the current account deficit, the US assumed an entrepot function for global markets. Excess flows into dollar assets triggered sizable outflows for investment in higher-yielding emerging market assets (US Department of Commerce, 2006). As an excess of dollars from foreign investment on top of current account surpluses flooded their markets, central banks in those countries responded by buying dollars to limit their conversion into local currencies. While these sterilized intervention strategies helped moderate a build-up in domestic liquidity, they also helped mitigate an appreciation of their currencies.

However, needing to invest the dollars they had acquired, emerging market countries bought US Treasury securities and other dollar assets and re-exported the problem back to the United States. The accumulation of dollar reserves by these countries augmented the highly liquid conditions in US financial markets, exerting downward pressure on medium- and long-term interest rates and fueling another round of capital outflows from the United States back to emerging markets as well as continued binge borrowing by US residents.

While 2005 was an extraordinary year in terms of rising liquidity and debt, the pattern of capital flows that year was not unique. Net foreign lending in US credit markets had averaged about 15 per cent of the annual supply of funds from the mid-1990s through 2007 (Federal Reserve System, 2008). Nevertheless, the advent of monetary easing after 2001 introduced a new dynamic: the generation of liquidity through the spill-over effects of leveraged cross-border investment flows. The round-robin nature of those flows constituted a sorcerer's apprentice scenario that was bound to lead to crisis when uncertainty—from whatever cause—threatened the highly leveraged financial sector's need for funding.

Meanwhile, the rising debt levels of private financial and non-financial sectors were threatening to burst the asset bubbles they had created. The housing bubble that had become apparent in the United States, and was to burst in the second half of 2007, had been fueled by an extraordinary growth in debt with outstanding credit reaching 352.6 per cent of GDP by the end of 2007, up from 255.3 per cent in 1997. The rise in household debt over the same decade (from 66.1 to 99.9 per cent of GDP) was both a key indicator of the debt bubble and of the growing threat it posed for future spending as debt service took a larger share of disposable income. But the most dramatic development was the jump in the debt of the US financial sector to 113.8 per cent of GDP from 63.8 per cent only a decade earlier (ibid.). While the increased borrowing by financial institutions signaled the rise in speculative leverage, it also reflected new funding strategies adopted by a profoundly changed financial system. Those changes and their implications for monetary policy implementation constituted another critical development the Fed ignored.

The slipping transmission belt for monetary policy

Over the past thirty years, the US financial system has been transformed by a shift of household savings from banks to pension/mutual funds and other institutional investment pools. Between 1977 and the end of 2007, the assets of all depository institutions plummeted from 56.9 per cent to 23.7 per cent of total financial sector assets. Meanwhile, spurred in part by the funding requirements of the Employee Retirement Income Security Act (ERISA) of 1974, the assets of pension funds and mutual funds rose from 21 per cent to 37.8 per cent of the total as these institutional investors came to provide the dominant channels for household savings and investment flows (Table 7.1).[3]

The shift in individual savings from banks to pension and mutual funds produced a symmetrical increase in business borrowing through capital markets. Credit flows to households also moved into the capital markets as mortgage originators such as banks, savings and loan institutions, and brokers bundled individual mortgages into pools and sold securities based on those

Table 7.1 Outstanding assets held by financial sectors

Amount ($ billions)	1957	1967	1977	1987	1997	2007
Depository Institutions[1]	287.0	625.1	1,716.6	4,455.9	6,546.5	13,737.4
Insurance Companies[2]	104.7	181.8	354.2	1,042.7	2,090.3	3,444.2
Pension Funds[3]	64.4	194.3	580.8	2,458.5	6,479.2	10,699.1
Mutual Funds[4]	13.1	51.8	56.8	815.3	4,177.8	11,170.4
GSEs & Federally Related Mortgage Pools	8.0	25.9	162.7	1,043.8	2,927.1	7,626.4
Issuers of Asset-backed Securities	0.0	0.0	0.0	118.3	905.0	4,221.0
Nonbank Lenders[5]	21.5	51.8	140.4	470.3	799.3	1,911.2
Security Brokers and Dealers	5.5	14.7	30.0	137.9	779.2	3,095.3
Others[6]	0.1	0.8	5.1	198.9	524.4	2,033.9
Total	504.3	1,146.2	3,046.6	10,741.6	25,228.8	57,938.9
Percentage of Total Financial Sector Assets						
Depository Institutions[1]	56.9	54.5	56.3	41.5	25.9	23.7
Insurance Companies[2]	20.8	15.9	11.6	9.7	8.3	5.9
Pension Funds[3]	12.8	17.0	19.1	22.9	25.7	18.5
Mutual Funds[4]	2.6	4.5	1.9	7.6	16.6	19.3
GSEs & Federally Related Mortgage Pools	1.6	2.3	5.3	9.7	11.6	13.2
Issuers of Asset-backed Securities	-----	-----	-----	1.1	3.6	7.3
Nonbank Lenders[5]	4.3	4.5	4.6	4.4	3.2	3.3
Security Brokers and Dealers	1.1	1.3	1.0	1.3	3.1	5.3
Others[6]	-----	0.1	0.2	1.9	2.1	3.5

[1] Includes commercial banks, savings institutions, and credit unions.

[2] Includes life and property-casualty insurance companies.

[3] Includes private pension funds, state and local government retirement funds, and insured pension assets.

[4] Includes money market mutual funds, closed-end funds, exchange-traded funds, and other mutual funds.

[5] Includes finance companies and mortgage companies.

[6] Includes real estate investment trusts and funding corporations.

Source: Federal Reserve System, *Flow of Funds Accounts of the United States*.

pools to investors. Government-sponsored enterprises (GSEs) such as Fannie Mae and Freddie Mac, and federally related mortgage pools played major roles in facilitating this securitization process. Meanwhile, asset-backed securities (ABS) issuers used securitization techniques to fund car loans and other consumer receivables. In the twenty-year period between 1987 and 2007, the assets of GSEs and mortgage pools—primarily holdings of mortgages for single-family housing—rose from $1.0 trillion to $7.6 trillion, while assets of ABS issuers jumped from $118.3 billion to $4.7 trillion.

The implications of these shifts in saving and credit flows radically altered the way the financial sector functions by reducing the role of direct lending in favor of trading, investment and asset management. Their impact on the transmission of monetary policy initiatives has been profound and was already evident in 1993. At that time, former Fed Chairman Greenspan made the following observation:

> the fairly direct effect that open market operations once had on the credit flows provided for businesses and home construction is largely dissipated [and while the Fed] can still affect short-term interest rates, and thus have an impact on the cost of borrowing from banks, from other intermediaries, and directly in the capital markets . . . this effect may be more indirect, take longer, and require larger movements in rates for a given effect on output. (Greenspan, 1993, p. 3)

At the same 1993 conference, former Bundesbank Vice President Hans Tietmeyer's view was somewhat gloomier. He argued that, in a number of countries, deregulation and financial innovation had altered the transmission mechanisms for monetary policy to the real economy and had "generally made it more difficult for monetary policy makers to fulfill their stability mandate" (Tietmeyer, 1993, p. 407).

Subsequent events have underscored the accuracy of these remarks. In the fifteen years since they were made, however, the major central banks have taken no steps to improve the monetary transmission mechanism. On the contrary, they countenanced further innovation and deregulation, and promoted the view that market-based regulations—the Basel Agreement on capital requirements, for example—could replace the quantity controls (reserve and liquidity requirements, lending limits, and capital controls) that had been targeted for removal by the advocates of liberalization.

After quantity controls were dismantled, the major central banks were left with a single policy tool: the ability to change the short-term policy rate. They lost control over the supply of bank credit and, over time, their influence over the demand for credit also weakened. As the banking system's share of credit market assets shrank, central banks' continued reliance on banks as the base for policy implementation weakened the link between the policy rate and other short- and long-term rates.

The build-up in banks' leverage was a direct result of the removal of quantity controls. But the extraordinary growth in leverage in other financial sectors and on the balance sheets of households and businesses was due to central banks' unwillingness to confront the implications of changes in financial structure that moved the dominant share of saving and borrowing from banks to the capital markets. The outcome of their failure to repair the transmission belt for monetary policy is the current slow and painful process of deleveraging within the financial system and the real economy.

As the BIS and others have argued, a prerequisite for stabilizing the crisis-stricken global economy is reinstating counter-cyclical policy initiatives. We argue that this will require the introduction of counter-cyclical regulatory reforms and extending their reach to all segments of the financial system. The following sections discuss how the introduction of comprehensive, counter-cyclical regulatory strategies will bolster the effectiveness of monetary policy implementation by addressing the inherently pro-cyclical bias of the market-based financial system that has evolved in US and global markets over the past thirty years.

Criteria and principles for financial regulatory reform

As discussed in the introduction, there are two broad principles, comprehensiveness and counter-cyclicality, that need to be adhered to, so that financial regulation is effective in helping ensure financial stability and avoid crises.

Regulation has to be comprehensive

One of the main causes of the current crisis is the fact that effective regulation covers a diminishing share of total capital and banking markets. As Damon Silvers, Counsel to the American Federation of Labor and Congress of Industrial Organizations (AFL-CIO, 2008), put it, "the regulatory system is a kind of Swiss cheese, where the regulatory holes gradually get larger."

As is often the case, it has been true in this crisis that the parts of the financial system that were not regulated at all, or were regulated too lightly, have generated more problems. Because of regulatory arbitrage, growth of financial activity (and risk) moved to unregulated mechanisms (Structured Investment Vehicles—SIVs), instruments (derivatives) or institutions (hedge funds). However, though unregulated, those parts of the shadow financial system were *de facto* dependent on systemically important banks via provision of credit, guaranteed liquidity lines or other commitments.

A clear example of when the lack of capital requirements led to excessive growth of unregulated mechanisms is in the case of SIVs. It is very interesting that Spanish regulatory authorities allowed banks to have SIVs, but required Spanish banks to consolidate these special purpose vehicles in their accounting, implying that they had the same capital requirements as their other assets (Cornford, 2008; interview material). This eliminated the incentive for such vehicles to grow in Spain and thus prevented them from becoming a major problem for banks as SIVs were in the United States.

It is positive that Basel II, unlike Basel I, requires banks to set aside capital to support liquidity commitments to those vehicles. However, such commitments have lower capital requirements for short maturities;

furthermore, the Basel Committee is reportedly planning to strengthen these capital requirements to reduce regulatory arbitrage incentives (Financial Stability Forum, FSF, 2008). Though positive, such measures would only be partial. A more comprehensive solution would be for all vehicles and transactions to be put on banks' balance sheets; then there should be no regulatory arbitrage, as risk-weighted capital requirements would be equivalent for all balance sheet activities; furthermore, transparency could automatically become far more comprehensive for banks.

This discussion of SIVs illustrates the fact that the only solution is for comprehensive and equivalent transparency and regulation of all institutions and instruments. This would discourage or even hopefully eliminate regulatory arbitrage and help prevent the build-up of excessive systemic risk, which is essential for financial stability. As discussed in the Introduction, the widening of last resort facilities—both national and international—that has recently occurred further justifies the need of a corresponding increase in comprehensiveness of regulation to avoid moral hazard.

The task of defining equivalent regulation on assets for all financial institutions and activities, both for solvency and liquidity, is essential.[4] To be more specific, all entities that invest or lend on behalf of other people—using other people's money and providing some type of leverage—need to have both relevant transparency requirements and need to be regulated. Within institutions, all their activities need to have equivalent regulation. Therefore, institutions like hedge funds need to be brought into the regulatory domain, as do all off-balance sheet activities of banks.

Specific steps have already been taken towards more comprehensive regulation; US authorities are addressing regulatory gaps in the oversight of entities that originate and fund mortgages, which is clearly welcome. Equally importantly, there is increasing support, even by G-20 leaders and finance ministers, for comprehensive regulation. However, important differences remain about the desirable extent of coverage of regulations, as well as the extent to which this important principle will be implemented in practice.

For example, an influential European Union report (European Parliament, 2008) argues that financial regulation should be comprehensive; it especially emphasizes the need to regulate hedge funds and makes specific recommendations to limit the leverage of hedge funds to preserve stability of the EU financial system. Some of the most influential mainstream commentators (see, for example, Roubini, 2008, and Wolf, 2008) are forcefully arguing for comprehensive regulation of all relevant institutions and activities. For example, Martin Wolf writes, "If regulation is to be effective, it must cover all relevant institutions and the entire balance sheet in all significant countries. It must focus on capital, liquidity and transparency." Furthermore, it is very encouraging that the March 2008 US Treasury Blueprint for Financial Regulatory Reform (US Treasury, 2008), though flawed in some aspects, put forward the idea that financial regulation should be comprehensive, and include hedge funds and other private pools of capital.

A key precondition for comprehensive regulation is comprehensive transparency of relevant variables. Transparency also has advantages for other actors such as investors, other market agents and macroeconomic authorities.

Reducing asymmetries of information between market actors and regulators

In many cases, regulators genuinely do not know the extent to which risks are increasing, and how these risks are distributed. The more complex and large the financial system becomes, the greater the opaqueness and difficulty to obtain information. Building on the work of Stiglitz (for example, Stiglitz and Weiss, 1981) there is a whole theoretical literature that shows market failures and incorrect incentives lead to private underprovision of information and monitoring by private actors, which gives a rationale for official sector intervention (see Kambhu, et al., 2007, for a view from the Fed).

One example is complex and totally opaque Over-The-Counter (OTC) derivatives, which reach massive levels, as highlighted for example by the 2008 FSF report. Possible solutions would be to attempt to standardize such instruments but above all to channel them through clearing house based exchanges, as Soros (2008) suggests for the $45 trillion credit default swap contracts; at the time of writing, those that hold the contracts do not even know whether those counterparties are properly protected with capital. This establishment of clearing houses or exchanges should become obligatory for all OTC derivatives. This would have the benefit of ensuring appropriate margin and capital requirements on each transaction, as well as many other advantages.

It is interesting that an emerging country, Brazil, has been effective in using regulations and other measures to encourage derivatives to move to established exchanges (Dodd and Griffith-Jones, 2008).

Another, somewhat related, example for the need for increased transparency is in the case of hedge funds; on this, there is growing consensus—including by the hedge fund industry itself—that improved information on hedge funds and other Highly Leveraged Institutions (HLIs) would also be valuable to investors and counterparties, as well as regulators. As pointed out in a previous paper (Griffith-Jones et al., 2007), it seems appropriate for hedge funds to report market, liquidity, and credit risk, as the Fisher II working group recommended. It also seems essential that hedge funds report aggregate worldwide and country positions, the aggregate level of leverage, and especially the level of long and short positions, and others, such as the level of trading.

In this context, it is encouraging that in June 2008, the UK's Financial Services Authority (FSA) introduced a tough disclosure requirement for anyone "short-selling" a significant amount of stock in a company conducting a rights issue; the requirements were stringent in that they obliged short sellers to disclose such positions if they amounted to more than 0.25 per cent of the total shares outstanding. This rule was introduced due to the strong suspicion that hedge funds were short-selling the stock of companies in the middle of rights issue, thus undermining the ability of banks to recapitalize themselves, which was essential for financial stability at the time.

It would seem desirable that such disclosure requirements on short and long positions remain, be more comprehensive and become the international norm.

It is also important to decide with what periodicity and to whom information is to be disclosed; additional important questions are whether this information should be provided by all hedge funds or only those that are systematically important.

In regards to periodicity of reporting, positions can be reported in real time or with a lag. Real time reporting would be particularly useful, but it could potentially be costly, though much of this information must already be privately available. Real time reporting, if publicly available, can enhance market stability by encouraging contrarian positions; however, it also risks encouraging herding if other market actors mimic the positions of large actors, e.g. hedge funds (for a good discussion, see De Brower, 2001). The problem of fixed point in time disclosure is the risk of window dressing for the particular moments. The solution may be to also require maximum and minimum positions during this period to avoid such window dressing.

It would seem best if information would be made publicly available, e.g. on the internet. It may be sufficient if positions are reported in aggregate by class of institution, e.g. bank, securities firms, hedge funds, other HLIs. The aggregate reporting would avoid revealing individual positions.

It seems important to find an institution that would be efficient at collecting and processing such data in a timely manner without compromising confidentiality. The institution with the best experience in similar data gathering would be the BIS, which already collects detailed information on banks and other financial institutions. The reputation of the BIS would also ensure confidentiality of individual positions.

Though we have discussed issues of transparency and disclosure in relation to the most opaque actors (hedge funds) and transactions (derivatives), similar criteria need to apply to other opaque actors and especially to the opaque parts of the banking system.

Regulation has to be counter-cyclical

It would seem that the most important market failure in financial markets, through the ages, is their pro-cyclicality. Therefore, it is essential that regulation attempts to compensate and curb this (particularly during booms when excessive risk is created) by pursuing counter-cyclical regulation. It is encouraging that finally there is growing agreement among academics, institutions like the

BIS (which in its 2008 Annual Report very forcefully argues for counter-cyclical regulation), and regulators about the need for introducing counter-cyclical elements into regulation. It is noteworthy that the 2008 BIS Annual Report rightly argues that the trends toward globalization, consolidation, and securitization increase the probability of both excessive behavior in the boom and costs in the bust, thus *increasing* the *dangerous* and *negative* side effects of financial market pro-cyclical behavior. This adds *additional urgency to introduce counter-cyclical regulation*. The questions now are not so much about if, but about how and when counter-cyclical regulation is introduced.

In regards to banks, Goodhart and Persaud (2008) have presented a specific proposal: increase Basel II capital requirements by a ratio linked to recent growth of total banks' assets. This is very important because it provides a clear, simple, and transparent rule for introducing counter-cyclicality into the regulation of banks. Another virtue of this proposal is that it could be fairly easily implemented because it builds on Basel II. Finally, it has the advantage—which lies at the heart of the concept of counter-cyclicality—of linking micro to macro stability.

If such a rule is introduced, it is important that it is simple and done in ways that regulators cannot loosen the regulations easily to avoid them from becoming "captured" by the general over-enthusiasm that characterizes booms.

Three issues arise. Should the focus just be on increase in total bank assets, or should there also be some weighting for excessive growth of bank lending in specific sectors that have grown particularly rapidly (such as real estate)? Often crises have arisen due to excessive lending during boom times to particular sectors or countries (e.g. emerging economies). However, most systemic bank failures have also been preceded by excessive growth of total bank assets.

Second, is the best way to introduce counter-cyclicality through modifying capital adequacy requirements through time? Would not the alternative of increasing provisioning against future losses—as done in Spain and Portugal—be a good option, given that it has much merit, as argued by Ocampo and Chiappe (2001) as well as others? An advantage of using provisions is that their objective is precisely to finance expected losses (in this case through the business cycle) as distinguished from capital, whose objective is to cover for unexpected losses. A disadvantage of using provisions is that accountants object to provisioning of expected losses.

As global accounting rules are defined, it would be desirable that they pay far more attention to balancing the aim of what is effective for individual and systemic bank stability with their current emphasis on providing information to investors.

Finally, there is the crucial issue of timing. It seems imperative to approve such changes soon while the appetite for regulatory reform remains high. However, their introduction should be done with a lag to avoid increased capital requirements (especially linked to the weighting given to growth in recent years in the Goodhart-Persaud formula, which would be high) putting pressure on currently weak banks and accentuating the credit crunch. Indeed, leverage has to be reduced, but this needs to be done gradually.

Some of the least regulated parts of the financial system may have some of the strongest pro-cyclical impacts. One such example is the role that hedge funds and derivatives play in carry trade; there is increasing empirical evidence that such carry trade has very pro-cyclical effects (on over or under shooting) on exchange rates of both developed and developing economies, with negative effects often on the real economy (see Brunnermeir, Nagel, and Peterson, 2008, for developed economies; see also, Dodd and Griffith-Jones, 2008 and 2006, for evidence on Brazil and Chile respectively). During 2008, reversals of the carry trade played a large role in significantly weakening the currencies of countries like Brazil and Mexico.

For regulation to be comprehensive, as argued above, there should be minimum capital requirements for *all* derivatives dealers and minimum collateral requirements for *all* derivatives transactions to reduce leverage and lower systemic risk. Collateral requirements for financial transactions function much like capital requirements for banks.

This issue of timing is crucial for introducing greater capital regulations for other actors, just as discussed above in the case of bank regulation. Regulations need to be approved now, given greater appetite for regulation, but may need to be introduced with a lag, when financial institutions are stronger; doing so now could weaken financial institutions further and/or accentuate the credit crunch.

An issue to explore is whether regulation of derivatives' collateral and capital requirements should also have counter-cyclical elements. This would seem desirable. It would imply that when derivatives positions, either long or short, were growing excessively (for example, well beyond historical averages), collateral and capital requirements could be increased. An issue to explore is whether this should be done for all derivatives (a far greater task, but consistent with our principle of comprehensiveness) or for derivatives that regulators think can generate systemic risk (shorting of banks' shares) or policy-makers believe can have negative macroeconomic effects (carry trade leading to over or under shooting of exchange rates). The latter, more manageable approach may unfortunately allow growth of derivatives that can have negative externalities, of which financial regulators and economic authorities are unaware of at the time.

More broadly, counter-cyclical criteria of regulation may need to be applied to regulations of all transactions and institutions. Besides doing this at the individual institution or transaction level, it may be necessary, as the BIS (2008) argues, to put greater focus on systemic issues, such as many institutions having similar exposures to common shocks, and risks of contagion between markets and institutions. This is technically challenging because regulatory needs for individual institutions would need to reflect not only their own behavior, but also the behavior of other system-wide developments, such as increasing property prices.

Finally, as argued below, counter-cyclical financial regulation is an increasingly important complement in the modern economy to counter cyclical monetary policy. Currently, counter-cyclicality is insufficiently used, both in financial regulation and monetary policy, though more widely accepted in fiscal policy, especially in developed economies.

Regulation needs to be as tightly coordinated internationally as possible

One of the easiest ways to do regulatory arbitrage is to move activities to other less regulated countries, especially offshore centers. This is particularly, though not only, true for OTC derivatives and hedge funds.

The international community has made important and valuable steps toward global coordinated regulation. However, its efforts are clearly insufficient given the speed and depth of the globalization of private finance and its often negative spillovers on innocent bystanders.

The discussion of a global financial regulator needs to be put urgently on the international agenda (Eatwell and Taylor, 2000; Kaufman, 2008). In the meantime, efforts at increased coordination among national regulators require top priority. It is also urgent that developing country regulators participate fully in key regulatory fora, such as the Basel Committee. Recent inclusion of G-20 developing countries is welcome, though not sufficient.

Compensation of bankers and fund managers needs to be self-regulated or regulated

As Stiglitz (2008) points out, incentive problems are at the heart of the boom–bust behavior of financial and banking markets. A large part of bonuses are tied to short-term profits and are one sided, positive in good times and never negative, even when big losses occur (Roubini, 2008). Such asymmetries seem even stronger in institutions such as hedge funds where managers' fees rise very sharply if profits are very high, but fall mildly with poor performance, encouraging excessive risk-taking and leverage (Rajan, 2005; and Kambhu et al., 2007).

There is increased consensus that high remuneration, and its link to short-term profits, contributes to boom–bust behavior of financial markets. Thus the FSF Report (2008) stated that "Compensation arrangements often encouraged disproportionate risk-taking with insufficient regard to long-term risks." Several senior figures in Wall Street and the City of London are arguing for a radical rethinking of compensation schemes (Lewitt, 2008). It is interesting that even the Institute of International Finance (which represents major banks) recognizes distortions caused by compensation schemes, though as could be expected, it is opposed to regulators reforming compensation models.

It is positive that the FSF Report recommends that regulators should work with market participants to mitigate risks due to inappropriate incentive structures. This is very encouraging, but it seems unclear whether market participants will voluntarily accept such changes due to collective action and other problems.

There is another negative effect of short-term bonuses that is less often highlighted. In good times, banks and other financial institutions have very high profits, but a large part of these are not capitalized or paid to shareholders. They are paid as very high bonuses. As Wall Street analyst Lewitt (2008) put it "Too much capital is allowed to exit banks in the form of cash compensation." Banks are bled of capital in good times making less capital available in bad times. When a crisis comes, bail-outs occur to help recapitalize the banks, paid by the public sector and ultimately by taxpayers. *It, in fact, could be argued that taxpayers are paying ex-post for excessive bonuses*. This gives an additional rationale for regulating compensation structure. In fact, very high short-term bonuses are creating moral hazard for three reasons. First, they encourage excessive risk-taking. Second, by bleeding banks of potential capital, they make the need for costly public bail-outs more likely. Finally, if banks have losses due to excessive risk-taking, they may well, in the future, pay fewer taxes. These two latter effects are not traditionally reflected in the literature.

There could be easy solutions to this problem including providing only a fixed basic salary on a monthly basis and accumulating bonuses in an escrow account such as a short-term pension fund. These could be cashed only after a period equivalent to an average full cycle of economic activity has taken place—independent of whether the person stays with the firm or not. The incentives would change towards making medium- or long-term profits, and the excessive risk-taking linked to short-term bonuses—where large payments are obtained upfront and no costs are paid when losses take place—would be significantly reduced.

There are of course some technical issues on how this could best be implemented. These could be quite easily overcome. However, the key problem will be political to overcome the resistance of bankers and fund managers. Given the magnitude of the current crisis and its damaging effects on the real economy—especially in major developed countries—now may be the best of times to move forward. The self regulatory route (by the industry itself) could be tried, but we are skeptical it would bring meaningful results; action by regulators seems essential. In the long term, financial institutions and the financial system will actually benefit from a change in compensation schemes. It is the problems of externalities, collective action, and principal agency that may inhibit market agents from reaching a better outcome from their collective perspective. Regulators therefore need to do it for them. This would benefit financial and macroeconomic stability and even the stability of individual financial institutions. As argued above, there is also a case for regulating compensation to protect taxpayers from possible future bail-outs, and from reduced tax payments by banks due to future losses.

Liquidity and solvency

Reform proposals put forward by national and international regulatory authorities have tended to call for banks and investment banks to raise capital to offset losses and write-downs on mortgages, mortgage-backed securities and other assets that have fallen in value. In these discussions, capital is viewed as the sole cushion for financial institutions and their shrinking capital base is increasingly viewed as a threat to systemic solvency. The ongoing pressure on capital is also seen as impeding efforts to revive credit flows and maintain economic activity.

The severity of the threat to institutional solvency led many to question the ability of the Fed and other central banks to defuse the credit crunch and stem the decline in asset prices. Many assumed that the US problem had shifted from a liquidity crisis to a solvency crisis. While a continuation of liquidity support is seen as necessary, that support appears to be of limited value in terms of either ending the crisis or moderating its current and potential negative impact on the real economy. Solutions have increasingly turned to proposals for government intervention to protect the solvency of systemically important institutions.

But beyond the immediate issue of crisis management, the complementary roles of central bank liquidity, as well as capital and holdings of liquid assets as cushions for private financial institutions, remain critical issues for reform. As discussed in the previous section, reform proposals must include ways to restructure capital and liquidity requirements for depository institutions to moderate their pro-cyclical impact and make them function as a counter-cyclical instrument of sound regulation. And, as discussed, we believe that, given the sizable shift in savings and investment flows from banks to institutional investors, the transmission belt for both regulatory and monetary policy initiatives must be extended to reach all segments of the financial system. In this section, we expand these discussions of institutional capital and liquidity and the liquidity cushion provided by central banks to indicate the direction we think further reform proposals should take to restore and bolster financial stability.

The role of capital in a market-based system

Assessments of the role capital plays in guarding the soundness of the financial system have tended to focus on the balance sheets of depository institutions. It should be noted, however, that before 1983 there had been no statutory basis in the US for prescribing the amount of capital banks were required to hold against assets, and capital requirements had tended to be ignored in most other countries as well. With the threat of default and the proliferation of non-performing loans on developing country debt in the early 1980s, the US Congress directed the Fed to set limits on banks' assets in relation to capital and this, in turn, led to negotiations with other developed countries that resulted in the adoption of the Basel Agreement on Capital Adequacy in 1988.

But rules governing capital adequacy for banks have not provided the systemic protection that was expected. Because of the rapid increase in outstanding securitized mortgages and other asset-based securities as well as the explosive growth of derivatives, trading and investment in marketable securities has become the dominant activity in US financial markets. However, as has been demonstrated repeatedly since the crisis erupted in mid-2007, marketability does not mean that an asset can be sold at the expected price—or even sold at all—and the wider applicability of regulations associated with trading activity may have intensified the inherent pro-cyclical bias of the market-based system that has evolved over the last several decades in the United States.

One of the requirements applicable to traded assets is that they be marked to market as prices change. Unlike bank loans held in portfolio at face value, traded assets—including those held by banks—require charges against capital when their prices drop. As a result of the wider applicability of capital charges, the shrinkage in credit flows through banks and their re-channeling through capital markets tended to exacerbate the pressure on capital as the subprime mortgage crisis spread. Moreover, it increased the potential that this credit crisis would deteriorate into a solvency crisis more rapidly than in earlier periods and affect a wider group of institutions.

Indeed, the resulting threats to the solvency of systemically important non-depository institutions have made clear that the focus on banks' capital position is incomplete. The role of capital in a transformed, market-based system is a parallel concern. Thus we argue that there is need to reexamine the role of capital in a systemic context and ensure that counter-cyclical capital requirements are developed which will bolster the soundness of all financial institutions and activities. But we note that when and how much capital should be held by individual institutions is increasingly related to the level of liquidity in the system as a whole, as well as the level of liquidity in individual institutions.

Maintaining liquidity in a market-based system

Because capital is a scarce resource and one that is automatically depleted when losses are written off, liquidity requirements were used by central banks and regulators as a critical tool to protect capital in the period before deregulation made such quantitative measures suspect. The Federal Reserve's recent call for investment banks to shore up their balance sheets with more liquid assets underscores the belated recognition that capital alone is an insufficient cushion against the threat of insolvency (Guerrera and van Duyn, 2008). However, the Fed's concern about illiquid balance sheets may come too late. The systemic nature of the current crisis suggests that efforts by individual institutions or sectors to increase their holdings of liquid assets may be ineffectual if the central bank is unable to inject liquidity into critical markets.

Designing a counter-cyclical regulatory system will require reexamining the role and effectiveness of liquidity requirements for individual institutions and sectors, as well as the channels the central bank uses to provide liquidity. The shift from a bank-based to a market-based system has obscured the fact that, in the US before the 1980s, the systemic cushion for the financial sector was bank reserves. One of the major reforms of the Federal Reserve Act of 1913 was to require banks to hold a given percentage of their reserves with their regional Federal Reserve banks rather than as deposits with larger private banks in "reserve cities." As the Federal Reserve System grew and evolved during the 1920s and 1930s, the Fed no longer required banks to pay in reserves; it created and extinguished those reserves by undertaking open market operations on its own initiative. Changes in reserves became the primary tool that allowed the Fed—as former Fed Chairman William McChesney Martin phrased it—to take away the punch bowl when the party got rowdy and bring it back in when spirits were flagging. In other words, the overreaching objective that had evolved within the Fed itself in its formative years was a commitment to counter-cyclical monetary policy using bank reserves and open market operations as the tools for implementing that objective.

In 1951, when banks held 65 per cent of financial sector assets and liabilities, their reserve balances with the Fed accounted for 11.3 per cent of bank deposits and constituted a remarkably comfortable cushion for a segmented financial system in which banks loaned to other financial sectors with which they were not then in competition. Fifty years later, however, the shift in credit flows away from banks and banks' use of borrowed funds and strategies, such as sweep accounts to reduce holdings of deposits subject to reserve requirements, had virtually wiped out that cushion. By the end of 2001, banks reserve balances had shrunk to 0.2 per cent of their deposits and banks' holdings of credit market assets had fallen to less than half the share they held fifty years back.

The missing monetary cushion has weakened individual financial institutions and made them more vulnerable to stops in external funding. Borrowing and lending among financial institutions through repurchase agreements— another rapidly expanding market developed as the system evolved—has ceased to be an efficient channel for distributing liquidity as institutions' confidence in the solvency of their financial counterparties has eroded. But the missing monetary cushion has also impeded the Fed's ability to provide liquidity to the system as a whole. The Fed is attempting to address the collapse of liquidity in funding markets by continuing to swap treasuries for riskier securities, extending its emergency borrowing program to investment banks, and continuing to provide term loans to banks.

A cushion of reserve balances owned by financial institutions but held by the Fed would be a far more effective way to alleviate the ongoing credit crunch. The soundness of payments among financial institutions made by transferring reserve balances would not be questioned. Moreover, reserve balances would retain their face value despite the erosion of asset prices. Thus, an established pool of financial sector reserves held with the central bank would act as a more effective liquidity buffer than the Fed's current ad hoc lending facilities because it would keep open the channels for private funding.

But such a cushion would serve other important purposes as well. The objective of the Fed's current program of liquidity support is to moderate the pressure for asset sales, stem the decline in their prices and thus protect institutional capital. While capital is and will remain a critical tool of sound regulation as a cushion against insolvency for individual institutions, capital alone cannot protect the financial sector as a whole in the event of a systemic crisis. The Fed's struggle to ensure a systemic reach for its efforts to provide liquidity suggests that, in the future, central banks should attempt to build a source of systemic funding within the monetary system that, like reserves, is renewable and will be immediately available to all financial sectors in a downturn. Meanwhile, a new, system-wide reserve management regime would also restore the effectiveness of counter-cyclical monetary strategies— a reform we believe is no less important than the regulatory reforms we and others have proposed.[5]

In summary, we argue that there is a critical link between liquidity and solvency; that liquidity protects solvency, and that financial stability will require reforms that include comprehensive, counter-cyclical regulatory and monetary strategies like those we offer here.

Notes

1. We thank Kevin Jason for his effective research assistance.
2. Low interest rates in one national market provided an incentive for carry trade strategies that used borrowings in that currency to fund investments in higher yielding assets denominated in other currencies.
3. The combined assets of pension and mutual funds as a share of financial sector assets were actually higher in 1997 (42.3 per cent) when pension fund assets were 25.7 per cent of the total than in 2007 when pension funds' holdings slipped to 18.5 per cent.
4. The technical aspects of how to calculate equivalent liquidity (e.g. reserves) and solvency (e.g. capital) requirements across different institutions and activities requires further study, both by institutions like the BIS and FSF, by national regulators from both developed and developing countries, and by academies.

5. For discussions of proposals to extend reserve requirements to all financial institutions and the balance sheet changes that would be required, see Thurow (1972); D'Arista and Schlesinger (1993); Pollin (1993); D'Arista and Griffith-Jones (1998); Palley (2000, 2003); and D'Arista (2002, 2008).

References

Andrews, E. L. (2007) 'In Reversal, Fed Acts to Tighten Mortgage Rules.' *New York Times*, December 19.

Bank for International Settlements (2002, 2003, 2004, 2005a, 2008). *Annual Report*. Basel, Switzerland: Basel Committee on Banking Supervision.

—— (2005b) *Quarterly Review: International Banking and Financial Market Developments*. Basel: Basel Committee on Banking Supervision (June).

—— (2006) *Quarterly Review: International Banking and Financial Market Developments*. Basel: Basel Committee on Banking Supervision (March).

Borio, C. and Lowe, P. (2002) 'Asset Prices, Financial and Monetary Stability: Exploring the Nexus.' BIS Working Papers, No. 114. Basel: Basel Committee on Banking Supervision.

Brunnermeir, M., Nagel, S., and Pederson, L. (2008) 'Carry Trades and Currency Crashes.' *NBER Macroeconomics Annual*, 23.

Cornford, A. (2008) 'An Agenda for Financial System Reform.' SUNS-South-North Development Monitor, No. 6511, July 7.

D'Arista, J. (2002) 'Rebuilding the Transmission System for Monetary Policy.' Howardsville, VA: Financial Markets Center.

—— (2008) 'Broken Systems: Agendas for Financial and Monetary Reform.' In *17th Annual Hyman P. Minsky Conference: Credit Markets and the Real Economy: Is the Financial System Working?* Annandale-on-Hudson, NY: Levy Institute, Bard College.

—— and Griffith-Jones, S. (1998) 'The Boom of Portfolio Flows to Emerging Markets and Its Regulatory Implications.' In S. Griffith-Jones et al. (eds.), *Short-Term Capital Movements and Balance of Payments Crises*. Helsinki: World Institute for Development Economics Research.

—— and Schlesinger, T. (1993) 'The Parallel Banking System.' In G. A. Dymski et al. (eds.), *Transforming the US Financial System: Equity and Efficiency for the 21st Century*. Armonk, NY: M. E. Sharpe.

De Brower, G. (2001) *Hedge Funds in Emerging Markets*. Cambridge: Cambridge University Press.

Dodd, R. and Griffith-Jones, S. (2006) *Report on Chile's Derivatives Markets: Stabilizing or Speculative Impact*. Institute of Development Studies.

—— (2008) *Brazil's Derivatives Markets: Hedging, Central Bank Intervention and Regulation*. Research sponsored by ECLAC/CEPAL and funding provided by the Ford Foundation.

Eatwell, J. and Taylor, L. (2000) *Global Finance at Risk: The Case for International Regulation*. New York: The New Press.

European Parliament, Committee on Economic and Monetary Affairs (2008) *Draft Report with Recommendations to the Commission on Hedge Funds and Private Equity*. Brussels, Belgium (April 18).

Federal Reserve System (2008) *Flow of Funds Accounts of the United States*. Washington, DC: Board of Governors of the Federal Reserve System.

Financial Stability Forum (2008) *Report of the Financial Stability Forum on Enhancing Market and Institutional Resilience.*

Goodhart, C. and Persaud, A. (2008) 'A Proposal for How to Avoid the Next Crash.' *Financial Times*, January 31.

Greenspan, A. (1993) 'Opening Remarks.' *Changing Capital Markets: Implications for Monetary Policy.* Kansas City, MO: Federal Reserve Bank of Kansas City.

—— (2005) *Testimony on the Federal Reserve Board's Semi-annual Monetary Policy Report to Congress.* Committee on Banking, Housing and Urban Affairs, US Senate (February 16).

Griffith-Jones, S., Calice P., and Seekatz C. (2007) *New Investors in Developing Countries: Opportunities, Risks and Policy Responses, the Case of Hedge Funds* <http://www.stephanygj.net> accessed September 24, 2008.

Guerrera, F. and van Duyn, A. (2008) 'Fed Presses Wall Street Banks on Liquidity.' *Financial Times*, August 11.

Kambhu, J., Shuermann, T., and Stiroh, K. J. (2007) 'Hedge Funds, Financial Intermediation, and Systematic Risk.' *The Economic Review*, 12(3), pp. 1–18.

Kaufman, H. (2008) 'The Principles of Sound Regulation.' *Financial Times*, August 6, p. 11.

Lewitt, M. E. (2008) 'How to Fix It.' *HCM Newsletter*, August 6.

Ocampo, J. A. and Chiappe, M. L. (2001) 'Counter-Cyclical Prudential and Capital Account Regulation in Developing Countries.' Paper prepared for Swedish EGDI.

Palley, T. (2003) 'Asset Price Bubbles and the Case for Asset-Based Reserve Requirements.' *Challenge*, 46(3).

—— (2000) *Stabilizing Finance: The Case for Asset-Based Reserve Requirements.* Howardsville, VA: Financial Markets Center.

Pollin, R. (1993) 'Public Credit Allocation Through the Federal Reserve: Why It Is Needed; How It Should Be Done.' In G. A. Dymski et al. (eds.), *Transforming the US Financial System: Equity and Efficiency for the 21st Century.* Armonk, NY: M. E. Sharpe.

Rajan, R. G. (2005) *Has Financial Development Made the World Riskier?* Proceedings, Federal Reserve Bank of Kansas City (August), pp. 313–69.

Roubini, N. (2008) 'The Shadow Banking System is Unraveling.' *Financial Times*, September 20.

Silvers, D. (2008) 'Some Thoughts on the Progressive Reform of the Financial Regulatory Structure.' Paper prepared for the AFL-CIO, Washington, DC.

Soros, G. (2008) *The New Paradigm for Financial Markets: The Credit Crisis of 2008 and What it Means.* New York: Public Affairs.

Stiglitz, J. E. (2008) 'The Financial Crisis is the Fruit of Dishonesty on the Part of Financial Institutions.' *The Guardian*, September 16.

—— and Weiss A. (1981) 'Credit Rationing in Markets with Imperfect Information.' *The American Economic Review*, 71(3), pp. 393–410.

Thurow, L. (1972) 'Proposals for Re-channeling Funds to Meet Social Priorities.' *Policies for a More Competitive Financial System.* Conference proceedings of the Federal Reserve Bank of Boston.

Tietmeyer, H. (1993) 'Overview.' *Changing Capital Markets: Implications for Monetary Policy.* Kansas City, MO: Federal Reserve Bank of Kansas City.

US Department of Commerce, Bureau of Economic Analysis (2006) 'The US International Investment Position.' *Survey of Current Business.* Washington, DC.

US Treasury Department (2008) *Blueprint for Financial Regulatory Reform.* Washington, DC (March).

White, W. R. (2007) 'The Need for a Longer Policy Horizon: A Less Orthodox Approach.' In J. J. Teunissen and A. Akkerman (eds.), *Global Imbalances and Developing Countries: Remedies for a Failing International Financial System.* The Hague: Forum on Debt and Development (FONDAD).

Wolf, M. (2008) 'The End of Lightly Regulated Finance has Come Far Closer.' *Financial Times*, September 17.

8

The Role of Policy and Banking Supervision in the Light of the Credit Crisis

Avinash D. Persaud[1]

Introduction

The zeitgeist of finance over the last decade was "marketization"[2]: the switch from bank finance to market finance as loans were originated and securitized by banks, rated by agencies and then relocated to investors. A cynic may say that a better description of what went on was regulatory arbitrage. Risks were transferred, on paper at least, from the regulated sector to the unregulated sector.[3] But it is important to recall that bank supervisors in Europe and elsewhere welcomed the marketization of financial risk. They saw it as a way of spreading risks. They saw risks being removed and distributed away from a small number of large and systemically important banks to a large number of investors. The marketization of finance was as much a conspiracy of the Gnomes of Basel as it was of the Gnomes of Zurich.[4] It is part and parcel of the approach to banking embedded in the new Basel accord on credit risk (Basel II).

The marketization of risk was associated with the greater use of market prices in the measurement and control of risks—a feature of the new Basel accord on capital adequacy (Basel II). During quiet or normal times, market-based finance appeared to offer greater liquidity, lower risk premiums and sophisticated risk management incorporating high frequency reporting. All this reinforced the view of bank supervisors that this was the future and that the future was bright. Nonetheless, the reason why we regulate the banking sector, above and beyond standard corporate regulation, is that financial markets often fail, with disastrous consequences for others—as we are seeing with the 2008 crisis.

When the financial markets failed to accurately assess credit risk, given the pre-eminent role of market price in the measurement, control and reporting of risks and estimation of capital adequacy, it initially led to a redoubling of imprudent lending and later to the inevitable, systemic crash. There had been warnings before that the marketization of risks contained a Faustian bargain: greater liquidity, lower risk premia, and the appearance of sophisticated risk management were delivered early, to the detriment of future resilience of the financial system (Persaud, 2008). Bank supervisors brushed these warnings aside at the time.

One of the consequences of making market prices central to the management and control of risks and capital is that when markets fail and prices disappear, the authorities are left with no option but to intervene to set a floor in the market price of assets. They find themselves guaranteeing purchases and prices of assets they would not normally purchase because of the level of market and credit risks. The marketization of finance has been associated with a switch in the role of the central bank, from lender of last resort to buyer of last resort.[5]

Beneath the wreckage, there is a coherent system at work. In the responses of bankers and regulators to the crisis,[6] there are only now some signs of an amendment to the system. The system is as follows. Risks are marketized. This is associated with the increasing use of market pricing in accounting and risk management. During the calm, liquidity is strong, risk premia falls and in response, there is market pressure for innovations that widen the inclusiveness of finance (the securitization of sub-prime mortgages was part of that process). But every five to seven years, markets fail. In the ensuing crisis, through the role of prices in valuation and risk management, declines in prices feed further declines in prices. The government is inevitably forced to underwrite risks in the financial sector until such time as there is a period of calm, and the cycle repeats itself. Some policy makers argue that the greater benefits from those seven years or so outweigh the costs of the crisis year. There is a legitimate trade-off to consider; however, I am not convinced and the crisis of 2007–9 seems particularly costly relative to the benefits.

The full consequences of the "credit crunch," which started in 2007, are yet to be realized. Estimates of the first round effects of losses amounted to around $250 billion in the middle of 2008, but these figures are likely to rise.[7] Then there are the likely and potentially more serious second round effects. During a surprisingly lengthy period from July 2007 to July 2008, banks lost confidence in other banks, hoarded liquidity, and distanced themselves from each other. It is therefore likely that private individuals will have a lasting loss of confidence in the banking sector, which may lead to a reduced willingness to use financial instruments to save, with negative spillover effects for investment in the productive sectors. Recall that the housing market boom in the United States and Europe was partly a result of investors eschewing mutual funds after the dot-com "bezzle" of 1999–2001. It is a serious measure of public disillusionment with financial markets when real estate agents are more trusted than fund managers. It would be reasonable to expect banks to respond to recent developments with a lower risk appetite and reduced lending, which in turn would threaten levels of economic activity more generally. Genuine initiatives to make the benefits of finance more inclusive will also likely fall victim to this new conservatism.

This litany of woes does not include issues of moral hazard, as the authorities take necessary hasty efforts, deep in the fog of war, to preserve the financial system. Bad banks as well as good banks will be saved by the rising tide of government guarantees. Furthermore, today, taxpayers are underwriting risks, created by bankers who paid themselves substantial bonuses before retiring. There is a widespread suspicion that these bonuses are often lightly taxed, offshore. It is understandable, therefore, that the political response to the credit crunch is fuelled by moral outrage. The clear and present danger is that this understandable moral outrage leads to a regulatory response that is too distracted by the ethical failure of the private sector to deal effectively with the government failure.[8] The scale of today's credit crunch could have been avoided by central bankers and supervisors, who had both sufficient information and the necessary instruments to respond, but failed to do so for a variety of reasons. These reasons include an absence of political will and a convenient intellectual entanglement with the prevailing zeitgeist of finance.

Systemic risks and the role of monetary policy and bank supervisors

Over the past ten years, bank supervisors have been given so many things to do that their real purpose has been lost. The mission creep includes anti-money laundering and anti-terrorist financing. These are important initiatives that need to be undertaken by somebody, but they are pervasive activities and they have encouraged pervasive regulation. Among the regulated sectors, financial regulation is heavy-handed, expensive, and ill focused. A measure of that ill focus is that supervisors were able to look at Northern Rock in the UK and Deutsche Industriebank in Germany, just a few months before they failed, and give them a good mark for compliance, when they were quite transparently engaged in the systemically dangerous activity of borrowing short-term paper from the international money markets and lending over 100 per cent loan-to-value mortgages.

The principal reason why we regulate banks above and beyond the way we regulate other industries is that bank failures can be systemic. If the high street shoe store fails, surrounding shoe stores profit. Shoe store failures are not systemic. If the high street bank fails, the loss of confidence and panic could cause a run on the other banks. The reason why banks are systemic are many, but most importantly, banks run substantial liquidity risk (banks borrow money over the short term, but lend it over the long term) and, as a bank deposit at one bank can be collateral for other loans, the failure of one bank can directly undermine the solvency of another. Today's regulation was born out of the devastating consequences of bank runs and the resulting systemic failure of payments and credit systems in the past.[9] Deposit insurance is specifically designed to reduce the risk of systemic bank failures.

Because the wider effects of one bank's failure are far greater than the private costs to the owners of a single bank failing, banks left to their own devices would "underinvest" in preserving systemic stability. They would put aside less capital than they would if the focus of their concern was not the viability of one institution, but the risks of the failure of one institution leading to systemic failure. This is a serious externality. As a result, banking regulators should be focused on the systemic activities of financial institutions. Regulators should intervene so as to cause bank shareholders to invest more in systemic stability than they would otherwise do (thereby internalizing the externality). Banking regulation has lost sight of this goal. It does not draw clear distinctions between systemic and non-systemic activities. It tries, oddly, to mimic what a "good" bank would do on its own,[10] motivated purely by private motives, and it encourages homogeneity of behavior through common standards that adds to systemic risks. Such banking regulation may be in the narrow interests of bank shareholders—and may be seen as protecting them against what might be in the interests of managers with their peculiar incentive structures—but not of the system and its other stakeholders.

The principal source of systemic crises is the economic cycle. Financial crashes do not stem from the random failure of an institution—though this is the implicit assumption of banking regulation. Crashes follow booms, and the credit cycle is often an appendage of the economic cycle. Consequently, any focus on systemic failure has to put the credit and economic cycles at the heart of financial regulation—moderating excesses in a credit boom and the following credit contraction. Yet in banking regulation today, in the European Capital Requirements Directive (CRD) and Basel II, the economic cycle is absent.

Regulators often respond to this criticism by saying two things. They either say that it is up to monetary and fiscal policy to address the economic cycle or they say that national supervisors can impose contra-cyclical measures under Basel II. Pillar II of the new accord provides for discretionary supervisory intervention if supervisors feel that banks are not sufficiently capitalized. Neither response is satisfactory.

Dealing with the cycle: institutional arrangements

The problem with relying on monetary and fiscal policy to address booms and crashes is that the level of interest rates or taxes required to curb an asset market bubble in one sector of the economy would cripple the rest of the economy. Imagine a housing market bubble, where home prices have risen by 20 per cent per year for the past few years and they are expected to continue doing so, where loan-to-value mortgages are close to 100 per cent and the market is well developed with home owners regularly re-mortgaging. Raising interest rates from 4 to 8 per cent would push the manufacturing sector into recession, but would do little to curb the housing boom. A rate hike of this order may even increase the flow of funds into housing as it becomes one of the few sectors of the economy able to grow amid these higher interest rates. It would take interest rate levels closer to 20 per cent to definitively curb the housing boom. But that would eviscerate the economy. More effective would be a regulatory intervention that, through direct or indirect levers, lowered the permitted loan-to-value ratio of mortgage lending.

In the European context, the scope for monetary and fiscal policy to address the pumping up, and subsequent deflation of asset market bubbles is even more limited than in the United States. The European Central Bank (ECB) has an uncompromising focus on inflation, and fiscal policy is limited to some extent by the 1997 Stability and Growth Pact. That is not to say that monetary and fiscal policies have no responsibility in managing the economic cycle. At a minimum, monetary and fiscal policy should try not to encourage the creation of asset market bubbles. In this regard, European macroeconomic policy has scored better than US macroeconomic policy. Nevertheless, the ECB and national Treasuries cannot shoulder the burden of reducing the financial excesses of the credit cycle. The problem is that bank supervisors have not been very good at taking on this burden either.

Supervisors have discretion to raise capital charges on banks if they feel a bank is not sufficiently capitalized. But this discretion is seldom used for political reasons.

It was former Fed Chairman McChesney Martin who argued that the authorities should remove the punch bowl before the party gets going. But parties are fun. Underpaid supervisors cannot easily squeeze past powerful and rich lenders, borrowers with seemingly worthy projects and politicians taking credit for the good times, to take away the bowl of punch. (Goodhart and Persaud, 2008)

Supervisors must shoulder the principal burden of dampening the worst excesses of a credit cycle, but they need some rules to help them resist the substantial political pressure for doing nothing.

One example of a contra-cyclical rule would be to have a minimum capital adequacy requirement for banks that is not fixed across time, as is currently the case, but rises and falls with the cycle. One appropriate measurement of the cycle would be the rate of growth of bank held assets—this moves pro-cyclically. We could start off with a capital to risk adjusted assets ratio of 8 per cent.

Rather like income tax each bank would have a basic allowance of asset growth which could be linked to the inflation target, the long-run economic growth rate, and some allowance for structural changes in the bank lending/GDP ratio. This formulation allows regulators and central banks to better link micro to macro stability. Growth in the value of bank assets would be measured as a weighted average of annual growth. To emphasize more recent activity, exponential weights could be used. Growth above the basic allowance over the past 12 months would have a 50 per cent weight; growth over the preceding year would have a 25 per cent weight and so forth until 100 per cent is approximated. Regulatory capital adequacy requirements could be raised by 0.33 per cent for each 1 per cent growth in bank asset values above the basic allowance. For example, if bank assets grew at a rate of 21 per cent above the growth allowance, minimum capital requirements would rise from, 8 per cent, to 15 per cent. (Goodhart and Persaud, 2008)[11]

One of the other implications of putting the credit and economic cycle back at the heart of financial regulation is that the distance between the central banks and bank supervisors should be narrowed further. Both institutions should house representatives of the other and new committee structures that better integrate macro financial and micro financial issues should be constructed.

The integration of banking supervision among the ECB, Federal Reserve, and Bank of England, though likely to be politically unpopular, should also be reconsidered. If systemic risk is the key focus of banking regulation, as it ought to be, it is best done close to the institution with the greatest systemic expertise and operational capacity. Moreover, key components of dealing with a systemic crisis, deposit insurance or a public lender or buyer of last resort are not within the scope of supervisory institutions but within the realm of the central bank, either as an agent for the Treasury, an advisor, a principal or all three.

Systemic risk and deposit insurance

The experience of the UK in September 2007 was that the existing deposit insurance arrangements had become "out of date." The level of full coverage had become too small for the average depositor and the "haircut" that depositors suffered on larger amounts contributed to the panic that led to the run on Northern Rock and other UK building societies. The government's response was to effectively announce a 100 per cent guarantee on all deposits.[12] It is not clear how this would work formally, but it would seem that a 100 per cent guarantee on depositors is required today to halt incipient bank runs. The idea of "co-insurance" between the taxpayer and the depositor has been found wanting.

There are clear moral hazard issues in offering blanket insurance. One alternative approach that maintains the insurance but reduces the moral hazard is to follow the example of the government approach to car insurance. Having car insurance cover is mandatory to be allowed to drive, but the insurance is provided by the private sector and high risks are priced accordingly. Taking this over to banking, it could be a requirement of any deposit-taking institution that they have some minimum level of insurance for their depositors, but they must buy this insurance themselves from the private sector or some combination of private and public sector. Insurers would try to differentiate good and bad risks and hopefully the greater the risk, the greater the premiums. Some institutions will not be able to be insured at all and would therefore be forced to consider alternative lines of business.

Macro financial problems of micro financial efficiencies

The focus of banking regulation historically has been on identifying good practices at banks and making these practices a standard for others to comply with. In the section above we have highlighted how this does not address the social externality, where a focus on a bank's private interests will lead to an underinvestment in systemic stability, nor does it address the systemic aspects of the pro-cyclical behavior of banks during credit cycles. While best practices may be insufficient to mitigate systemic risks, it is commonly thought that high and common standards are a good and necessary thing. But this is not as clear-cut as you might imagine. To appreciate the problem it is important to understand that financial market liquidity is not about how big a market is, but how diverse it is. If a financial market has two people in it, whenever one wants to buy something and the other wants to sell it, it is a very liquid market. If a market had one thousand people in it, and they are all using the best practice valuation, risk-management, and accounting system so that when one wants to sell something, in response to their risk management, valuation and accounting systems, so does everyone else. At any one time there will only be buyers or sellers; but you need both for liquidity. The market that is bigger with common standards is thinner in terms of liquidity.

An inclusive financial system has natural diversity in it. A pensioner, a young saver putting aside savings for a distant future, an insurance company and a charitable endowment all have different investment objectives and different capacity for risks and these should be reflected in different valuation and risk management systems. For example, an illiquid five-year bond backed by good collateral would be a risky asset for an investor funded with overnight money, but a relatively safe asset for an institution with no cash commitments over the following five years, like a young pension fund. The risk management, valuation and accounting system that the institutions with overnight funding use should be different than the one the long-term investor should use. The trend, however, for the same transparency, valuation, accounting and risk management rules reduces this natural diversity and increases systemic fragility. Some of the Structured Investment Vehicles (SIV) that were forced to sell assets in the credit crunch, and thus adding to the turmoil, were forced to do so, not because their funding dried up, but merely because they were using the same accounting and risk rules that the banks used even though they had longer-term funding commitments.

One of the key lessons of the crisis is that a critical factor in systemic risks is funding liquidity. When the system freezes, those with short-term funding topple over. Those with long-term funding are the system's stabilizers. They are risk absorbers. However, by using common mark-to-market accounting, valuation and risk rules we do not make any distinctions between those with a funding liquidity issue and those without, between risk traders who are short term and risk absorbers who, as a result of long-term funding liquidity, have a capacity for market and liquidity risks. It is not overly stylized to say that the risk management strategy of a risk trader is to sell before others do, while the risk management strategy of a risk absorber is to diversify risks through time. This absence of any distinction at the regulatory and accounting level has encouraged the growth of risk traders at the expense of risk absorbers as short-term funding is cheaper, and this has increased the systemic fragility of the financial system.

One of the problems with the originate, rate and relocate model is that risks were transferred to a varied group of investors, who may have structurally had different objectives, but through common valuation, accounting and risk systems, they ended up behaving as if they were one investor. We ended up with a greater spread across legal entities, but less diversity of behavior. The trend of common standards is actually championed by the banks under the guise of equal treatment. Their interest is to reduce any advantage others may have in the financial system and allow them to set up investment subsidiaries. But if that advantage is based on a different capacity for risk, through a genuinely different funding structure, then this difference should be preserved for systemic reasons, not removed. Accounting, valuation, risk management and transparency standards, and the equality of treatment are all generally good, but it must be understood that in some cases there is a trade-off with macro financial stability. If standards are a force for more homogeneity in the financial system then we must think again about how they are derived and implemented.

Broadening regulation, counterparty risk

The crisis has been an occasion for renewed calls for the greater regulation of independent hedge funds and private equity firms. Our analysis so far points to two issues in consideration of the greater regulation of these institutions. First, these firms did not play a pivotal role in the crisis. The credit crunch centered on the banks and the banks' own in-house investment vehicles. Second, spreading these common rules across from banks to hedge funds, private equity firms, pension and insurance firms and others while continuing to ignore the distinction between risk absorption and risk trading will make the financial system even less safe because it is within this group of investors that some of those with long-term funding—the natural stabilizers of the financial system—reside.

Where hedge funds and more recently private equity funds can contribute to systemic risks is through their use of leverage. Hedge funds and investment banks in general are far more leveraged than commercial banks. When things go wrong, de-leveraging has systemic and contractionary consequences. However, hedge funds, private equity funds, and investment banks do not generate their leverage on their own; they get leverage from the commercial banks. It is therefore possible to regulate the most important part of what these institutions do, by regulating the way commercial banks give them leverage. This would be a far more effective form of regulation of institutions that for a variety of reasons are often domiciled in offshore locations and where their principals are footloose.

Indeed, part of the systemic problem has been that the supply of leverage to these institutions is regulated by their counterparties, the commercial banks, in a homogenous manner. The common rules that turn on and off leverage from the commercial banks to hedge funds, investment banks and private equity firms, and the common approach that these rules take to value and manage risk is a major source for a reduction in diversity of behavior and an increase in financial fragility. Where hedge funds have been a point of stress over the past twelve months it is often as a result of price declines in a market, causing its counterparty bank using its internal, short-term model of risk and value to cut lending to funds, that are then forced to offload assets on to an already weak market. This is a mechanism for spreading and increasing systemic risks. Some of the regulation being proposed to extend regulation to these counterparties of banks may in fact reinforce these systemically risky processes, not disrupt them.

The solution to these issues is two-fold. First, if capital requirements are counter-cyclical this should also regulate the flow of leverage to bank counterparties. Second, regulators should resist calls for identical treatment of all financial institutions; a distinction needs to be made between those financial institutions, whatever they are called, that have short-term funding, less than 12–24 months say, and those that have longer term funding. Those with short-term funding would be required to follow bank capital adequacy requirements. Those with long term funding will have a different regulatory regime. They will be required to provide disclosures to the regulators that make them comfortable that they do not have a funding liquidity risk. They must have a long-term "solvency" regime that takes into account their long-term obligations and the long-term valuations of their assets. This would focus regulation on systemic activities and it would incentivize long-term investors to behave like long-term investors. The fact that different classes of investors would then behave differently would help stabilize the overall system.

Risk absorption, pension funds and banks

There is an understandable instinct that wishes to shield pension funds from risk. But of course pension funds can only generate returns for their members by taking some risk. Therefore, the issue is more: what is the right risk for a pension fund to take? It is my contention that regulation is pushing pension funds to take the wrong kind of risk and exposing them to inappropriate danger. In thinking about what is the right kind of risk to take, it is important to understand that there is not one kind of risk, but several and that "riskiness" has less to do with instruments and more to do with behavior.

As we have discussed above, a "risky" instrument held by a bank may be a "safe" instrument if it is held by a pension fund. There are broadly three types of risk: market risk, credit risk and liquidity risk. The way to diversify market and liquidity risk is through time. The way to diversify credit risk is actively across different types of credit. A young pension fund has the ability to earn the market and liquidity premium, but clearly not the credit risk premia. It should therefore invest in high quality credits with poor liquidity[13]—assets with strong long-term prospects but much short-term volatility or uncertainty.

What they should not do is buy highly liquid instruments and low volatility instruments with large credit premia. Yet this is the route they are chased down by accounting and regulatory standards. A pension fund required to match the duration of its assets to its pension liabilities, to mark-to-market its assets, and to earn a high yield to minimize contributions is inexorably led to buy liquid instruments with poor credit. In buying liquid instruments, it is paying for a liquidity that it does not need, and in poor credits it is earning a risk premia it does not have a natural capacity to earn because it does not have cheap access to natural hedges of credit risk. The person who loses from this unnatural asset allocation is not the consultant, actuary, or manager, but the pensioner.

In a similar vein, banks have been pushed towards the wrong kind of risks. A bank has short-term funding. It therefore has little capacity for liquidity and market risks. However, it has much capacity for credit risks as it is an expert in credit origination and through its origination activity is able to actively source and hedge across a variety of credit risks. Yet, what do banks do today? They sell their credit risk to pension funds and they fund private equity and hedge funds that effectively take on liquidity and market risk—and in a sense, a large part of this risk is passed back to the banks, as we have seen. We have said that we need to put the credit cycle at the heart of financial regulation—we also need to include there the concept of risk capacity, with different risks flowing towards institutions with a capacity for that risk.

Conclusions, off balance sheet instruments and a new supervisory framework

The current process of regulation is that we begin with the banks and regulate them for holding risk. Regulation is like a tax (as perceived by each firm; though the regulations may actually be good for the sector as a whole) and like all businesses, commercial banks tried to avoid the tax—in this case, through regulatory arbitrage and by shifting risks to, say, investment banks. So, we regulate the investment banks; that in turn shifts risk to SIVs and hedge funds. So we plan to regulate these, but they will only shift risks to some other place. What is the logical conclusion of this game? That the system will be heavily regulated, but that it will not hold much risk; risk will instead have shifted, and shifted until it has arrived at a spot where it can no longer be seen. This does not strike me as a good model.

We saw an element of this during the 2008 credit crisis. Banks shifted credit risks to off balance sheet investments where they were not very visible. Basel II correctly addresses off balance sheet instruments by requiring banks to hold capital against contingent liabilities that may arise from these off balance sheet holdings and vehicles. But while this responds to the specific issue of off balance sheet instruments, it does not really address the more general problem that the old distinctions of instruments and institutions are less relevant today than when bank regulation started. What matters is whether an activity is systemic, not whether it is called a bank or an SIV. Activities where there are a mismatch between funding liquidity and asset liquidity are likely to be systemic. Activities where there is substantial short-term leverage are likely to be systemically important.

A better model of banking regulation would be based on three pillars. The first pillar of supervision would be about doing away with distinctions based on legal entities of banks or investors, and instead focusing on a capacity to absorb risks on one hand and on systemic risks on the other. In some regards, this would be a broader regime—incorporating institutions, off balance sheet and other investment vehicles not currently regulated—but also a more focused regime. Those institutions with little funding liquidity (like a traditional bank) have little capacity to hold market and liquidity risk and should follow a capital adequacy regime. In calculating the value of risk-adjusted assets under the capital adequacy regime, short-term measures of value and risk, mark-to-market accounting and high standards of transparency would apply. This would be pro-cyclical, but this would be addressed explicitly by a counter-cyclical second pillar.

Those institutions with long-term funding liquidity (like a traditional pension fund or endowment fund) can be exempt from the capital adequacy regime in return for disclosures that satisfy the regulator that this is appropriate and adheres to a new "solvency regime" that allows institutions to use long-term measures of valuation and risk in determining and reporting their solvency. The quid pro quo of not being required to follow mark-to-market price and value systems is the greater disclosure of assets and perhaps the requirement to use their party custodians to hold assets, reducing the scope for fraud. Banks will attack this approach for creating an unlevel playing field. But the approach seeks to support the natural diversity in the financial system and draws on the systemically beneficial role of risk absorbers—those that have a capacity to diversify risks across time.

The second pillar of supervision would be about putting the credit cycle back at the heart of the capital adequacy regime. Capital adequacy requirements should rise and fall with the overall growth in bank assets. Contra-cyclical mechanisms face tough political resistance and they should be supported with clear rules. They should be formulated closely and perhaps in conjunction with the monetary authorities.

The third pillar of supervision would be about maximizing transparency where it will benefit investor protection, with the constraint of not reducing heterogeneity in the behavior of all market participants.

The related but separate issue of investor protection can be managed by requiring institutions that take in depositors' money to have some minimum, transparent level of deposit insurance, which is provided privately. This may serve to reduce the moral hazard of deposit insurance.

These three ideas should form the basis of efforts to reform current banking regulation. This crisis like almost all crises before was associated with embezzlement and fraud, especially in the brokerage of mortgages, but even if there was no fraud, the crisis would still have happened. It was an inevitable consequence of the economic cycle, modern finance and its regulation. Moreover, while there is a limit to what we can do about the ethical standards of bankers, there is much we can do about the way we regulate the financial system.

If the three regulatory pillars above were in place in 2007, the crisis would have been ameliorated in three ways. First, the scale of the previous boom would have been moderated by counter-cyclical charges that would have made lending and borrowing more costly, and as a result, kept them in greater check. Second, as a result of these counter-cyclical charges, banks would have been far more capitalized than they were—perhaps doubly so—providing a greater capital cushion for losses when the crash struck. Third, while banks and hedge funds with short-term funding were selling assets to raise fresh capital, pension funds, private equity firms, insurance companies and other long-term investors would have been buying these assets which on long-term valuation metrics had become cheap. This buying would have reduced the scale of the market price falls, which in turn would have reduced the depletion of bank capital and reduced the amount of forced selling. In a financial crisis there are multiple equilibriums. The price-based system prevalent in 2007 forced the financial markets into loss spirals that delivered a low price equilibrium and associated insolvency and illiquidity.

The three pillars described here would not eliminate the cycle, but they are more likely to have delivered higher price equilibrium, with less insolvency and illiquidity. Let us not wait for another crash before we try it.

Notes

1. Chairman of Intelligence Capital Limited, Chairman of the Warwick Commission, Co-Chair of the OECD EmNet, and Professor Emeritus, Gresham College.
2. I first heard the term the "marketization of finance," as well as the term "macroprudential" risks, from one of the leading experts in this field, Claudio Borio.
3. Professor Charles Goodhart makes the important point that one of the problems with the originate, rate, and relocate model is that many banks were too greedy to relocate the risks very far and often put them into their own bank sponsored Structured Investment Vehicle or hedge fund. Indeed, the collapse of Bear Stearns started with a collapse of a Bear Sterns hedge fund.
4. The Gnomes of Zurich is a disparaging term for bankers. The British Labour Party politician Harold Wilson, then shadow chancellor, coined the term in 1964 when he accused Swiss bankers of pushing sterling down on the foreign exchange markets by speculation. Basel is the home of the Basel Committee of G-10 Bank Supervisors who developed the Basel accords on bank capital adequacy.
5. I was led to this idea by Professor Willem Buiter, who was one of the first people to write about central bankers becoming buyers of last resort.
6. See, for example, the White House Draft Financial Regulation Proposals, a version of which is available at <http://documents.nytimes.com/draft-of-president-obama-s-financial-regulation-proposal#p=1> accessed on June 29, 2009.
7. Public loans to Northern Rock alone has already cost close to $100 billion.
8. It is argued that this was the fate of efforts in the US in 2001–2 in response to the major corporate accounting scandals, which culminated in the Sarbanes-Oxley Act of 2002.
9. "Prior to the passage of deposit insurance legislation in 1933, banking panics were a recurrent feature of US banking history" (see Wicker, 2008).
10. One of the stated goals of Basel II is to better emulate the economic capital models that the banks use themselves. But if regulation was merely about emulation and not about addressing market failures, why would we need it?
11. The original Goodhart and Persaud (2008) article assumed that this exercise would be carried out for individual banks, but as suggested above, this approach could be used to estimate a country or region wide capital adequacy requirement.
12. On September 17, 2007, the UK Chancellor of the Exchequer Alistair Darling said:

   I want to put the matter beyond doubt. I can announce today that following discussions with the governor [of the Bank of England] and the chairman of the FSA [Financial Services Authority], should it be necessary, we, with the Bank of England, would put in place arrangements that would guarantee all the existing deposits in Northern Rock during the current instability in the financial markets

   Later this guarantee was extended to all UK banking institutions.
13. Since there will be little need for them to sell these assets in the short run.

References

Goodhart, C. A. E. and Persaud, A. (2008) 'The Party Poopers Guide to Financial Stability.' *Financial Times*, June 4.

Persaud, A. (2000) *Sending the Herd Off the Cliff Edge: The Disturbing Interaction of Herding and Market-Sensitive Risk Management Practices*. London: State Street Bank <http://www.bis.org/publ/bppdf/bispap02l.pdf>.

—— (2008) *'Sending the herd off the cliff edge: the disturbing interaction between market sensitive risk management and the herding of investors.'* Jacques de Lanosier Prize Essay, 2000, IIF Washington.

Wicker, E. (2008) *Banking Panics in the Gilded Age*. Cambridge: Cambridge University Press.

9

How, If At All, Should Credit Ratings Agencies (CRAs) Be Regulated?[1]

C. A. E. Goodhart[2]

Introduction

The role of credit ratings agencies (CRAs) is to forecast the probability that the issuer of a debt liability will default on the due repayment (its probability of default, PD). In this respect, CRAs are one of a large set of institutions and people who seek to forecast certain aspects of the future.[3] As a generality, the *only*, or at any rate the most important, requisite of a forecast is its accuracy. So long as the forecast is accurate, it is largely beside the point how the forecasters behave otherwise, whether they lead a blameless life, or alternatively are rude to their parents, beat their children, or cheat on their spouses, etc. Moreover, in the case of CRAs, (unlike the Delphic oracle), the forecast is not only *relatively* clear in content, (though we shall consider later how it could, and should, be made even clearer), but also the status of the event being forecast, i.e. whether the issuer defaults, or not, on due repayment, is also relatively clear—and any remaining ambiguity often becomes subject to a legal decision. So the forecasting activities of CRAs should be susceptible to *ex post* accountability. Compare forecast with out-turn; assess and publish the comparative accuracy of the various CRAs and leave competition to do the rest.[4] We shall review what extra steps need to be taken to enhance such *ex post* accountability, comparing forecast with outcome, and comment briefly on how, perhaps, to enhance competition.

  If the time gap between forecast and out-turn was very short, as for example in the case of someone tipping horses for that day's races (though even here the tipster may have a separate agenda—a principal/agent problem), it is arguable that proper *ex post* accountability is all that is needed. A cause for concern with CRAs is, however, that the lapse of time between forecast and out-turn is often rather long, measured in years rather than days. Hence, if the CRA is paid by the issuer of the debt, it may pay the current CRA executives to shade their forecast in a more favorable light. By the time that their more enthusiastic prediction is shown to be *ex post* over-optimistic, these executives will have probably moved on to another job, or retirement, having pocketed enhanced earnings along the way. Even if such concerns among the users of ratings are exaggerated and misplaced, as they probably are, they serve to damage CRAs' credibility. The mechanism for making payments to them should place them beyond suspicion. Again, we shall discuss how this might be done below.

In this chapter, I shall start with a brief record of the recent history of the attempts to regulate the CRA. Then I consider whether the current payment system does involve conflicts of interest, and, if so, what to do about that. In the third section I briefly discuss why, besides conflicts of interest, there may be a case for some kind of official intervention, and what forms it should *not* take, i.e. some other proposals for reform. The fourth section describes how, and why, existing ratings are systematically misused by *investors*, and then go on to unveil my main recommendation, which is the establishment of an independent body (to be paid for by the CRAs), to assess and publish reports on the relative accuracy of such CRAs. In the sixth section, I review whether there is a case for additional, pecuniary, penalties on CRAs with a forecasting record worse *ex post* than they have advertised *ex ante* (to try to establish truth in advocating/ forecasting). In the seventh section, I consider what effects these proposals may have on competition among, and entry into, the set of CRAs. In the eighth section, the question of how ratings *transitions* should be estimated and reported is discussed. This chapter concludes with a summary of recommendations.

Some recent history

The most important market for CRAs is the United States. In the United States, CRAs have come under the oversight of the Securities and Exchange Commission (SEC).

Since 1975, the SEC has relied on credit ratings from 'market-recognised credible' rating agencies in order to distinguish between grades of creditworthiness in various regulations under the US federal securities laws.[5]

These credit rating agencies, known as "nationally recognized statistical rating organizations" or "NRSROs," are recognized as such by SEC staff based on, among other things, acceptance of a firm's credit ratings by predominant users of securities ratings. While eight firms have been recognized as NRSROs to date, consolidation has resulted in the following four NRSROs at present: Moody's Investors Service, Inc., Fitch, Inc., Standard & Poor's, a division of The McGraw-Hill Companies, Inc., and Dominion Bond Rating Service Limited.

During the past thirty years, SEC staff has developed a number of objective criteria for assessing NRSRO status. Under current practice, the SEC staff reviews a credit rating agency's operations, position in the marketplace, and other specific factors to determine whether it should be considered an NRSRO.

The single most important factor in the SEC staff's assessment of NRSRO status is whether a credit rating agency is "nationally recognized" in the United States as an issuer of credible and reliable ratings by the predominant users of securities ratings. The SEC staff also reviews the operational capability and reliability of each credit rating agency. In view of the growing importance of credit ratings to investors and other market participants, and the influence credit ratings have on the securities markets, in recent years, the SEC and US Congress have reviewed a number of issues regarding credit rating agencies and, in particular, the subject of their regulatory oversight. (CESR, 2005)

What sparked the first round of concern with CRAs in the current century was the collapse of Enron and of several other companies which were found to be fraudulent after the bust of the NASDAQ (National Association of Securities Dealers Automated Quotations) bubble in 2001. The CRAs had been patently slow in spotting these, and some maintained that they should, and could, have done better in this respect. Moreover, any such shortcomings among CRAs were becoming more worrying in view of their potentially enhanced role under the standardized version of Pillar 1 of Basel II.

So the aftermath of the Enron debacle led to a flurry of exercises to explore what might be done to improve the workings of CRAs, both nationally and internationally. Nationally, the most important study was done by the SEC,[6] though France and the UK also participated via the AFTE (Association Francaise des Tresoriers d'Entreprise) and ACT (Association of Corporate Treasurers) respectively in such exercises. Since the main CRAs all operated internationally, arguably the more important forum became the Technical Committee of the International Organization of Securities Commissions (IOSCO), which formed a taskforce, under the Chairmanship of Commissioner Campos of the SEC "to examine certain key issues regarding the role CRAs play in securities markets" (IOSCO, 2003a). This issued two reports in September 2003; the first, above-mentioned, report provided a general, and excellent, description[7] of the work of CRAs, informed by a questionnaire to, (among others), and discussions with the CRAs. The second report was the more important. Its main content was a Statement of Principles to be used by CRAs, as indicated by its title, 'IOSCO Statement of Principles regarding the Activities of Credit Rating Agencies' (2003b).

No serious rationale was provided to explain why a code of conduct or statement of principles would be helpful.[8] Admittedly, regulators were then so engaged in the process of drawing up standards, codes of conduct, principles, etc.—all to be checked by the IMF (International Monetary Fund) in its ROSC (Report on Observance of Standards and Codes) exercises—that any justification may have seemed otiose. There were four main principles discussed.

(1) Quality and integrity of the rating process: CRAs should endeavor to issue opinions that help reduce the asymmetry of information among borrowers, lenders, and other market participants.

(2) Independence and conflicts of interest: CRA ratings decisions should be independent and free from political or economic pressures and from conflicts of interest arising due to the CRA's ownership structure, business, or financial activities, or the financial interests of the CRA's employees. CRAs should, as far as possible, avoid activities, procedures, or relationships that may compromise or appear to compromise the independence and objectivity of the credit rating operations.

(3) Transparency and timeliness of ratings disclosure: CRAs should make disclosure and transparency an objective in their ratings activities.

(4) Confidential information: CRAs should maintain in confidence all non-public information communicated to them by any issuer, or its agents, under the terms of a confidentiality agreement or otherwise under a mutual understanding that the information is shared confidentially.

In the introduction, I claimed that there were two key issues for forecasters—CRAs' *ex post* accountability and conflicts of interest—with a third important question of competition. The only sub-heading on *ex post* accountability left it to the CRAs themselves what to publish.[9] The key section on conflicts of interest was a perfectly reasonable statement of objectives rather than providing any guidance on how to identify and remove such conflicts.[10] There was no mention of competition between CRAs. Since there is no international law on issues such as this, international bodies, such as IOSCO or BCBS (Basel Committee on Banking Supervision), cannot and do not discuss the question of sanctions for non-performance or how to enforce any such principles, except by peer pressure.

Following this Statement of Principles, the main CRAs issued their own individual codes. What changes of behavior followed, if any, are difficult to ascertain. In particular, they have not prevented the CRAs from coming under renewed attack in the past couple of years, notably for having over-optimistic ratings for mortgage-backed structured products,[11] in some part, it is alleged, because of continuing conflicts of interest.[12]

Nevertheless, until at least very recently, the IOSCO code of conduct has remained the centerpiece of such regulatory efforts and discussion, vis-à-vis the CRAs, as have continued. In December 2004, IOSCO extended the Principles into "a more specific and detailed code of conduct giving guidance on how the Principles could be implemented in practice" (IOSCO, 2004a). This took the four main principles, with the wording marginally revised, and expanded the number of sub-headings to 18, 16, 18, and 2 respectively. There was some additional material on conflicts of interest (in Sections 2.5 and 2.8).[13] How far these extra clauses altered CRA procedures would be difficult to discover without an in-depth exercise. The one section on checking outcomes (now 3.8), remained essentially unchanged, and there continued to be nothing about competition.

Other reviews, apart from that of the Technical Committee of IOSCO, have been done by the Committee on European Securities Regulation (CESR), which has published three such reports, the first in March 2005, on "CESR's technical advice to the European Commission on possible measures concerning credit ratings agencies." This report largely rubber-stamped the earlier IOSCO reports. There were two more recent studies on "The role of credit rating agencies in structured finance" (2008a) and its consultation paper on the same topic (2008b).[14] This latter continued to advocate making a voluntary code of conduct the centerpiece of regulatory oversight, but now to be overseen by an additional monitoring body.[15] How anyone can monitor such a verbose set of pious objectives is far from clear.

Meanwhile, the Technical Committee of IOSCO has now also reported in March 2008 with a consultation paper on "The Role of Credit Rating Agencies in Structured Finance Markets" (2008a). In this paper, the Committee proposed a number of minor modifications to its original code of conduct (see the section on 'Recommendations'). It has followed this with a Final Report (2008b). Apart from a new section on 'Competition' (pp. 13–14), which does not provide any recommendations, it offers yet another marginal re-write of the Code of Conduct.

But not everyone remained convinced that a revamp of the existing codes of conduct would do. In the *Financial Times* on June 16, 2008, Nicki Tait and Gillian Tett reported on a forthcoming speech by Charlie McCreevy, the EU internal markets commissioner entitled "Brussels to Crack Down on Ratings Agencies."

Mr McCreevy is to make clear that nothing short of regulatory supervision will do. "I am now convinced that limited but mandatory, well-targeted and robust internal governance reforms are going to be imperative to complement stronger external oversight of rating agencies...I have concluded that a regulatory solution at the European level is now necessary to deal with some of the core issues."

The announcement comes just weeks after the IOSCO proposed changes to the industry code of conduct, a code Mr McCreevy will make clear falls far short of what is needed.

In withering language, Mr McCreevy will describe the code as "a toothless wonder" and point out that "no supervisor appears to have got as much as a sniff of the rot at the heart of the structured finance rating process before it all blew up." He will say that he is "deeply skeptical" about its usefulness. "Many of the recent IOSCO taskforce recommendations do not appear enforceable in a meaningful way," he will suggest.

Similarly, Andrew M. Cuomo, the Attorney General in New York State, moved to introduce new constraints on CRAs' pricing of their services in respect of rating structured products. It is to this subject that we now turn.

Conflicts of interest: notably in the ratings of structured products

There are two dimensions to criticism of CRAs in their relationship with issuers of structured products, one that I regard as largely invalid, but one that may have some force.

Let us turn now to the first, mainly incorrect, allegation—that CRAs provided undue assistance to issuers of securitized products. This is a misplaced criticism, not because the CRAs did not provide such help, but because it was their duty to do so. Thus, IOSCO's own code of conduct, Sections 3.5 and 3.7 states:

> the CRA should inform the issuer of the critical information and principal considerations upon which a rating will be based and afford the issuer an opportunity to clarify any likely factual misperceptions or other matters that the CRA would wish to be made aware of in order to produce an accurate rating.

In short, a CRA is obliged to inform issuers of the details of the techniques used to assign ratings and to answer questions of clarification about such methodologies. Of course, issuers of structured products can, and will, use such assistance to place their product *just* above some desired threshold.

Irrespective of the fact that IOSCO's own code of conduct requires CRAs to assist issuers of securitized products with information to enable them to structure their product so as to achieve a desired rating, why might this practice be undesirable? More information is better than less. Only if CRAs, and issuers, jointly apply a rating that CRAs believe is too high is there a problem. So long as CRAs assess PDs correctly, and make that information public, then this question of inappropriate relationships, and conflict of interest, can be seen as a canard.

The second issue is the main one. Might conflicts of interest lead to a distortion of publicly stated ratings of securitized products, especially since ratings agencies are paid by the issuers, not by investors? In general, the accuracy of a CRA's ratings is protected by its need to maintain its reputation. The importance of reputation was spelt out in IOSCO's September 2003 Report (pp. 10–11).

> The most common conflict of interest cited by taskforce members was that larger CRAs receive most of their revenue from the issuers that they rate. Where a CRA receives revenue from an issuer, the CRA may be inclined to downplay the credit risk it poses in order to retain the issuer's business. The CRAs responding to the taskforce's questionnaire stated that they are aware of this potential conflict of interest and attempt to mitigate its influence by ensuring that no particular issuer constitutes any significant portion of the CRA's overall revenue. These firms claim that, because credit ratings from a particular firm are only valuable insofar as the firm maintains a reputation for independence, accuracy and thoroughness, CRAs would be unwilling to risk damaging their reputations just to retain a single client. Furthermore, while issuers may prefer to use a credit rating from a firm with relatively lax rating standards, investors are unlikely to accord such ratings much weight and the issuer would pay higher costs for the capital it is trying to raise.

CRAs also note that CRA analyst compensation is not linked to issuer fees. According to the CRA respondents, this, combined with the use of rating committees, removes the likelihood that the rating process will be inappropriately influenced.

Competition is also important. Insofar as debt issuers are rated by two or more agencies and/or that identical products are rated by different agencies, a tendency for one agency to become systematically lax should become evident quite quickly, even before actual default events could demonstrate the relative accuracy of the CRAs. Of course collusion is possible, but the damage to reputation, if caught, would be overwhelming.

So, the essential question is whether there are some features of the process of rating structured products that make the standard safeguards of reputation and competition less effective in their case. This may be so. The incentive to over-rate to gain a fee is negligible on traditional corporate business. Corporate rating fees are quite small—why risk the company's reputation to gain a fee? But structured issues are different in two respects. First, it was a new business and has been earning super-normal profits—especially for the investment bankers proposing the issues, but also (in a smaller way) for the CRAs. With fees generally higher in relation to marginal costs than is the case for a corporate rating, the incentive to over-rate to secure a fee is that much greater. (And the investment bankers proposing a deal can be demanding—they want their high bonuses for getting the issue away.) Second, whereas a company would normally want to be rated by all the major agencies—or at least two of them— structured issues are often rated by only one or two agencies. The company seeks out the agency that will give the highest rating (or demand the least credit enhancement to achieve the desired ratings); the other agencies are then not used. That indicates a prima facie case for bias.

This analysis suggests potential remedies, much along the lines already proposed by New York Attorney General Andrew Cuomo (Dow Jones News services, June 6, 2008). First, all issuers must pay for advice and analysis separately from the rating to prevent issuers asking several CRAs for their ratings assessment, and then only paying the agency offering the most optimistic rating. Second, there must be more precise disclosure of ratings' fees. Third, all issuers of structured, securitized products, must obtain, and publish, a rating from two or more, CRAs. This latter obligation would also be justifiable on the grounds that such products are more complex and opaque. It could also encourage more competition among CRAs. Finally, there is a major need, as elaborated below, for an independent assessment body to check on the accuracy of CRAs' predictions of PD.

An alternative approach has been proposed in the consultation document issued by the SEC (2008).

To address this conflict . . . as a condition to the NRSRO rating a structured finance product the information provided to the NRSRO and used by the NRSRO in determining the credit rating would need to be disclosed through a means designed to provide reasonably broad dissemination of the information. The intent behind this disclosure is to create the opportunity for other NRSROs to use the information to rate the instrument as well. Any resulting unsolicited ratings could be used by market participants to evaluate the ratings issued by the NRSRO hired to rate the product and, in turn, potentially expose an NRSRO whose ratings were influenced by the desire to gain favor with the arranger in order to obtain more business.

While there are several features to be applauded in this proposal, notably the use of *ex post* accountability rather than codes of conduct, the encouragement of competition and the reliance on market mechanisms rather than government intervention, I doubt they would work for several reasons. First, it requires any issuer, either directly or via its CRAs of such a product, to provide full details of any new structured product to *any* potential CRA. What might happen if a competitor were to set up a subsidiary CRA with the purpose of discovering competitive details? Could such details be kept confidential in such a regime? I wonder whether issuers of structured products would be willing to accept such a disclosure obligation.

Second, the proposal would work by having CRA competitors undertake more conservative (i.e. less favorable) unsolicited ratings. A representative sample of such products would have to be rated by the unsolicited CRA in order to establish that the initial (solicited) CRA had a pattern of excessively optimistic ratings. This would be quite expensive. Insofar as ratings were paid for by issuers, it is not clear why the publication of such "knocking copy," in the guise of lower unsolicited ratings, would ever gain more commissions.

So this proposal could only benefit those CRAs whose receipts came from the "buy-side," such as Egan-Jones. While it might provide them with an enhanced marketing benefit, it would lead to another problem. Suppose that those unsolicited ratings, sold onto subscribers, were in some sense superior. Then these subscribers would be in command of relevant market information not available to others. In line with the SEC's own disclosures rules, unless specifically amended to promote buy-side CRAs, such unsolicited ratings would have to be publicly published. In which case they would be valueless, and there would be no incentive for such "unsolicited ratings" to be undertaken.

The SEC and IOSCO have then faced a conundrum. It could promote buy-side CRAs, enhance competition and encourage cross-checking of accuracy, but only if it is prepared to soften its own rulings of common disclosure of market relevant information. Alternatively, it could stick by its own disclosure rules, and then these proposals would fail to achieve their intended purpose.

Other proposals for reform

In the pantheon of villains, on whom the current financial crisis is blamed, CRAs usually now receive a (dis)honorable mention, if not quite pride of place. This has led to a wild variety of proposed "reforms."

Perhaps almost as serious from the standpoint of the CRAs, their reputation has been damaged, and reputation is the key to their brand name.

It would be easy enough to put CRAs out of business, and some of the proposed reforms for them could do just that. The problem is that CRAs do perform a public service. It would be a massive waste of time if all investors had to run a complete information-gathering exercise (due diligence) on all of their investments, however small a share of their overall portfolio. They could not, and would not, do that. So it represents a huge economy of time and effort to delegate such information gathering, sifting and dissemination to specialists, *so long as one can trust them.*

This latter is quite a qualification. How does one ensure that CRAs are trustworthy? There are numerous suggestions. Most of them are, I believe, unworkable. Some of the more common suggestions follow.

Involve the government, either as supervisors or as promoting an additional CRA to compete with the private CRAs

To many, the idea that a public sector CRA would be more trustworthy than a private sector CRA when rating public sector debt, a local "national champion" or a failing company of political significance is an oxymoron. Who would, for example, trust a French publicly established ratings agency to rate a French "champion" objectively? More generally, any public sector involvement with CRAs as supervisor or overseer would tend to be held, by the public, as leading to public sector responsibility for the accuracy of CRA forecasts/opinions. If a public sector body was to supervise a CRA in any way, it would be held to have given its approval of such forecasts.

Make the CRAs legally liable for their forecasts/opinions

I cannot help wondering what would happen if governments, central banks, think-tanks and economists were also to be made legally liable for their fore-casts and opinions. I cannot see how such forecasting could continue. Once legal liability is applied, the potential for open-ended damages, especially in the US legal system, would, I believe, make the whole business model of CRAs non-viable. Those who press this line of attack need to explain how legal liability can remain sufficiently constrained to enable the services of CRAs to continue.

Although the most virulent attacks on CRAs have mostly come from the United States, the CRAs are, perhaps, more at risk from legal challenge in Europe where the constitutional defense has less resonance.

Prevent debt issuers paying CRAs, so the CRAs are forced to seek payment from investors (the buy-side)

The problem with this approach is that information, once publicly revealed, becomes a free public good. In principle, every investor could subscribe individually and privately to one or more CRA *and* promise not to pass on that information.[16] However, that promise would be hard to enforce. Hundreds of employees at many financial institutions would have access to such ratings and could undercut the CRAs by making secondary markets. Moreover, the information content in the ratings could soon be deduced from the actions of subscribing investors. Newspapers would have an incentive to glean and publish accurate estimates of CRA ratings.

Furthermore, in a context in which transparency is desired in almost all cases, is it appropriate to move to a system in which the business of providing ratings can only work if these are maintained privately by individual subscribers?[17] Also, how do you price subscriptions so that retail investors can afford to see ratings, while banks/Other Financial Institutions (OFIs) pay massively more? Not impossible, but it would be difficult and costly to get right. Such a system would also be more difficult and time-consuming to run than the present one.

Some failings in the use of CRA ratings

Much of the problem with CRA ratings resides with their misuse by users rather than the mechanisms of their provision.

Misuse of forecasts

Forecasts tend to be systematically misused by their recipients (NB this is usually only partially the fault of their providers). Recipients of forecasts tend to focus unduly on the modal (or mean) forecast while ignoring or discounting the wide probability distribution (the higher moments), especially the uncertainty (confidence limits) and skewness of the forecast. This has been encouraged by CRAs by the emphasis placed on the particular rating, for example A or BBB, rather than the probability distribution of implied credit default or the potential volatility of ratings migration in each case.

When he introduced the Inflation Report in the UK in 1992–3, Mervyn King, then Chief Economist at the Bank of England, tried to wean the recipients of his forecasts away from focusing on the most likely modal outcome by refusing to publish a specific number and publishing a fan chart instead. It may well be the case that CRAs would have been prepared to publish similar fan charts of the one-sided probability of default for each rating notch had investors asked for that. But they did not. I believe that such forecast data can and should be made available. I would propose that all ratings *should* be accompanied by a fan chart showing not only the prospective default probabilities attached by that CRA to that rating for each year of the rated product's life, but also a measure of the uncertainty of that measure.[18] An example is provided in Figure 9.1, where X is a central tendency of PD, mean or mode and + and * are one-sided estimates, e.g. confidence interval, of the upward uncertainty relating to that forecast of PD. Here, + shows the confidence interval for the mortgage-based structured product, while * gives the same confidence interval for a corporate bond. The two have a completely different time path, even when the expectation of mean PD is, by construction, taken to be the same. Under normal circumstances, uncertainty increases and confidence limits widen as the time horizon lengthens, i.e. the further into the future one looks. This is, however, not so with mortgage-based structured products, as Mason and Rosner report (2007, Part III, pp. 34–51).

In summary, because RMBS [Residential Mortgage Backed Securities] are constructed on the basis of mortgage pools that consist of static portfolios of fixed-income investments that become seasoned over time, performance over time becomes increasingly predictable. That increased predictability results in RMBS ratings that telescope in quality towards either default or AAA. Furthermore, all the tranches of securities associated with a specific mortgage pool will migrate toward default or AAA together. This all-or-nothing

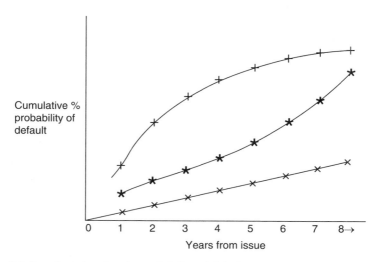

Figure 9.1 Fan chart showing the probability of default over time

nature of the risk in structured finance is the source of relatively high AAA yields (and yields across the credit spectrum) that attract investors to the sector, as well as the source of concentrated defaults that have historically hit various ABS and RMBS sectors to date. The problem with rating RMBS therefore is not that the future is hard to predict. The problem is that the traditional ratings process, when applied to RMBS, is being used to do things for which it is not designed. (Mason and Rosner, 2007, p. 48)

It is in this sense that RMBS have been sometimes described as "economic catastrophe" bonds. It has yet to be completely determined how far the CRAs systematically underestimated mean PDs for RMBS, mainly by giving too little weight to the probability of housing price declines throughout the United States, and to the subsequent effect on default—jingle mail.[19] But what is clear is that once conditions started to deteriorate with RMBS, the volatility of ratings was far more extreme than for plain corporate debt. My assertion here is that differences in essential characteristics can only be met by CRAs publishing additional detail on the prospective confidence limits (volatility) of their forecasts.

There may be little initial enthusiasm among investors for such extra information. What most forecast users want is a simple mental crutch in the guise of a point forecast, rather than a more careful assessment of uncertainties. Investors are ordinary people, and ordinary people are lazy. Some may also have been complicit, in that they know that structured product ratings had greater risk, but consciously sought to move further along their return/risk curve than their own investment constraints normally allowed. Investors *should*, as a matter of public policy, be made aware of the uncertainties surrounding future forecasts of PD. Suggestions have been made that ratings of structured products carry a different symbol. That does not really catch the point that the risks of ratings migration are quite different and in a way that can be quantified and estimated, for RMBS as compared with corporate debt.

The rating applied to a structured product cannot *imply the same probability of default as an exactly similar rating applied to an underlying instrument*

The point is that a structured product is precisely structured to achieve a particular ratings level. Thus, in the aggregate of such structured products, the mass is right at the bottom of the set of allowable conditions. So the expected PD of a portfolio of structured instruments, all of which are correctly awarded an A rating, can potentially be higher than that of a portfolio of original underlying instruments of the same A rating. Again, the proper way to handle this is to require CRAs to publish fan charts of PDs over the expected life of each product. Then it will immediately become obvious that an AA rating assigned to a structured product is not, and cannot, be the same as an AA rating assigned to an underlying product.

CRAs will be unduly pressured to provide ratings too soon

Because of information asymmetries, a market for innovative investment products needs to have these rated. Almost by definition, such products will be launched in favorable conditions. So the CRAs will not know what will happen to correlations, PDs, etc., in adverse times for such instruments. But they will nonetheless be under great pressure to issue such ratings, and their self-interest will tempt them to proceed despite the lack of sufficient time and life history.

Once more, the correct approach is not to ban ratings of new products, but to require the CRAs to expose their uncertainty by publishing fan charts, applicable to any rated new product, in which the upper line, recording uncertainty, should deviate much further from the modal forecast. Of course, CRAs may fail to appreciate this problem (of too short of a data set) or knowingly publish tighter fan charts as a sales mechanism, but that is where the assessment and perhaps the penalties or pre-commitment mechanism kicks in. If their estimate of PDs turns out to be overly optimistic, they are penalized.

No mechanism for ex post evaluation of ratings

The CRAs keep a record of the outcome of all their rated instruments, (default and when, or not). They need this to revise their own methodologies. Moreover, they mostly publish an account of their default and transition studies, though in some cases with full access limited to subscribers. For example, Fitch's latest reports on structured and corporate ratings are available on its website.[20]

But what CRAs publish is what they independently choose to publish, which may incorrectly evoke some public cynicism. Moreover, such independent publication of results makes comparison of relative accuracy *between* CRAs difficult or impossible.

Therefore, comparisons of relative forecast accuracy among CRAs cannot be made. Moreover, there is relatively little call among investors for such comparative exercises to be done. After the event, individual issuers and investors have no further *individual* interest in providing a public record of what happened and of how accurate the CRAs were. However, there is a *public* interest in achieving *ex post* accountability.

An independent assessment institution

This leads directly to my main proposal, which is the establishment of an independent assessment institution to assess the accuracy of CRA estimates of PD and to publish comparative studies of such accuracy. It would *not* have a wider responsibility for monitoring compliance with a code of conduct. Indeed, as noted at the outset, so long as the forecasts are accurate, the behavior of the forecaster in other respect is largely immaterial. A subsidiary proposal, therefore, is that IOSCO's code of conduct be scrapped.

What is needed is a small independent body—a CRA Assessment Center (CRAAC). All CRAs in every country should be required to place with CRAAC a record of each product rated and an initial quantified forecast of expected PD and a measure of the uncertainty of that forecast annually through the life of that product. At the extinction of the product (default, payment or repackaging) the CRA would again inform CRAAC. The Center would be essentially a data handling centre with few staff. Members could have the ability to cross-check the validity of CRA information. It would be global in scope. It would have to be set up under a specific country's national law and there should be a right of judicial appeal. It should have the right to request information from CRAs.

Unfortunately, it would not be credible for the industry to set up such a body under its own direct control. It would be for discussion whether the industry could finance a third party, perhaps a large accounting firm, to set up and establish the CRAAC or whether it would have to be done by governments. As Willem Buiter has noted, "Self-regulation is to regulation, as self importance is to importance." Moreover, penalties, some combination of reputation and pecuniary loss, may be necessary to insure that CRA estimates of PD are both as honest and accurate as possible, and are seen to be such.

The key issue is to ensure that the product, a securitized instrument, is correctly rated at the outset when it is originated and sold. At first sight, it might seem a reasonable idea, insofar as such ratings are based on fallible models, for the CRAAC also to be asked for a second opinion on model architecture and assumptions, but that would be dangerous since (a) there are fashions and common errors in model construction techniques as in most everything else; and (b) it would tend to make CRAAC complicit, rather than independent, in assessing model outcomes. There may be a case for having such an independent body also assess the relative speed and accuracy of ratings transitions, but that could be left for later when the assessment body had been properly established, and was running effectively.

Again, it may be helpful to compare and contrast the proposal here with that contained in the SEC's June 2008 consultation paper. The SEC would have CRAs provide sufficient extra data to allow assessments of *ex post* accountability to be undertaken, but they would have the data made available to everyone whereas we would only require the CRAs to send it confidentially to CRAAC. So the CRAs themselves would, I believe, find our proposal more acceptable.

Then, having obtained this massive accumulation of data, the SEC would leave it to:

the marketplace to use the information on the history of each credit rating [to] create the opportunity for the marketplace to use the information to develop performance measurement statistics that would supplement those required to be published by the NRSROs themselves in Exhibit 1 to Form NRSRO.[21]

Whilst the intention and objective is laudable, and in line with our own proposal, I doubt whether it is practicable to leave it to "the marketplace." Doing such comparative exercises would have to be continuous and consistent; it would also be expensive. Who would pay for it? The "free rider" problem would be huge. It *has* to be a separately established independent agency, though exactly who establishes it, either the government or the private sector, could be for discussion.

As a primarily statistical body, *without* concern for conduct, it should be possible to set a CRAAC up quite cheaply. The industry would, I assume, initially pay for it pro rata to earnings. Perhaps in subsequent years, the payment/premium could be related to the assessed relative accuracy, with those who did worst paying most. Note that there are two dimensions to such accuracy: first, how close was mean predicted PD to actual average outturn PD; second, did the expected number of defaults lie within the upper confidence band. Some method of weighting those two dimensions would need to be found.

This is not such a large step and, indeed, the SEC, as noted above, is considering imposing even stronger data reporting requirements. Moreover, IOSCO has requested CRAs to publish information on historical default rates "in such a way to assist investors in drawing performance comparisons between different CRAs" (2008a).[22] Again and perhaps more important, the CESR Report (2008a, p. 17) records the following:

The Participating CRAs continue to meet to discuss and develop potential initiatives and measures aimed at promoting confidence in the credit rating process and structured finance market. In their latest update[23] the group is presenting a number of recommendations that the members are committed:

- Plainly stating that the Participating CRAs do not and will not provide consulting, or advisory services to the issuers they rate, nor do their analysts make proposals or recommendations regarding the structure or design of structured finance products.

- Conducting regular, periodic reviews of staffing needs, training and competences, as well as formal, internal reviews of remuneration policies and practices to ensure that they do not compromise analyst objectivity.

- Working with market participants on measures that could enhance the quality and transparency of information regarding assets underlying structured finance securities available to the investing public.

- Creating an industry portal to house the participating CRAs' performance studies and other relevant data.

- Providing more disclosure about key model and methodology assumptions and stress-testing of assumptions.

Perhaps the key difference here is the insistence that the comparative assessment body should be independent of the CRAs themselves.

Penalties and pre-commitment?

What is being proposed here is a quantification of ratings, so that *ex post* accountability can be more easily achieved in two dimensions. The first and easiest is a numerical estimate of the mean expected cumulative PD, annually over its stated life for a debt instrument assessed as being within a given ratings class. The second is a measure of the confidence with which that forecast is held, expressed as an upper band, which the distribution of defaults should only breach, say, 1 per cent or 2.5 per cent of the time. Both sets of data, on central tendencies and expected variance of PDs, provide necessary information for investors.

Pure concerns of reputation are likely to provide sufficient incentive for CRAs to aim to achieve the best possible point forecast so long as the initial forecast can be properly compared with actual outcome and comparisons between CRAs are published by an independent assessor. But one of the problems with forecasts, especially with forecasts of PDs for innovative products, is that recipients have little idea of the uncertainty of such forecasts. There is little incentive for the CRAs to reveal just how uncertain they may be.

So there is a case for requiring the CRAs not only to report an upper band, beyond which they expect defaults for any given asset class to fall very rarely (say 1 per cent or 2.5 per cent of the time) but also to pay a modest penalty if this is breached more often than expected. This would be akin to the pre-commitment approach devised by Paul Kupiec for application to bank capital in several articles in the 1990s (see in particular Kupiec and O'Brien, 2003). The purpose of the penalties would be to provide a balance between CRA desire to indicate confidence in their own forecast by implying little uncertainty for promotional reasons against the cost and shame of having to pay such a penalty if the upper band was breached.

If the occasion of such a penalty being levied were to be published, as I would advocate, the cost to reputation would be greater and the actual amount of the pecuniary penalty kept small. It could then be applied to meet the running costs of the independent assessment body (the CRAAC).

An alternative and possibly preferable approach, which I owe to Professor Perry Mehrling (see Chapter 10 in this volume), would be to require CRAs to purchase credit default swaps on the issues that they rate at the date of issuance and configured so that a default rate on such products greater than the upper confidence limit predicted by each CRA would generate a transfer to the current holder of that product.[24] While this is a nice idea, whether credit default swaps (CDS) could in practice be so configured is an issue beyond the limits of this paper.

Competition

There are only two big US-based CRAs—Moody's and Standard & Poor's—and one European-owned rival, Fitch. This is not enough to provide proper competition. The NRSRO procedure is not helpful (a kind of Catch 22).[25] As argued earlier, government-backed agencies would not be credible.

The proposal here to provide independently assessed and quantified comparisons of *ex post* accuracy might help generate more competition. A new entrant could establish a track record for greater accuracy (this is *independently assessed*) in a particular niche by exploiting a comparative advantage, perhaps rating one particular product line, with a small staff, and then build from that. What investors want is forecast accuracy. At present, they have no simple or straightforward way of assessing that (though large investors might do so by comparing the historical records of each of the large CRAs). Consequently, most investors fall back on reliance on brand names which reinforces oligopoly.

Ratings transitions

The main role of CRAs is to give a credit rating to *new* debt issues at the time of issuance. One of the criticisms of CRAs is that they lag badly behind events in adjusting ratings in response to subsequent changes in the condition of such instruments. While that charge is surely justified and has been empirically demonstrated, it is a misperception to expect CRAs to do much better than now. They do not get paid for making ratings transitions, and hence have neither the incentive nor the staff to monitor continuously the idiosyncratic behavior of a myriad individual debt issues.[26] They do have Merton-type time to default models, e.g. Moody's KMV, but these by definition lag behind market data and given model uncertainty, the CRAs would not necessarily rush to use such model estimates to make rating transitions. If the issuer of existing debt instruments should issue a new instrument, that also may give a CRA grounds for revising earlier ratings; but issuers, in conditions where they face a potential downgrade, may defer new issues.

There may be a better way. Banks have more incentive to maintain continuous monitoring of all their credit claims. Moreover, under Basel II the larger banks are adopting the two Internal Ratings Based (IRB) approaches. Why not require the IRB banks to confidentially report their current ratings assessments on a limited number of representative credit holdings? The independent assessment body (CRAAC) would then average these, and publish them.[27] It would have much in common with the publication of London Inter-Bank Offer Rate (LIBOR) estimates from individual bank data.

This would provide a service to the banks that could compare their own assessment with the industry average. It would provide a service for CRAs which would become free of an expensive and poorly provided requirement to provide subsequent ratings transition. It would provide a service to investors who should then receive quicker and better information on ratings transitions.

Summary of recommendations

1. All CRAs should be required to provide confidential details of their ratings in a numerically quantified format to the Credit Rating Agency Assessment Centre (CRAAC), an independent assessment body.
2. CRAAC should maintain *ex post* accountability of CRAs by comparing forecasts with out-turn and publish reports on comparative accuracy.
3. CRA forecasts should have two numerical dimensions, central tendency and a measure of uncertainty (forecast confidence). The latter may need support from a modest pre-commitment penalty or by some other equivalent mechanism.
4. Ratings transitions should come from an averaging of IRB internal ratings, not from CRAs.
5. The industry should pay the costs of CRAAC.
6. Because of the long lag between forecast and out-turn, conflicts of interest do remain a valid concern. This can be handled by appropriate adjustment of the payment mechanism and by requiring all products to be rated by two or more CRAs.
7. The IOSCO Code of Conduct is best forgotten. No other government intervention is necessary or desirable *except* to insure that CRAAC is independent, not captured by CRAs and adequately resourced from the industry. Whether the CRAAC would be set up by the private sector or by the government would be for discussion, but it *must* be independent of the CRAs themselves.

Notes

1. My thanks are due to, among others, Jon Danielsson, Perry Mehrling, Robin Monro-Davies, and Lionel Price for advice and suggestions, but all opinions and errors remain my own.

2. Financial Markets Group and London School of Economics.

3. The forecasting profession is, however, by nature somewhat disreputable. Since all the available evidence is historical experience, the basic assumption is that the future will be like the past, i.e. that the world and the economic/financial system within it is stationary; that assumption is most often invalid (black swans, etc.). Moreover, available data are either too short to allow accurate statistical inferences, at least of extreme events, or so long as to include major structural regime changes, thereby making the earlier data irrelevant, or both at the same time.

4. One common complaint of regulators is that there is no central coordinating body for the CRAs, with which regulators can communicate; no Self Regulating Organization (SRO). Given the importance of clean competition among CRAs, especially when there are so few, their reluctance to form a common organization is understandable and even commendable. Making communications easier for regulators should not be a high priority.

5. While the SEC found the output of the CRAs to be useful for this purpose, the SEC otherwise left them largely unsupervised and on their own prior to the Enron debacle. Between 1975 and then, there were virtually no visits to NRSRO SRAs by the SEC. Rosner and Mason (2007) state that "The SEC examines the ratings agencies every five years" (p. 29).

6. See CESR (2005, pp. 8–9). This Concept Release and the SEC study formed the basis for the CRA Reform Act, which became effective in June 2007. Nine CRAs had registered as NRSROs under this legislative framework, as of May 2008: A.M. Best Company, Inc., DBRS Ltd., Fitch, Inc., Japan Credit Rating Agency, Ltd., Moody's Investor Service, Inc., Rating and Investment Information, Inc., Standard & Poor's Ratings Services, LACE Financial Corp., and Egan-Jones Rating Company. See also CESR (2008a, p.11).

7. Ibid., p. 2.

8. Ibid., p. 1.

9. IOSCO (2003b), Section 3.4: "CRAs should publish sufficient information about the historical default rates of CRA rating categories and whether the default rates of these categories have changed over time, so that interested parties can understand the historical performance of each category and if and how ratings categories have changed."

10. Ibid., Section 2.4:

> Reporting lines for CRA staff and their compensation arrangements should be structured to eliminate or effectively manage actual and potential conflicts of interest. A CRA analyst should not be compensated or evaluated on the basis of the amount of revenue that a CRA derives from issuers that the analyst rates or with which the analyst regularly interacts.

11. Whereas the spate of downgrades of such ratings is evidence of that failure, we do not yet have complete data on the incidence of default, so the full story has yet to unfold.

12. In my view, the main problem was the failure of the model-builders in the CRAs to attach sufficient probability to a generalized price decline in US housing, on the grounds that it had not previously occurred in the historical data set that they were using.

13. Ibid., Section 2.5:

> The CRA should separate, operationally and legally, its credit rating business and CRA analysts from any other businesses of the CRA, including consulting businesses that may present a conflict of interest. The CRA should ensure that ancillary business operations which do not necessarily present conflicts of interest with the CRA's rating business have in place procedures and mechanisms designed to minimize the likelihood that conflicts of interest will arise.

See also Section 2.8:

> The CRA should disclose the general nature of its compensation arrangements with rated entities. Where a CRA receives from a rated entity compensation unrelated to its ratings service, such as compensation for consulting services, the CRA should disclose the proportion such non-rating fees constitute against the fees the CRA receives from the entity for ratings services.

14. See also Daenen (2008).
15. See the Conclusion in CESR (2008a, p. 3).
16. There is at least one agency, Egan-Jones, working on this principle, and it now has SEC approval. The proprietors point to some good "calls" (though of course we do not know what bad calls they have made) and it seems to be making a profit. But the business may work only because it is tiny—few enough subscribers not to spill the beans, but too few analysts to provide comprehensive coverage.
17. This was noted by the Technical Committee of IOSCO in their September 2003 Report, pp. 13–14.
18. Requiring the CRAs to do this annually would help to resolve the tedious, and often unhelpful, distinction between "through the cycle" (TTC) and point in time (PIT) ratings. At issue the estimate of PD over the next few years would have to be, in effect, PIT, whereas the estimates over the longer run would revert to TTC, as would be both desired and expected. For a brief discussion of subsequent ratings' migration estimates, see the subsequent section on ratings transitions.
19. In the US, unlike the UK and most of Europe, mortgage lending is "without recourse," which means that once the lender has recovered possession of the house from a defaulting borrower, the lender cannot make any further claims on that borrower's other assets or income. So, when mortgage borrowers in the USA found themselves in negative equity, they would often walk away, posting the keys of the house back to the mortgage originator. Mail with keys in it jingled; hence the term "jingle mail".
20. <http://www.fitchratings.com/corporate/reports/report_frame.cfm?rpt_id=38310>.
21. See SEC (2008), pp. 67–9.
22. "A CRA should publish verifiable, quantifiable historical information about the performance of its rating opinions, organized and structured, and, where possible, standardized in such a way to assist investors in drawing performance comparisons between different CRAs."
23. "Credit Rating Agencies' Statement and Progress on Initiatives to Strengthen CRA Performance and Enhance Confidence in the Credit Rating Process," April 2008.
24. A credit default swap requires the protection seller, in this case the CRA, to pay over the nominal value of the bond in the event of that bond defaulting, to the protection buyer. The purpose of the exercise is to impose a financial loss on the CRA giving the rating, should the outcome of that class of bonds be significantly worse than the CRA had predicted.
25. As recorded in IOSCO (2008b), p. 13.

26. This needs some minor qualification: 15 per cent of CRA income comes from their general research activities which includes the work that would lead to ratings' migration. The CRAs regard this as an integral part of their (research) role. Even so, as long as it is not, and probably cannot be, a profit center for them, they do not have sufficient incentives to carry out this task.
27. The CRAAC would also have to propose a common numerical scale for PD ratings in order to be able to average the separate ratings.

References

Committee on European Securities Regulation (2005) 'CESR's Technical Advice to the European Commission on Possible Measures Concerning Credit Rating Agencies_05–139b.'

—— (2008a) 'CESR's Second Report to the European Commission on the Compliance of Credit Rating Agencies with the IOSCO Code and the Role of Credit Rating Agencies in Structured Finance.' CESR/08 – 277.

—— (2008b) 'CESR Consultation Paper: The Role of Credit Rating Agencies in Structured Finance.'

Daenen, P. (2008) 'Rating and Regulation: Current Turbulent Conditions Could be an Opportunity to Reform.' Paper presented at the Finlawmetrics Conference at Bocconi University, Milan (June 12–13).

International Organization of Securities Commissions (2003) 'Report on the Activities of Credit Rating Agencies.' IOSCO: Madrid, Spain.

—— (2004a) 'Code of Conduct Fundamentals for Credit Rating Agencies.' Technical Committee of IOSCO, Madrid, Spain.

—— (2004b) 'Public Comment on Code of Conduct Fundamentals for Credit Rating Sections 3.5 and 3.7.'

—— (2008a) 'The Role of Credit Rating Agencies in Structured Finance Markets.' IOSCO Technical Committee (March).

—— (2008b) 'The Role of Credit Rating Agencies in Structured Finance Markets: Final Report.' IOSCO Technical Committee (May).

Mason, J. R. and Rosner, J. (2007) 'Where Did the Risk Go? How Misapplied Bond Ratings Cause Mortgage Backed Securities and Collateralized Debt Obligation Market Disruptions.' <http://ssrn.com/abstract=1027475>.

—— (2008) 'How Resilient Are Mortgage Backed Securities to Collateralized Debt Oblication Market Disruptions?' New York: Hudson Institute.

Securities and Exchange Commission (2008) 'Amendments to Rules for Nationally Recognized Statistical Rating Organizations.' 17 CFR Parts 240 and 249b, RIN 3235 – AK14.

10

Credit Default Swaps: The Key to Financial Reform

Perry Mehrling

Sir, George Soros ("The false belief at the heart of the financial turmoil," April 3) suggests establishing a credit default swaps clearing house or exchange as an institutional mechanism for reducing counterparty risk in this $45,000 bn (notional) market. We have been here before also.

Walter Bagehot's *Lombard Street* explains how a bank's acceptance of a bill of exchange (in effect a CDS) turned an illiquid asset into a liquid one. The key to the system, as Bagehot made clear, was the central discount facility at the Bank of England. In Bagehot's time, the CDS was bundled with the bill, and the entire bundle was eligible for discount. In our time, the two instruments trade separately, and the CDS part has no access to the lender of last resort.

Perry Mehrling, Financial Times, April 7, 2008.

Commentary about the credit crisis has identified a wide range of culprits: faulty risk models (both at banks and at rating agencies) that relied on historical frequencies during a time of changing practice; faulty underwriting driven by the skewed incentives of the new originate-to-distribute model; faulty regulatory oversight based on imagined effectiveness of private policing of counterparty risk; faulty monetary policy that kept interest rates too low for too long, so sparking a credit-fueled asset bubble that was bound to collapse. Deeper causes have also been suggested: a regulatory regime that focused on capital adequacy and that did not encompass the burgeoning shadow banking system; a pattern of global imbalances that was sustained in the short run by sending the supposedly best dollar assets (Treasuries and Government Sponsored Enterprises, GSEs) to Asia, leaving a vacuum on the balance sheets of American and

European financial intermediaries that was filled by the new untested products of structured finance.

All of this commentary is well taken, but little of it goes to the heart of the matter. In my view, the current crisis is best seen in broad terms as a test of the brave new world that we have been building in the image of the theory of modern finance. Here is one early and remarkably prescient characterization of the world that could be:

> Thus a long-term corporate bond could actually be sold to three separate persons. One would supply the money for the bond; one would bear the interest rate risk; and one would bear the risk of default. The last two would not have to put up any capital for the bonds, although they might have to post some sort of collateral.

This is Fischer Black writing in 1970 and the world he is imagining is very much the world that has come to be, some forty years later. The instruments he is suggesting are what we know today as interest rate derivatives and credit derivatives, and more specifically interest rate swaps and credit default swaps (CDS). It is this world that is now being tested.

Credit default swaps were first developed, just as Fischer Black imagined, as a way of separating out the credit risk in a particular corporate bond. But nothing in the underlying technology prevented anyone from selling credit risk in this way even if they did not own the underlying bond referenced by the swap. This free-floating character of CDS proved to be important for market development. For one, it became possible to create a *synthetic* corporate bond simply by packaging together a riskless security and a CDS— such a bond was supposed to trade just as though it were the liability of the referenced corporation, though of course it was no such thing. Further, it also became possible to create *index* CDS that referenced an index of corporate bonds (such as the CDX index[1]), and so to trade generalized corporate credit risk exposure. Here again the swap was a derivative contract, a kind of side bet between consenting adults, not the liability of any of the referenced corporations.

All of this apparatus was developed first for single-name corporate bonds, but nothing in the underlying technology prevented it from being applied to other fixed income instruments. The most important extension in this regard was undoubtedly to so-called CDOs of Asset Backed Securities (ABS)—collateralized debt obligations issued against a portfolio of asset backed securities. Just as a corporation might fund itself with debt of varying capital structure seniority, ranging from AAA to BBB for example, so too a Special Purpose Vehicle could fund its holding of mortgage-backed securities by issuing securities with more or less senior claim to the cash flows of the underlying collateral. Once these securities were created, the credit risk on each tranche could be carved off and sold separately using the CDS technology. Indeed, CDS could be written that referenced a particular tranche even if the writer did not own that tranche, and such CDS could be used to create synthetic CDOs of ABS. Index CDS that referenced an index of CDO tranches from separate securitizations (such as the ABX index[2]) were the next logical development.

The ostensible purpose of all this technology was by making credit risk tradable to make it also cheaper, and hence to make the underlying credit cheaper and more available to the ultimate borrower. All indications are that this purpose was achieved, but it is important to understand how exactly it worked. The underlying securities were never very liquid, though corporate bonds were always more liquid than CDO tranches. CDS were more liquid than the underlying referenced instrument, and index CDS were the most liquid instrument of all. Thus, in terms of price discovery, we can think of the price of general credit risk as being determined in the index CDS market. This price then fed into the pricing of individual CDS, and then ultimately into the price of the underlying referenced instrument (BIS, 2008).

From this point of view, the market-making apparatus for CDS was of critical importance. So long as investment banks (such as Lehman Brothers) stood ready to serve as dealers in that market, offering to buy or sell at a reasonably tight spread, everything worked fine. And they were quite ready to serve, so long as there was an ultimate buyer of credit risk (such as American International Group, Inc.) willing to absorb any excess net exposure. In this way, the market-making apparatus facilitated a transfer of risk from the banking sector to the insurance sector, and everyone understood that. The problems came only when this market-making apparatus stopped working, specifically when Lehman Brothers was allowed to fail and AIG was placed on life support in September 2008.

It could be said, indeed it will be argued explicitly in what follows, that AIG should never have been in this business. By focusing its exposure on the super senior AAA tranches, it was in effect writing insurance against systemic risk, since the only time when truly AAA assets would ever be threatened was when the system as a whole was threatened. Only the government can deliver on such a promise, as we subsequently discovered. We can understand the Financial Stability Plan put forward by Treasury Secretary Timothy Geithner on February 10, 2009, as recognition of this fact.

From this point of view, the most important piece of the Geithner plan is the Consumer and Business Lending Initiative, which uses the Federal Reserve's Term Asset-Backed Securities Loan Facility (TALF) to support the AAA tranches of new securitized lending. The government is not writing explicit CDS, or even making explicit the credit risk exposure that it is absorbing. But make no mistake about it, from March 25, 2009, the government has taken the place of AIG as the ultimate buyer of credit risk, starting with consumer loans but expanding to mortgage-backed securities, starting with a target exposure of $200 billion but expanding to $1 trillion, or perhaps more as needed.

To be sure, the program is carefully tailored to limit the credit risk taken on by the government. First there is a "haircut" applied to the collateral offered, so that the owner of the collateral takes the first loss of approximately 10 per cent. The second loss is then absorbed by the Treasury using funds appropriated under the Troubled Asset Relief Program (TARP) legislation. But everything else, all the tail risk, is absorbed by the Federal Reserve Bank because its lending is explicitly "non-recourse." It might lend $90 against collateral value of $100, but in the worst case scenario it can recover only the value of the collateral. The haircut is there for moral hazard reasons, but it also makes sure that the government is ensuring only what it alone can insure, namely systemic risk. Implicitly the government is already on the hook for such risk. The TALF mechanism makes that exposure explicit, and charges for it, 100 basic points over the London Inter-Bank Offer Rate (LIBOR) on most TALF lending.[3]

So far the program covers only new securitizations, and that is a serious limitation. A large overhang of legacy securitizations remains on bank balance sheets as a continuing obstacle to financial recovery, and hence economic recovery as well. But, as noted by William Dudley, newly appointed President of the New York Fed, the TALF approach is very general. "In principle, it could be applied to other distressed asset classes... it could be used to fund older vintage assets."[4] That seems to be the direction in which we are heading.

The upshot is that the government is providing the ultimate credit insurance backstop needed to stabilize the system. In the short run, this buys time while we reorganize the market-making apparatus that supported the CDS market and hence also the securitization of mortgages and other types of lending.[5] The most important innovation in this respect is clearly the development of a proper clearing system for credit default swaps, which will increase transparency and reduce problematic counterparty risk. As of this writing (March 13, 2009) such a clearing system is scheduled to begin momentarily, and it will start (reasonably enough) with corporate CDS. In principle though, the same approach could be applied to other CDS as well. That too seems to be the direction we are heading.

To the extent that the market-making apparatus depends on an ultimate backstop for systemic risk, these new programs also represent the first steps toward establishing a permanent facility to support the brave new world that Fischer Black envisioned back in 1970. We have discovered a key weak link, and are now in the process of fixing that link for the future. Back in 1873, Walter Bagehot identified the weak link in the bank lending credit system of his own day, and proposed his famous Bagehot Principle for addressing financial crisis in that system: Lend freely but at a high rate of interest (Bagehot, 1873, p. 197). The modern system of securitized credit markets requires an updated principle: insure freely but at a high insurance premium.

Discovering the weak link

In its efforts to put a floor under the downward spiral that began in August 2007, the Federal Reserve soon found that standard interest rate policy did little, not even when augmented by a new Term Auction Facility (introduced December 12, 2007). It was only when the Fed announced its readiness to swap bona fide Treasury securities for private name mortgage backed securities that markets stabilized (technically the swap was structured as a collateralized loan). However the significance of this new Term Securities Lending Facility (TSLF, introduced March 11, 2008) was not widely noted, perhaps because it was overshadowed by the immediately subsequent failure of the investment bank Bear Stearns. Attention focused instead on the new Primary Dealer Credit Facility (PDCF, March 16, 2008) and on the unprecedented acquisition by the Fed of $30 billion of Bear Stearns' least attractive assets.

In the event, even this stabilization proved to be only temporary. On September 7, the Treasury nationalized Fannie Mae and Freddie Mac, in effect swapping Treasury bills for all existing GSE bonds, but also (and more significantly) taking over all of their mortgage guarantees in return for equity ownership of both entities. Subsequently the Treasury refused to step in to save Lehman Brothers, preferring instead merely to widen the range of collateral acceptable at both the TSLF and the PDCF (September 14, 2008) in an attempt to limit the fallout from Lehman's failure. But the fallout nevertheless soon brought down the insurance company AIG, and on September 16, 2008, the Fed stepped in to take over its wide-ranging book of credit derivatives in return for an 80 per cent equity stake in the company.

The significance of this new form of government intervention—credit insurance in return for equity participation—has not been widely noted, perhaps because it was overshadowed by the $700 billion "bail-out" proposed by Treasury Secretary Henry M. Paulson and turned into emergency legislation by Congress.[6] The ensuing political drama in which the bill was defeated in the House, resurrected in amended form in the Senate, and then successfully passed in the House (October 3, 2008) has framed most discussion of the AIG deal. No press accounts seem to have noticed, but the credit insurance dimension of the AIG deal is explicitly authorized in the legislation, in Section 102 "Insurance of Troubled Assets" which follows immediately after Section 101 "Purchases of Troubled Assets," which authorizes Paulson-style outright purchases.

A further reason that the emerging insurance dimension of government intervention has not been more widely noticed is that the most dramatic interventions since passage of TARP have been focused elsewhere. The Fed has been the principle actor, and it has more than doubled its own balance sheet in an attempt to substitute for frozen money markets, both domestically and internationally. In the domestic market, the Fed began paying interest on bank reserves, and subsequently excess reserves ballooned to over $500 billion. In the international market, an intervention of similar scale through currency swap lines with foreign central banks substituted for direct lending in private markets. Meanwhile, the Treasury abandoned plans to buy troubled assets, and instead embarked on a $250 billion Capital Purchase Program intended to recapitalize troubled banks, while the FDIC intervened to insure bank debt generally (not just deposits).

Notwithstanding all this, behind the scenes the Fed has quite clearly been muddling its way toward a kind of discount facility for CDS—in other words, a reinsurance facility for disaster risk—without perhaps even realizing that it is doing so. Since March 11, 2008 the Fed has been swapping AAA mortgage-backed securities for Treasuries, and since September 14, 2008 it has broadened that swap facility to encompass all investment grade debt securities; the risk exposure in such an operation is exactly that of a credit default swap. Back in March 2008 the Fed in effect sold credit insurance on the most toxic assets of Bear Stearns, while lending J.P. Morgan the money to buy the insurance. In the government's subsequent September intervention in Fannie, Freddie, and then AIG, the Treasury and then the Fed took over explicit credit insurance contracts written by others and accepted equity shares as payment. There can be no question that the government is in the credit insurance business.

Recently, the insurance character of certain interventions has become even clearer. On October 21, 2008 a new Money Market Investor Funding Facility was announced under which the Fed essentially provides a price floor at 90 per cent of amortized cost for highly rated money market assets held by Money Market Mutual Funds. This is insurance, and the premium is the difference between the primary credit rate charged to the Facility and the target Fed Funds rate, a difference of 25 basis points in March 2009, the time of writing.

Even clearer was the extension of the insurance structure to $306 billion of mortgage-related assets owned by Citigroup. In this deal, Citigroup paid an explicit insurance premium of $7 billion for a policy that has the following features: $29 billion deductible and 10 per cent co-payment for losses greater than that deductible.[7] A similar deal was subsequently used for $138 billion of assets held by Bank of America. Both of these were "interregnum" deals, put together to handle crisis situations in the period between the election and the inauguration. But they were important learning experiences, and they prepared the way for the more systematic plan that is now being developed under Secretary Geithner. The government is now in the credit insurance business for real. It began by taking over policies written by private parties who got into trouble, but now it is writing new policies.

What is needed now is recognition of why this kind of intervention has proven necessary and, building on that analysis, the construction of a less haphazard system for determining which insurance policies the government will issue and which it will not, in order to create appropriate tiering in the market. Whatever governments say *ex ante*, they may have to provide insurance *ex post*, as we have discovered. This is especially so in the case of systemic risk, because only the government can provide insurance against systemic risk. The crisis that we now face has its origin, in part, in the fact that private agents like AIG were writing (and mispricing) systemic risk insurance on which they could not deliver. And the continuing freeze that we now face has its origin, in part, in the fact that government has not yet fully taken on the task of writing systemic risk insurance. This is where government most needs to substitute for private markets, not just in providing liquidity to the money market.

So far, government insurance interventions have been focused on supporting individual institutions rather than markets, and on insuring specific portfolios of assets rather than general categories of risk. So far, government interventions have been focused on fighting fires rather than systematic intervention, and on the immediate crisis rather than permanent institutional reform. In this respect, a careful examination of how the system of structured finance works will make clear both why credit insurance is the answer to the crisis, but also why public credit insurance as a standing facility must be part of any lasting financial reform.

Brave new world

Suppose that a person buys a corporate bond and then engages in the following balance sheet entries (Table 10.1). Bracketed items are "mirror" bonds that offer the same cash flow as some other bond, but with a different counterparty.[8]

The second line represents a kind of credit default swap, in which Person 1 commits to make all the payments that the corporation makes on its bond, while Person 2 commits to make all the payments that the US Treasury makes on a bond of the same maturity. Thus, after the swap of IOUs, Person 2 is now bearing the risk of default on the corporate bond.[9]

The third line represents a kind of interest rate swap, in which Person 1 commits to make all the payments that the US Treasury makes on a long-term bond, while Person 3 commits to make all the payments that the US Treasury

Table 10.1 Credit risk transfer using "mirror" bonds

	Person 1		Person 2		Person 3
Assets	Liabilities	Assets	Liabilities	Assets	Liabilities
Corp. Bond					
[Treas. Bond	Corp. Bond]	[Corp. Bond	Treas. Bond]		
[Treas. Bill	Treas. Bond]			[Treas. Bond	Treas. Bill]

makes on a short-term bill (rolled over at maturity until the maturity of the long term bond). Thus Person 3 is now bearing the interest rate risk on the corporate bond.

Although Person 1 still holds title to the corporate bond, in effect he or she has swapped the cash flows on that bond for the cash flows on a sequence of Treasury bills. He or she is the one funding the corporate borrowing, but Person 2 and Person 3 bear the credit risk and interest rate risk respectively, just as Fischer Black imagined. If the bond defaults, then Person 2 is on the hook for the loss. If short-term interest rates rise above the fixed long-term rate, then Person 3 is on the hook for the loss. No matter what happens, Person 1 gets the return on a riskless Treasury bill.

Actual credit default swaps and interest rate swaps operate just like this swap of IOUs, except that the bilateral payments are netted. Market convention treats Person 1 as the "buyer" of a credit default swap, and the "buyer" of an interest rate swap, so we treat these long swap positions as assets and rewrite our balance sheet relationships as in Table 10.2.

This market convention can be a bit confusing since being long a swap means being short the associated risk exposure. It is thus helpful to think of the long swap as an insurance policy owned by Person 1. For Person 1, short positions in credit risk and interest rate risk exactly hedge the long exposures embedded in the bond, so the net exposure to both risks is zero. By means of the swaps, credit risk has been transferred to Person 2 and interest rate risk to Person 3. They are short their respective swaps, but long the underlying risk.

It is straightforward to extend this analysis to other kinds of fixed income claims, such as mortgages. In this case the interest rate exposure is a bit more complicated because of the right of the mortgage borrower to prepay—the system of MBS tranches was originally developed to manage this problem. Also the credit risk exposure is a bit more complicated because individual mortgages are so heterogeneous and small—the system of pooling mortgages into mortgage-backed securities was developed to handle this problem. (In practice, these two adaptations got a bit muddled, as the tranche system got used for default risk as well as interest rate risk. Clarification of this muddle is likely to be one consequence of the crisis—see Davies, 2008.)

Table 10.2 Credit risk transfer using CDS

Person 1		Person 2		Person 3	
Assets	Liabilities	Assets	Liabilities	Assets	Liabilities
Corp. Bond					
CD Swap			CD Swap		
IR Swap					IR Swap

The devil is in the details in these matters, and we can expect that many details will be revised as a consequence of the current crisis. For our purposes the important point to hold on to is that all this apparatus exists essentially to carve off the interest rate risk and credit risk and sell them separately. This is the brave new world of modern finance, and I take it as a maintained hypothesis that this world is here to stay, notwithstanding a certain amount of tinkering.

Counterparty risk

This system of risk distribution depends crucially on each of the counterparties fulfilling their commitments. For example, in the credit default swap Person 1 promises to make payments that match the payments on the underlying corporate bond. So long as Person 1 actually holds the bond, this commitment could be iron-clad, since it involves nothing more than transferring a payment received. But if Person 1 sells the bond, or even has the right to do so, then there will be counterparty risk.

Similarly, in the interest rate swap, Person 1 promises to make payments that match the payments on a Treasury bond. Here again, Person 1 is in line to receive exactly the same payments (as the other side of its credit default swap), but in this case the payor is Person 2 not the Treasury, so we can hardly say that Person 1's commitment is iron-clad since Person 2 may fail to pay. And there is the further problem that Person 1 might sell the credit default swap, so there is counterparty risk in this transaction as well.

In both cases, appropriate margin requirements might mitigate counterparty risk, and such requirements were apparently standard practice, although the details were subject to negotiation.[10] This is the "collateral" that Fischer Black imagined might be necessary in order to ensure performance. In practice, the vast majority of credit default swaps that were written were hedged with another credit default swap going the other way, and perhaps with yet another written on the immediate counterparty exposure. The result was a chain of linked exposures in which no one knew exactly what all the links were between them and the ultimate insurer.[11]

What was widely known was that, in general, the system moved credit risk away from banks, including investment banks such as Lehman Brothers, and onto the balance sheets of insurers such as the monolines and AIG (IMF, 2008, p. 79). Thus, when the crisis reached AIG, there was really no choice but for the government to step in. So many chains of linked exposures ended there that the cascade of defaults could not have been contained. The US government now stands behind all those chains, so there is no more risk that a failure somewhere in the middle can bring down the whole system.

But that is true only for existing contracts. Now that AIG is gone, there is no party writing new contracts at the base of the chain, and this poses a problem for the survival of the entire system of structured finance, which depended crucially on credit derivatives as a means of controlling risk. Credit derivatives were used to hedge underlying credit risk—you might have trouble selling your complicated CDO but you could always put a floor on your losses by buying credit insurance. And they were used to hedge the counterparty risk involved in the CDS contract itself. But the CDS mechanism only passes the risk along to someone else, and it only works if there is some place in the system where that risk finally comes to rest.

The lack of an ultimate insurer has produced predictable consequences. Everyone wants to buy insurance and no one wants to sell, so the result is upward pressure on the price of insurance. In a mark-to-market accounting system, that consequence has a way of becoming self-fulfilling since the rising price of insurance seems to indicate a falling value of the insured asset. And falling values only redouble the demand for insurance to put a floor under losses, and so the downward spiral proceeds. Note well that this channel of contagion depends not at all on irrational waves of panic, but only on the interlinked character of balance sheets.[12]

The point to hold on to is that, as in any scramble, liquidity can be a problem, and prices can be pushed rather far from underlying values. I take it that one of the central reasons for LOLR intervention is to set outer bounds for such liquidity-driven price distortions. The classic Bagehot Principle recommends lending freely at a penalty rate against collateral that would be good in normal times. The central problem facing us today is how to extend this principle to the instruments at the core of modern financial markets. It seems that we need a kind of discount window backstop for credit default swaps.

The Bagehot Principle tells us that the backstop can and should be expensive, but elastically supplied. Potential public exposure from such an explicit facility will be large, but no larger than the public exposure from our current haphazard implicit backstop facility. The government is the only body able to backstop systemic risk, and as such it will inevitably be called into service anyway. Better that we make this commitment explicit, and collect insurance premiums before the fact. That way we can force private actors to take account of the systemic consequences of their private actions.

Regulation and structured finance

Basel I (and II) requires banks to maintain capital reserves against their risky asset portfolio, in proportion to the riskiness of that portfolio. Critics always emphasized the pro-cyclical character of this regulatory framework. In good times, bank capital increases and so also does the bank's ability to expand its balance sheet, both by making more loans and by making more risky loans. In bad times, the same effect works in reverse. What the critics feared would happen is what in fact did happen.

Indeed, if anything, the critics *underestimated* the pro-cyclical character of the regulatory framework, because of the way that the capital adequacy regulations created incentives for off-balance sheet expansion. The consequence of these incentives was that effective capital cushions actually fell during the boom (leverage increased), as credit expanded on balance sheets that the Basel regulations did not reach. One possible direction for reform is to extend the Basel framework to include these new balance sheets—or equivalently to forbid off balance sheet activity (as D'Arista and Griffith-Jones propose in Chapter 7)—so it is important to understand why that extension has not been done previously.[13]

One way for banks to avoid the capital adequacy requirement is by doing their lending off balance sheet, by establishing a Special Purpose Entity (SPE) to hold the loans, which entity issues its own debt and equity to fund the holdings.[14] SPEs are not banks and so not subject to the Basel regulations. This loophole was intended, one supposes, to provide a way for new capital to finance banking activity without diluting existing ownership. It was imagined by the regulators that the buyers of the debt and equity would be long-term investors.

Table 10.3 shows how this worked. Mortgages are packaged into Residential Mortgage Backed Securities, with various tranches, and then those securities are further packaged into a CDO with various tranches of its own. To fix ideas, we can stipulate that the AAA tranche was held by banks and insurance companies, the AA tranche by pension funds, and the equity tranche by hedge funds.[15]

The balance sheet makes clear how this method of financing mortgage loans evades the capital adequacy restrictions of Basel. Indeed, that was its main purpose. When people speak of the "shadow banking system," they are usually emphasizing that capital adequacy regulations are no obstacle to expansion of mortgage (and other) lending. Indeed, quite the contrary, they provide an incentive to move that lending off balance sheet.[16]

Table 10.3 Regulatory arbitrage

	Assets	Liabilities
Bank	Mortgages	Deposits
		Equity capital
Special Purpose Entity	RMBS	AAA CDO tranche
		AA CDO tranche
		Equity tranche

The key point to emphasize is that, in practice, the credit default swap was absolutely key to making this system work. Regulators might look askance at a bank that was investing in CDOs, even the AAA tranche, but once AIG wrote credit insurance on that CDO it was deemed to pass muster (Union Bank of Switzerland, 2008).[17] The same concerns played out in a similar way for investors in the lower tranches, and the credit default swap was the grease that made the whole system work for a time.

CDS and system liquidity

Given this analysis, it is really not surprising that government intervention has increasingly taken the form of writing credit insurance, or taking over insurance contracts written by others. By providing this insurance, the government is in effect putting a floor under the price of the referenced assets, and so stabilizing the balance sheet of the institution holding the assets. Call this the Paulson-Bernanke CDS put.

The problem with the Paulson-Bernanke CDS put is that it is both too broad and too narrow, both too temporary and too permanent. It is too broad insofar as it provides a floor under the value of portfolios containing a very wide range of securities, and too narrow insofar as it is focused on portfolios held by particular market participants rather than on the markets themselves. It is too temporary insofar as it envisions no continuing support for markets, and too permanent in that it envisions long-term government exposure to the referenced assets.

The underlying problem is that the Fed is operating on the securities themselves, rather than on the relevant swap. No doubt one reason is a fear of supporting swaps that do not arise from any real funding operation—this is the modern equivalent of the ancient banker's idea that confining discount to "real bills," and avoiding "finance" bills, was the way to ensure safety. What is needed is a recognition that swaps are here to stay, and need their own discount facility.[18]

The general outlines of such a facility are clear, although there will be myriad operational details to fill in. The key point to appreciate here is that the risk in the AAA tranches of credit and their derivatives is not diversifiable; it is systemic risk.[19] It follows that government involvement in credit insurance should focus here. Perhaps we want a standing facility, with a rather wide bid-ask spread, in order to allow room for some private insurance of the first loss. The bounds of the facility might operate to make sure that insurance does not get too cheap, so facilitating an unsustainable credit expansion, but also that is does not get too expensive, so sparking a spiral in the other direction. The model, obviously, is the standing facility through which modern central banks provide liquidity to the money market. Like that facility, we could set the price as a policy variable, and change it according to changing circumstances.

In Bagehot's day, the bill of exchange was the significant instrument for short-term borrowing, and acceptance of the bill by a bank or bill broker provided a kind of credit insurance that made it possible to discount the bill for current cash. In Bagehot's day, the credit default swap traveled with the bill, and the entire package was the asset acceptable for LOLR discount at the Bank of England. Since Bagehot's day, we have learned the value of extending discount eligibility to long-term bonds—no one today argues "bills only." But long practice of confining central bank activity to government liabilities has gotten us out of the habit of thinking about credit risk as appropriate for discount. We have gotten over "bills only" but not "Treasuries only." The current crisis is forcing us to change, and rapidly, by adapting the verities of Bagehot's time to the new financial order of our own time.

Notes

1. The CDX indices are composed of CDS on the debt issue of an assortment of US corporate names.
2. The ABX index is composed of the twenty most liquid CDS on US home equity ABS.
3. Is this the right price? We'll have to learn from experience.
4. "Financial Market Turmoil: The Federal Reserve and the Challenges Ahead" (March 6, 2009).
5. This helps to put some perspective on the government's continuing engagement with the problems of AIG. It is not merely a bail-out, but rather an attempt to hold together the old system while a new and better system is being put into place. For details see the testimony of Donald Kohn, Vice Chairman of the Board of Governors, before the Senate Committee on Banking, Housing, and Urban Affairs (March 5, 2009).
6. But see Kotlikoff and Mehrling (2008).
7. This simple economic structure is unfortunately obscured by the somewhat convoluted structure of the deal, so that the insurance dimension is still not widely appreciated. After the first loss of $29 billion, the Treasury is on the hook for the next $5 billion only, the FDIC for the $10 billion after that, and the Fed for everything else. Further complicating the deal, the insurance piece was packaged with a recapitalization of $20 billion, funded from the Treasury's TARP funds.
8. The following explication of the economics behind the credit default swap owes inspiration to Duffie and Singleton (2003, p. 180). See also Lando (2004) and Meissner (2005).
9. It will be recognized that the Fed, by lending Treasuries for mortgage-backed securities, has in effect been behaving something like Person 2. The MBS are supposed merely to be collateral for the loan, so the credit risk remains in principle with the borrower not with the Fed, but if there are any problems with repayment the Fed is on the hook for the credit risk in the collateral.
10. In this respect, a key piece of the AIG story was its AAA rating, which allowed it to write CDS without posting collateral.

11. Here is the reason behind the push to set up a central clearinghouse to net exposures, or perhaps even an exchange to be the central counterparty to all CDS contracts (CRMPG, 2008; Soros, 2008, chapter 8).

12. One way to avoid this self-fulfilling death spiral is to avoid marking to market, but one man's "fair value" accounting is another man's "number juggling." Just so, observes Charles Morris (2008, p. 132): "Midquality subprime CDO tranches are carried at 90 at the Swiss bank UBS and 63 at Merrill, while the ABX, a widely used index of such CDOs, trades at 40. Similar indexes on CMBS, leveraged loans, and credit default swaps all suggest that internal marks should be much higher."

13. This is the general direction being pushed by the Financial Stability Forum.

14. Another way to avoid capital adequacy regulations is to do your lending on your trading account, where assets attract much lower capital requirements (as UBS, 2008). The analysis of this section applies directly to that case as well, and so is omitted. The practice of funding these trading account assets in the short-term money market by using them as collateral for repurchase agreements met the same fate as the SIVs.

15. The best available source on the system of credit risk transfer is the report of the Basel Committee on Bank Supervision (2008), especially Appendix A, B, and C. See also J.P. Morgan (2006).

16. This is the origin of proposals by FASB/IASB to require stricter accounting for off balance sheet exposures.

17. If the regulator continued to look askance, another way to avoid capital adequacy regulations was to set up a Structured Investment Vehicle to buy the AAA paper, funding the purchase by using the paper as collateral for issue of so-called Asset Backed Commercial Paper. In this way, the SIV created a short-term asset that could be bought by money market mutual funds, and so ultimately held by businesses, households, and government entities who were looking for a higher-yielding alternative to a bank deposit account. These SIVs also required a kind of insurance to make them work, most importantly a backup line of bank credit in case it proved impossible to roll over the commercial paper at maturity. These structures proved to be weakest link in the system, and as of this writing they have all been unwound, with the assets finding their way back onto the balance sheet of the sponsoring bank where they prove to be a continuing source of funding challenge. This is the origin of much of the trouble at Citigroup.

18. Even more, what is needed is recognition that the proposed Paulson-style outright purchase of troubled assets using Section 101 is in fact a kind of credit default swap, since the fund winds up long credit risk and short Treasuries. We could do the same thing more efficiently using Section 102.

19. See Basel Committee on Banking Supervision (2008, Appendix C) for details.

References

Bagehot, W. (1873) *Lombard Street, A Description of the Money Market*. London: H.S. King.

BIS (Bank for International Settlements) (2008) 'Credit Risk Transfer: Developments from 2005 to 2007.' Basel Committee on Banking Supervision ["Joint Forum"].

Black, F. (1970) 'Fundamentals of Liquidity.' Mimeo.

Claudio, B. (2008) 'The Financial Turmoil of 2007–? A Preliminary Assessment and Some Policy Considerations.' Bank of International Settlements Working Paper No. 251.

Counterparty Risk Management Policy Group ["Corrigan Report"]. (2008) 'Containing Systemic Risk: The Road to Reform' (August).

Davies, P. (2008) 'BIS Report Heralds Demise of Key Security Behind Subprime Crisis.' *Financial Times*, April 2.

Dudley, W. (2009) 'Financial Market Turmoil: The Federal Reserve and the Challenges Ahead' (March 6) <http://www.newyorkfed.org/newsevents/speeches/2009/dud090306.html>.

Duffie, D. and Singleton, K. J. (2003) *Credit Risk: Pricing, Measurement and Management*. Princeton, NJ: Princeton University Press.

IMF (International Monetary Fund) (2008) *Global Financial Stability Report: Containing Systemic Risks and Restoring Financial Soundness*.

J.P. Morgan (2006) 'Credit.' *Derivatives Handbook*.

Kotlikoff, L. and Mehrling, P. (2008) 'Bagehot plus RFC: The Right Financial Fix' (September 25) <http://blogs.ft.com/wolfforum/2008/09/bagehot-plus-rfc-the-right-financial-fix/>.

Lando, D. (2004) *Credit Risk Modeling: Theory and Applications*. Princeton, NJ: Princeton University Press.

Meissner, G. (2005) *Credit Derivatives: Application, Pricing, and Risk Management*. Malden, Mass.: Blackwell.

Morris, C. R. (2008) *The Trillion Dollar Meltdown: Easy Money, High Rollers, and the Great Credit Crash*. New York: Public Affairs.

Soros, G. (2008) *The New Paradigm for Financial Markets The Credit Crisis of 2008 and What It Means*. New York: Public Affairs.

Union Bank of Switzerland (2008) *Shareholder Report on UBS's Write-Downs* <http://www.ubs.com/1/ShowMedia/investors/shareholderreport?contentId=140333&name=080418ShareholderReport.pdf>.

199

11

Governing the Global Regulatory System[1]

Marion Williams[2]

This chapter is set against a background in which the regulatory world is grappling with the realization that its regulatory regimes have been less than adequate to cope with the fast changing pace of financial innovation, sophisticated securitization, and unfettered financial liberalization.

The existing regulatory system

A quick review of the existing system and its overlapping structures is useful to first set the current situation in perspective. There is no single international regulatory body in the financial world. The earliest institution which comes closest to being described as a global oversight body was the Bank for International Settlements (BIS). This was the first international (but not global) financial institution and was established in 1930. It originated after the First World War as a means of handling reparation payments imposed on Germany, but emerged into an international institution which focused on cooperation among central banks, though for many years it also comprised many non-banks as its members. For many years its representation excluded developing countries and emerging markets, and was principally European-focused. Currently, representation on its Board is from major European countries, US and Canada with three other members—China, Japan, and Mexico. Its fifty-five member central banks are mainly from Europe, whether significant or not, and from significant non-European emerging markets. In more recent years, membership of its subcommittees has been extended to include several emerging market countries. It retains, however, mostly a developed country focus, principally European. While attendance at its annual meetings includes all central banks, some developing countries have observer status.

The most influential group linked to, but separate from, the BIS is possibly the Basel Committee on Bank Supervision (BCBS), a committee that provides a forum for cooperation on banking supervisory matters. This Committee develops guidelines and supervisory standards. The Committee describes itself as being best known for its international standards on capital adequacy; the Core Principles for Effective Bank Supervision and the Concordat on cross-border banking supervision. The Committee's members were from Belgium, Canada, France, Germany, Italy, Japan, Luxemburg, the Netherlands, Spain, Sweden, Switzerland, the United Kingdom, and the United States, but have recently widened to include some emerging market economies. South Africa is the only African country on the Committee. Countries are represented either by their central bank, or regulator where the regulatory function is not performed by the central bank.

The guidelines set by this group have become international guidelines and are copied by many supervisors across the world. Financial markets, as well as the IMF and World Bank (through their conditionality), have tended to influence/push developing countries to adopt this standard even though they do not participate in its design. The Basel II recommendations that are presently being implemented by many countries were devised principally by this group.

Formal channels for coordinating with supervisors of non-bank financial institutions include the Joint Forum established in 1996. The BIS describes this forum as a senior group of supervisory standard setters. It includes the chairman and secretaries general of the International Organization of Securities Commissions (IOSCO) and the International Association of Insurance Supervisors (IAIS).

Other supervisory groups have developed to cater to geographical needs. For example, the Advisory Group for Bank Supervisors and Securities Regulators comprises securities regulators and bank supervisors of the APEC group (Asia) and ADB (Asian Development Bank) countries. Similarly, the Caribbean Group of Bank Supervisors performs this function for the Caribbean, while in Latin America the ASBA group (the Association of Supervisors of Banks of the Americas) performs this function for the Americas.

The International Monetary Fund (IMF), set up after the BIS, through the Bretton Woods agreement, was founded in July 1944. Originally comprising 45 countries, it played a key role in the international monetary system. The Fund itself notes that in an era of fixed exchange rates and the gold standard and in a context where many developing countries were establishing their own currencies and their own central banks, there was an important role for the IMF in providing lender of last resort (LOLR) facilities to many developing and developed countries. In addition to LOLR functions, it also provided and continues to provide an important economic and financial monitoring function through its Article IV consultations and, in more recent years, Financial Sector Assessment Programs (FSAPs), which review the wider financial sector beyond commercial banks and central banking. A third function, a technical assistance function has become a very important role of the IMF. The Fund has also been very critical in assisting the Heavily Indebted Poor Countries (HIPC) in obtaining debt forgiveness from their major creditors, and serves as a forum for intellectual discussions on the international financial system.

Several other international financial oversight entities have emerged, most with specific responsibilities or areas of interest. IOSCO is an organization of regulators of the securities industry which aims to cooperate in order to promote high standards of regulation, exchange information, provide mutual assistance, and generally protect the integrity of the securities markets.

Other international organizations have developed in order to promote common international standards in finance or related areas. Among these is the International Financial Reporting Standards (IFRS) body which issues standards adopted by the International Accounting Standards Board (IASB). Many of the standards forming part of the IFRS were issued by IASB between 1973 and 2001. In providing comprehensive guidelines for accounting professionals, auditors, financial managers and users of financial statements, this organization influences the balance sheet statement and reported income of financial entities and is therefore important in influencing what regulators see as the value of the assets and liabilities of financial entities.

The Financial Stability Forum (FSF) is of much more recent vintage. It was convened in 1999 and describes its objective as principally to promote international financial stability through information exchange and cooperation in financial supervision and surveillance by bringing together, on a regular basis, national authorities responsible for financial stability in significant international financial centers. Its first major initiatives related to offshore centers.

The FSF has made recommendations and calls for their implementation in financial centers of both emerging markets and in developing countries. The FSF has comprised in recent years 12 countries (G-7 plus Australia, Hong Kong, the Netherlands, Singapore and Switzerland) including related institutions in those countries and nine international standard setting organizations. The FSF Secretariat is housed in the BIS.

It has not included developing countries among its members, though all of the G-20 became members following the G-20's April 2009 meeting in London. At the meeting, it was agreed that the FSF would become the Financial Stability Board, and would have more power.

The Financial Action Task Force (FATF) is an intergovernmental body which describes its purpose as that of developing and promoting national and international policies to combat money laundering and terrorist financing. The FATF is a policy-making body created in 1989 that works to bring about legislative and regulatory reforms in these areas. The FATF has published forty-nine recommendations in order to meet these objectives. The FATF members were originally sixteen and now number twenty-eight. They comprise principally

European and North American countries with subsequent additions of Japan, Mexico, Singapore and South Africa. Several international organizations have observer status.

There are other relevant international regulatory organizations, among them the Committee on the Global Financial System (CGFS) chaired by the Vice Chairman of the Federal Reserve Bank of New York. This Committee monitors developments in global financial markets for the Central Bank Governors of the G-10 countries. The Committee sees itself as having a mandate to identify and assess potential sources of stress in global financial markets, to further the understanding of the underpinnings of the financial markets, and to promote improvements in the functioning and stability of these markets. The CGFS, formerly known as the Euro Currency Standing Committee, was set up in 1971, initially to monitor the currency markets, mainly the Eurodollar market, and principally the rapid growth of offshore deposit and lending markets. The Committee was renamed and its mandate revised in February 1999.

The Financial Stability Institute (FSI) is another arm of the BIS. Its primary role is to improve the coordination between national bank regulators through holding seminars and acting as a clearing house for information on regulatory practice.

The Institute for International Finance (IIF), a global association of private financial institutions, provides comment on international events and hosts seminars and conferences on financial topics on a regular basis, from a private sector perspective.

From time to time, other ad hoc committees are set up to deal with specific issues, for example, the Senior Supervisors Group comprising financial supervisors from five countries was set up to review disclosure practices of financial services firms concerning their exposures to certain financial instruments that the market considered to be high risk.

These groups sometimes coordinate with each other both through formal and informal channels, but the group with the most representative membership is the IMF, which currently comprises 185 members. However, up until recently, the IMF had not concentrated its resources on regulation of banks or on monitoring or evaluating the innovations in the financial system and exploring its implications. It is unclear whether it should increase its role in this area, as the BIS and FSF may be better suited for this role, if the latter's membership is expanded. Naturally, the IMF should play some role, especially in macro-prudential issues.

While the Financial Stability Forum is active, it tends to function in an issue-oriented fashion. It seems to have overtaken the role of the Committee on the Global Financial System, a Committee set up to monitor developments in global markets for Central Bank Governors of G10 countries, following concerns about the growth of offshore deposits and lending markets. The FSF, if it widened its mandate to continual monitoring rather than an issue-based approach, could come closest to the kind of entity which has the track record needed to coordinate regulatory and oversight functions of bank regulation, securities, insurance, accounting rules and payment system issues and monetary and financial stability issues.

There is an admission that there has been a dramatic increase in cross border flows, sovereign wealth funds, outward investment from developed countries and inward investment into North America from China and other developing countries and, more recently, in equity support from non traditional sources for financial institutions. Given this accepted interdependence, there is a basis for more meaningful international dialogue, with a greater role for developing and emerging countries.

This was recently recognized at a historic meeting of the G-20 held on April 2, 2009 in London, when it was agreed that the Financial Stability Forum would be expanded, given a broader mandate to promote financial stability and re-named the Financial Stability Board. It was given a stronger institutional basis and its capacity was enhanced. This was meant, among other objectives, to strengthen regulatory and supervisory capabilities, enhance global capacity to assess vulnerabilities, promote coordination and strengthen policy development.

The impact of innovation and the challenge for regulators

It is against the background of this regulatory framework and in the context of a philosophy of financial liberalization and integration of financial markets that innovative financial technologies took off. Financial technologies, however, rapidly went beyond the regulatory framework and it is now fairly well acknowledged that regulatory frameworks have not kept pace with financial innovation.

In recent years, advancing technology has allowed for far-reaching structural changes in global financial markets. Financial innovation has manifested itself in various ways, the most prominent being the growing importance of new and complex financial instruments, new business models which focus on multiple financial activities facilitated by financial liberalization, and significant developments in the area of securitization and disintermediation. This is compounded by the rising importance of relatively new, largely unregulated players, such as hedge funds, private equity firms, conduits and structured investment vehicles (SIVs). Financial innovation seemed limitless and regulators were left behind in the process.

This rapid innovation led to major structural changes in financial intermediation which affected the global financial system, and financial market activity had expanded at a tremendous pace. Simultaneously, the push for capital market integration and deregulation rapidly gained strength. According to McKinsey and Company (2008), global cross-border flows as a percentage of global GDP jumped from 4.8 per cent in 1990 to 15.4 per cent in 2005. As a result, the likelihood of contagion effects became even greater.

However, dependence on capital markets and on sustained market liquidity also increased (as discussed by Turner in Chapter 6), as banks and other intermediaries placed greater reliance on their ability to 'originate and distribute' loans and other financial products. They also depended on the market to manage their risk positions dynamically as economic and financial conditions changed, many through the use of credit derivatives.

This placed additional pressure on the robustness of financial market infrastructure to handle large changes in trading volumes and to cope with periods of strain. The coincidence of greater levels of deregulation and integration of capital markets implied that if a major problem arose it was more likely to spread quickly across borders.

Combined with strong returns in the capital market, the profitability of major financial institutions ballooned. This environment encouraged an increase in risk-taking as many players "hunted for yield." Estimates of the hedge fund industry note that the industry grew by leaps and bounds from $497 billion in assets under management in 2000 to $1,868 billion in 2007. Interestingly, the composition of the investors also changed.

Measuring risk where credit can be sliced and diced

The widespread use of structured credits effectively lowered the compensation for bearing credit risk and market risk to historically low levels. It was during this time that a market for bearing risk through complex structures of credit derivatives flourished. There were a few warning signals, particularly about hedge funds, but not many warnings about securitization generally. Regulators were caught napping and the rating agencies did not spot the weaknesses.

There are two aspects to this problem. One is the absence of oversight bodies which were monitoring and had authority to forestall this problem. The other was the absence of rules or processes that would help to prevent its occurrence. There was also clearly a need for internal corporate ground rules at the operational level. However, cessation of securitization as an investment tool is not an option. Securitization is here to stay. It is a critical factor in achieving financial flexibility in a world of global flows. However, it is important that credit originators bear greater responsibility for the credit worthiness of the credits they originate. Because of the difficulty of tracking risks in securitized loans which have been leveraged several times, loan originators should be required to take more responsibility, by keeping part of the loans and to suffer some penalty for failure of the loans they originate.

Concentration and risk management

Developing guidelines for risk management and requiring compliance to them are a core remedy for the concentration of risk. Developing internal risk management measures and processes at the level of the firm are very important. Portfolio concentration seems also to be an important area that requires attention. Both sectoral and instrument concentration are risk areas for which guidelines need to be developed.

Regulatory slips

In addition to the national oversight level, there were serious failures with global regulatory and oversight systems. The IMF did not see itself as having specific responsibility for these developments. The BIS—while it did see itself as an entity with some responsibility for the stability of the financial system, did not directly have regulatory tools—was a European-dominated organization, and most of its clients were not, at the time, experiencing problems to the same degree as in the US (that is less clear now). It did draw attention to the risks, largely in the area of hedge funds, but did not appear to display serious alarm and was perhaps too hesitant in requesting remedial measures from US regulators, in whose jurisdiction the problem was escalating most. Furthermore, the BIS does not have authority over national regulators.

The initiatives which had been taken in the late 1990s, when offshore centers were flourishing, and that gave rise to the FSF and the FATF did not replicate themselves with the same aggression nor lead to concerted action, as in the case of the offshore centers issue, nor did regulators evaluate the nature of the problem sufficiently quickly. Even in the case of offshore centers, it became increasingly important that both market participants and policy-makers improve their understanding and assessment of threats to financial stability, and take steps, where appropriate, to contain and reduce them.

The FSF and the IMF, with their emphasis on macro-prudential indicators and early warning systems, have recently been active in the development of models to identify and assess potential sources of major vulnerability to the financial system. This involves greater dialogue between regulators and practitioners, to better understand current approaches to measuring risks, and to encourage improvements and the sharing of best practices in stress testing techniques. The FSF lacks the network for so doing. The IMF has that network, but presently lacks the track record of analyzing financial markets, instruments, structures and flows with a view to quickly improving risk management techniques.

Size, market share and mega-financial institutions

The extent to which mega-financial institutions were at risk has become evident during the recent financial crisis. This has made it clear that there is a need to focus more on size, governability, adequacy of internal controls and internal information flow as increasingly important aspects of financial governance are conducted by oversight bodies of mega-banks. Some large banks have increased their capital by going to the market, some tapping into sources outside of their jurisdictions. There may be some issues here of too light a regulatory hand and over confidence in the role of the market. Responsibility rests with the CEOs as was evident in the firing of CEOs of large financial institutions in the US. It emphasizes that information flow, internal oversight systems, distributed decision-making and incentive systems that support good governance need to be an integral part of review by regulators, particularly so in mega-financial institutions where distance from the operation can be a problem.

Innovation, financial market development and monetary policy

The role for central banks in influencing macroeconomic outcomes has also changed as a result of the inter-connectedness of capital markets and the internationalization of financial flows. The development of deeper, more complete and more competitive financial markets has strengthened the pass-through effect of central bank interest rates to market interest rates, and has led to a closer relationship between market and bank interest rates. Consequently, the deepening of financial markets has served to amplify the effects of monetary policy on bank interest rates, and *ceteris paribus* other variables such as inflation.

However, a countervailing truth has also been evident. The major monetary policy transmission channel through bank lending has become less important, but new regulations are still focusing on the quality of bank credit. The widespread use of credit derivatives has meant that banks could respond more flexibly to changes in financial market conditions, and may therefore not pass through each and every change in the central bank's official short-term interest rate. Moreover, financial developments have not only broadened banks' options in terms of responding to interest rate changes; they have also broadened borrowers' financing opportunities, reducing their dependency on bank loans.

These developments have meant that there is a more urgent need for adequate amounts of data and regulatory mandate to provide policy-makers with sufficient ammunition to maintain financial stability. Indeed, in some jurisdictions, investment banks, the key institutions in this securitization boom fell outside the prudential purview of key financial regulators.

Measuring stability

Initiatives to build robust financial stability indices have thus far not been good enough or easily understandable by the market. Moreover, interpreting them with sufficient precision in order to focus in on remedial areas in need has been a fuzzy exercise.

The concept of financial stability involves various financial intermediaries, financial market segments and infrastructure, for which a whole host of different quantitative and qualitative indicators can be used. As a consequence, determining the degree of financial stability remains a highly integrated and complex task. It therefore means that the governance system which has responsibility for ensuring financial stability must be able to monitor information and analyze developments in several financial sectors and not just in commercial banks.

Recognition of the multi-faceted nature of ensuring financial stability contributed to the concept of a single regulator as evidenced in the establishment of financial services authorities in some jurisdictions and was intended to help to deal with the problem of the widening scope of financial transactions and interconnectedness. It is beginning to appear that it is becoming increasingly difficult for a single regulatory authority to fully grasp all the intricacies of securities regulation, insurance, banking, and derivatives use and all other financial institutional arrangements simultaneously. It seems, therefore, that not only greater depth of understanding by regulators in each specific financial area is required, but also more specialization, together with greater collaboration among regulators with a view to ensuring greater stability in the systems as a whole. As Stiglitz proposes in Chapter 5, the latter function could be performed in the US by a Financial Stability Commission.

The role of calculating the feedback effects between financial system behavior and the real economy has long been conducted by central banks on a national scale and by the IMF on a global scale. The latter still retains a very important role. The IMF may be well positioned to evaluate these effects, but it is not clear that it is best positioned to set regulatory criteria.

Therefore, there seems to be a role for an oversight monitoring body with multiple oversight responsibilities, but with the ability to access a wide range of inputs from various regulatory bodies with regulatory responsibilities. The bodies which come closest to this are the BIS and FSF, despite the drawback that they are not truly global institutions (but it is encouraging that that the G-20 committed in November 2008 to expand its membership). It is useful to note here that the BIS is in some ways the engine room of the FSF.

Given that feedback effects play a crucial role in assessing a financial system's vulnerability to contagion, and system-wide stress, vulnerability is an area that an international oversight body needs to concentrate on more intensively. Since this requires continuous monitoring and interactive dialogue and risk management skills, a joint FSF/IMF/BIS collaboration may be the best route.

Data availability and relevant data identification

With the exception of market prices and regulatory information, only a limited set of data is available in a timely manner and in a manner that facilitates international comparison. For instance, financial intermediaries' financial reporting contains little or vague information on risk transfer mechanisms, and the use of off balance sheet financial derivatives.

New regulatory issues can also arise either from the changing nature of the domestic financial system or the challenges arising from globalization and financial integration across borders. Therefore, the data needs for studying the latter problems need to be more aggressively analyzed and translated into data identification and reporting.

In addition, methods need to be devised for handling the shifting demand for data in an environment in which financial markets are constantly undergoing change. This is the regulators' challenge. At present, stability forecasting is often scattered with respect to risk categories, financial market segments and structural or regulatory issues. While every national regulator should be involved in this process, global recognition may be needed at the global level. This must not be confused with any doubts about the skills and knowledge of such special geographic groupings.

Central bank as regulator or financial services authority?

Having set guidelines, the issue of compliance is important. Over the years there has been a simultaneous shift from a direct and administered system to market-determined and marked-based systems of determining interest rates, exchange rates and other key financial variables. However, the regulator or policy-maker must still remain vigilant at all times to ensure that private owners and management of financial intermediaries operate within defined risk parameters, observe the standards, guidelines and codes diligently, comply with prudential regulations and norms, and follow the best corporate governance practices. The regulator who has responsibility for compliance may not necessarily be the regulator who sets the guidelines, since guidelines can span regulatory authorities. The need for coordination is therefore essential.

Even the role of governments in the process of underwriting balance sheets has been an issue. In the UK it was the government that gave assurances to depositors about the safety of their funds following the Northern Rock problem. In the US, the questions also arose around the issue of appropriateness of central banks bailing out financial institutions (which were not banks) and the use of funds which would otherwise be available to the Treasury. This issue of bailing out financial institutions which central banks do not regulate also has implications for reporting obligations and raises the question of the wisdom and practicality of a single regulatory authority and the moral hazard of an institution which regulates, but does not provide financial support, and the information and regulatory needs of the authority which does. It is noted that Northern Rock was regulated by the FSA but was bailed out by the Bank of England.

Importance of real time information

The use of technology to produce an updated management information system on a real time basis, and the re-engineering of business processes and systems, are the tools, which can help regulators to remain on top of the potential problems. In many instances, the ability to regulate effectively is also dependent on the robustness of governing legislation, rules and regulations, as well as the ability of legislators to act quickly in changing such laws and regulations.

Very often financial regulators and legislators take years to enact laws and regulations, while financial activity is changing rapidly. In this situation, the regulatory system can be made irrelevant in the face of fast-paced financial developments.

In this context, the content, characteristics, embedded risks and the accounting of the ever growing array of financial instruments, particularly derivatives, hedge products and similar products, as well as the risks they generate, have to be fully understood so that guidelines governing them may be revised and made relevant, and this has to be done quickly. However, while some of these rules may be set by securities regulators, it is banks which use securities. The absence of appropriate rules by securities regulators is affecting the stability of banks and near-banks who answer to different regulators, and who may need in extremity to be bailed out by the central bank.

Common standards and disclosure requirements

Regulators have to insist that there are common standards for valuation of assets and liabilities, with common yardsticks for measurement. However, it is not clear that these standards should necessarily be accounting standards. Transparency and disclosure standards have to be kept under constant watch and suitably upgraded so that the innovators are obligated to provide the full range of information required to evaluate risks. While the regulators should not stifle all financial innovation, they should have the capacity to understand the risks involved and disseminate them to the market participants. However, if innovations create danger of systemic risk, they need to be regulated.

The traditional approach toward regulation, which is mainly compliance-oriented with an emphasis on the review of portfolios rather than the evaluation of processes, has diminished effectiveness in the present dynamic landscape. The imperatives of market innovation demand a departure from the current predominant approach towards a more proactive approach that forces banks to recognize issues when they occur or, preferably, even ensure that the probability of their occurrence is known and the risks contained. This approach puts more emphasis on examining the bank's risk measurement and management processes instead of simply reviewing its assets portfolio. It demands that a bank's risk management processes should be scaled to reflect risk appetite and complexity of operations. Specifically, the bank which engages in more complex business lines should be expected to have in place credible internal risk measurement models and should assess and maintain economic capital adequate to cover the underlying business risks.

Capital adequacy

The emphasis on adequate capital has helped a great deal in the past, but cannot in itself ensure solvency and stability of the financial system in all situations. The prevailing Basel Capital Accord was an initial step towards achieving capital adequacy. However, there are some inherent rigidities which fail to cover many of the risks that banks assume in their business operations. This explains the shift towards less rigid capital adequacy concepts, which have however been undermined through regulatory capital arbitrage. The sub-prime crisis in the US is testimony to the effects of regulatory arbitrage and the impact of regulatory loopholes, which can occur in even the most developed financial system.

While the BIS has been the most proactive body in trying to stay on top of these aspects of risk measurement in the industry, it too has fallen behind. This could principally be because the BIS has been concentrating primarily on commercial banks, whereas many of the weaknesses in the financial systems had moved to the securities markets.

Measuring fair value

Accounting and bank regulation guidelines do not always coincide. Recent accounting mark-to-market rules of the IFRS are a case in point. Indeed, the role that mark-to-market accounting may have played in the evaluation of assets of financial institutions in recent months, and in hampering the ability of creditor financial institutions to organize workouts of debt with their customers, has been a matter of some discussion. Accounting rules tend to make the decision to reschedule or reorganize debt workouts a matter for greater provisioning by the financial institution, thus discouraging workouts and the long-term prospect of recovery.

In the recent US case, government intervened and mandated that some customers must be given time to reorganize their debts. However, accounting rules do not predispose to making arrangements with one's creditors. The verdict is out on how the Spanish solution of dynamic provisioning has solved the problem. The counter-argument is that these systems prolong the period over which debt is collectable and in the meanwhile might be misrepresenting the value of the asset. Discussion and dialogue with the accounting associations seem to be critical to resolving this problem which has the potential for preventing recovery of debt over the longer term. Regulators need therefore to work closely with international accounting standard-setting bodies to ensure that accounting guidelines do not aggravate financial crises.

Review of the Basel II Accord

The Basel II Accord was expected to eliminate some of prior-mentioned market anomalies, but also has serious problems. For example, the accord includes definitions for the measurement of operational risk and legal risk, but there is no definition or little interpretation for a major risk such as reputational risk. Still, Basel II covers a more comprehensive range of risks, and better aligns regulatory capital to underlying risks than Basel I. It also integrates capital requirement into a larger framework and provides for the role of supervisors in evaluating risk and market discipline. However, it may further encourage pro-cyclical bank lending, by putting rating agencies and banks' own models at the heart of determining capital adequacy.

Since it provides options to banks, it appears to encourage improvements in the risk management processes. Policy-makers have already realized the importance of this new accord, and presently it is in different stages of implementation across the globe. However, the implementation in itself demands even more concentrated efforts and capacity-building both by regulators and stakeholders. However, following the mortgage market sub-prime crisis in the US there are growing concerns about the advanced approach which gives banks flexibility to develop their own risk assessment systems, in light of what occurred in the investment banking community when these institutions had total autonomy to do so and failed.

The role of the market needs to be enhanced to discipline businesses indulging in excessive risk-taking. But this is not going to be an easy task nor will it be sufficient. This is especially true in the economies that have built-in safety nets which translate to negative incentives, and which hamper market discipline on the one hand and in turn encourage excessive risk taking by financial institutions on the other.

Moral hazard and market discipline

The usefulness of market discipline in augmenting the supervisory roles cannot be overlooked, but has to be reworked. While some safety nets are indispensable, we should seek ways to reduce associated moral hazard, and to perfect the market discipline framework to complement supervisory practices. Market discipline itself is, however, being questioned and it is becoming clearer that there must be penalties for inappropriate and risky behavior which threaten system stability.

Market discipline basically centers on responses to provision of adequate information and incentives for market participants to act in the interests of market stability. We need to identify the information that could enhance market discipline. This must include a requirement that banks entering the global arena need to meet international standards with respect to transparency and disclosure and face penalties for failing to do so.

Improved disclosure about the risk profile, risk management practices and performances, and related matters facilitates market discipline by enabling the market participants and supervisors to assess the soundness of a bank given the level of risks it assumes. The market assessment of the bank's soundness as reflected in the pricing of its products by the market could be used as an indicator for devising effective policy responses.

A great deal of effort has been put into the introduction of Basel II by the Basel Committee and in most organizations there is a tendency to protect one's creation. However, it is important that, given the questions that have been raised about certain aspects of Basel II in the context of the sub-prime crisis and the moral hazard of self assessment, the architects of Basel II revisit some of the major tenets of the new proposed regulatory framework, especially the advanced approach.

The role of ratings

In a Basel II regulated world, and in a world where market discipline matters greatly, ratings will become even more important. Ratings should reflect risk and prompt more responsible behavior by financial institutions which value their ratings and the investors who rely on them. This too has its challenges, since in many instances pricing is based on a risk rating, itself the product of analysis of information that has been provided to the ratings agency by the specific issuer. Following the sub-prime fallout, the validity of ratings, rating agency modeling, methodology and compensation have been called into question. Therefore, any enhanced program aimed at improving the governance of the global financial system may require some changes to the ratings infrastructure and the extent to which ratings reflect risk and are not overly influenced by massive corporate profits of high-risk institutions (see Chapter 9, by Goodhart). Indeed a special rating for risk may be appropriate—one that refers both to the risk in the firm and transferred risk—namely risk transferred by the firm to the system. There needs to be a series of major changes to plug the loopholes in the system and regulators need to ensure that they are as proactive as possible.

Global liquidity management

Over the past few years, the liberalization of the financial system has created the need for liquidity to be provided, not to governments through the IMF as was the case in the past through stabilization programs, but directly to financial institutions. The internationalization of finance and the existence of mega-banks emphasize the need for liquidity support across large financial institutions (see Chapter 6, by Turner). This may very well be beyond the capability of monetary authorities. There is a need to identify how this problem can be solved and how that liquidity can be provided before the problems occur. What is more serious is that where these problems are systemic and are not restricted to any individual bank, access to liquidity could be very problematic. This eventuality needs to be considered before it occurs.

Towards a revised global governance structure

The question of developing a multi-pronged over-arching monitoring body is an important factor in a revised governance system. The nucleus of this exists in the BIS, the FSF, and the IMF. Around the BIS there already are, in addition to the Basel Committee on Banking Supervision, several useful sub-committees, for example, the Policy Development Group which has a number of sub committees—on Risk Management and Modeling, Liquidity, Definition of Capital, Trading Book Matters, and Cross-Border Bank Resolution. The downside of this arrangement is the degree of possible tunnel vision since most of the subcommittees arose out of the Basel II Accord, which it now appears needs some modification in light of recent events. It also has problems of representation of emerging and developing countries.

The recently established International Liaison Group is the group with the widest representation, as it includes a number of emerging markets supervisory authorities. In addition, the existence of the Joint Forum which includes securities and insurance could form the nucleus of a multi-pronged monitoring entity. The issue here is global acceptability. Most of these groups, even the International Liaison Group—which has the widest representation—falls short of the international representation of an organization such as the IMF, which has 185 members. The question is: how much is lost in terms of global stability by the exclusion of these countries? Is their inclusion in the IMF—albeit even in a notional way—enough, or are they destined to continue to be excluded on the grounds that they are not systemically important? There seem to be losses, both in terms of efficiency and legitimacy, from such exclusion.

The Financial Stability Forum (now Board) attempts to function as a critical issues forum with representation beyond banking. This forum, which in April 2009 was finally broadened to all G-20 countries, includes a number of international financial regulatory organizations, including the International Association of Insurance Supervisors (IAIS), the International Organization of Securities Commissions (IOSCO), the International Accounting Standards Board (IASB), the Committee on Payments and Settlement Systems (CPSS), the IMF, World Bank, and BIS. The forum is not considered to be an arm of BIS, but is housed in BIS. This comes closest to being a multi-purpose oversight body, but lacks global representation and clear authority (though both aspects have shown some improvement in recent decisions). This needs to be remedied further if the forum wants to be considered an effective global body with the ability to speak to other countries with authority. The group, therefore, by reporting to the IMF would possibly be able to give itself some legitimacy. The report of the FSF of April 2008 on enhancing market and institutional resilience is an example of its work: a good analysis with general recommendations and with specific recommendations promised later. However, which entity will determine whether and how the recommendations are implemented is the key question? The IMF? The BIS?

Summary

This chapter attempted to analyze the international financial governance system, its strengths and weaknesses. In the course of the chapter, a number of issues were ventilated and a number of recommendations made. The chapter does not call for a total revamp of the financial governance structure, but rather for a number of improvements; including dealing with the issue of legitimacy and, also importantly, since some of these issues had been identified prior to the current difficulties, ensuring that systems and regulated entities accelerate their responses to the recommendations.

Notes

1. Paper prepared for Initiative for Policy Dialogue Task Force on Financial Market Regulation, July 1–2, 2008, Manchester University, UK, coordinated by Columbia University.
2. Governor of the Central Bank of Barbados.

References

BIS (Bank for International Settlements) (1988) 'International Convergence of Capital Measurement and Capital Standards.' Basel Committee on Banking Supervision (July).
—— (2006) 'International Convergence of Capital Measurement and Capital Standards– A Revised Framework.' Basel Committee on Banking Supervision (June).
FSF (Financial Stability Forum) (2008) 'Enhancing Market and Institutional Resilience' (April).
IASB (International Accounting Standards Board) (2001) 'The Framework for the Preparation and Presentation of Financial Statements.'
IMF (International Monetary Fund) (2009). 'Containing Systemic Risks and Restoring Financial Soundness.' *Global Financial Stability Report* (April).
McKinsey & Company (2008) *Mapping Global Capital Markets: Fourth Annual Report* (January).

Part III

Developing Country Perspectives

12
The Management of Capital Flows and Financial Vulnerability in Asia[1]

Yılmaz Akyüz[2]

Introduction

It has been more than a decade since a virulent financial crisis has devastated several East and South East Asian economies with excellent track records in economic development and macroeconomic stability. The crisis was generally considered the outcome of a combination of misguided capital account and exchange rate policies, coupled with overreaction of foreign lenders and investors to temporary shortfalls in international liquidity, rather than vulnerabilities emanating from structural payment imbalances and excessive external indebtedness. There is now almost a collective determination across the region never to allow a repeat of the crisis. There is also an increased awareness that vulnerability to financial contagion and shocks depends in large part on how capital inflows are managed, and that governments may have limited options in addressing the sudden stops and reversals that often mark short-term capital flows.

As the current global financial crisis brews, it is natural to ask how it will affect emerging markets, especially those in Asia. How have the changes in global financial markets and emerging markets affected their vulnerability? The first draft of this chapter was written before the calamitous events of September 2008. In early 2008, there was much discussion of decoupling, that the problems in the United States would not spread to Europe. Part of that hope was that the emerging markets, especially those in Asia, were sufficiently robust that their growth would be sustained and that growth would, in turn, sustain global growth. Many of the countries had instituted regulatory reforms. Some of these reforms had involved strengthened regulation, but some, following the prevailing "conventional wisdom," had liberalized. Some feared that the liberalization measures would make them more vulnerable while others hoped that the increased reserves and regulatory reforms would enable these countries to withstand the global storm. By late 2008, it was clear that this hope would not be realized. The crisis had spread to emerging markets. This chapter helps explain why the policies pursued in the past decade may have made Asia's financial markets less vulnerable to the problems that afflicted the region a decade ago, but perhaps more vulnerable to the kind of shock that confronted the global economy in 2008.

The recurrent currency, balance of payments, and financial crises in emerging markets, including the 1997 Asian crisis, suggest that there are at least four areas of vulnerability associated with surges in capital flows: (i) currency and maturity mismatches in private balance sheets and especially those of financial institutions; (ii) credit, asset and investment bubbles; (iii) unsustainable currency appreciations and external deficits; and (iv) reliance on the International Monetary Fund (IMF) for help and policy advice rather than self-insurance against sudden stops and reversals of capital flows.[3] These lessons for crisis prevention—namely, the need to prevent fragility in private balance sheets and external payments, to check financial and investment bubbles, and to build adequate self-insurance at times of surges in capital inflows—appear to be widely held among the policy-makers in the region, including by countries not directly hit by the 1997 crisis.

After a brief interruption, capital flows to emerging markets recovered strongly in the earlier years of this decade, growing constantly and, in recent years, surpassing previous peaks. Asia has been among the main recipients. These flows have been greatly influenced by the very same factors that led to a surge in speculative lending in the United States and elsewhere in the developed world—notably, ample global liquidity resulting from a policy of easy money and search for yield. With the bursting of the sub-prime bubble, these flows have declined drastically and have even been reversed in several cases, and many emerging markets have become vulnerable to financial shocks and contagion in different ways and degrees.

This chapter discusses the management of the recent surge in capital flows in Asia with the aim of identifying existing financial fragilities and vulnerabilities to external financial shocks, notably the current turbulence triggered by the sub-prime crisis. Particular attention is paid to China and India because together these countries account for about four-fifths of the total output and two-thirds of the total trade of developing countries in the region. Examining the volume and composition of capital inflows and capital account regimes, the chapter shows that in recent years Asian policy-makers did not generally opt for tighter restrictions over capital inflows as a means of reducing the likelihood of a repeat of the 1997 crisis. In fact, Asian capital accounts are invariably more open today than they were during the 1997 crisis—with few exceptions, they are almost fully open to non-residents and have become increasingly open to residents.

Rather than applying tighter counter-cyclical restrictions over capital inflows, most countries in Asia have chosen to relax restrictions over resident outflows and to absorb excess supply of foreign exchange by intervention and reserve accumulation. In this way, most of them have successfully avoided unsustainable currency appreciations and payments positions, and accumulated more than adequate international reserves to counter any potential current and capital account shocks without recourse to the IMF. However, they have not always been able to prevent capital inflows from generating asset, credit and investment bubbles or to improve the resilience of domestic financial markets to adverse spillovers and contagion from financial instability abroad. These policies now expose them to certain risks, but not necessarily of the kind that hit the region in the 1990s.

Recent capital flows to Asian emerging markets

Beginning in the early years of the decade, the world economy went through a period of easy money policy as interest rates in major industrial countries, notably the United States and Japan, were brought down to historically low levels and international liquidity expanded rapidly.[4] These, together with stagnant equity prices in most mature markets, led to a search for yield by creditors and investors and played a major role in the strong recovery of capital flows to emerging markets. After falling to some $100 billion at the beginning of the millennium, private flows picked up rapidly reaching $929 billion in 2007 before falling drastically to an estimated level of $465 billion in 2008 (Table 12.1).[5]

The increase until 2008 was accompanied by a rapid narrowing of spreads on emerging-market sovereign debt. The average spread, which had climbed to 1,400 basis points after the Russian crisis and fluctuated between 600 and 1,000 basis points during the early years of the millennium, fell constantly from mid-2002 onwards reaching 200 basis points in the first half of 2007.[6] It started to edge up in 2008 with the deepening of the sub-prime crisis, exceeding 400 basis points at the end of the year (IMF, 2008a, Box 1.1).

The strong and favorable global "push" factors explain why recovery in private capital flows has been broad-based. But country-specific conditions (the pull factors) explain why inflows have been stronger in certain parts of the developing world than in others.[7] International financial markets have not always differentiated among countries with respect to economic fundamentals (such as growth and price stability, and external payments, debt or reserve positions), but focused occasionally on opportunities for short-term capital gains and arbitrage profits.

Such flows can be divided into three categories which assume different importance in different parts of the world. The first category is capital attracted

Table 12.1 Private capital flows, current account balances and changes in reserves in emerging markets[1] ($ billion)

	Private Capital Flows					Current Account Balance					Reserve Increases				
	2004	2005	2006	2007	2008	2004	2005	2006	2007	2008	2004	2005	2006	2007	2008
Emerging markets	348.8	519.6	564.9	928.6	465.8	150.2	274.1	383.9	434.0	387.4	398.2	442.2	554.8	948.7	444.3
Asia	165.6	220.5	258.9	314.8	96.2	115.2	181.0	289.5	420.2	386.4	296.1	270.6	337.5	587.8	373.1
Latin America	41.8	70.0	51.5	183.6	89.0	22.3	41.1	54.4	27.2	0.3	22.5	29.7	49.3	129.1	36.8
Europe	131.1	204.1	226.3	392.8	254.2	5.7	35.8	24.9	-23.5	-29.8	60.8	116.5	130.7	193.5	25.5
Africa/ Middle East	10.4	25.0	28.2	37.4	26.4	6.9	4.0	15.1	10.1	30.5	18.7	25.5	37.3	38.3	8.9

[1] 2008 data are estimates.
Source: Institute for International Finance.

by carry trade profits due to large interest rate differentials with industrial countries, notably Japan, of which highly-leveraged hedge funds have been among the main beneficiaries.[8] The second category is capital inflows seeking gains from prospective currency appreciations in countries with undervalued exchange rates and large current account surpluses, notably China. The third category is investment in asset markets, which has been a common feature of capital flows to emerging markets in different regions.

It is notable that during 2004–8 emerging markets in Central and Eastern Europe received more foreign private capital than those in Asia, even though their total income is one-fifth of the total income of Asia. In several countries in that region, the combination of high interest rates with floating exchange rates has resulted in currency appreciations and growing current account deficits which reached on average 7.1 per cent of GDP in 2008 (IMF, 2008, Table A12). High interest rates in some larger emerging economies (e.g. Turkey and Brazil) attracted large amounts of capital linked to carry trade. There have also been considerable intra-regional carry trade activities in these regions where funds borrowed in low interest currencies have been invested in the same region in higher interest currencies. High local interest rates have also attracted international investors to domestically issued local currency debt, as these investors have become more willing to assume the exchange rate risk in return for much higher yields.[9]

In gross terms, capital inflows to Asia as a proportion of GDP have been close to historical highs, but in net terms they have been around the long-term average due to increased resident outflows (IMF, 2007b; IIF, October 2007). The share of equity investment in total private capital inflows has been higher in Asia than in most other regions. Since 2003 more than two-thirds of these equity inflows to Asia have been in direct equity and one-third in portfolio equity.[10] Equity flows have been particularly strong in China and, more recently, India. But most of India's equity investments have been portfolio rather than foreign direct investment (FDI). This is also true for Malaysia where cumulative portfolio inflows between 2002 and 2007 were nine times the cumulative inflows of FDI (Khor, 2008).

Following the cutback in bank lending after the 1997 crisis, international bank inflows to Asia started to exceed repayments in the early years of the decade. While restrictions on foreign participation in domestic bond markets have generally been maintained, in countries such as Malaysia and Indonesia there have been marked increases in foreign holding of local currency debt instruments. In the region as a whole, local claims of foreign banks including local bond holdings, as a percentage of all foreign banks' claims, more than doubled since the beginning of the decade.

While capital flows to emerging markets as a whole fell by one-half between 2007 and 2008, the decline in Asia was more marked, having fallen by more than two-thirds (Table 12.1). Although direct investment flows remained relatively resilient, due to the deepening of the credit crunch in the United States and Europe, there was a sharp drop in commercial bank credits (from $156 billion to an estimated $30 billion) and this is expected to turn negative in 2009 (IIF, January 2009). Net portfolio equity flows to Asia, including outflows by residents, were already negative in 2007 and they are expected to have become even bigger in 2008, reaching $55 billion.[11] Redemption by highly leveraged hedge funds from the United States and United Kingdom appears to be an important reason for this expected increase. These institutions were very active in Asian equity markets in the earlier years, with assets managed by them being estimated to have grown sevenfold between 2001 and 2007. These institutions have been hit hard by the crisis, and their de-leveraging appears to be a main reason for the exit of equity portfolio investment, not only from Asia, but from emerging markets as a whole.[12]

Credit, asset, and investment bubbles

Vulnerability to a sudden stop and reversal of capital flows is often assessed on the basis of short-term external foreign-denominated liabilities.[13] Thus the increased fraction of capital inflows to Asian emerging markets in the form of equity (as well as local currency debt) is generally considered to be more favorable to stability because with foreign investment in equity and local currency debt the exchange rate risk is assumed by investors.

However, for vulnerability what matters is not simply currency denomination but also liquidity of liabilities. A move by non-residents away from domestic equity and bond markets could create significant turbulence in currency and asset markets with broader macroeconomic consequences, even though losses from asset price declines and currency collapses fall on foreign investors.[14] This potential source of instability naturally depends on the relative importance of foreign participation in local financial markets. Extensive foreign participation raises exposure to adverse spillovers and contagion from financial instability abroad. The increased correlation between global and emerging-market equity returns since 2004 is consistent with financial market integration and the increased exposure to such spillovers.[15]

Figures for *net* equity inflows understate the rapid increase of foreign presence in Asian equity markets because, as noted, there has also been a rapid growth of resident outflows—and it is this increased foreign presence, together with the liberalization of resident outflows, which generates the increased vulnerability. Available evidence shows that non-resident holding of Korean equities reached almost one half of market capitalization (McCauley, 2008). In China, foreign share as a per cent of market capitalization rose from 2.5 per cent in 2001 to 23.2 per cent in 2006, and in India from 6.6 per cent to 10 per cent in the same period (BIS, 2009, Table E1). According to a recent study on foreign net purchases and net sales of equities in Asian markets, the share of foreigner transactions in 2005 in average daily turnover was around 20 per cent in Korea, 30 per cent in Thailand, and 75 per cent in Taiwan (China).[16]

There is also strong evidence that foreign investors tend to move in and out of some of the different Asian markets simultaneously. This may be because of "bandwagon effect"—foreign investors' perceptions of various Asian markets move together, and seeing some investors move into or out of one Asian country, others investors do not want to be left behind; or because of correlated changes in returns to Asian markets.[17]

For most of the countries in the region, equity inflows appear to have been driven not so much by gains from anticipated currency appreciations as by local market returns. However, a relatively large proportion of financial inflows to China appears to have been motivated by expectations of appreciation of the yuan (Setser, 2008; Yu, 2008). Some of these are reported to have entered the country through over-invoicing of exports. According to some market participants, the "hot money" amounted to $5–10 billion a month during 2007 (Anderlini, 2007).

Large capital inflows to equity markets—together with the consequent expansion of liquidity resulting from, inter alia, incomplete sterilization of currency market interventions, discussed below—have been both the cause and effect of sharp increases in stock prices in several Asian markets.[18] This is also suggested by a strong correlation between changes in net portfolio equity flows and stock prices in Asia—much stronger than that observed in Latin America (IIF, October 2007, chart 13). For the region as a whole, the equity market index increased by almost fourfold between 2002 and 2008, with increases exceeding 500 per cent in China and India. The price/earnings ratios also rose rapidly until 2008, and seemed unrelated to improvements in underlying fundamentals—suggesting a bubble in the making (IIF, March 2005, p. 4). China increased the stamp duty on stock market transactions in order to restrain the bubble, only to reverse it after the decline resulting from the fallout from the sub-prime crisis. Indeed, the bubble has now burst with equity prices in China and India losing almost half of their values in 2008 due to global retrenchment in risk appetite and exit of foreign capital from emerging market funds.

The two largest countries, China and India, which have seen the strongest surge in capital inflows and the largest increases in stock prices, have also experienced a boom in the property market. Again, liquidity expansion resulting from capital inflows and foreign demand for property played an important role. During 2002–6 in real terms residential property prices rose by over 8 per cent per annum in China and 10 per cent in India.[19] In these countries the price-to-rent ratio rose by more than 20 per cent during the same period. There was also an acceleration of property price increases in Korea (15 per cent), Singapore, and Vietnam during 2006–7. While these were not as dramatic as increases in the United States—where the price-to-rent ratio rose by 30 per cent over the same period—there are large pockets in China, India, Korea, and the Philippines where increases were comparable and even greater.[20] In some cases, house prices also outstripped strong growth in incomes.[21]

These booms in property markets too are now coming to an end. In China, house prices declined in December 2008 for the first time since the government started releasing the data in 2005, and urban fixed asset investment has been falling since September 2008. The government is now taking measures to revive the property market (Forbes.com, 2008; Xinhuanet, 2009a). In Korea, the slump that started in 2008 is now threatening to set off a process of debt deflation, reminiscent of the 1997 crisis when housing prices fell by some 13 per cent (Citigroup, 2009).

Such boom–bust cycles in asset markets generate considerable instability in economic activity. There is evidence, not only from industrial countries, but also from a number of Asian emerging markets, including Hong Kong (China), Indonesia, Korea, Malaysia, the Philippines, Singapore, and Thailand, that asset booms (defined as periods in which asset prices exceed their trend by more than 10 per cent) significantly raise the probability of output being eventually pushed below its potential level and the price level above its trend with the bursting of the bubble (Gochoco-Bautista, 2008). This implies that monetary and capital account policies should not neglect developments in asset markets since their longer term consequences may undermine economic stability and growth. That is, of course, precisely what happened in the United States and elsewhere.

Rapid domestic credit expansion and low interest rates have played an important role in bubbles in equity and property markets in Asia. As in some mature economies, monetary policy has been highly expansionary and real policy interest rates have been considerably lower than those in other regions. However, the surge in capital flows is part of the reason for rapid expansion of liquidity since interventions in foreign exchange markets could not be fully sterilized. After 2003, private credit growth in real terms reached nearly 9 per cent per annum in China and 5 per cent in other countries.[22] The failure to adequately regulate and control capital inflows thus was an integral part of the macroeconomic story.

The ample liquidity not only fed into asset prices, but translated, especially in the case of China, into investment levels that may not be sustained over the longer term with the return to normal financial conditions.[23] This increase appears to have been associated with considerable excess capacity and wastage of capital: 40 per cent of China's state-owned industrial enterprises are reported to have been running losses and facing declining rates of return on capital (BIS, 2007, p. 56). It is expected that in the event of a sharp upward adjustment in the exchange rate and a severe downturn in exports, the capacity built in some industries may become unviable, with attendant consequences for the banking system.[24]

Current account balances, exchange rates, and reserves

While major Asian emerging markets have not been able to prevent capital inflows from making an important contribution to asset and investment bubbles, they have been more successful in managing their impact on exchange rates and the current account. Developing countries of the region taken together had a current account surplus of 7 per cent of GDP in 2007 and over 5 per cent in 2008, up from 1.5 per cent in 2001. This is largely due to China's strong export performance, but a number of other countries have also been enjoying surpluses. By contrast India, Pakistan, and Vietnam have been running growing current account deficits since 2006, while Korea started to run deficits on its current account in 2008 for the first time since 1997 (IMF, 2008, table A12), and these are expected to widen further in coming years with the severe downturn in the world economy.

Since the Asian crisis, several countries in the region have moved towards more flexible exchange rate arrangements. But they have followed various shades of managed floating rather than leaving their currencies entirely to the whims of international capital flows. Most countries have strived to absorb excess supply of foreign exchange generated by strong capital inflows and/or current account surpluses in reserves through interventions in foreign exchange markets, rather than allowing them to push up currencies to unsustainable levels and undermine their trade performance. To keep liquidity expansion and inflation under control, attempts have been made to sterilize such interventions, mainly by issuing government and/or central bank debt and by raising reserve requirements in the banking system, and these attempts appear to have been reasonably, though not fully, successful.[25] In China, where for much of the early years of this decade the worry was about deflation, capital inflows did not lead to inflation in goods and services, but, as noted earlier, contributed to the increases in asset prices.

There have been relatively sizeable appreciations in some countries, but these are moderate in comparison with those in other emerging markets where exchange rates are left to float. Moreover, appreciations in Asia have occurred under much more favorable current account positions and faster economic growth.[26]

In China, government control over the financial system has allowed it to keep the fiscal cost of intervention down.[27] Reserve requirements of banks were constantly raised from 7 per cent in 2003 to 17.5 per cent in 2008, and banks have come to hold over 80 per cent of central bank securities issued for that purpose, with their share in total bank assets exceeding 20 per cent (Yu, 2008; BIS, 2009, box D4). In India the cash reserve ratio was also increased in several steps, from 4.75 per cent in 2003 to 7.5 per cent in 2008, but because of higher interest rates, the cost of intervention is reported to have reached 2 per cent of GDP in 2007—more than half of the central government deficits.[28]

Table 12.2 Current account and reserves[1] ($ billion)

	Asia	China
Reserves		
2008	2,830.4	2,201.3
2001	379.5	216.3
Increase	2,450.9	1,985.0
Current account 2002–08[2]	1,458.9	1,331.8
Borrowed reserves 2002–08[3]	992.0	652.3
Import coverage[4]		
2001	4.9	6.6
2008	9.4	13.8

[1] 2008 data are estimates.
[2] Cumulative current account balance over 2002–8.
[3] Difference between increases in reserves and cumulative current account balance over 2002–8.
[4] Months of imports covered by reserves.
Source: International Monetary Fund (2008).

As of the end of 2008, total reserves in developing Asia (excluding Newly Industrialized Economies, NIEs) exceeded $2.2 trillion and 86 per cent of these were generated after 2001 (Table 12.2).[29]

Asian reserves now account for more than half of total reserves of the developing world. The twin surpluses that the region as a whole has been running on its balance of payments (that is, on both current and capital accounts) have been fully converted into reserves.[30] Of the $2.4 trillion reserves accumulated after 2001, 60 per cent are earned from current account surpluses. The rest is accumulated from capital inflows; that is, they are "borrowed" in the sense that they accompany increased claims by non-residents in one form or another, including direct and portfolio equity investment, which entail outward income transfers. This stands in sharp contrast with most other regions where reserve increases came mostly from capital inflows. However, excluding China, almost three-quarters of Asian reserves in recent years were also from capital inflows. In countries running current account deficits, such as India, reserves are 100 per cent "borrowed."

Asian reserves are greater than required for preventing a crisis, under the Greenspan-Guidotti rule noted above. They are several times the total short-term external debt of the region, which stood at around $400 billion at the end of 2008, and more than twice the total external debt of some $1,160 billion (IMF, 2008, tables B21–22). They now cover more than nine months of imports, much higher than the three months of imports traditionally considered as adequate for addressing the liquidity problems arising from time lags between payments for imports and receipts from exports.

A policy of accumulating reserves at times of strong capital inflows and using them during sudden stops and reversals might appear to be a sensible counter-cyclical response to instability in international capital flows. By intervening in the foreign exchange market and accumulating reserves, a country facing a surge in capital flows can both reduce its external vulnerability by preventing appreciations and trade deficits—or at least reducing their magnitudes—and secure self-insurance against possible speculative attacks. In other words, if inflows are believed to be temporary, at first blush, it might be rational to resist an inward transfer that would result in an increase in domestic consumption and/or investment.[31] However, such a strategy implies that a country is borrowing from abroad to buy short-term foreign assets—which typically yield a lower return than the borrowing costs[32]—in order to pay back the lenders and investors when they exit.

In previous decades the current account in Asia was generally in deficit so that a very large proportion of reserves held at the beginning of this decade was "borrowed" rather than earned reserves. If this is added to reserves accumulated from capital inflows since 2001, about half of the total stock of reserves in Asia now would be "borrowed" reserves. This is a little more than the existing stock of external debt of the region. Assuming a moderate 500 basis point margin between the interest cost on debt and the return on reserves, this would give an annual carry cost of some $60 billion for the region as a whole.[33] This is how much the region as a whole could save per year by paying up its external debt by drawing on reserves.[34]

Some Asian central banks appear to have invested an important part of these reserves in debt issued by the United States Government Sponsored Enterprises, including mortgage firms Fannie Mae and Freddie Mac.[35] Had the United States government not bailed out these institutions, losses would have been severe.[36] Moreover, should the dollar come under pressure, countries with a large stock of dollar reserves stand to incur considerable exchange rate losses.

The high carry cost of reserves in excess of possible liquidity needs, together with the risk of exchange rate related losses, raise the question of alternative investments in higher yielding foreign securities, as done by several fuel exporters and Singapore through sovereign wealth funds (SWFs). Like China, fuel exporters as a group also generate large current account surpluses, but unlike China, they run deficits in their capital accounts. About two-thirds of oil surpluses generated since 2002 have been used for reserve accumulation and one-third for investment abroad. Many of these have recently been acquiring high-risk equity in Western banks hit by the sub-prime crisis, thereby acting as a global force for stability while suffering significant losses.

SWFs in fuel exporters and Singapore are established from earned reserves and fiscal surpluses except that in the former case reserves are directly acquired by the government from oil exports while in the latter they are purchased from private exporters. These are quite distinct from SWFs that could be established with borrowed money—that is, where reserves come from capital inflows not current account surpluses, and governments acquire them by issuing domestic debt rather than generating fiscal surpluses, as has been the case in India. Investing these into foreign equity would seriously expose the economy to deterioration in global financial conditions, which could not only lower the value of investment but also raise the need for reserves by leading to sudden stops and reversals in capital flows and/or sharp increases in current account deficits. In such countries the case for not borrowing them in the first place (rather than investing them in highly volatile assets) is strong.

In this respect, China stands in between fuel exporters and India in that its reserves are largely earned from current account surpluses but acquired by the government by issuing domestic debt. At some $200 billion, the assets of the recently established China Investment Corporation (CIC) are only a fraction of the total reserves of the country, and only a small part of these appear to have been used for investment abroad.[37] There is certainly scope for considerable expansion of Chinese investment abroad, including for securing greater control over supply of natural resource based commodities, notably minerals. However, given the deep suspicion and misgivings about Chinese government investment in some advanced countries, a large proportion of its reserves cannot be expected to be quickly translated into investment in more lucrative, less risky assets in these countries.[38] An alternative would be to recycle them in the region for, inter alia, infrastructure projects in low income countries in need of development finance. This may best be achieved through a genuinely regional development bank, established and owned by the developing countries of the region along the lines of the recent Banco del Sur in Latin America or the previously existent Corporación Andina de Fomento.

Capital account measures

From a "flow of funds" perspective, it makes little sense for a country to hold excess reserves beyond its liquidity needs and even less sense for it to borrow from abroad to hold money in reserves—which are in effect lent abroad at lower interest rates. There are external effects from foreign borrowing, both in terms of exposure to foreign exchange rate changes, with the attendant macroeconomic consequences, and in terms of the requisite offsetting reserve holdings.[39] At the very least, these external costs should be imposed on capital inflows. This brings up the broader issue of measures to manage the capital account—regulations that would affect emerging market exposure to global financial market volatility.

Many Asian emerging markets are incurring high reserve costs and facing macroeconomic policy dilemmas mainly because they have chosen to keep their economies open to the surge in capital inflows, rather than imposing tighter counter-cyclical measures of control.[40] Indeed, capital accounts in the region are more open today than they were during the Asian crisis.[41] In China, for instance, one of the countries with the tightest restrictions, calculations based on an IMF formula are said to show that 80 per cent of the capital account has been liberalized.[42]

In several cases the opening to inflows has been selective, such as raising the limits on the QFII (qualified foreign institutional investors) in China. Countries such as India have liberalized sectoral caps on FDI. Foreign banks have generally been allowed greater freedom to operate, with many domestic borrowers receiving funding from such banks directly from abroad or through their local offices.

However, there have been some efforts to bring greater transparency to capital inflows. For instance, in 2007, in a move that was designed not so much to relieve the upward pressure on the rupee as to bring greater transparency by restricting the activities of hedge funds, India adopted a proposal by the Securities and Exchange Board to restrict the foreign buying of shares through offshore derivatives, despite an adverse initial reaction from the stock market.

There have been, to be sure, some efforts to curb excessive inflows in order to ease the upward pressure on their currencies. In 2006 China extended to foreign banks the restriction over borrowing abroad to fund domestic dollar assets. In 2007 its foreign exchange regulators felt obliged to take action against ten international banks for breaching capital account regulations by "assisting speculative foreign capital to enter the country disguised as trade and investment" (Anderlini, 2007). Exporters have been required to park their export revenues in temporary accounts in order to enable the officials to check and verify that invoices are backed by genuine trade transactions.

In December 2006, Thailand imposed a 30 per cent unremunerated reserve requirement on capital inflows held less than one year, including portfolio equity flows, in order to check continued appreciation of the currency by reducing the effective return on capital inflows. This provoked a strong reaction from the stock market, forcing the government to exempt investment in stocks from the requirements. The remaining restrictions were removed in March 2008. With a continued surge in capital inflows, India reversed the liberalization of the limits on external commercial borrowing, tightening them in 2007. Similarly, Korea restricted external funding of domestic lending by foreign banks and reintroduced limits on lending in foreign currency to domestic firms.

However, the main response to the surge in capital inflows has been to liberalize outward investment by residents. This is partly motivated by a desire to allow national firms to expand abroad and become important players in world markets. This has particularly been the case in China and India. However, while in China assets acquired abroad are financed from trade surpluses, in India these are, in effect, funded by capital inflows.[43] As remarked by an observer:

the global flood of money (and attendant hubris) has enabled Indian companies like Tata to buy themselves a place on the world stage rather than earning it through export success or technological advance. (Bowring, 2008a)

There has also been considerable liberalization of portfolio outflows. For instance, China took a decision to permit investment by its residents in approved overseas markets and raised the limits on corporate and individual purchases of foreign currency for mitigating the pressure for appreciation through its QDII (qualified domestic institutional investor) scheme. The share of portfolio investment in the total international assets of China in 2006 was three times that of FDI abroad.

In Malaysia where limits on foreign assets held by some institutional investors were increased significantly, cumulative portfolio outflows during 2004–7 were slightly below cumulative portfolio inflows and nine times direct investment abroad. In 2007 there was a net outflow of capital (excluding reserve accumulation) which absorbed as much as half of the current account surplus (Khor, 2008). India, Korea, and Thailand have all liberalized rules limiting portfolio investment abroad and Thailand abolished the surrender requirement for exporters.

Capital account opening for residents as a response to a surge in inflows is clearly an alternative to sterilized intervention and has the advantage of avoiding carry costs for reserves. But, like interventions, it effectively does nothing to prevent currency and maturity mismatches in balance sheets, or instability and vulnerability to shocks associated with greater presence of foreigners in domestic asset markets. Its rationale as a longer-term strategy for closer integration with global financial markets is highly contentious. Besides, in countries such as China where property rights are not clearly defined, liberalization of resident outflows could encourage asset stripping and money laundering (Yu, 2008). As a counter-cyclical measure, it can be even more problematic—once introduced for cyclical reasons, it may not be easily rolled back when conditions change. Thus, unlike official reserves, these do not provide self-insurance against payments and currency instability and may even aggravate them when market sentiments change.

Conclusion

The Asian emerging market economies are now much more closely integrated into the international financial system than they were in the run-up to the 1997 crisis. Foreign presence in Asian markets has increased not only because of historically high non-resident portfolio inflows, but also because of increased penetration of foreign-owned banks and other financial firms. Furthermore, due to liberalization of resident outflows, portfolio investment abroad has reached unprecedented levels.[44] Closer integration has resulted in greater fragility of the domestic financial system by contributing to asset, credit and investment bubbles. It has also increased the susceptibility of the Asian economies to shocks and contagion from the current global financial turmoil even though payments and reserve positions of many countries in the region are strong enough to provide insurance against balance of payments and exchange rate instability of the kind experienced during 1997.

Several Asian countries, notably China, India, and Korea, experienced bubbles in equity and property markets after the early years of this decade, with price increases going well beyond levels justified by fundamentals. These have also been accompanied by rapid and unprecedented increases in investment in China and India, not only in construction and property, but also in industry. The surge in capital flows made an important contribution not only directly, but also by giving rise to a rapid liquidity expansion, since central bank interventions in foreign currency markets aiming at preventing appreciations could be only partially sterilized. However, monetary policy stance also played an important role. Although, unlike the United States, some efforts were made to cool the bubble in asset markets, monetary policy has generally been loose, resulting in rapid credit expansion.

It appears that asset bubbles have now come to an end, particularly in equity markets. The global retrenchment of risk appetite and the exit of foreign investors have no doubt played a key role. This cycle in Asian asset markets has many features reminiscent of those in the 1990s, but is different in an important respect. In the current cycle, asset deflation is not associated with currency crises and interest rate hikes, but with severe trade shocks. The combination of asset deflation with sharp drops in exports and consequent retrenchment in investment can no doubt wreak havoc in the real economy.[45] This explains why in Asia "the slump in industrial production has been more significant and more rapid than in 1997–98."[46]

It is important to avoid destabilizing feedbacks between the real and financial sectors, particularly in China because of its wider regional ramifications. A sharp drop in growth can threaten the solvency of the banking system given the high degree of leverage of many firms, which can in turn lower growth further.[47] It remains to be seen whether or not the massive fiscal package proposed by the government will prevent such an outcome In any event, the challenge faced by China is not only to overcome the deflationary impulses from the sub-prime crisis, but also to shift to a growth trajectory led by the expansion of domestic consumption.[48]

Even though the region as a whole has strong payments and reserve positions, the behavior of capital flows, including resident outflows, is likely to continue to exert a strong influence on the space available for policy response to external shocks and hence the performance of several economies of the region. Because of the sharp slowdown in total capital flows and reversal of portfolio flows, several currencies that had faced constant upward pressure against the dollar (and the yuan) after 2003, particularly the Indian rupee, Korean won, and Thai baht, have been falling sharply against both currencies since mid-2008. Given strong deflationary impulses from the crisis, this may be viewed as a welcome development, and unlike in 1997, governments now seem to be wary of throwing all their reserves into stabilizing their currencies. However, in some of these countries, notably India and Korea, reserves have been declining rapidly as a result of exit of capital and growing current account deficits. For such countries the deepening of the global crisis can pose serious risks for currency and payment stability.[49]

It seems that Asia may have learned some lessons from the last crisis. It improved domestic regulation. It improved transparency. It strengthened external payments. It accumulated large reserves. These put it in better stead than it otherwise would have been in the current turmoil. But its greater integration into the global financial system seems to have brought "risk without reward" (Stiglitz, 2002). The large gross private inflows and capital market integration—with low levels of net flows—means that Asia has been exposed to greater risk, with little direct gain from access to more capital. Prior to the financial meltdown, some might have claimed that it was buying "intermediation services"—i.e. Western banks did a better job in credit assessment, monitoring, and enforcement. But today, it is hard to make such a claim. More importantly, Asia allowed itself to be more integrated into the global financial system, without putting into place counter-cyclical regulatory mechanisms that would have provided protection against the vicissitudes of global financial markets. It focused on internal macro-management, failing to note that many of the disturbances come from abroad. It failed to note the macro-externalities that arise from capital inflows. This has not put the region in a good position to withstand this particular storm coming from the United States and Europe.

Notes

1. This chapter draws on the Third World Network research project "Financial Policies in Asia." An earlier and more detailed version was included in a paper prepared for ESCAP (Akyüz, 2008a). I am grateful to Martin Khor, Joe Stiglitz, Andrew Cornford, Stephany Griffith-Jones, the staff members of ESCAP, and the participants of the IPD Meeting of the Task Force on Financial Market Regulation at the University of Manchester's Brooks World Poverty Institute, July 1–2, 2008 for comments and suggestions. The usual caveat applies.
2. Special Economic Advisor, South Centre, Geneva. Former Director, Division on Globalization and Development Strategies, UNCTAD, Geneva.
3. Not all Asian countries hit by the crisis manifested vulnerability in all these areas—see UNCTAD TDR (1998) and Akyüz (2000).

4. See IMF (2007c) for the notion of global liquidity and the role of monetary policy in advanced economies and financial innovation in global liquidity expansion and risk appetite. See also BIS (2007, pp. 8–10) for a similar discussion.

5. The underlying figures in Table 12.1 are on net-net basis for equity flows and gross basis for debt flows; that is, net outflows of FDI and portfolio equity by residents are deducted from net inflows by non-residents. Thus, the current account balance plus private capital flows minus net lending by residents (and errors and omissions) would give changes in reserves—see IIF (October 2007, box 3). The countries included are: China, India, Indonesia, Malaysia, Philippines, South Korea, and Thailand in Asia; Argentina, Brazil, Chile, Colombia, Ecuador, Mexico, Peru, Uruguay, and Venezuela in Latin America; Bulgaria, Czech Republic, Hungary, Poland, Romania, Russian Federation, Slovakia, Turkey, and Ukraine in Europe; and Algeria, Egypt, Morocco, South Africa, and Tunisia in Africa/Middle East. The latest figures are from IIF (January 2009).

6. See World Bank (2007) and IMF (2007a). That improvements in underlying economic fundamentals in the recipient countries are not always the main reason for this unprecedented decline in spreads was also recognized by the IMF (2004, p. 66).

7. That the push factor is generally more important in boom–bust cycles in international capital flows is also noted by the World Bank (2003, p. 26): the "dynamics of net capital inflows and the changes of official reserves over the cycle do indeed indicate that the push factor is more important for middle-income countries, while the pull factor dominates in high-income countries."

8. On different forms of carry trade and interest differentials, see BIS (2007, pp. 83–8), UNCTAD TDR (2007, chapter I) and IIF (October 2007).

9. The proportion of domestic currency sovereign debt held by non-residents in emerging markets is estimated to have reached 12 per cent—see Mehl and Reynaud (2005) and De Alessi Gracio, Hoggarth and Yang (2005). The expansion appears to be particularly rapid in Latin America due to high levels of sovereign debt. Available data shows that foreign investment in local currency government securities went from less than $15 billion at the beginning of 2003 to $200 billion by the end of 2006—see Tovar and Quispe-Agnoli (2008). Moreover, some Latin American countries have been able to issue local-currency-denominated global bonds at rates below those in domestic markets because of lower jurisdiction spreads (IMF, 2005; Tovar, 2005).

10. For further discussion of components of capital flows to Asian emerging markets, see BIS (2007), IMF (2007d and 2007e), and McCauley (2008).

11. Net portfolio investment outflows in 2008 from emerging markets as a whole is estimated to have been $89 billion (IIF January 2009). It appears that all of the money that came into emerging markets funds in 2007 came out again in 2008 (Citigroup 2008).

12. *Wall Street Journal*, October 17, 2008; see also RGE Monitor (2008). The tendency of investors to liquidate their holdings in emerging markets in order to cover mounting losses and margin calls means that, as suggested by McCauley (2008, p. 1), emerging markets are providing "liquidity under stressed conditions to portfolios managed in the major markets."

13. For instance, according to the so-called Greenspan-Guidotti rule formulated after the Asian crisis, in order to avoid a liquidity crisis, international reserves in emerging markets should meet short-term external (foreign denominated) liabilities, defined as

debt with a remaining maturity of up to one year. For a discussion of the adequate level of reserves, see UNCTAD TDR (1999, chapter V). For an attempt to empirically determine the optimum level of reserves based on welfare criteria, see Jeanne and Rancière (2006). For a discussion of the underlying theory, see Furman and Stiglitz (1998).

14. The degree of vulnerability in this sense can be measured in terms of stock of foreign portfolio investment as a percentage of reserves. In 2008 this ratio was greater than unity in Korea, Indonesia, and the Philippines and exceeded 80 per cent in Singapore, Russia and Malaysia; see ESCAP (2008).

15. See BIS (2007, p. 51) which points out that this correlation has been higher during the most recent periods of global market volatility.

16. See Chai-Anant and Ho (2008). The evidence is from six emerging Asian markets: India, Indonesia, Korea, the Philippines, Taiwan (China), and Thailand.

17. IMF (2007e) finds that institutional investors introduce considerable volatility in equity prices in emerging markets because of herd behaviour. BIS (2009, p. 69) argues that increased market liquidity resulting from greater participation of foreigners in equity markets tends to reduce day-to-day volatility, but notes that "even highly liquid markets do not insulate EME equity markets from a global retrenchment in risk appetite or a withdrawal of foreign investors."

18. In China the equity market is segmented between residents and non-residents in A-share and B-share markets, with the former being reserved exclusively for residents. Both residents and non-residents are allowed to use foreign exchange to invest in B shares. Large inflows of capital, together with growing current account surpluses, affect A-share equity prices mainly through liquidity expansion.

19. For an analysis of developments in Asian housing markets, see IMF (2007b) which somewhat underplays the extent of the bubble and the risks involved, but nevertheless points out that speculative dynamics cannot be ruled out, notably in China, India and Korea.

20. Korea and United States data from OECD (2007, annex table 60). For the others, see BIS (2007, p. 50) and IMF (2007b). In Korea bank lending to households grew rapidly after 2005, and household debt has reached 140 per cent of disposable income—above the level of household indebtedness in the United States (ADB, 2007).

21. In some cases, authorities did not directly take actions to dampen the bubble, in others, they did. Concerned by the growing speculative spree, China adopted a number of measures to stem increases in property prices, including higher interest rates and larger downpayments on both residential and commercial property loans (ESCAP, 2007, p. 10). Even before the global financial meltdown, housing prices in parts of China began to soften (Forbes.com, 2008).

22. For credit conditions and interest rates in Asia, see BIS (2007, pp. 39–41), Mohanty and Turner (2006, p. 43), and IMF (2007c, p. 5).

23. In China gross fixed capital formation has been growing four to five percentage points faster than real income, with the share of investment in GDP now reaching 46 per cent and exceeding the share of consumption. Similarly, in India growth in investment has been faster than GDP by more than five percentage points per annum, with the investment ratio rising to over 30 per cent of GDP from less than 24 per cent in the early years of the decade. Investment rates in most other Asian countries did not fully regain their pre-crisis levels.

24. See Goldstein and Lardy (2004), Nagaraj (2005), and Branstetter and Lardy (2006) on excess capacity, waste and sustainability of the investment boom in China.

25. See various studies in BIS (2005), notably, Disyatat and Galati (2005) and Mihaljek (2005). See also Mohanty and Turner (2006). These findings stand in contrast to a recent IMF study which argues that sterilized intervention in emerging markets is likely to be ineffective when the influx of capital is persistent, and tends to be associated with higher inflation (IMF, 2007c, pp. 122–4).

26. Most Latin American and European emerging markets have experienced sizeable appreciations in real effective exchange rates—see UNCTAD TDR (2007) and IIF (October 2007). According to UNCTAD figures, real effective exchange rates were relatively stable in India and China during 2002–6 while Indonesia saw an appreciation of over 20 per cent and Malaysia close to 10 per cent. Appreciations in Korea and Thailand were in the order of 10 per cent—see also BIS (2007). India, the Philippines, and Thailand saw relatively strong appreciations in 2007.

27. Ignoring exchange rate changes, the fiscal (or quasi-fiscal) cost of each dollar of reserves acquired through intervention can be written as: $i_g - i_r = (i_g - i_x) + (i_x - i_r)$ where i_g, i_r and i_x are the rates, in common currency, on government domestic debt, reserve holdings and external borrowing, and typically $i_g > i_x > i_r$. The margin between i_x and i_r is determined mainly by the credit risk and between i_g and i_x by the exchange rate risk. When non-resident claims are only in foreign currencies, the first term on the right-hand side of the equation is captured by the holders of public debt at home and the second term is the net transfer abroad—what Rodrik (2006) calls the social cost of foreign exchange reserves. For the distinction between the two types of transfers and costs see UNCTAD TDR (1999, chapter V). Mohanty and Turner (2006) provide some estimates of fiscal cost of intervention in emerging markets.

28. Fiscal cost from ESCAP (2007, p. 21) and central government deficits from IMF (2007d, p. 20).

29. It should be noted that reserve figures are subject to a valuation effect which can be large because of sharp changes in cross rates among reserve currencies.

30. Here capital account surplus is used in the conventional sense; that is, surplus on non-reserve financial account.

31. See Williamson (1995) on the rationality of reserve accumulation under such conditions. Polak and Clark (2006, p. 555) refer to fear of floating in explaining reserve holding in China, Korea and Singapore.

32. In fact, it is more so for equity flows for the acquisition of ownership rights of existing assets since rates earned by transnational companies exceed the cost of international borrowing by a very large margin (UNCTAD TDR 1999, chapter V).

33. This figure appears quite modest if one takes the average spread over the full boom–bust cycles in capital flows to emerging markets. For instance the average spread of emerging-market bonds exceeded 700 basis points during the 1990s and never fell below 400 basis points. For similar calculations of the cost of reserves, see Rodrik (2006) and Stiglitz (2006).

34. Since "borrowed" reserves of some countries fall short of their total external debt, realization of this aggregate benefit would require lending by countries with excess reserves to those with deficits at rates earned on reserves.

35. Holding by central banks outside the United States of such debt is estimated to be in the order of $1 trillion and large amounts are also known to be held in private portfolios. China's holding of United States agency debt is estimated to be at least 10 per cent of its GDP, mostly in Fannie Mae and Freddie Mac assets (Pesek, 2008).

36. The Bank of China is reported to have lost some $2 billion on its holdings of collateralized securities, including those backed by United States mortgages (Pearlstein, 2008). Standard Chartered, in which Singapore's sovereign wealth fund, Temasek, owns a 19 per cent stake, is reported to have been walking away from its $7.5 billion SIVs sold in Asia and the Middle East (Bowring, 2008b).

37. Its first batch of investment abroad in the Blackstone Group has not been very lucrative but quite controversial in China; see Bradsher (2007).

38. Such investment is sometimes considered as cross-border nationalization; see Weisman (2007). Several commentators including Summers (2007) and Truman (2007) call for greater transparency and accountability—something visibly missing in the case of western institutional investors and hedge funds. Others such as Wade (2007) see SWFs as "a partial redress to the unlevel playing field."

39. These are discussed at greater length in Stiglitz (2003) and Korinek (2008).

40. These include direct restrictions over foreign borrowing by residents and access of non-residents to domestic securities markets, supplemented by market-based or administrative restrictions over maturity and currency mismatches in banks' balance sheets and restrictions designed to limit exchange rate related credit risks—for a discussion, see Akyüz (2008b).

41. For recent measures in Asia, see BIS (2007), IMF (2007b, 2007e), and McCauley (2008).

42. See Yu (2008). It has been argued that China's capital controls remained substantially binding during the period of a de facto dollar peg until July 2005, as suggested by sustained and significant gaps between onshore and offshore renminbi yields. It is also found that since July 2005 there has been a partial convergence between onshore and offshore yields; see Ma and McCauley (2007).

43. For a discussion of inward and outward FDI in India, see Chandrasekhar (2008).

44. This pattern of integration is quite different from that pursued by Korea and Japan, where resident portfolio investment abroad emerged at a much later stage of development, after a global expansion of highly successful indigenous firms through direct investment. Japanese corporations had already established themselves as global players through direct investment abroad and sustained surpluses in manufacturing trade long before its financial and savings institutions were allowed to invest freely in foreign assets as a result of financial liberalization brought about by the 1984 United States–Japan accord. A key provision of that accord was relaxation of restrictions on the purchase of foreign bonds by Japanese residents—see Osugi (1990).

45. On some accounts, on its own, the bursting of asset bubbles in China would lower growth only by a couple of percentage points; see Chancellor (2008).

46. IIF (January 2009, p. 11). According to preliminary estimates, as of January 2009, some Asian countries, notably Korea and Singapore, experienced severe contraction in output during the last quarter of 2008. In China where manufacturing output also dropped and loss of employment reached some 20 million, more recent indicators seem to be more encouraging; see Xinhuanet (2009b).

47. BIS (2007, p. 56) notes that in China the bulk of recorded profits are earned by relatively few enterprises while the rest have high leverage so that if growth slows significantly a substantial proportion of bank loans can become non-performing.
48. The only viable alternative to exports is domestic consumption and this requires faster growth in wages and higher share of wages in GDP, see Akyüz (2008a).
49. For the behaviour of reserves in India and Korea during 2008 see Obstfeld, Shambaugh, and Taylor (2009) and RGE Monitor (2009a, 2009b).

References

Asian Development Bank (2007) 'Asian Development Outlook.' *Policy Research Report.*

Akyüz, Y. (2000) 'Causes and Sources of the Asian Financial Crisis.' Paper presented at the Host Country Event: Symposium on Economic and Financial Recovery in Asia. UNCTAD X, Bangkok. Reprinted in TWN Global Economy Series, No. 1.

—— (2008a) 'The Current Global Financial Turmoil and Asian Developing Countries.' Paper prepared for the United Nations Economic and Social Commission for Asia and Pacific (ESCAP) and presented at the Ministerial segment of its 64th commission session, Bangkok, April 29. Reprinted in TWN Global Economy Series, No. 11.

—— (2008b) 'Managing Financial Instability in Emerging Markets: A Keynesian Perspective.' *METU Studies in Development*, 2008(1).

Anderlini, J. (2007) 'China hits out over "hot money." *Financial Times,* June 27.

BIS (Bank for International Settlements) (2005) 'Foreign exchange market intervention in emerging markets: motives, techniques and implications.' BIS Papers, 24.

—— (2007) *Annual Report.*

—— (2009) 'Capital Flows and Emerging Market Economies.' CGFS Paper 33.

Bowring, P. (2008a) 'Asia Won't Get Away Clean.' *Asia Sentinel*, January 25.

—— (2008b). 'StanChart Leaves Investors Out in the Cold.' *Asia Sentinel*, February 12.

Bradsher, K. (2007) 'Feeling the Heat, Not Breathing Fire.' *New York Times*, August 3.

Branstetter, L. and Lardy, N. (2006) 'China's Embrace of Globalization.' NBER Working Paper, 12373.

Chai-Anant, C. and Ho, C. (2008) 'Understanding Asian Equity Flows, Market Returns and Exchange Rates.' BIS Working Paper, 245.

Chancellor, E. (2008) 'Bursting Chinese Bubble Could Hurt.' *Independent Investor,* January 18.

Chandrasekhar, C. P. (2008) 'India and the World Economy' <http://www.networkideas.org>.

Citigroup (2008) 'Equity Strategy. EM Funds Flows. How Much Foreign Money has left EM?' December 3 <http://www.citigroup.com>.

—— (2009) 'The Asia Investigator. Korea: Asset Deflation Impact on Construction and Banking.' January 19 <http://www.citigroup.com>.

De Alessi Gracio, C., Hoggarth, G., and Yang, J. (2005) 'Capital Flows to Emerging Markets: Recent Trends and Potential Financial Stability Implications.' *Bank of England Financial Stability Review* (December), pp. 94–102.

Disyatat, P. and Galati, G. (2005) 'The Effectiveness of Foreign Exchange Intervention in Emerging Market Countries.' BIS Papers, No. 24, pp. 97–113.

Economic and Social Commission for Asia and the Pacific (2007) *Key Economic Developments in the Asia-Pacific Region 2008.*

—— (2008) *Macroeconomic Policy Brief. Volume 1: Financial Crisis, No. 1.*

Forbes.com (2008) 'China Seeks to Revive Property Market.' December 30 <http://www.forbes.com>.

Furman, J. and Stiglitz, J. E. (1998) 'Economic Crises: Evidence and Insights from East Asia.' *Brookings Papers on Economic Activity*, 2, pp. 115–35.

Gochoco-Bautista, M. S. (2008) 'Asset Prices and Monetary Policy: Booms and Fat Tails in East Asia.' BIS Working Paper, 243.

Goldstein, M. and Lardy, N. R. (2004) 'What Kind of Landing for the Chinese Economy?' Policy Brief 04–7. Washington, DC: Institute for International Economics.

Institute of International Finance (various). *Capital Flows to Emerging Markets.* Various issues <http://www.iif.com>.

International Monetary Fund (2004) *Global Financial Stability Report.*

—— (2005) *Global Financial Stability Report.*

—— (2007a) *World Economic Outlook* (April).

—— (2007b) *Regional Economic Outlook. Asia and Pacific* (April).

—— (2007c) *World Economic Outlook* (October).

—— (2007d) *Regional Economic Outlook. Asia and Pacific* (October).

—— (2007e) *Global Financial Stability Report* (October).

—— (2008) *World Economic Outlook* (October).

Jeanne, O. and Rancière, R. (2006) 'The Optimal Level of International Reserves for Emerging Market Countries: Formulas and Applications.' IMF Working Paper 06/229.

Khor, M. (2008) 'Financial Policy and the Management of Capital Flows: The Case of Malaysia.' Paper presented to the TWN-CAP workshop on "Global financial turmoil, capital flows and policy responses." Penang, August 26–28.

Korinek, A. (2008) 'Regulating Capital Flows to Emerging Markets: An Externality View.' Unpublished paper, University of Maryland.

Ma, G. and McCauley, R. N. (2007) 'Do China's Capital Controls Still Bind? Implications for Monetary Autonomy and Capital Liberalisation.' BIS Working Paper, 233.

McCauley, R. (2008) 'Managing Recent Hot Money Flows in Asia.' ADBI Discussion Paper, 99.

Mehl, A. and Reynaud, J. (2005) 'The Determinants of "Domestic" Original Sin in Emerging Market Economies.' European Central Bank Working Paper, 560.

Mihaljek, D. (2005). 'Survey of Central Bank Views on Effectiveness of Intervention.' BIS Papers No. 24, pp. 82–96.

Mohanty, M. S. and Turner, P. (2006) 'Foreign Exchange Reserve Accumulation in Emerging Markets: What Are the Domestic Implications?' *BIS Quarterly Review,* September, pp. 39–52.

Nagaraj, R. (2005) 'Industrial Growth in China and India: A Preliminary Comparison.' *Economic and Political Weekly,* May 21.

OECD (Organisation for Economic Co-operation and Development) (2007) *Economic Outlook,* 82.

Obstfeld, M., Shambaugh J. C., and Taylor, A. M. (2009) 'Financial Instability, Reserves, and Central Bank Swap Lines in the Panic of 2008.' Paper presented at the ASSA Meetings, San Francisco.

Osugi, K. (1990) 'Japan's Experience of Financial Deregulation since 1984 in an International Perspective.' *BIS Economic Paper*, No. 26.

Pearlstein, S. (2008) 'More Room to Fall.' *Washington Post*, January 22.

Pesek, W. (2008) 'Asia is About to Give US a Kick in the Fannie.' Bloomberg, September 3 <http://www.bloomberg.com>.

Polak, J. J. and Clark, P.B. (2006) 'Reducing the Costs of Holding Reserves. A New Perspective on Special Drawing Rights.' In I. Kaul and P. Conceição (eds.), *The New Public Finance. Responding to Global Challenges*. Oxford: Oxford University Press.

RGE Monitor (2008) 'Hedge Funds in Asia: More Redemptions?' RGE Monitor, December 8 <http://www.rgemonitor.com>.

—— (2009a) 'Reserve Increase: Is Korea Pulling Back from the Brink of Currency Crisis?' RGE Monitor, January 23 <http://www.rgemonitor.com>.

—— (2009b) 'India's Declining Forex Reserves: Capital Outflows and External Deficits Posing Risks?' RGE Monitor, February 6 <http://www.rgemonitor.com>.

Rodrik, D. (2006) 'The Social Cost of Foreign Exchange Reserves.' NBER Working Paper, 11952.

Setser, B. (2008) 'The Debate Over the Pace of Hot Money Flows into China.' RGE Monitor, February 20 <http://rs.rgemonitor.com/blog/sletser>.

Stiglitz, J. E. (2002) 'Capital Market Liberalization and Exchange Rate Regimes: Risk without Reward.' *The Annals of the American Academy of Political and Social Science*, 579, pp. 219–48.

Summers, L. H. (2007) 'Funds that Shake Capitalistic Logic.' *Financial Times*, July 29.

Tovar, C. E. (2005) 'International Government Debt Denominated in Local Currency: Recent Developments in Latin America.' *BIS Quarterly Review*, December, pp. 109–18.

—— and Quispe-Agnoli, M. (2008) 'New Financing Trends in Latin America.' BIS Papers, 36.

Truman, E. M. (2007) 'Sovereign Wealth Funds: The Need for Greater Transparency and Accountability.' Policy Brief 07–6, Peterson Institute of International Economics, Washington, DC.

UNCTAD TDR (various) *Trade and Development Report*.

Wade, R. H. (2007) 'Sovereign Funds a Useful Weapon for Poorer Nations.' Letter to the Editor, *Financial Times*, August 10.

Weisman, S. (2007) 'US Fears Overseas Funds Could "Buy up America."' *International Herald Tribune*, August 21.

Williamson, J. (1995) 'The Management of Capital Flows.' *Pensamiento Iberoamericano*, January–June.

World Bank (2003) *Global Economic Prospects*.

—— (2007) *Global Development Finance*.

Xinhuanet (2009a) 'Chinese Housing Prices Decline for the First Time Since 2005.' January 10 <http://news.xinhuanet.com/english>.

—— (2009b). 'Chinese Policymakers Need Caution to Counter Financial Crisis.' February 6 <http://news.xinhuanet.com/english>.

Yu, Y. D. (2008) 'Managing Capital Flows: The Case of the People's Republic of China.' ADBI Discussion Paper, 96.

13

Regulation of the Financial Sector in Developing Countries: Lessons from the 2008 Financial Crisis

Y. V. Reddy

This chapter aims to draw some practical lessons and raises some issues from the 2008 financial crisis for regulation of financial sectors in developing countries. At the time of writing, the crisis is far from over and the aftermath is still unclear. The chapter is divided into five sections. The first section gives an overview of considerations that are important in drawing lessons from the crisis, especially from the point of view of developing economies. The second section addresses the major issues of scope for, and limits to, counter-cyclicality in regulation, in view of the widely perceived need for such an approach to avoid similar crisis in the future. The third section addresses an issue which has been in focus since late 2008—the idea of comprehensiveness in the regulatory scope of the financial sector. The fourth section explores possible improvements in regulatory structures that are provoked by the recent crisis. The concluding section lists several broader issues that need to be kept in view while considering improvements in regulation of financial sectors for the future.

The observations made in this chapter are essentially from a practitioner's perspective. Furthermore, several comments are based on the author's experience as Governor of the Reserve Bank of India (RBI), which is the Central Bank in India. Consequently, such comments have an advantage of pragmatism but may not necessarily carry universal validity.

Lessons to be learned

There are extensive analyses on the origins and the evolution of the current financial crisis that are valuable for learning lessons. At the same time, several aspects of the crisis are yet to be fully comprehended. Hence, all lessons from the current crisis should be recognized as very valuable, but subject to possible modifications as greater insights into the events are gained. Moreover, while some generalizations about the crisis are possible, they have to be contextualized to the particular economy under consideration, as developing economies are very diverse and at various stages of development regarding their financial sectors and their integration into the global economy. It is equally important to recognize that the financial sectors in various economies have been affected by different degrees of intensity. For example, the extent to which the crisis has gripped the United States is in contrast to its neighbor Canada, which has been considerably less affected despite having a fairly developed financial system and an open economy; this seems to be linked to better regulation of the Canadian Financial System. In other words, lessons need to be taken not only from the experience of those countries that are seriously affected and hence under intense scrutiny as this chapter goes to press, but also from those advanced and developing economies, which are less intensely affected.

It is noteworthy that in terms of first-order effect, at the time of writing, the financial institutions in developing economies are less affected than in advanced economies. This could partly be attributed to the fact that the financial sectors in the developing economies are dominated by banks that still conduct traditional banking business and do not host complex financial products that could be riskier. The credit crunch and volatility in equity markets in the advanced economies have certainly had an impact on institutions in developing countries, but this is essentially in the nature of contagion, especially if such markets or institutions happen to be over-leveraged. The contagion is, in any case, being transmitted though liquidity and credit crunch. To the extent that money and credit markets in the developed world cause a squeeze on the credit available for cross-border trade, there is a similar squeeze on the availability of trade credit to exporters and importers in the developing countries. In addition, this poses greater pressure on the domestic money and spot foreign exchange (forex) markets as importers seek to borrow domestic currencies to purchase forex to honor their obligations.

The banks in developing countries may be sound and well-functioning, but financing import–export trade with advanced economies requires similar well-functioning banks at their end too. For example, opening and honoring a letter of credit requires cooperation between the two relevant banks. In some developing economies, the weakening of local investor confidence in bonds and equities may be severe. However, in economies where there is a high presence of foreign banks, the contagion through the financial sector can be more intense.

The second-order effect, which has been very evident since late 2008 and is currently high on the agenda of developing economies, was caused by the volatility in capital flows that seriously impacts exchange rates. The third-order effect, which is already influencing the level of confidence in developed and developing economies, is via linkages with the real sector, especially linkages in trade. At the same time, there is extraordinary volatility in several commodity prices with severe impacts on many developing economies. In this regard it might be better to distinguish between oil and non-oil commodities. Moreover, the impact would vary depending on whether a country is a commodity exporter or importer. No doubt, the impact would also differ depending on the movements in the exchange rates of the countries. These have the potential to generate non-performing assets on the balance sheets of banks in developing economies. Furthermore, non-performing loans could also arise from the wealth effect channel of market risk being translated into credit risk. It is also likely that remittances from non-resident workers to developing economies may diminish in due course and, hence, economies heavily dependent on such remittances may experience pressures on exchange rates, especially if this is accompanied by outflows of capital. Similarly, there could be lowering of aid and donor flows to low income countries. All of these developments have consequences for the real sector. In brief, the causes and the cross-border transmission of the crisis may significantly differ between developed and developing economies, as well as among developing economies. Appreciation of these differences is critical for drawing out appropriate lessons from the crisis by developed and developing economies.

The impact on developing countries of the volatility in capital flows may be particularly severe by the mere fact that their economies are still nascent. However, the soundness of the regulatory structures, policies or economic fundamentals should also be factored in. For example, developing economies have limited access to international currency reserves (see Chapter 16, by Ocampo). Furthermore, the scope for coordinated intervention akin to that by the G-7 economies is limited for developing economies. Moreover, international financial markets view the risk-reward frontier in developing economies differently than those in developed economies.

In terms of policy responses to the current crises, there are several features common to *all* economies: a focus on fiscal stimulus to growth, injection of liquidity and reduction in policy interest rates. But there are differences among them too. The most visible is the magnitude of the injection of capital into banks and other financial intermediaries. The most affected advanced economies took recourse to coordinate action by major central banks and their governments while the seriously affected developing economies approached multilateral agencies, in particular the International Monetary Fund (IMF), for support. It is noteworthy that some other developing countries have command over significant amounts of forex reserves.

In order to draw the appropriate lessons from this crisis for future regulation of financial sectors, it is essential to look beyond the financial sector, not only because the crisis is now no longer solely a financial problem—it is in fact now an economic crisis—but also because the crisis itself reflects the prevalence of several macroeconomic imbalances and political economy considerations.

However, despite these complexities, for the purpose of this chapter it is necessary to focus on factors directly relevant to the financial sectors while drawing lessons from the crisis.

The prevailing standards of capital regulation for financial intermediaries, with some degree of acceptance at the global level, are the Basel II standards. It has been argued that the crisis is in some ways a reflection of the inadequacy of the Basel II framework, though it has been developed by the regulators of developed economies working over several years. It is also worth noting that the origin and the initial intensity of the crisis in the financial sector have been substantially concentrated in the two leading international financial centers. Hence, the current problems may not be significantly reflective of financial regulation in many other economies. In other words, it can be held that an incentive for softer regulation may exist when there is competition among a few countries to attract the financial services industry.

The regulators' willingness to tolerate savings in risk capital employed by the regulated entities, and excessive reliance on self-regulation, may be considered mechanisms adopted by some regulators to attract activity to the jurisdiction concerned. In this process, the regulators may have underestimated the risks to the system and the costs of a bail-out. In theory, over a long period, markets should be able to perceive the risks emanating from self-regulation in a particular country; though in practice, the incentives and the relevant time horizons may lead to underestimation of such risks by market participants for a prolonged period.

The reliance on self-regulation by market participants—the principle-based approach to regulation involving limited use of prescription or rules, and the tolerance of shadow banking systems, as well as rapid innovations—may also be reflective of the attitudes of regulators, the incentive for the regulated, and the stakes for public policy. The associated entities, such as Credit Rating Agencies (CRAs), may also have vested interests in a framework that is conducive to their expansion as well as continued dominance.

In this regard, it is essential to recognize that the eagerness to have a thriving international financial center is often, explicitly or implicitly, a decision of broader public policy. In the normal course, the regulatory framework may have to align itself to such a stance of public policy, thus attracting several political economy considerations. In India, a committee was appointed by the government to recommend measures to develop Mumbai as a regional financial center. The recommendations were far reaching and involved the whole gamut of fiscal, monetary and prudential measures for the country as a whole. There is an implicit assumption that the financial center in India will not only provide employment and generate output, but also lead real sector development throughout the entire country. Development of the financial sector of course plays a critical role, but not necessarily the leading role, in facilitating growth with stability; hence, there is a need to persevere with reforms in the financial sector along sound lines, including sufficient and effective regulation that serves the main goals of the real economy. In this regard, the 2008 financial crisis has generated debates on several fronts, but with regards to this chapter, the three important areas specific to regulation of the financial sector include the following: the relevance of counter-cyclical regulation, the need to make regulation more comprehensive, and the scope to refashion the regulatory structures.

Counter-cyclical regulation

Several arguments have been advanced in favor of injecting elements of counter-cyclicality into regulation. In particular, senior officials at the Bank for International Settlements (BIS) have in recent years been advocating for greater attention to the rapid growth of credit, deterioration in the quality of credit and steep acceleration in the prices of assets. The RBI and a few others, such as the Central Bank of Spain, have taken recourse to various instruments of counter-cyclical prudential regulation. RBI had adopted neutral or tight monetary policy in an uninterrupted fashion, from 2004 up until the third quarter of 2008, using both direct and indirect instruments of monetary policy. Similarly, the RBI had been using prudential measures relating to foreign currency exposures of all financial intermediaries under its jurisdiction as part of the management of the capital account. Furthermore, a range of monetary, prudential and fiscal instruments have been used to influence the overall liquidity in the markets. On the basis of this limited experience (described more below), operationally it may be feasible to design instruments for counter-cyclical regulations, and use them effectively, consistent with objectives regarding growth in output, inflation and overall stability of the financial sector.

The case for counter-cyclical policies in regard to developing economies is stronger than others, owing to the fact that higher weight has to be accorded to stability in these economies. Growth is essential for the eradication of poverty in such economies, but the gains from growth typically occur to the poor with a time lag. However, the pains of high inflation, as well as financial instability, affect the poor instantly. Furthermore, there is empirical evidence that costs in terms of increases in poverty are higher if output falls, than the reduction of poverty for an equivalent rise in output. Moreover, the poor have marginal capabilities and resources to manage or mitigate risks, while most governments in developing economies have very few mechanisms for social safety nets. At the same time, designing and implementing a counter-cyclical policy is more complex in developing economies. The cycles are not easily identifiable, especially if a significant structural transformation is underway in the economy. In some countries with persistent fiscal deficits, like India, the room for maneuver for expansionary fiscal policy may be limited. The transmission of monetary policy is constrained by several factors, in particular the development of financial markets. The environment of public policies, especially through administered interest rates and directed credit, makes the transmission more complex. The effectiveness of prudential measures depends on the standards of governance in financial institutions operating in that country. Above all, a relatively open capital account makes transmission of monetary policy muted. There is, therefore, in developing countries, a special case for harmonized counter-cyclical policies in the three spheres of policies: monetary, prudential regulation and fiscal.

It is well recognized that identifying the construction of asset bubbles is difficult. But the issue of operational purposes is where the judgment should sit when there are doubts. Perhaps in all developing economies, the decision may have to be to protect, at a minimum what may be considered critical financial institutions, namely banks, from the serious ill effects of the bubble if it were to build up and burst. Banks stand out as most critical: a common person, particularly in developing economies, seeks an institution, traditionally banks, where his personal savings are safe. It is essential for public policy to assure such a facility, and recent events have shown that the governments would be obliged to make such a facility available even *ex post* crisis. In brief, there is a strong case, based on the experience of the 2008 events, to ensure that bank depositors are protected from the ill effects of volatile business cycles. In response to rapid growth of credit and asset prices, RBI took temporary measures that included generally increasing the risk weights, seeking additional provisioning, imposing quantitative limits and engaging in supervisory review of select banks to protect them, as much as possible, from the possibility of a serious downturn in asset prices. The quantitative limits on exposures and a few other prescriptions were flexible with regard to any specific institution, provided its risk containment policies were to the satisfaction of the regulator.

Comprehensiveness in regulatory scope

There is a plea for greater comprehensiveness in the institutions that are subject to regulation. First, while the regulators focused their attention on the commercial banks, the crisis essentially originated from non-banks, especially investment banks, and in some ways the non-regulated parts of commercial banks, as well as hedge funds or private equity funds. Second, the relationships between banks and non-banks were not adequately regulated; with the result that the assurance of liquidity support from banks implicit in such relationships was not properly monitored. The consequences of the "originate and distribute" model partly reflected this weakness. Third, while regulating the commercial banks, their excessive dependence on resources other than deposits was not monitored. Fourth, large corporate magnates have emerged as big players in financial markets, but financial regulators have failed to regulate them. Some of the players operated in a way that their operations became too big to fail. Fifth, the risk of individual financial institutions could have been assessed by each institution, to the satisfaction of the regulator. But the exposures of institutions to each other within the financial sector might have been largely ignored. It may be noted that this phenomenon is different from consolidated supervision of conglomerates, in the sense that it relates to exposures of conglomerates to each other collectively. Sixth, financial innovations appeared to spread the risk widely, and often away from regulated entities like banks and institutional companies. In reality, however, such innovations removed the risks from regulators' radar, while substantively reverting to the banking system under stressful conditions. Correspondingly, the off balance sheet obligations of financial institutions might have been seriously underestimated by the regulators.

There are several issues of costs and benefits associated with more comprehensive regulation, but the financial crisis of 2008 has enlarged the scope of central banking in terms of institutions dealt with and instruments used by them, especially in regards to their function as lender of last resort. In a way, therefore, comprehensiveness in financial regulation has perhaps come to stay. But what is needed is a well thought out redrawing of the boundaries and intensity of financial regulation across financial institutions and their activities.

The RBI had attempted to address these issues in several ways even as the problems were building up in the global financial sector. The RBI retained its jurisdiction to regulate approximately 30,000 non-banking financial companies (NBFCs), but operationally it focused only on deposit-taking institutions and systemically important ones, defined on the basis of the size of the balance sheet. The regular monitoring of systemically important NBFCs ensured that corrective measures were undertaken in a timely manner, particularly in terms of enhancing capital requirements in 2006. Furthermore, the extent of direct and indirect exposures of the banking system to such NBFCs was also regulated. The NBFCs themselves were divided into several categories and regulatory regimes were fine-tuned to suit each category. Noticing tendencies of banks to hold each others' equities on their books, a limit of 5 per cent of total equity was placed on any bank holding in any other single bank. The guidelines on securitization issued in 2006 provide a conservative treatment of securitization, exposures for capital adequacy purposes, especially in regards to the credit enhancement and liquidity facilities. In order to reduce the extent of concentration of banks' liabilities, guidelines were issued which placed prudential limits on the extent of interbank liability. In addition, guidelines were issued in order to contain risks arising out of banks' investment portfolio, in particular non-government securities. Banks were specifically advised not to be solely guided by the ratings assigned to these securities by the credit rating agencies, which was in the nature of moral suasion only. Articulation of issues relating to financial stability in the public domain, moral suasion, supervisory review of over extended individual banks, and emphasis on regulatory comfort rather than mere regulatory compliance were some important instruments used in regard to several areas of regulatory concern. In brief, the experience of RBI indicates that it is possible to dynamically define boundaries of regulation depending on evolving conditions in the financial sectors provided that the regulators have the mandate, skills, and above all, real operational freedom. A comprehensive coverage, as per mandate with operational freedom, executed in terms of exhaustive monitoring, but with selectivity in prescriptions and intervention, appears to add to the capacity of the regulators to dynamically redefine the boundaries of their activities.

Regulatory structures

There is a view that the current crisis was essentially caused by regulators' inability to cope with the pace of financial innovation and partly on account of weaknesses in regulatory structures at the national and international level. In this regard, it is useful to note that the most seriously affected financial institutions are those which were reputed to have the best capabilities in risk assessment and risk management. Similarly, the reportedly high regulatory standards of the most seriously affected countries were not adequate to avert a crisis. Consequently, it is held that the fault may be with the structures of regulation, and hence a case is made for improvements in regulatory structures. At a very general level, it can be argued that there is no convincing evidence of serious shortcomings in the regulatory environment of developing economies as far as the current crisis is concerned. Therefore, the focus should be on the issues of regulation in advanced economies and on global regulatory structures, in view of the globalization of finance that has also contributed to the crisis.

The current debates on appropriate national level regulatory parameters are also of interest to developing economies due to their goals of aligning with internationally set standards of globalization of finance. First, it is suggested that a single regulator for the financial sector would avoid regulatory arbitrage and add to stability, while the central bank would be responsible for monetary policy and financial stability. Another view is that, ideally, the central bank itself could assume the responsibility of a single regulator, combining the monetary and regulatory functions. Yet another view, particularly relevant for developing economies, is that the regulation of banking should lie with the central bank, and the regulation of others could be separated. The empirical evidence so far appears very mixed. Hence, it may not be appropriate to take a definite view on the issue of single versus multiple regulators. However, whatever the structure is, close coordination between regulatory functions is critical, irrespective of whether they are located in single or multiple authorities. In India, the RBI, in addition to regulating banks, regulates NBFCs, money, and government securities markets and payment systems. Regulation of other activities in the financial sector is distributed among capital market, insurance and pension funds regulators. However, to ensure coordination within the financial sector, a High Level Committee on Capital and Financial Markets (HLCCM) has been constituted. This is presided over by the governor of the RBI, and includes the membership of the heads of the regulatory bodies in the financial sector and the Permanent Secretary of Ministry of Finance. The HLCCM has in turn constituted standing technical committees to ensure coordination on operational issues and provide assistance to the committee. In summary, the Indian experience points to the desirability of establishing standing mechanisms for close and continuous coordination of regulation in the financial sector, irrespective of the fact that statutory compulsions do not exist for new mechanisms.

There is also a view that regulation of the financial sector has often been left to experts in finance, money or economics, and that such an approach encourages an inward looking view of regulation, which potentially ignores the implications and externalities for other stakeholders, including depositors, borrowers or consumers of financial services. On the other hand, it is also recognized that regulation of the financial sector is highly specialized and technical in nature. In India, the Board for Financial Supervision (BFS) within the RBI has been established to make regulation and supervision somewhat autonomous within the RBI. The Board advises and guides the RBI in all matters relating to the regulation and supervision of banks and NBFCs. The Board, which meets at least once a month, is presided over by the Governor of the RBI, and in addition to the Deputy, has four non-official, part-time independent members. These members are eminent individuals who are from such diverse fields as accounting, macroeconomics, the corporate sector, and civil society associated with non-governmental organizations. It is interesting to note that the BFS identifies any bank whose operations give rise to regulatory discomfort, and carries out monthly monitoring of its functioning. Yet another set of institutions are the Technical Advisory Committees, which address issues relating to regulation, and whose members comprise of academics, representatives from self-regulatory organizations, industry associations and select representatives of the regulated entities. These committees meet less frequently than the BFS, and unlike the BFS, have no statutory backing. While the BFS has been very effective, the contributions of Technical Advisory Committees have been mixed, depending on the nature of the subject. For example, the committees on monetary policy and financial markets were more active than the ones on financial regulation.

Finally, there is a view that it is desirable for central banks to have a formal mandate for ensuring financial stability. In India, the RBI has no formal mandate for financial stability, but it has interpreted its mandate on monetary stability to include operational purposes—both price and financial stability in addition to growth. The general approach has been to pursue multiple objectives with explicit statements of relative priorities, from time to time, depending on the circumstances evidenced by multiple indicators. In fact, the regulation of banks is one of the multiple instruments used for operational purposes of RBI's policy objectives.

Some broader issues

There are several broader issues which need to be kept in view while considering changes in the regulatory structures of regimes within developing economies in light of the recent financial crisis. During the crisis, whatever has to be done must be done promptly, comprehensively and effectively to bring stability; but in rewriting regulatory structures, some broader issues need to be considered. Most developing economies recognize the continuing need for reforms in their financial sector. However, the crisis of 2008 raises doubts as to the efficacy of known and existing models of financial sectors in advanced economies. Thus, in the future, reforms in the financial sector may have to be cognizant of the evolving understanding of the subject, and hence, gradualism commends itself. Furthermore, the fundamental changes in regulatory regimes do require acceptance by political authorities and indeed legislative actions.

In this regard, it is necessary to extract the right lessons from the crisis. Some observers think that the experience with sub-prime lending in the United States shows that providing finance to those who cannot afford it is not desirable. Financial inclusion should mean ensuring access to all relevant financial services, to all sections of the populace, and it should not be equated with aggressive lending or simple provisions of micro-credit with profit motives driving the process. In fact, the 2008 crisis shows that banks with a significant retail base tended to be more resilient.

Recent debates on the 2008 crisis have focused on the role of tax havens, and in this regard, developing economies have a high stake in view of the large share of capital flows through such tax havens. Some of them are brought about by bilateral agreements among countries, often as part of free-trade agreements. In addition, enforcement of financial regulation is made particularly difficult by the inadequate attention to "know your investor" in some jurisdictions, and tax regimes that encourage cross-border round-tripping of funds by residents.

The role of CRAs has also received considerable adverse attention. The relevant issues for regulators in developing economies are: the appropriate regulatory frameworks governing them, use of credit ratings by the regulators, and more importantly, the desirability of encouraging domestic CRAs that could serve the growing needs of the developing economies. Such domestic CRAs could have the potential to compete with existing international agencies.

One of the most important lessons from the crisis is the need to recognize links between the financial sector and the real sector. In view of the recent experience with what may be termed as "excessive financialization of economies," should there be a review of the sequencing and pacing of reforms in the financial sector relative to the fiscal and the real sectors in developing economies? In light of the observed volatility in capital flows and also of commodity prices, how should the policies relating to the financial sector in the developing economies provide cushions against such shocks? Similarly, should there be a review of sequencing various elements in the development of domestic financial systems in the developing economies, and their integration into the global financial system? Finally, is it inevitable that the relationships between government, central banks and financial regulators will be redrawn in view of the very serious consequences of the present crisis?

14

Economic Development and the International Financial System[1]

Roberto Frenkel[2] and Martin Rapetti[3]

Introduction

At the beginning of the new century, let us say up until 2002, the insertion of the emerging market economies into the global financial system—that had been evolving since the mid-1970s—seemed to have become a burden on economic growth and a source of instability for these emerging countries. There was little room for optimism about the prospects of these countries. The following five main stylized facts supported this view.

First, financial and currency crises in emerging market economies were increasingly frequent and intense. Considering only the major crises since the early 1990s,[4] the list encompasses the cases of Mexico and Argentina in 1995, the five East Asian economies in 1997–8, Russia and Brazil in 1998–9, and Argentina and Turkey in 2001. Even the most favorable observers of the financial globalization process, such as the managing directors of the International Monetary Fund (IMF) at that time, assumed the continuity of this trend and the emergence of new crises in emerging market economies to be an intrinsic characteristic of the global financial system (Camdessus, 2000; Köhler, 2002).

Second, there was striking evidence of the volatility of capital flows and the propensity for international contagion. These characteristics were first observed with the repercussions of the Mexican crisis in 1995 and gained wide recognition with the strong global financial impacts of the Asian and Russian crises.

Third, the extreme cases of highly indebted countries, like Argentina and Brazil, weighed heavily in the diagnosis. At the end of the 1990s, both economies were locked in financial traps (Frenkel, 2008), with high country risk premia, slow growth (e.g. Brazil) or recession (e.g. Argentina), and great external financial fragility. The Argentine crisis erupted in 2001 and was followed by the default on its external debt. Brazil had experienced a currency crisis in 1998–9 without defaulting on its external debt; however, even though the Brazilian exchange rate policy became more flexible after that episode, economic policy and performance were still locked in a financial trap at the beginning of the current decade.

Fourth, most of the emerging market economies seemed to have entered the global financial system in a segmented way (Frenkel, 2008). This phenomenon was evident in the highly indebted countries. However, several emerging market economies that had managed their policies in order to avoid high debt and financial traps also experienced segmented integration. Even after participating in the financial globalization process for a long time (almost three decades in the case of the Latin American economies), the financial assets of these countries constituted a class of assets whose yields included a considerable country risk premium. The country risk premia had reached a minimum level in 1997, just before the devaluation in Thailand occurred. But since then, country risk premia have increased and were still high at the beginning of 2000. Hence, given that the sum of the risk-free international rate and the country risk premium sets the floor for domestic interest rates, financial integration seems to have doomed emerging market economies to systematically higher interest rates than those of developed countries, with negative consequences for growth and income distribution.

There is one last negative aspect of the situation at the beginning of the current decade that is worth mentioning: the reversal of the initiatives for international reform that followed in the wake of the crises in the mid and late 1990s. At that time, some initiatives were taken in order to improve the "international financial architecture," to reduce volatility and contagion, to prevent crises and to improve the international management of potential future crises. However, since 2001, the US administration and the newly appointed authorities at the IMF have held on to the belief that the very existence of multilateral support mechanisms creates incentives for over-indebtedness and increases the probability of crises. Around this time, the IMF began to work on the Sovereign Debt Restructuring Mechanism (Krueger, 2002), but this initiative, originally suggested by the new US administration, was abandoned shortly thereafter. Simultaneously, interest in the "international financial architecture" also became fainter. By the early 2000s, the stability of the international financial linkages of emerging markets became more reliant on the spontaneous behavior of the markets than ever before.

In sum, far from delivering on its promise of greater stability and growth—as touted by the promoters of financial liberalization and opening—the process of financial globalization in most emerging market economies seemed to have created a new source of volatility and a burden on growth. In order to deal with the resulting volatility, these countries had to implement their own preventive and defensive measures without the support (and in many cases even against the orientation) of multilateral financial institutions. As already mentioned, these circumstances did not leave much room for optimism.

At that time, one of the authors of this paper (Frenkel, 2002) attempted to synthesize the difficulties confronted by emerging market economies as follows:

A country that intends to implement capital market and capital account regulations to avoid an unsustainable financial integration path has to confront the IMF and the pressure of financial markets. It is a difficult task, but some countries have managed to do it. With regard to this issue, the target is well defined. We should put our efforts into promoting the appropriate changes in the rules and conditionality of the IMF and other multilateral institutions.

In contrast, without an important effort of international cooperation it seems difficult to find ways out of the highly indebted emerging market countries' situation, and more generally, to establish an institutional context capable of neutralizing the segmented integration. The essence of the problem lies in that there is an inconsistency between the Nation States and an international financial system that lacks most of the institutions that have been developed over time at national systems to improve their stability and the way they work.

The above diagnosis was not wrong, given the evidence accumulated up to 2002, but the pessimism was not justified *a posteriori*. Actually, in the next few years the countries found unforeseen ways to avoid unsustainable financial paths and high debt financial traps without confronting the IMF. Interestingly, the segmentation of emerging market assets almost vanished in the following years without any improvement in the international institutional setting. Those unforeseen novel trends have been associated with a remarkable change in emerging market economies' financial integration and in the global system; in particular, the fact that developing countries started to become less dependent on foreign saving and that many of them actually became net suppliers of savings. This change first became apparent in 2002, and was more marked from 2003 onwards.

This chapter aims to describe and discuss the main characteristics of this new way in which emerging market economies participated in global financial markets, as well as its implications for their economic performance. The section following this introduction describes the recent economic performance of emerging market economies associated with changes in the way in which they participate in global financial markets. It also surveys empirical evidence on the relationship between foreign saving, foreign exchange reserve accumulation and economic growth. The third section discusses at a theoretical level the role of competitive real exchange rates (RER) in the performance of emerging market economies and then surveys empirical evidence regarding the relationship between RER and economic growth. The major theoretical explanations for the RER–growth link are evaluated in the light of evidence provided by a set of recent studies. The final section concludes by arguing that the agenda for global capital markets reform should aim to incorporate the lessons learned from the period 2002–8. The main message here is that a deep reform should push for an international agreement on real exchange rate levels and exchange rate regimes that help developing countries follow export-led growth trajectories.

The new trends in global financial markets

The changes in the global financial system with respect to the aforementioned trends are well represented by two facts. First, up until mid-September 2008 there were no new crises in emerging market economies, in spite of the emergence of various episodes of financial turmoil in the period 2002–8. Remarkably, the sub-prime crisis in the United States did not trigger a financial crisis in any emerging market economy up until the collapse that followed the Lehman Brothers bankruptcy. Second, country risk premia have followed a declining trend since late 2002, and by mid-2005 they fell below the minimum value registered in the pre-Asian crisis period. In mid-2007, country risk premia, measured by the Emerging Markets Bond Index elaborated by J.P. Morgan (EMBI+), reached their historical low, significantly lower than the minimum level of the pre-Asian crisis period and also significantly lower than the spread of US high-yield bonds. Country risk premia only started to rise in July 2007, once the concerns about the sub-prime crisis emerged. However, since that moment up until the Lehman Brothers bankruptcy in mid-September 2008, the EMBI+ remained at levels comparable to the low records of the pre-Asian crises period, showing a fairly robust relative performance of emerging markets' financial assets. It was only after the Lehman Brothers collapse that country risk premia increased substantially, reaching a peak of 860 basis points (bp) in October 2008 and then remaining around a mean of 680 bp until early 2009.

It should also be mentioned that parallel to these two developments in the global financial system, there has been a substantial acceleration of developing countries' growth rate. Between 2002 and 2008, developing countries' GDP had been growing at an average annual rate of 6.7 per cent; a substantial acceleration compared to the average annual growth rate of 4.8 per cent during the period 1991–2001.

These changes have occurred simultaneously with a shift in the exchange rate regimes of emerging market economies. Flexibility is the key characteristic shared by the exchange rate policies of most of these countries. Traditionally, flexibility has meant that the exchange rate is determined in the foreign exchange market and the monetary authority in these markets is not bound to intervene. But in the present context of developing countries, flexibility also means that the monetary authority reserves the right to intervene in the foreign exchange market.

One advantage of this regime is its preventive role, as it cannot be a victim of speculative attacks. The regime combines the advantages of a floating regime, with the degrees of freedom of the monetary authority, to react to changes in the domestic and international contexts, and to accordingly adjust the exchange rate behavior and the monetary policy to the changing needs of economic policy. In practice, if not *de jure*, in the recent experience of most of the emerging market economies we find the above mentioned exchange rate regime, which is generally called "managed floating" (Williamson, 2000; Bofinger and Wollmerhäuser, 2003).

The movement toward greater exchange rate flexibility by many developing countries has certainly contributed to the development of the above mentioned facts. In our view, however, the main change in the process of financial globalization has been wrought by another factor; namely, the reversal of net capital flows now moving from developing to developed countries.[5] Many of the emerging market economies, which had initially entered the system as recipients of capital inflows financing current account deficits, have in recent years started to generate current account surpluses—or to reduce significantly the previous deficits—and to persistently accumulate foreign exchange reserves.

In a set of twenty-nine emerging market economies,[6] only four showed a current account surplus in 1997. In the same set, the number of countries with current account surpluses was fourteen in 2001, eighteen in 2004 and fourteen in 2006. In the same set of countries, the ratio between the aggregate amount of the surpluses and the absolute value of the aggregate amount of the deficits was 0.35 in 1997, 1.40 in 2001, 3.93 in 2004, and 4.64 in 2006. Excluding China, the ratio was 0.04 in 1997, 1.13 in 2001, 2.73 in 2004, and 2.15 in 2006.

There was a turnaround in the circumstances under which these countries entered the international financial system—they shifted from being absorbers of external savings to becoming exporters of savings and intermediaries of international capital flows—and this changed their position in the global financial system. It is our claim that this reduction of foreign saving dependence in the period 2002–8 helped developing countries reduce the chances of facing external crisis, lower their risk premia and enhance economic growth. Our claim requires an explanation of the channels through which this has occurred.

Current account surpluses and the availability of large amounts of foreign exchange reserves are indicators of external robustness, as they indicate a low probability that the country will face difficulties in meeting its external commitments. These indicators are used by international investors in their portfolio decisions. Research has also shown that they perform well at predicting the probability of balance of payment crises (Kaminsky et al., 1998). It is therefore not difficult to see why both the perceived risk and the risk premia followed downward trends in the cases where the current account showed a surplus.

The emergence of a number of surplus countries can have beneficial effects on countries whose current account deficits still persist, and can benefit the system as a whole. Having fewer numbers of deficit countries in a context where many emerging market economies show surpluses diminishes the risk of herd behavior and contagion, and thus reduce the perceived risk of the deficit countries. The emerging market asset class is more heterogeneous, and many of these assets correspond to robust economies. This configuration benefits the risk perception of deficit countries and the risk perception of the whole asset class.

Let us illustrate with two Latin American cases how the new trends in the balance of payments helped developing countries find ways to overcome the hard constraints confronted at the beginning of the present decade. The strong improvement in Brazil's current account was the key factor that allowed the country to climb out of the financial trap in which it had been caught since the beginning of the new century. This improvement reduced the external financial fragility and induced a reduction of the country risk premium. The consequent fall in the international interest rate confronted by the country decelerated the growth of its external and public debts, and improved its sustainability prospects. Therefore, the shift from current account deficit to surplus led to a virtuous circle instead of the vicious circle configured by the financial trap.

Argentina's debt restructuring illustrates a case where a country benefits from the emergence of a group of economies with current account surpluses. The default on the external debt was declared in December 2001, before the improvement in international financial market conditions. In early 2003, the government launched an initiative that offered a 75 per cent haircut on the face value of the original debt. More than 76 per cent of the debt under default accepted the swap. The success of the restructuring was surprising, given both the dimension of the restructured debt and the level of the haircut; the highest recorded in the recent globalization era. It is clear that the novel international financial conditions contributed to this result. The debt swap took place while country risk premia in emerging markets were falling, thus making it a sufficiently attractive offer, which just a few months earlier had been considered "unacceptable."

The emergence of current account surplus (or reduction in current account deficits) and the accumulation of foreign exchange reserves have affected developing countries' performance not exclusively by reducing risk premia and the perceived risk of crises. A recent and increasing series of comparative international studies suggest that these variables are key factors explaining recent economic growth acceleration in developing countries. This empirical literature shows that current account and foreign exchange reserves accumulation are positively correlated with economic growth. For instance, the influential work by Prasad et al. (2007) has shown that there is a positive correlation between current account balances and economic growth among non-industrial countries for the period 1970–2004. Similar results have been obtained by Bosworth and Collins (1999) and the United Nations Conference on Trade and Development (UNCTAD, 2008). On the other hand, the positive correlation between foreign reserve accumulation and economic growth has been documented by Polterovich and Popov (2002) and Levy-Yeyati and Sturzenegger (2007), among others.

Even when the positive correlation between these variables seems to be a well documented empirical fact, the mechanisms through which both current account surpluses and foreign exchange reserves accumulation favor economic growth are not necessarily obvious. One possible channel is related to the discussion above. International capital markets suffer from many imperfections that make financing to developing countries volatile and subject to sudden stops. This feature can affect growth in at least two ways. Massive capital outflows may lead to external crises with negative long-lasting effects on the economic structure and thus undermine long-run growth (Stiglitz, 2000). Even if crises could be avoided, the inherent volatility of capital flows may affect investment decisions and growth. By reducing volatility and the probability of crises, current account surpluses (or lower deficits) and foreign exchange reserves accumulation may contribute to economic growth. These seem plausible stories. In fact, the work by Prasad et al. (2007) suggests that one of the reasons why higher growth was observed in countries that relied less on external savings is that they did not suffer from external crises. However, their study also indicates that the association between growth and the current account does not follow exclusively from avoiding crises, provided that the correlation also holds for sub-periods in which no crises were observed. This result suggests that the effects of current account surplus and foreign exchange reserve accumulation on economic growth do not operate exclusively by reducing volatility and the chances of crises.

Foreign savings, real exchange rate, and economic growth

In the previous section, we argued that developing countries have found a novel way to enter the international financial markets by becoming net suppliers of capital. The consequent improvement in their current account balance has led to an acceleration of their rate of foreign assets accumulation. There seems to be a wide consensus that the main motivation behind this strategy is countries' willingness to maintain competitive real exchange rates, or at least to avoid overvaluations. The findings of the literature surveyed above corroborate that both current account surpluses and reserve accumulation are highly and positively associated to competitive (or undervalued) real exchange rates (see, for example, Prasad et al., 2007). One hypothesis that has recently gained an increasing number of advocates is that both current account surpluses and the accumulation of foreign exchange reserve impact economic growth by making the RER competitive. The results of a new series of research on the RER–growth link provide substantive support of this view.

In an early work, Razin and Collins (1999) show that competitive (undervalued) real exchange rates appear to be associated with more rapid economic growth for a sample of 93 countries over the period 1975–92. Aguirre and

Calderon (2005) use dynamic panel data techniques for a data set of 60 countries between 1965 and 2003. They find that moderately undervalued real exchange rates enhance economic growth. A recent work by Rodrik (2008) uses a panel data of 184 countries for the period 1950–2004 and also finds that these two variables are positively correlated. The estimated coefficients are significant for the whole period and for different sub-periods, which indicates that the relation is independent of the period under consideration. Using a two-stage panel growth regression, Rodrik also finds that competitive real exchange rate is associated with growth in industrial economic activities, and that the expansion in this sector correlates positively and significantly with aggregate economic growth. The result suggests that the effects of the real exchange rate on growth operate (at least partially) through the expansion of industrial (tradable) activities. The result is also important because it is free from reverse causation problems; at a firm level the real exchange rate can be interpreted as exogenous, something that cannot be assumed in aggregate cross-country analyses. With a similar objective, Eichengreen (2007) finds that—in a sample of 28 industries for 40 emerging markets countries in the period 1985–2003—undervalued real exchange rates are positively correlated with growth of industrial employment. Other studies obtaining similar results between competitive (undervalued) RER and growth are Hausman et al. (2005), Gala (2007), Prasad et al. (2007), and Bhalla (2008).

The literature reviewed so far suggests that the novel way in which countries entered international capital markets, via the generation of current account surpluses and the accumulation of reserves, enhances economic growth not only by reducing volatility and the risk of external crises, but mainly through its effect on the level of the real exchange rate. This seems to be a widely shared view both among academics and policy-makers. What remains under dispute are the channels through which the real exchange rate affects economic growth.

At the macroeconomic level, the debate revolves around whether economic growth in developing countries is supply or demand constrained. Under the former view, the intellectual roots of which go back to the neoclassical growth model (Solow, 1956), growth acceleration requires an increase in the savings rate, which will then be transformed into higher investment rates and capital accumulation. Ideally, in an open economy it would not matter whether the sources of savings are domestic or foreign. Moreover, if neoclassical production functions are a good description of the real world, one would expect savings to flow from rich countries with high capital–labor ratios to poor countries with low capital–labor ratios. Evidence has systematically run counter to this prediction. A common explanation for this "paradox" (Lucas, 1990) points to the existence of multiple imperfections in both domestic and international capital markets. As already mentioned, it is usually admitted that because of imperfections in the international capital markets, flows of finance to developing countries are volatile and prone to sudden stops. Similarly, it is argued that underdeveloped domestic financial markets typically do a poor job at intermediating foreign savings and channeling them into productive uses. If these premises are reasonable enough, advocates of the supply-constrained view plausibly expect that countries with higher *domestic* saving rates would grow faster. The relevant question then concerns the causal channel going from more competitive real exchange rates to higher domestic saving rates.

Levy-Yeyati and Sturzenegger (2007)—following the well-known result of the standard Kalekian-structuralist model—point to the redistributive effects of devaluation. The transition to a more competitive real exchange rate implies a transfer of income from workers to firms via a decline in real wages. In an economy with financially constrained firms, higher saving rates, capital accumulation, and growth would follow.

Inspired by the recent Chinese experience, Dooley et al. (2004a and 2004b) suggest another possible channel. An undervalued real exchange rate implies a subsidy to exports relative to imports, which generates an increase in domestic saving relative to absorption, and consequently a current account surplus. In order to maintain the internal balance, a rise in the domestic interest rate is needed. In a financially repressed economy, the government would be able to set the domestic interest rate to restrain absorption and increase the saving rate. The resulting current account surplus and reserve accumulation in turn serve as collateral required to support the flows of foreign direct investment that sustain rapid growth.

Irrespective of the validity of the theoretical arguments, the RER–saving link seems to find little empirical support. Montiel and Serven (2008) test the correlation between the two variables for a set of 94 countries over the period 1975–2005. Using the (log) GDP deflator from the Penn World Tables as a proxy for the RER, the unconditional correlation analysis shows that a higher saving rate is strongly associated with a more *appreciated* real exchange rate. When they control for the level of income per capita, the correlation coefficient changes signs; namely, higher savings correlate with undervalued RER. However, the coefficient is very small and statistically significant only for the ten-year frequency, and not for the thirty-year frequency. The authors conclude that "saving is unlikely to provide the mechanism through which the real exchange rate affects growth."

Proponents of the demand-constrained view are inspired by the Keynesian vision in which effective demand is the main driver of economic growth in economies with unemployed and/or underemployed workers. In an open economy, a competitive real exchange rate would lead to an increase in the demand for exports and import substitutes, and the additional demand to additional domestic production and income. Higher production would in turn lead, through the accelerator principle, to higher investment and growth. Additionally, the acceleration in aggregate demand growth has a reinforcing feedback effect on labor productivity growth, sometimes called the "Kaldor-Verdoorn law" (Frenkel and Taylor, 2007). Furthermore, it is not difficult to show within the Keynesian framework that a depreciation of the real exchange rate leads to higher saving and investment rates, together with an improvement in the current account. This result fits the stylized facts.

In a closed system the source of the aggregate demand pull is not as relevant as in an open one. This distinction is well known in many parts of the developing world where economic growth has been recurrently constrained by shortages of foreign currency. This is a key aspect of the export-led growth strategy: the demand-pull is obtained simultaneously with a relaxation of the external constraint. Proponents of the export-led growth view, with John Williamson (2003 and 2006) as a notable example, have been pointing out for a long time the importance of a competitive real exchange rate as a key element in a development strategy that seeks to overcome the foreign exchange constraint.[7] Interestingly, Keynesian economists of the balance of payment (BoP) constraint school have largely undermined the possibility that a competitive RER could contribute to relax the external constraint. A key assumption for such a conclusion is that income elasticities of exports and imports are fixed in the long-run (Thirlwall, 1979). This assumption may be too stringent if one is willing to consider relatively long RER departures from "equilibrium." Barbosa-Filho (2006) suggests that with the reasonable assumption that trade elasticities can be altered by changes in the real exchange rate, the BoP constraint is no longer immutable as suggested in the standard model.

Levy-Yeyati and Sturzenegger (2007) are skeptical about export growth and import substitution being the factors explaining the positive correlation between competitive real exchange rate and growth. Their view rests on the finding that exports are negatively (and imports positively) correlated with reserve accumulation.

A third line of argumentation emphasizes the existence of positive externalities associated with the production of traded goods. Many appealing stories are possible, but all share the notion that a temporary undervaluation of the real exchange rate may solve the standard private versus public benefit dilemma. With higher profitability, tradable firms would find incentives to invest. Capital accumulation and productivity growth arising from the positive externality would follow. If this process is long enough, the tradable sector would have acquired a productivity level that would turn it profitable at the original relative prices. This type of idea has a long tradition in development economics. For instance, the use of competitive RER to protect infant industry can be explained along these lines. The Dutch disease problem shares the same logic but it is applied to the opposite case: real appreciation and shrinking the tradable sector.[8]

Rodrik (2008) is a notable example of this third line of argumentation. He shows that a competitive real exchange rate can function as a second best solution to compensate for the institutional and market failures that keep tradable firms from exploiting positive externalities. In his explanation, however, it is not clear why these failures affect tradable activities more proportionally than non-tradable ones (Eichengreen, 2007).

It seems fair to conclude this section by stating that there is robust evidence suggesting that a key channel through which current account surplus and foreign exchange reserve accumulation foster economic growth is by maintaining real exchange rates at competitive levels. However, we still need more research to assess, with higher precision, the channels through which the competitive RER–growth link operates.

Broadening the pending agenda of reforms

Under the light of the evidence shown in the previous section, the period 2002–8—with numerous developing countries exhibiting current account surpluses, financial robustness and accelerating rates of growth—can be seen as an amplification of a historical pattern. In the recent phase, more developing countries have followed paths that showed both current account surpluses and higher rates of growth. In some cases, those outcomes resulted from policies explicitly oriented to foster growth through the management of competitive exchange rates that simultaneously contribute to generate higher rates of growth, current account surpluses and the accumulation of reserves. In other cases, those outcomes resulted mainly from international factors that were exogenous to the countries' economic policies (i.e. low international interest rates, high expansion of the US economy, rising commodity prices). However, even in cases where the outcomes cannot be attributed to domestic policies, the authorities aimed to strengthen external robustness throughout the accumulation of reserves. Thus, the recent pattern followed by numerous developing countries seems to have been an a posteriori confirmation of the policy lessons implicit in the above mentioned studies.

Regardless of the particular impact on individual countries, an important feature of the configuration in the period 2002–8 was its positive effects on the workings of the global financial system vis-à-vis the emerging market economies as a whole. This configuration significantly alleviated the most negative aspects that financial globalization had shown until the early 2000s. However, its benefits for developing countries have not been recognized by the multilateral financial institutions. The official doctrine of the IMF does not seem to see the virtues of that configuration in terms of financial robustness and growth. For instance, the institution continues officially to promote macroeconomic policies based on free floating and inflation targeting. Free floating could lead to exchange rate appreciation and therefore threaten external balance robustness, and economic growth.

The current global financial and economic crisis has brought the discussion about the international financial architecture back. The depth and length of the crisis seem to have persuaded political leaders and their advisors about the potential dangers of unregulated financial markets and free capital mobility. The emerging debate at international forums has so far focused on the degree of regulation of global financial markets and potential reforms of multilateral financial institutions. These initiatives seem to share the spirit of the proposals of the late 1990s and early 2000s, which were developed as a result of the crises in emerging markets economies. Regarding developing countries, those proposals focused on one of the most prominent failures of global financial markets, namely, the instability that affected emerging market economies. The proposals called for building institutions capable of preventing, managing and compensating for the instability of the system. This agenda is still valid today, as was vividly illustrated by the contagion effects of the developed countries' financial crisis on the emerging markets' economies from late 2008. However, it should be broadened to take into account the lessons from the period 2002–8.

One important lesson underlines the key role of markets for developing countries' exports. The experience of financial globalization tells us that capital inflows and external savings are by no means substitutes for growth-cum-exports. Therefore, together with institutional reforms aimed at stabilizing the workings of the global financial system, developing countries should also call for a deeper reform, intended to consolidate the positive features of the 2002–8 configuration. For instance, they should pursue an international agreement on real exchange rates and exchange rate regimes that would allow developing countries to follow paths of high rates of growth-cum-exports.[9]

One common objection to the proposal of targeting competitive RER, current account surplus and foreign exchange reserves accumulation is that it implies a fallacy of composition. Certainly, this kind of strategy cannot be followed by all countries at the same time. However, there is a priori no inconsistency in proposing it only for developing countries as a group. Furthermore, the prediction derived from standard neoclassical growth theory that rich countries would tend to provide savings to poor countries in their development process has been criticized on many grounds, but it has never been accused of inconsistency. Our proposal simply states the opposite direction of saving flows, by interpreting empirical evidence as suggesting that developed countries can best contribute to poor countries' development by providing markets for their (infant) products, instead of providing savings. Many historical experiences show that developing or poor countries have benefited from having a competitive RER and exporting to developed countries. These include the recovery of Western Europe and the development of Japan after the Second World War and the East Asian miracle since the mid-1960s. A priori, there are no significant differences between those experiences and the more recent cases, of which China is the most popular one.

Although not inconsistent, the proposed strategy may not be entirely effective if product competition among developing countries is high. Razmi and Blecker (2008), for instance, found that most developing countries compete with other developing country exporters of low-technology products rather than with industrialized country producers. In such a context, an uncoordinated strategy where all developing countries try to maintain a competitive RER may end up in a fallacy of composition. A situation like this would certainly call for international coordination, in order to reach an agreement on real exchange rate levels among developing and developed countries and avoid fallacy of composition effects. But even without coordination, developing countries may still find it useful to maintain a competitive RER to foster activities that face developed country competition.

It has also been argued that the 2002–8 configurations implied a "global imbalance." By the mid-2000s, some analysts argued that those imbalances would require an adjustment, which could end up in a severe global crisis (i.e. a "balance of financial terror"). It would be a mistake to think, as some analysts still do, that the current global financial crisis is the predicted crisis. The so-called global imbalances were by no means responsible for the current situation; the crisis resulted instead from the massive underestimation of risks by financial institutions and the very poor regulation of financial markets by the governments of developed countries (Dooley et al., 2009).

The implementation of the deeper reform we are suggesting is not an easy task. Garnering support for this reform in the international arena would require reviving the spirit of Bretton Woods in a setting in which developing countries should have the voice and the weight they presently lack within the international financial institutions. But every journey begins with a first step. In this case, the first step should be the acknowledgment of the lessons from the history of financial globalization and of the beneficial effects that an agreement on exchange rates would have both on developing and developed countries.

Notes

1. A previous version of this chapter was presented at The Initiative for Policy Dialogue Meeting of the Task Force on Financial Markets Regulation at the University of Manchester's Brooks World Poverty Institute, July 1–2, 2008. The authors would like to acknowledge the collaboration of Eleonora Tubio and thank the Ford Foundation for financial support.
2. Principal Research Associate at CEDES and Professor at the University of Buenos Aires.
3. Research Associate at CEDES and PhD candidate at the University of Massachusetts, Amherst.
4. In fact, the sequence of crises in Latin America had started much earlier. Many of these countries had been participating in the process of financial globalization since it came into existence during the second half of the seventies. All of the Latin American

economies that were financially integrated at that time (i.e. Argentina, Bolivia, Brazil, Chile, Colombia, Mexico, Uruguay, and Venezuela) suffered external and financial crises (the so-called Latin American external debt crisis) in 1981–2. The smallest economies (Bolivia, Chile, and Colombia) started to recover a few years later, but for the biggest economies (Argentina, Brazil, and Mexico) the recovery did not start until the early 1990s.

5. In the 1980s, there was also a trend of net capital flows moving from low income to high income countries. But this was a transitory consequence of the external sector adjustments of Latin American economies after their crises. In the course of renegotiations of Latin America's defaulted external debts, which lasted from 1982–90, there was no voluntary lending from private sources and most of these countries went through current account adjustments in order to pay some proportion of the interest dues.

6. The data set comprises 24 out of 25 countries included in the Emerging Markets index elaborated by MSCI Barra (Argentina, Brazil, Chile, China, Colombia, Czech Republic, Egypt, Hungary, India, Indonesia, Israel, Jordan, Korea, Malaysia, Mexico, Morocco, Pakistan, Peru, Philippines, Poland, Russia, South Africa, Thailand, and Turkey) in addition to Bulgaria, Ecuador, Panama, Ukraine, and Venezuela.

7. Not to mention Bela Ballasa (1971) and Carlos Díaz Alejandro (1975). UNCTAD (2008) is also worth a mention.

8. Dutch disease models with these characteristics have been used to illustrate deindustrialization processes, such as in the UK under Margaret Thatcher's government (Krugman, 1987) and in Latin America during the 1990s (Ros and Skott, 1998).

9. Suggestions for the implementation of an international agreement on real exchange rates have recently been presented by John Williamson (2006).

References

Aguirre, A. and Calderón, C. (2006) 'The Effects of Real Exchange Rate Misalignments on Economic Growth.' Mimeo. Central Bank of Chile: Santiago.

Balassa, B. (1971) 'Trade Policies in Developing Countries.' *American Economic Review*, 61(2).

Barbosa-Filho, N. (2006) 'Exchange Rates, Growth and Inflation.' Paper submitted to the Annual Conference on Development and Change. Campos do Jordão, Brazil (November 18–20).

Bhalla, S. (2008) 'Economic Development and the Role of Currency Undervaluation.' *The Cato Journal*, 28(2).

Bofinger, P. and Wollmershäuser, T. (2003) 'Managed Floating as a Monetary Policy Strategy.' *Economics of Planning*, 36(2), pp. 81–109.

Bosworth, B. and Collins, S. (1999) 'Capital Flows to Developing Economies: Implications for Saving and Investment.' *Brookings Papers on Economic Activity*, 1, pp. 143–69.

Camdessus, M. (2000) 'An Agenda for the IMF at the Start of the 21st Century.' Speech at the Council on Foreign Relations, New York (February 1).

Díaz Alejandro, C. (1979) 'Algunas vicisitudes históricas de las economías abiertas en América Latina.' *Desarrollo Económico*, 19(74).

Dooley, M. P., Folkerts-Landau, D., and Garber, P. M. (2004a) 'Direct Investment, Rising Real Wages and the Absorption of Excess Labor in the Periphery.' NBER Working Paper, 10626 (July).

—— (2004b) 'The US Current Account Deficit and Economic Development: Collateral for a Total Return Swap.' NBER Working Paper, 0727.

—— (2009) 'Bretton Woods II Still Defines the International Monetary System.' NBER Working Paper, 14731.

Eichengreen, B. (2007) 'The Real Exchange Rate and Economic Growth.' Paper prepared for the Growth Commission.

Frenkel, R. (2002) 'Capital Market Liberalization, Growth and Stability.' Opening remarks to the Initiative of Policy Dialogue Capital Market Liberalization Task Force Meeting, Columbia University, New York (September).

—— (2008) 'From the Boom in Capital Inflows to Financial Traps.' In J. A. Ocampo and J. E. Stiglitz (eds.), *Capital Markets Liberalization and Development*, Initiative for Policy Dialogue (IPD) Book Series. Oxford: Oxford University Press.

—— and Taylor, L. (2007) 'Real Exchange Rate, Monetary Policy, and Employment.' In J. A. Ocampo, K. S. Jomo, and S. Khan (eds.), *Policy Matters: Economic and Social Policies to Sustain Equitable Development*. London: Zed Books.

Gala, P. (2007) 'Real Exchange Rate Levels and Economic Development: Theoretical Analysis and Empirical Evidence.' *Cambridge Journal of Economics*, March 2008, 32, pp. 273–88.

Hausman, R., Pritchett, L., and Rodrik, D. (2005) 'Growth Accelerations.' *Journal of Economic Growth*, 10(4), pp. 303–29.

Kaminsky, G., Lizondo, S., and Reinhart, C. (1998) 'Leading Indicators of Currency Crisis.' IMF Staff Papers, 45(1).

Köhler, H. (2002) 'Working for a Better Globalization.' Conference on Humanizing the Global Economy, Washington, DC (January 28).

Krueger, A. (2002) 'A New Approach to Sovereign Debt Restructuring.' International Monetary Fund.

Krugman, P. (1987) 'The Narrow Moving Band, the Dutch Disease, and the Competitive Consequences of Mrs Thatcher.' *Journal of Development Economics*, pp. 41–55.

Levy-Yeyati, E. and Sturzenegger, F. (2007) 'Fear of Floating in Reverse: Exchange Rate Policy in the 2000s.' Mimeo.

Lucas, R. (1990) 'Why Doesn't Capital Flow from Rich to Poor Countries?' *American Economic Review*, 80, pp. 92–6.

Montiel, P. and Serven, L. (2008) 'Real Exchange Rates, Saving and Growth: Is There a Link?' World Bank Policy Research, Working Paper No. 4636.

Polterovich, V. and Popov, V. (2002) 'Accumulation of Foreign Exchange Reserves and Long Term Growth.' Working Paper, New Economic School, Moscow.

Prasad, E., Rajan, R., and Subramanian, A. (2007) 'Foreign Capital and Economic Growth.' *Brooking Papers on Economic Activity*, 1, pp. 153–209.

Razin, O. and Collins, S. M. (1999) 'Real Exchange-Rate Misalignments and Growth.' In A. Razin and E. Sadka (eds.), *The Economics of Globalization: Policy Perspectives from Public Economics*. Cambridge: Cambridge University Press.

Razmi, A. and Blecker, R. (2008) 'Developing Country Exports of Manufactures: Moving Up the Ladder to Escape the Fallacy of Composition?' *Journal of Development Studies*, 44(1).

Rodrik, D. (2008) 'The Real Exchange Rate and Economic Growth: Theory and Evidence.' John F. Kennedy School of Government, Harvard University (July).

Ros, J. and Skott, P. (1998) 'Dynamic Effects of Trade Liberalization and Currency Over-valuation Under Conditions of Increasing Returns.' Manchester School, pp. 466–89.

Solow, R. (1956) 'A Contribution to the Theory of Economic Growth.' *Quarterly Journal of Economics*, 70(1), pp. 65–94.

Stiglitz, J. E. (2000) 'Capital Market Liberalization, Economic Growth, and Instability.' *World Development*, 28(6), pp. 1075–86.

Thirlwall, A. P. (1979) 'The Balance of Payments Constraint as an Explanation of International Growth Rate Differences.' *Banca Nazionale del Lavoro Quarterly Review*, 128, pp. 45–53.

UNCTAD. (2008) *Trade and Development Report 2008*.

Williamson, J. (2000) *Exchange Rate Regimes for Emerging Markets: Reviving the Intermediate Option*. Washington, DC: Institute for International Economics.

—— (2003) 'Exchange Rate Policy and Development.' Paper presented at the Initiative for Policy Dialogue (IPD) Capital Market Liberalization Task Force, Columbia University, Barcelona (June).

—— (2006) 'A Worldwide System of Reference Rates.' Working Paper, No. 45, Bank of Greece, August.

—— (2008) 'Exchange Rate Economics.' Working Paper Series, WP 08-3, Peterson Institute for International Economics (February).

15

The Accumulation of International Reserves as a Defense Strategy

Fernando J. Cardim de Carvalho[1]

Introduction

The financial turmoil of the second half of the 1990s showed that even some of the most successful and fast-growing emerging countries risked suffering deep and widespread damages caused by balance of payments crises generated by capital flow reversals. In fact, as reflected in the contemporaneous debate, most of these countries suffered doubly, both from the crises themselves and from the burden of the rescue packages put together by the International Monetary Fund.[2] Stung by the costs of those crises and their resolution, emerging countries seem to have adopted in the 2000s a different strategy, dubbed "self-insurance." The central and most visible, although by no means the only, instrument of this strategy has been the relentless accumulation of international reserves.

Reserve accumulation by developing economies, however, has been a more complex phenomenon than has often been recognized. First, because reserves have been accumulated under very different circumstances, in response to different reasons, depending on the country one chooses to analyze. Second, because it is assumed by many analysts that these countries have better alternative uses for the resources that are being kept idle or semi-idle (invested in low yield securities as US Treasury bonds, for instance). Third, critics and defenders of reserve accumulation as a defensive strategy do not always properly evaluate the risks of new balance of payments crises. In any case, in the absence of adequate sources of liquidity that could offer emergency support on reasonable terms in the case of crisis, it should not be a surprise that developing countries tried to identify means to defend themselves.

In this chapter, we want to reexamine the set of defensive strategies recently adopted by emerging economies, of which reserve accumulation has been rightly identified as a central element. In doing so, we begin, in the following section, by examining the motives to hold reserves, based on the notion of liquidity preference proposed by Keynes in *The General Theory of Employment, Interest and Money* (2007), and discussing how it applies both at the international and domestic levels. The next section focuses on how reserve accumulation, as well as other instruments currently being adopted or proposed, fit into this theoretical approach. We distinguish the cases where reserve accumulation results from conscious precautionary strategies from those where it is a by-product of policies designed to achieve other goals. In the following section, we show that important vulnerabilities remain even if the country is successful at accumulating a very large amount of reserves. The last section concludes the chapter by examining some alternatives to reserve accumulation that could reduce vulnerabilities and minimize negative externalities.

Motives for demanding international liquidity

Quite apart from any need for *capital* or *external savings* of any nature, a nation demands *liquidity*, that is, *the command over international means of payment*, for reasons that are fundamentally similar to the demand for domestic money on the part of individuals and firms. If we adapt Keynes' well-known classification of motives to demand money[3] to the demand for international reserves, we may define:

A transactions demand. Domestically, this is the main reason behind the demand for money. As in the case of the domestic transactions demand for money, the amount of international means of payments a country needs to retain to cover its payments needs for goods and services depends primarily on the time profile of its cash inflows and outflows. *Normal* expenditures cover payments for imports of goods and services as well as factor incomes. Inflows are generated by the export of goods and services and by the import of capital. The latter may be too volatile to be counted on to guarantee cover for normal expenditures. On the other hand, it is extremely unlikely that cash inflows from exports of goods and services will materialize exactly when needed to pay the country's external obligations, given their own time patterns. The less dependent a developing country is on the export of a few agricultural or mining commodities, the smoother its export inflows should be. In this case, one would expect a transactions demand for reserves to emerge to guarantee the payment for normal imports of goods and services in the cases where normal inflows may be too irregularly distributed.

A precautionary demand. In contrast to the transactions demand for money, the precautionary demand refers to the liquid balances held against uncertainty, that is, to protect the country against the possibility of suffering adverse shocks. Supply shocks, like the oil price rises of the 1970s, may suddenly and sharply increase the import bill. Reversal of capital flows and capital flight may easily overcome the monetary authorities' abilities to maintain stability in the foreign currency market.[4] For a country, guarding against adverse shocks that may reduce or interrupt cash inflows or increase outflows may be the most important motive to retain reserves.

A finance demand.[5] Keynes defined this motive to demand money as applying to the case where an individual has an abnormal expenditure plan, as in the case of making an investment, for example, and thus has a temporarily higher need for means of payment. For a country, particularly if it is a developing country, there may be moments where the launching of a large-scale investment plan may create an extra demand for international means of payment, above and beyond the normal transactions demand for reserves. In this case, the country can satisfy this demand by borrowing, if it has access to foreign financial markets and loans are available, which increases its external liabilities, or by accumulating extra reserves in advance of the launching of the plan.

A speculative demand. In Keynes's theory, the speculative demand for money refers to money balances held by investors when they expect interest rates to rise. They prefer to hold money until the prices of securities go down to avoid a capital loss, buying them on the cheap when the interest rate finally rises as expected. Normally, one would not think of countries actually speculating with asset prices and therefore there would be no speculative demand for reserves. However, as the value of reserves held by emerging economies rose steeply in recent years, there arose some concern with the growing opportunity cost of maintaining those idle reserves. The possibility was then examined in many quarters of investing a fraction of those resources in reasonably safe but higher-yielding assets. But liquidity considerations should remain paramount in reserve management. Thus, to avoid mixing liquidity management with the search for higher returns, more and more countries decided to dedicate a fraction of their reserves to constitute Sovereign Wealth Funds (SWF) with the mission of increasing the overall return on reserves. The creation of SWF worked, thus, as an alternative to the definition of a speculative demand for international reserves, that is, to holding currency reserves in anticipation of some expected investment opportunity to materialize.

Thus, as in the case of domestic demand for money, demand for international reserves should be a function of the "normal" value of expenditures with goods and services and the time profile of cash inflows from exports (transactions motive), the level of uncertainty about the future (precautionary motive), and the existence and value of extra expenditure plans (finance motive). Expected changes in foreign interest rates and the price of securities (speculative motive) should influence the portfolio choices of SWF, rather than influencing directly the demand for foreign currency. The size of the demand for reserves, on the other hand, should depend on the existence of ready sources of international liquidity in case of need, and the conditions for accessing these sources. The easier the access to liquidity sources, the lower will be the demand for money since users will not need to maintain idle balances if they can obtain the money they need from existing facilities.

Two main features distinguish domestic and the international monetary systems with respect to liquidity provision. First, domestic monetary systems are run by specially-created institutions to manage the creation of money in line with the economy's needs, while no such institutions exist at the international level. Second, while domestic economies are usually endowed with one currency, in the international economy different currencies can actually co-exist and compete for the preference of private agents and governments, as it currently happens in the case of the US dollar and the euro.

In modern domestic monetary systems, high-powered money (legal tender) is created by central banks and multiplied into a larger volume of means of payment by the banking system. The provision of liquidity, at least in principle, is regulated so as to accommodate the increase in transactions that will follow the expansion of the economy, while safeguarding the value of money by combating inflation. This can be done in modern monetary systems because liquidity is ultimately created by a specific institution with the power *and* the mission to create means of payment in the necessary amount to allow trade to grow.

Modern international monetary systems, in contrast, are not governed by a specific institution with a mandate to support the legitimate demands for international means of payment. In the post Second World War world, the US dollar has played the role of international means of payment, even after the collapse of the fixed exchange rate system adopted in 1944 at the Bretton Woods Conference. This means that the provision of international liquidity has been a by-product of domestic monetary policies adopted in the United States, which are decided almost exclusively with domestic goals in mind. There is no reason to expect, of course, that international needs for means of payment will be served by such a policy. The Federal Reserve decides on policy having the US economy's needs in mind, not the world's. Only by accident, the pursuance of domestic goals will generate the money supply the rest of the world needs. The problem, of course, is not the predominance of the US dollar as such. The use of a *national* currency as an *international means of payment* would pose a similar problem were the euro or the yen the dominant currency.

In fact, as Robert Triffin explained in 1960, giving a national currency the role of international money inevitably creates a dilemma.[6] For a national currency like the US dollar to work as a means of payment in international transactions, it is necessary that other countries have access to dollars to make transactions among themselves. This is only possible if the United States generates deficits in its balance of payments with the rest of the world. If the value of transactions is growing, and the velocity of circulation of money is stable, balance of payments deficits have in fact to increase in order to increase international liquidity. The growth in the US balance of payments deficits, however, erodes the confidence on the stability of the value of the dollar, undermining its role as an international money of account and means of payment. This is the Triffin dilemma: controlling US balance of payments deficits could restore the confidence in the dollar, but at the cost of rationing international liquidity and creating obstacles to trade expansion. Accommodating the international demand for the international money, in contrast, accelerates the erosion of confidence in the same money.[7]

The provision of means of payment is not an exclusive responsibility of central banks. Domestically, high-powered money is multiplied by the banking system when the latter creates demand deposits. In addition, non-bank financial institutions can again multiply the ability of doing transactions with a given volume of means of payment. The smooth operation of the monetary system depends, thus, on the way the three types of institutions operate and relate to each other. The central bank influences the ability of banks to multiply the volume of means of payment and the banks influence the rest of the financial system in the creation of additional liquidity.

In the first two decades after Bretton Woods, the expansion of international liquidity was limited by the general acceptance of capital controls and other restrictions on international financial transactions. In particular, purely financial transactions were banned in a large number of cases. Even foreign direct investment was subject to legal or regulatory restrictions in many countries. Practically only trade credit, to support the expansion of international trade in goods and services, was accepted without reservations. Capital controls began falling out of favor in the 1960s. Their reach was increasingly restricted in the following decade and they practically disappeared among developed countries in the late 1980s. In the 1990s, it was the developing economies' turn to dismantle their capital controls, although the process somehow lost momentum at the end of the decade.

The rapid expansion of financial transactions following the liberalization of the capital account aggravated the fragility of a system already plagued by the Triffin dilemma. The fast growth of capital flows sharply increased the volatility of asset prices, interest rates and exchange rates, with significant impact on the "real" side of the economy. Increased volatility meant an increase in the uncertainty surrounding the behavior of the capital account and of the overall balance of payments position. All other things equal, the increasing uncertainty was bound to increase the precautionary demand for international money, stimulating the accumulation of reserves.

These increased uncertainties, naturally, affected much more strongly developing countries because external liabilities for these countries are mostly denominated in foreign currencies, for reasons discussed in the "original sin" literature.[8] Unable to service its liabilities in its own currency, a developing country has to be sure it will have access to, or will have in storage, the amount of foreign currency necessary to honor those obligations.

The situation is certainly potentially more dramatic in the case of developing economies, but they are by no means the only countries threatened by these developments. In fact, it was precisely the conscience of how serious this problem could be for the international economy that inspired the creation of the IMF in the 1944 Bretton Woods Conference. In its original conception, the IMF was to serve precisely as a supplier of "secondary" reserves to countries suffering from balance of payments deficits in a world where the only internationally accepted means of payment would be the dollar. It was only after a protracted debate, in the late 1940s and early 1950s that the Fund came to adopt its current practice of imposing (sometimes exacting) conditionalities on its support programs for countries in need.[9]

In the absence of supporting institutions providing international liquidity at reasonable terms (financial costs *and* policy conditionalities), countries were supposed to turn to private financial markets. The precariousness of this "solution," however, was repeatedly illustrated by the succession of crises initiated by the Mexican crisis of 1994.[10] On the other hand, the rescue packages by the IMF came to be seen, especially in Asian countries, as a burden in themselves, imposing heavy costs, hard to disentangle from the costs of the crises themselves. New strategies, more efficient in protecting these economies against the volatilities of the international economy just *had* to be devised.

Reserve accumulation and other instruments of "self-insurance"

The experience of the 1990s crises vividly illustrated to developing countries the risks of financial and capital liberalization. Both capital flow reversals *and* the rescue packages put together by the IMF imposed heavy losses to afflicted countries in terms of lost output and employment, bankruptcies, and the loss of policy autonomy resulting from the imposition of structural conditionalities that even the Fund itself ended up recognizing were excessive.[11] The sudden realization that international financial integration made the position of emerging countries exceedingly fragile led to two main results.

The first, and more immediate, impact of the succession of balance of payments crises since 1994 was the loss of momentum of the process of capital account liberalization that had been going on in force since the beginning of that decade among developing economies. The most dramatic of the crisis episodes, the 1997 Asian crisis, exploded precisely when the IMF was proposing a reform of its Articles of Agreement to consecrate the principle of capital account convertibility. After 1997 this process was decelerated, virtually to a halt, but it was not reversed.

The second was the realization that emerging economies had to find ways to deal with the possibility of capital flows reversals other than appealing to the IMF for support. It is in this context that several measures were adopted, among which the most visible so far has been the accumulation of reserves.

Capital flows reversals are particularly destructive for developing economies for at least four reasons. First, given the size disparities between world capital markets and those in developing countries, even marginal changes in capital flows in the world market can create great volatility in emerging economies.[12] Second, capital flows respond more frequently to changes in *source* countries than in *recipient*, developing economies. Third, both capital inflows and outflows into developing countries tend to induce vast changes in domestic policies in order to sterilize their effects on exchange rates. Fourth, finally, through their effects on exchange rates (or on interest rates as a result of attempts to sterilize their domestic impact), capital movements can generate important externalities, such as the deleterious effects on exports caused by exchange rate appreciation when inflows are excessive, or the impacts on the solvency of domestic borrowers in foreign currency, when the local currency depreciates as a result of capital flight.

In fact, both *capital flight* and *capital flood* create difficulties for developing countries (see Carvalho, 2008b). In an environment of free capital flows, even small changes in their intensity or direction can cause disproportional damage to the recipient economy.

Developing countries sought to implement measures directed at providing themselves some degree of protection. Short of reinstating capital controls, there were three main instruments for self-protection: the accumulation of increasing amounts of international reserves, to create a cushion against the risk of capital flight or to attenuate the pressures to overvaluation in the case of capital flood; the creation of regional monetary arrangements; and the development of domestic financial markets to accommodate demands for financial resources by local borrowers, including the government.

At first sight, the pace at which reserves have been accumulated by emerging economies these last few years is a very impressive proof of the popularity of the instrument. Table 15.1 shows that, for all developing countries, international reserves grew at a rapid pace in the 2000s, adding almost $2.5 trillion in the years 2004–7 alone. The perception that one could not count on alternative sources of liquidity should lead to an increase both in the transactions and the precautionary demand for money, intensifying reserve accumulation. One should be careful, however, in attributing all growth in reserves to a strategy of self-insurance. Until the outbreak of the sub-prime crisis in the United States, a large amount of reserves had been accumulated as a result of capital inflows that were beyond the control of recipient countries. In some cases, inflows were so intense that exchange rates appreciated strongly even while reserves were accumulated. In other cases, reserves were held precisely to avoid potentially

Table 15.1 Balance of payments and international reserves: all developing countries ($ billion)

	1999	2000	2001	2002	2003	2004	2005	2006	2007
Private creditors	1.5	5.8	−23.0	3.8	84.4	155.2	222.7	288.0	413.0
Net foreign direct investment	177.0	165.5	173.0	160.7	161.9	225.5	288.5	367.5	470.8
Net portfolio equity flows	11.4	13.5	5.6	5.5	24.1	40.4	68.9	104.8	145.1
Current account balance	−18.0	36.0	13.0	62.0	117.0	164.0	310.0	431.0	426.0
Addition to internal reserves	33.0	43.0	80.0	167.0	292.0	402.0	391.0	634.0	1,091.0

Source: World Bank (2008), *Global Development Finance*, part 1: Review, Analysis, and Outlook, table 2.1.

disruptive movements of the exchange rate. Table 15.1 also shows that, in parallel to an impressive growth of current account surpluses, developing countries also received increasing volumes of foreign capital. In fact, in 2006 alone, net private capital inflows reached about $600 billion. In 2007, net private capital inflows rose to slightly less than $900 billion. These inflows are not necessarily sought for, or even desired by developing countries: they simply cannot be stopped once capital controls have been dismantled. In some other cases, reserve growth is a by-product of an attempt to promote the expansion of net exports to compensate the slow growth of domestic expenditures, particularly in the presence of restrictive monetary and fiscal policies. In this case, growth of reserves is not a strategic goal, but just an unintended result of aggregate demand management policies.

Whichever way one measures the contribution of each of the three factors just discussed to the final result, the result is still very impressive in itself—that is, the accumulation of such a volume of reserves in a small period of time.

The creation of regional monetary funds is an attempt to create liquidity facilities that may be more member-friendly than the IMF. It is widely believed that the Fund took advantage of the crisis in Asian countries to promote structural reforms that seemed to be more in line with the demands of some developed countries than in the interest of the borrowing countries. Of course, it is accepted that monetary funds must seek guarantees that their loans will be repaid, but there must be clear principles and mandates to set the types of guarantees that are legitimate. The Fund itself seems to have concluded that it went beyond its mandate during the Camdessus tenure, since an immediate review of the reach of structural conditionalities was begun by his successor. How far the Fund is willing to go to recover its legitimacy is still to be tested, but the bad experience of the 1990s has stimulated many countries to look for alternative liquidity facilities where conditionalities could be more reasonable.

So far, however, only one of the experiments created recently has actually matured, in Asia, the Chiang Mai Initiative (see Park, 2004). The creation of other institutions is being examined, most notably the Banco do Sul in Latin America. The original proposal, advanced by the Venezuelan government, contemplated an institution that would simultaneously perform the roles of a regional monetary fund and of a development bank. The conflation of the two roles was, however, criticized by some potential members, most notably Brazil, which supports the creation of a development bank, but not of a monetary fund. Other relevant, and more immediately viable, initiatives comprise the adoption of local currencies in bilateral trade, as established between Brazil and Argentina, which can be extended to the remaining Mercosul partners (Paraguay and Uruguay), and the creation of swap lines that can economize the use of reserves in the region.

Finally, incentives for the expansion of domestic securities markets have been instrumental in reorienting the demand for financial resources on the part of public and private borrowers in domestic markets in order to reduce exchange rate risks. Of course, the development of domestic financial markets cannot solve problems related to the scarcity of foreign currency, when this is the case, but can keep foreign liabilities under control when foreign financial markets are accessed just because they are more liquid or the cost of capital may be lower. Again, a few countries have achieved a significant measure of success in creating domestic markets for public securities and/or stock exchanges, but this is still mostly a promise for the future.

Persistent vulnerabilities

Building up regional monetary arrangements or creating domestic securities markets are long-term processes that may or may not become efficient protective devices in the future. The accumulation of reserves, in contrast, is meant to protect economies against balance of payments disequilibria *right now*. They are expected to represent a liquidity cushion capable of accommodating sudden demands for foreign currency, giving some breathing space for government authorities to devise more consequent policies.

In fact, as shown in Table 15.2, the accumulation of reserves contributed to the general improvement in the external position of developing countries as a whole. However, a case can be made that, after the widespread process of capital account liberalization of the 1980s and 1990s, the traditional indicators reported in Table 15.2 may no longer give an accurate assessment of a country's external vulnerability.[13]

Of course, cushions are only efficient if they are available when one needs to use the resources. In this sense, it is important to distinguish between the cases where reserves result from the accumulation of current account surpluses and where they result from capital account surpluses in excess of current account deficits, since the latter implies an increase in foreign liabilities. *Borrowed*

Table 15.2 Debt indicators[1]: emerging and developing economies

	2000	2001	2002	2003	2004	2005	2006	2007	2008
Total debt service/exports of goods and services (%)	27.0	27.0	24.5	22.6	18.2	18.8	17.5	14.7	12.1
Reserves/debt service payments	1.79	2.06	2.50	2.88	3.68	3.59	4.19	5.83	7.04
Reserves/imports of goods and services (%)	44.9	49.7	55.4	60.6	62.8	66.3	73.5	83.5	84.7

[1] 2008 data are forecasts.
Source: International Monetary Fund (2008b).

reserves can become unavailable precisely when a country needs them most, that is, when capital flow reversals put pressure on the balance of payments, as was the case for Latin American countries in many occasions since the debt crisis of the 1980s. *Earned* reserves, on the other hand, resulting from the accumulation of surpluses in the current account, become the country's foreign *net worth*, which cannot be just taken away by creditors in the event of a crisis and can thus help keep the country solvent.

In practically all cases, net capital inflows have been an important source of reserves. Some countries, however, have accumulated reserves entirely, or almost entirely, out of capital inflows. In these cases, self-insurance may be largely illusory, since it is likely that creditors will call back their loans and portfolio investments in case of a BoP crisis, as has frequently happened in the past. The extensive substitution of debt securities placements for syndicated bank loans as a source of external finance that followed the debt crisis of the 1980s in Latin America and the appeal to foreign investors to acquire stock in local exchanges may have accentuated the fragility of the financial position of the countries in the region. However, although it is extraordinarily difficult to make any kind of prediction, capital flight has not been as dramatic a problem so far for countries like Argentina, Brazil, and Mexico. Capital movement reversals were somewhat strong in 2008, but there seems to be no evidence yet of the kind of sharp change in the demand for foreign assets among residents in those economies, which has signaled the beginning of a capital account crisis in the recent past.

The situation may be only marginally improved if capital inflows take the form of foreign investment rather than loans or portfolio investment. Foreign investments create *implicit* foreign liabilities that may be as much constraining as the *explicit* liabilities created by debt. In fact, they may even pose more difficult problems for the authorities since there is no pre-determined schedule of repatriation or of remittances of profits and dividends, which can be accelerated or decelerated according to changing evaluations made by investors. In any case, Table 15.3 shows that, among the major emerging economies, the situation, from this point of view, is less reassuring than it may look if one only pays attention to the amount of reserves. In fact, at least in the case of Brazil, the situation has clearly worsened since 2006. After a rapid fall of the current account surplus in 2007, the surplus was transformed into a deficit in 2008. The deficit has continued to grow very quickly, prodded initially by a over-valued currency and afterwards by the dramatic weakening of external demand, even after a sharp devaluation of the real exchange rate reversed the trend towards exchange rate appreciation that had been observed for some months.

Be it as it may, in the absence of capital flight, reserves may offer a good measure of protection against events like the reduction of exports, caused by a deceleration of trade or a reduction in the price of exported goods and services, particularly if they take place gradually. The use of reserves to maintain payments for *normal* imports and service external liabilities may avoid changes in exchange rates that would transmit the disturbances to other agents, running the risk of initiating a contagion process.

The accumulation of earned reserves may also be an efficient shock absorber in the current environment where foreign liabilities are mostly of private responsibility, in contrast with the dominance of public borrowers in the past. Private liabilities are spread throughout the economy, making a coordinated response to a given shock much more difficult than in the case of public liabilities, where a unified reaction by government can be articulated relatively quickly. The availability of an ample cushion of reserves may accommodate unexpected capital outflows without causing significant changes in exchange rates, for instance, that can influence the solvency of other local debtors. Of course, a cushion serves to attenuate shocks, to gain time while a more definite policy response is articulated; it is not a response in itself. But it can help to avoid contagion effects as it happens when a sudden outflow causes exchange rates to rise, thereby forcing other debtors to rush to try to liquidate their liabilities before rates rise even more, generating a self-feeding devaluation process.

The benefits of reserve accumulation do not come without costs, though. In the case of borrowed reserves, the pecuniary costs are relatively easy to calculate, comprising the spread between the rates of interest paid to service the external debt and the rates received as interest on the securities that are held by the country. As reserves are usually held in highly liquid, low-yield securities, as, typically, US Treasuries, this spread is certainly negative. In the case of earned reserves, the calculation is not as clear-cut, since it would involve the opportunity cost of maintaining those resources invested in low-yield securities, compared to their "best" possible alternative use, which is seldom calculable with certainty. In any case, one should notice that the main service offered by the accumulation of liquid reserves is not their yield, but the safety it provides.[14]

It is still important to notice, on the other hand, that the security reserves offer may be overestimated when one uses traditional indicators, such as those

Table 15.3 Current account balances ($ billion)[1]: selected emerging economies

	2000	2001	2002	2003	2004	2005	2006	2007	2008
Argentina	−8,955	−3,780	8,720	8,065	3,158	3,686	5,594	4,459	2,780
Brazil	−24,225	−23,215	−7,637	4,177	11,679	14,193	13,621	1,712	−29,215
China	20,519	17,405	35,422	45,875	68,659	160,818	249,866	371,833	399,325
Hungary	−4,010	−3,204	−4,642	−6,702	−8,589	−7,470	−6,861	−6,932	−9,960
India	−4,599	1,410	7,061	8,773	0.781	−10,285	−9,800	−15,494	−34,580
Mexico	−18,684	−17,697	−14,138	−8,573	−6,595	−5,207	−2,231	−5,813	−15,882
Poland	−9,981	−5,376	−5,009	−4,599	−10,118	−3,705	−9,200	−15,905	−26,805
Russian Federation	46,839	33,935	29,116	35,410	59,514	84,443	94,340	76,163	115,286
South Africa	−0.172	0.333	0.920	−1,806	−6,920	−9,773	−16,602	−20,557	−23,908

[1] 2008 data are estimates.

Source: International Monetary Fund WEO database <http://www.imf.org>.

listed in Table 15.2. In fact, most studies evaluate the adequacy of reserves in comparison either with imports of goods and services or with the value of *short-term foreign debt*. As difficult and uncertain as the estimation may be, one should also consider, in addition to debt, the possibility of repatriation and acceleration of profit remittances by foreign direct investors, which usually happens during a BoP crisis. In addition, the mass exit of portfolio investments by non-residents may also create strong pressures on reserves. The potential negative impact of these outflows on the level of reserves (or on the exchange rates) can at least be calculated. But the most fateful omission in the calculation of vulnerability indices based on the value of the short-term debt relates to the possibility of *capital flight by residents*. It is often forgotten that the liberalization of capital accounts opens up the possibility for residents to transfer their wealth abroad. Under these circumstances, the volume of reserves do not have to be just sufficient to allow repayment of non-residents' loans. Reserves actually have to be enough to also cover capital flight by residents. In fact, most of the BoP crises in emerging economies in the 1990s were triggered by capital flight by residents using the privileges obtained in the financial liberalization reforms.[15]

A final word must be reserved to notice that the increase in the number of reserve currencies, to include most notably the newly-created euro, in an international system of flexible exchange rates, introduces the exchange rate risk in the calculation of national authorities. An even more difficult Triffin dilemma of sorts emerges, because BoP disequilibria in countries issuing reserve currencies may influence the valuation of (and therefore the degree of protection afforded by) reserves through its impacts on current and expected exchange rates.

Conclusion: are there better alternatives?

Holding high volumes of reserves, particularly if they are earned reserves, serves to absorb moderate shocks, smooth the behavior of exchange rates in floating regimes, and to allow some breathing space for government authorities, postponing the operation of contagion channels, such as the impact of changing exchange rates on the balance sheets of borrowers in foreign currencies. So far, the availability of reserves seems to have given some measure of protection to economies like Brazil's, since they allow local authorities to face the pressures resulting from the international financial crisis and avoid major disruptions. The key feature of the current situation (as of early 2009), in the Brazilian case, seems to be that while foreign portfolio and direct investors are reducing their presence in the national economy, residents have not felt the push to substitute foreign for domestic assets that leads to uncontrollable capital flight.

Under current conditions, accumulating reserves may be a better strategy than just relying on the possibility of accessing institutions such as the IMF, or trying to establish emergency credit lines with private banks, as done by Argentina during the Tequila crisis, which may not be honored when the country needs them.

Nevertheless, reserve accumulation as a defensive strategy should be seen mostly as an option of last resort, to be adopted when better strategies are not available. It is potentially expensive for the country holding them, particularly in the case of developing countries that could find better capital accumulation strategies than just holding idle balances or low-yield securities. It is deflationary for the global economy, reducing global demand, output and employment.

The best alternative, doubtless, would be the organization of an international monetary system where a true international currency, free of the Triffin dilemma, could be created as the need for liquidity increased. In such a system, emergency liquidity facilities, accessible at reasonable terms, should be created to protect countries suffering adverse temporary shocks to their balance of payments. Finally, in the case of countries facing deeper disequilibria, institutions and formal procedures should be defined to allow restructuring of liabilities to be negotiated by the concerned parties without causing excessive disruption to the operation of their economies.

Of course, these were features (except for the third) of Keynes's plan presented at the Bretton Woods Conference of 1944, rejected by the United States delegation, which presented its own plan.[16] The White Plan[17] maintained the US dollar as the international means of payment, and created the IMF, not really as a liquidity provider of last resort, but as a financial intermediary demanding more and more exacting terms, as time passed by, to concede loans to countries in difficulties. Although the creation of international institutions and the attempts to formalize procedures represented a definite progress in the evolution of international monetary relations, the inadequacies of the chosen strategy became clearer through the years. Through time, these inadequacies led many economists to propose versions of Keynes's plan adapted to current conditions. Most of these proposals gave special attention to the need to overcome the Triffin dilemma and to create more flexible emergency liquidity provision mechanisms. Since the creation of SDRs, a favorite with reformers is the possibility of transforming this instrument into a true international currency.

There seem to be, however, some important political obstacles to the exploration of such a reform path. In contrast with the situation in 1944, there is no clear hegemony in the world economy that would give any country the power to impose solutions, no matter how enlightened they might be. On the other hand, there are no clear and convergent views among the leading economies as to the need for a new monetary and financial architecture or the lines along which the existing architecture should be reformed. In particular, there is nothing like the identity of concerns and goals that marked the two leading groups of participants in the Bretton Woods process, the "new dealers" of the US administration and the British delegation, under the intellectual leadership of Lord Keynes.

One should recognize that the IMF has been making an effort to streamline its loan conditionalities, after the widely criticized excesses under Michel Camdessus' directorship in the 1990s. New guidelines have been approved by the Executive Board, making an important distinction between policy changes and reforms that are *critical* to the success of a rescue plan and those that are only considered *relevant* by the Fund. The former would still be part of loan conditionalities, but the latter would just be *recommended* by the IMF. There is reason for skepticism, however, as to the efficacy of such guidelines, which have been mostly ignored by the Fund's staff in the past in their dealings with client countries. This is far from a dead subject and the Fund will again be an important institution when international liquidity dries up once more, as it most certainly will. The debate about the adequacy of its resources and of its loan procedures and conditionalities cannot be abandoned.

If global reforms in the international monetary architecture do not offer much promise in the current situation, it is inevitable that countries will keep pursuing individual solutions, particularly in the case of emerging economies. These economies are already highly integrated both financially and commercially into the world economy, but do not have the privilege of issuing liabilities in their own currency, at least not to a significant extent.

The main alternative to reserve accumulation is the reinstatement of capital controls. In principle, capital controls serve the same purpose as maintaining reserves. Restrictions on non-residents' capital inflows serve to avoid exchange rate appreciation in times of excess liquidity. Restrictions on capital outflows by residents absolve a country from the need to maintain reserves to allow these outflows to take place. However, no matter whether the costs of maintaining controls are greater or smaller than its benefits, after the liberalization process of the 1990s, reinstating capital controls, after private interests have already crystallized around the protection of their newly-acquired privileges, would require bold action by political leaders that seldom seem willing or capable of taking this path.

The orthodox view is that floating exchange rates alone should do the trick. Neither controls nor reserve accumulation would in fact be necessary if exchange rates could freely float in result of excess demands or supplies of foreign currency and converge to new equilibrium positions. Empirical evidence, however, has not supported the optimistic expectations of floating exchange rates defenders. These regimes have been marked by excess volatility, which causes domestic disequilibria, particularly in countries that exhibit a higher degree of financial and commercial integration into the world economy. Besides, under capital account liberalization, capital flows have become an important determinant of the behavior of exchange rates which means that monetary policies play an indirect but no less decisive role in the determination of exchange rates. Under these circumstances, it is difficult to make the case that exchange rates are really "freely" floating in response to pure market forces, unaffected by macroeconomic policies.

This brief examination of alternatives helps to understand why reserve accumulation has been seen, if not as the very best defensive strategy to deal with the volatility of the world economy, still as the best *available* strategy. On the one hand, it does not depend on a currently unlikely disposition of the international community to work towards a cooperative solution that contemplates the needs and priorities of developing economies. On the other hand, it is politically much easier to implement than reinstating capital controls, since reserve accumulation does not threat any group's privileges. There is a serious risk that the degree of protection afforded by this strategy may not be as high as some countries seem to think, but it doubtless seemed to be the least effort option available while the international economy operated relatively smoothly. Whether reserve accumulation can be enough in the face of capital flight episodes fed by major financial turmoil remains to be seen.

Notes

1. Professor of Economics, Institute of Economics, Federal University of Rio de Janeiro, Brazil.
2. For a review of the criticisms raised against the IMF performance in dealing with the Asian crisis, see Carvalho (2000).
3. Keynes (2007, pp. 195–7).
4. Capital flight may happen when non-residents return their investments to the source country (or, in fact, move them to some other recipient country) or when residents try to substitute foreign for the domestic assets they hold. In the absence of capital controls, governments try to hold enough reserves to prevent capital flight from disrupting exchange markets.
5. The finance motive to demand money was introduced by Keynes in his post-publication debate on The General Theory with Bertil Ohlin. See Keynes (1937, p. 246).
6. On the Triffin dilemma, see Ocampo, Kregel, and Griffith-Jones (2007, p. 141), and Ocampo (2007).
7. One should notice that an eventual replacement of the dollar by the euro as an international means of payment would not in any way solve the Triffin dilemma.
8. For a recent explanation of the original sin hypothesis, which states that developing countries cannot borrow in their own currency in international financial markets, see Panizza (2006).
9. Cf. Horsefield (1969). See also Carvalho (2008a).
10. In fact, the risks involved in turning to private financial markets had already been shown in the aftermath to the oil shocks of the 1970s, when Latin American countries borrowed from international banks to finance their balance of payments, which led to the debt crisis of the early 1980s.

11. Both Managing Directors Kohler and Rato, who succeeded Camdessus, emphasized the need to streamline structural conditionalities. A less circumspect criticism of the Fund's performance in the period can be found in Stiglitz (2002). Another critical evaluation, more focused on the political mistakes made by the IMF in the Asian crisis is offered in Blustein (2001).

12. According to the IMF (2008a, p. 144), total capital inflows to emerging markets and developing countries in 2006 was a little less than a quarter of the inflows to developed economies. Although precise comparisons between the sizes of domestic capital markets in developed and developing countries are very difficult (p. 147), the IMF informs that stock market capitalization in the US alone, for instance, was twice as big as markets for all developing and emerging economies. Similar ratios applied to other financial market segments.

13. Such criticism will be addressed at the end of this section.

14. The growing perception that these costs may be unreasonably high given the size reached recently by international reserves has led many countries to create or enlarge SWF. This denomination actually covers a widely heterogeneous set of institutions, including a restricted set of Funds created by developed countries, as is notably the case of Norway. Most of them were created by exporters of oil or other commodities who saw their export revenues increase steeply recently. A study prepared by J.P. Morgan Research estimated that at the end of 2007, assets detained by the fifty largest SWF reached between $3 and $3.7 trillion, making them as a group larger than hedge funds, for instance. The concern with the possibility that SWF investments may be politically motivated has led a few countries, led by the US, to press for regulation of their activities. A code for recipient countries is being prepared by OECD, and a set of "best practices" to promote self-regulation is being prepared by a working group led by the IMF. On characteristics of SWF, see Griffith-Jones and Ocampo (2008) and J.P. Morgan Research (2008). For the IMF's view of SWF, see Lipsky (2008) and Johnson (2007).

15. A working paper by IMF staff members on the Brazilian crisis of 1998/9 showed that capital flight actually began with residents taking their wealth out of the country, followed later by non-resident investors. Cf. Baig and Goldfajn (2000). A similar pattern is believed to have been followed at least in the cases of Mexico, in 1994, and Thailand, in 1997.

16. The Keynes Plan was rewritten many times to respond or incorporate criticisms. All its main versions can be found in volume XXV of Keynes' Collected Writings (Moggridge, 1980). A summary of its main propositions can be found in chapter 1 of Horsefield (1969).

17. Named after Harry White, the head of the US delegation to the conference.

References

Baig, T. and Goldfajn, Y. (2000) 'The Russian Default and the Contagion to Brazil.' IMF Working Paper 00/160.

Blustein, P. (2001) *The Chastening. Inside the Crisis that Rocked the Global Financial System and Humbled the IMF.* New York: Public Affairs.

Carvalho, F. J. C. (2000) 'The IMF as Crisis Manager: An Assessment of the Strategy in Asia and of its Criticisms,' *Journal of Post Keynesian Economics*, 23(2), pp. 235–66.

—— (2008a) 'Once Again, On the Question of IMF's Conditionalities.' Unpublished manuscript.

—— (2008b) 'Macroeconomic Policy with Open Capital Accounts.' in E. Hein et al. (eds), *Finance-led Capitalism? Macroeconomic Effects of Changes in the Financial Sector.* Marburg: Metropolis-Verlag.

Griffith-Jones, S. and Ocampo, J. A. (2008) 'Sovereign Wealth Funds: A Developing Country Perspective.' Unpublished paper presented at the workshop on Sovereign Wealth Funds organized by the Andean Development Corporation (February 18).

Horsefield, J. K. (1969) *The International Monetary Fund 1945–1965. Twenty Years of International Monetary Cooperation, Volume 1: Chronicle.* Washington, DC: International Monetary Fund.

International Monetary Fund (2008a) *Global Financial Stability Report* (April).

—— (2008b) *World Economic Outlook* (October).

Johnson, S. (2007) 'The Rise of Sovereign Wealth Funds.' *Finance and Development*, 44(3).

J.P. Morgan Research (2008) *Sovereign Wealth Funds: A Bottom–Up Primer* <http://www.morganmarkets.com> accessed on June 15, 2009.

Keynes, J. M. (1937) 'Alternative Theories of the Rate of Interest.' *The Economic Journal* (June), pp. 241–52.

Keynes, J. M. (2007) *The General Theory of Employment, Interest and Money.* London: Palgrave MacMillan, for the Royal Economic Society.

Lipsky, J. (2008) 'Sovereign Wealth Funds: Their Role and Significance.' Speech by John Lipsky, September 3, 2 <http://www.imf.org/external/np/speeches/2008/090308.htm> accessed on June 19, 2009.

Moggridge, D. (ed.) (1980). *The Collected Writings of John Maynard Keynes. Volume XXV: Activities 1940–1944. Shaping the Post-War World: The Clearing Union.* Cambridge: MacMillan and Cambridge University Press for the Royal Economic Society.

Ocampo, J. A. (2007) 'The Instability and Inequities of the Global Reserve System.' *International Journal of Political Economy*, 36(4), Winter, pp. 71–96.

—— Kregel, J., and Griffith-Jones, S. (2007) *International Finance and Development.* London and New York: Zed Books, with Orient Longman and TWN.

Panizza, U. (2006) '"Original Sin" and Monetary Cooperation.' In B. Fritz and M. Metzger (eds.), *New Issues in Regional Monetary Coordination.* London: Palgrave MacMillan.

Park, Y. C. (2004) 'Regional Financial Integration in East Asia: Challenges and Prospects, UN ECLA and DESA.' Seminar on Regional Financial Arrangements, New York (July).

Stiglitz, J. E. (2002) *Globalization and Its Discontents.* New York and London: WW Norton.

World Bank (2008) *Global Development Finance.* Washington, DC.

Part IV

Reforming the Global Monetary System

16

Reforming the Global Reserve System[1]

José Antonio Ocampo[2]

The magnitude of the ongoing world financial meltdown and its real economic effects have lessened the focus on another set of major international financial issues that had been the center of significant attention in recent years: large global imbalances and their links to the global reserve system. Rising public sector debts and the massive monetary expansion in the United States, coupled with the highly uneven macroeconomic policy stimulus taking place throughout the world are two major reasons why renewed attention has to be paid to these issues.

This chapter analyzes the basic deficiencies that the global reserve system exhibits and its links with global imbalances. It is divided into four sections. The first examines the basic deficiencies of the system. The second and third sections look in greater detail at the instability and inequities of the system. The last section considers how the reserve system could be reformed.

The deficiencies of the current system

The global reserve system exhibits three fundamental flaws. All of them are associated with the essential fact that the system lacks mechanisms to guarantee that balance of payments surpluses and deficits (i.e. global imbalances) compensate each other without having adverse effects on world economic activity. Most of the deficiencies generate global deflationary biases but some can also generate inflationary risks.[3]

The first problem, which was highlighted by Keynes during the debates that preceded the creation of the Bretton Woods arrangements, is that the current global monetary system—as all international monetary systems that preceded it—is tilted against deficit countries. This tends to generate a global deflationary bias: the adjustments that deficit countries have to adopt to balance their external accounts, when financing is not available in sufficient amounts (or if those deficits and associated financing are not deemed desirable), will not be matched by expansionary policies in surplus countries, which do not face a similar pressure to adjust. This bias becomes profound particularly during periods of generalized balance of payments crises, such as the one we are experiencing today. The Bretton Woods arrangements were born with this intrinsic imperfection since the International Clearing Union, the proposal by Keynes (in 1942–3) to create a more symmetric system, was not accepted. Its very imperfect substitute, the "scarce currency clause," has never been used. We will refer to this problem as the *anti-Keynesian bias*.

The second deficiency, which is generally referred to in the literature as the *Triffin dilemma* after the pioneering work of Robert Triffin (1961, 1968), is associated with the fact that an *international* reserve system based on a *national* currency (the US dollar)—and, more generally, on a limited number of national or regional currencies (the euro today)—has a built-in instability. The only way for the rest of the world to accumulate *net* dollar assets is for the US to run a current account deficit. However, US deficits and associated deteriorations in its net external balance sheet tend to erode confidence in the dollar as a reserve currency. This loss may then force adjustments to restore credibility—or, more generally, reverse dollar depreciation—but this could make the deflationary bias of the system felt.

It must be underscored that, aside from this "exorbitant privilege" (to borrow de Gaulle's characterization of the role of the dollar in the global reserve system) of receiving transfers from the rest of the world (appropriating seignorage powers and, more broadly, benefiting from the investment of other countries' reserves at low interest rates), its position at the center of the global reserve system gives the US the additional privilege of running a truly independent monetary policy. The basic reason for this is the perception (and consequent use) of US Treasury bills as the "safest assets" in the world economy, which implies that the determinants of US interest rates are relatively independent of the exchange rate of the US dollar against other currencies. This is contrary to what is usually assumed in open macroeconomic models, in which runs on currencies tend to be associated with upward pressures on domestic interest rates, a result that is consistent with the experience of most countries facing balance of payments crises.

The major constraint that the US faced in running an independent monetary policy was the possibility of other countries transforming their dollar reserves into gold, but this constraint was lifted in the early 1970s, when the system evolved from the "gold-exchange standard" to what is effectively a "fiduciary dollar standard"—and only secondarily a system of competing fiduciary reserve currencies. Given the lack of constraints, we are living in a world in which the monetary policy of the major reserve currency country can alternatively generate excessive liquidity in the international economy or cause contractionary global effects, which make themselves felt during different phases of the business cycle. In this sense, the generation of global liquidity has become even more "capricious" than under the original Bretton Woods system, to use a characterization that was common in the debates of the 1960s. As we will see below, this has been reflected in increasingly intense cycles of the US current account deficits, which have been closely linked with strong fluctuations in the real dollar exchange rate. Furthermore, to the extent that the US does not regard the actual or likely weakening of its currency as a problem to be corrected, the absence of any constraint on US monetary policy implies that, contrary to Keynes' classical views on the deflationary bias of the global reserve system, a fiduciary dollar standard can actually exhibit, over certain periods, the opposite phenomenon: an inflationary bias. However, although the US is able to spend generously, it does not totally capture the benefits of its expansionary policies, as they are "exported" to the rest of the world through deterioration in the current account of its balance of payments.

The third deficiency of the current reserve system is that it is inequitable, as the demand for foreign exchange reserves forces developing countries to transfer resources to the countries issuing those reserve currencies—a case of "reverse aid" (see the Zedillo Report, United Nations, 2001). We will refer to this problem as the *inequity bias*. It has been magnified in recent decades of financial and capital market liberalization by the pressures generated by strongly pro-cyclical flows that developing countries face in world financial markets, which in turn reduce their room to undertake counter-cyclical macroeconomic policies. These facts have led to a massive accumulation of foreign exchange reserves by developing countries as "self-insurance" or, better, "self-protection" against reversals in capital inflows. This adds up to the more traditional "precautionary" demand for reserves in commodity exporting countries against commodity price volatility and, more generally in today's export-led economies, against international trade volatility (see Carvalho's Chapter 15, in this volume).

The accumulation of foreign exchange reserves can also be seen as rational responses by individual countries to a system that lacks any well functioning "collective insurance" against balance of payments crises. Furthermore, the fact that the only available collective insurance, International Monetary Fund's (IMF) emergency financing, is deemed unacceptable by many countries due to its conditionalities, actually heightens the demand for self-protection. In this sense, self-protection by developing countries is the demand for foreign exchange reserves associated with both pro-cyclical capital account and trade shocks, *and* the perception that there are inadequate mechanisms at the global level to provide liquidity to developing countries during balance of payments crises. Although rational from each country's perspective, such protection generates "fallacy of composition" effects that tend to worsen global imbalances and generate deflationary bias in the global system. We will call this problem the *inequity–instability link*.

Although the inequities of the system were already built into its initial post-war design, they have been considerably heightened since the 1990s by the increased opening of developing countries—trade opening, domestic financial liberalization, and capital account liberalization—and the risks they generated. In fact, the major waves of foreign exchange reserve accumulation followed the two major crises experienced by the developing world—the Latin American debt crisis of the 1980s, and the succession of Asian, Russian, and Latin American crises of the late twentieth and early twenty-first centuries—which made evident that these risks are substantial.

Viewed from the perspective of creditors, pro-cyclicality is obviously a response to the "riskiness" associated with lending to developing countries. What this implies, however, is that this riskiness is not independent of the position these countries occupy in the global economy and in the global reserve system in particular. This is therefore, part of the essential asymmetries of the international economic system—that is, one of its "center-periphery" features, to use a concept that was made popular by Raúl Prebisch half a century ago, and one that is used commonly today, even in mainstream literature.

It is important to emphasize that the three basic problems the current system exhibits would not be solved if several national (or, in the case of Europe, regional) currencies compete for the status of international reserve currencies—which is a secondary feature of the current world monetary system. In particular, although such a multi-reserve currency arrangement would provide developing countries the benefit of diversification of their foreign exchange reserve assets, investment of those reserves would still benefit industrial countries, so that reverse aid would continue to be a feature of the system.

Exchange rate flexibility would allow a full-fledged system of competing reserve currencies to be resilient to the attacks on fixed parities that led to the collapse of both bimetallism in the late nineteenth century and of gold–dollar parities in the early 1970s. However, it adds an additional element of instability to a purely dollar-based system associated with the exchange rate volatility among major reserve currencies—a problem that is already present in the current system. Such volatility results in major gains and losses by central banks on their reserve holding, a feature that increases the risk associated with holding specific reserve assets and, therefore, their value as what they are meant to be: "safe" or low-risk assets. Equally important, if the central banks were to respond to exchange rate fluctuations by changing the composition of their international reserves, this would feed into exchange rate instability. Under these conditions, a full fledged multiple currency reserve system would generate growing calls for a fixed exchange rate arrangement (i.e. a return to a Bretton Woods type scheme, at least among reserve currencies), but fixing the exchange rates among major currencies in a world of large and free capital flows would be a daunting task. It must be added that, given their high demand for foreign exchange reserves, developing countries suffer disproportionately from the instability of the exchange rates of reserve currencies.

In any case, this will continue to be a secondary feature of the system so long as there is no alternative supply of safe assets in the world economy. The bonds of some European governments and Japan can be a substitute, but only a partial one, given the size and liquidity of the market for US Treasury bonds. This problem is magnified by the absence of a unified European bond market and the perception by many agents that the euro is backed by a heterogeneous group of countries, with unequal strength.

This implies that the major deficiencies in the current system can only be solved through an overhaul of the global reserve system. Although some other possibilities could be designed—such as Keynes' proposal for an International Clearing Union and similar solutions (see, for example, D'Arista, 1999)[4]—the most viable is completing the transition that was launched in the 1960s with the creation of Special Drawing Rights (SDRs). This implies putting a truly global fiduciary currency at the center of the system, completing a trend towards fiduciary currencies that has been at the center of national and international monetary systems since the nineteenth century (Triffin, 1968). Given the pro-cyclicality of finance towards developing countries, and the high demand for foreign exchange reserves that it generates, this has to be accompanied by reforms aimed at guaranteeing that SDR allocations are used to at least partly correct the problems that developing countries face under the current system.

The instability of the global reserve system

The cyclical recurrence of US imbalances is closely related to the nature of the current global reserve system. A global deflationary bias was evident in the early post-war period in the form of the "dollar shortage." The gradual accumulation of dollar reserves later generated a pressure on US gold reserves that major countries tried to avoid through the creation of the "gold pool" (Eichengreen, 2007). The failure of this arrangement and the increasingly inflationary bias that the system exhibited, associated with increasing US deficits, led to the abandonment of the gold–dollar parities in the early 1970s. In any case, during the gold-exchange standard, the US generally ran current account surpluses, and the provision of dollar liquidity to the rest of the world was made through the capital account.

In contrast, under the fiduciary dollar standard that followed, the current account deficits of the United States have been the rule rather than the exception. The system has also been plagued over the past three and a half decades by an increasingly intense cycle of expansion and contraction in the external deficit of the United States, which has been associated in turn with strong

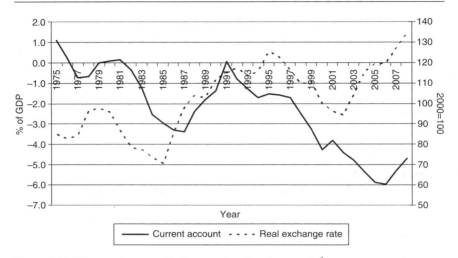

Figure 16.1 US current account balance and real exchange rate[1]
[1]The real exchange rate in this chart shows an increase when there is a real depreciation (the opposite convention to that used by the IMF). It is calculated as the inverse of the real exchange rate estimated by the Fund.

Source: International Monetary Fund, *International Financial Statistics*.

fluctuations of the real exchange rate of the major reserve currency (see Figure 16.1; and Ocampo et al., 2007, ch. 4). Although real exchange rate fluctuations have played an important role, corrections in the US current account deficit have also been associated with US slowdowns or recessions that have had major effects on the world economy.

The first but short cycle of this type was experienced in the second half of the 1970s: rising deficits in 1977–8 followed by the strong contractionary monetary policy adopted in late 1979, largely to fight inflation which, together with the real depreciation of the dollar, corrected the US deficit but generated a strong global slowdown. A longer and stronger cycle was experienced in the 1980s. During the first half of that decade, contractionary monetary policy, mixed with expansionary fiscal policy later on, led to a substantial appreciation of the US dollar, and a sharp deterioration of the US current account. The adjustment was initiated prior to but was accelerated by the 1985 Plaza Accord. The market response produced a sharp real depreciation of the dollar, and led to the Louvre Accord of 1987, which sought to stabilize the dollar.[5] Following two sharp falls in equity markets, in 1987 and 1989, the correction of the current account deficit was again the joint effect of real exchange rate depreciation and the US recession of the early 1990s. Deterioration of US economic activity led, again, to the global slowdown of 1989–91.

The adjustment of the deficit in the United States during the late 1980s was matched by a rebalancing of surpluses in Germany and a few other developed countries, a number of developing countries in Asia and, as a result of falling petroleum prices, in oil-exporting developing countries. In contrast, Japan's large external surplus remained stubbornly high, even though the yen had appreciated significantly against the dollar since the mid-1980s. This experience showed that currency appreciation in a surplus country may not necessarily correct external imbalances. The real appreciation may have actually fed into the asset price bubble, which contributed to the financial crisis and stagnation of the Japanese economy during the 1990s; the latter phenomenon in turn swamped the effects of real exchange rate on the current account.[6]

US deficits returned after the 1989–91 global slowdown, but were moderate during the first half of the 1990s. The renewed appreciation of the US dollar in the second half of that decade led to the strongest deterioration of the US current account in history. Although this had its counterpart in a deterioration of US domestic deficits, particularly of households, the large magnitude of the current imbalances also reflects events taking place outside the US economy. Particularly important in this regard was the sharp divergence between US and world economic growth during a conjuncture characterized by recession in many parts of the developing world and the transition economies induced by the Asian, Russian, and Latin American crises. As in the past, the strong US and global slowdown of 2001 led to a reduction in the US deficit, but such reduction was very small due to the aforementioned factors.

The renewed and sharp increase in the US deficit in the early 2000s can be attributed to the joint effect of domestic imbalances and events in the developing world, particularly the very strong demand for self-protection (see the next section). The 2003–7 world economic boom was therefore characterized by large current account deficits in the US, which continued to widen until 2006, matched by aggregate surpluses in a number of other countries, mainly developing countries in East Asia, commodity-exporting countries in the rest of the world, and Japan. The cumulative depreciation of the dollar since 2003 was strong but orderly. However, it was not accompanied, as in the second half of the 1980s, by a strong correction in US current account deficits. These imbalances only started to fall with the US slowdown of 2007, indicating again that major corrections in the US current account are joint effects of dollar depreciation and US slowdowns, which have global implications.

These trends have changed significantly during the recent global recession. As in previous recessions, the US current account deficit is narrowing. In turn, with the collapse of commodity prices, the surpluses of commodity exporting countries were significantly eroded. The collapse of world trade has had similar effects on the surpluses of Japan and many East Asian manufacturing exporters, with the major exception of China. Despite the still high current account deficit, the dollar has strengthened in late 2008 and early 2009 due to the "flight to safety" that has accompanied the world financial collapse, and the demand for dollars to finance withdrawals from non-banking financial institutions in the US (an important part of the strong de-leveraging process underway). The yen has also been strengthening due to the reversal of Japanese carry trade (a phenomenon similar to the demand for dollars generated by de-leveraging), but the major alternative reserve currency, the euro, has shown its incapacity to offer an adequate supply of safe assets.

This short narrative of US imbalances and exchange rates during the three and a half decades under the fiduciary dollar standard indicates also that the role as the center of the global reserve system has had both positive and negative aspects for the United States. On the positive side, the most important advantage is the monetary independence that it confers. The fact that the US is both the global reserve currency and means of payments generates a demand for dollar reserves that are usually held in deposits and liquid instruments paying relatively low interest rates, which also enhance the role of the US as the world's banker.

Under the current system, the United States faces an additional advantage. Whereas economies that have external liabilities denominated in other countries' currencies experience a net wealth (real balance) loss when their currencies depreciate,[7] this effect is absent in the US. In contrast, the US experiences a positive wealth (real balance) effect when the dollar depreciates, as such change increases the value of foreign assets owned by US residents, while their liabilities remain invariable. This implies that the depreciation of the US dollar will have weaker effects in terms of rebalancing global current account imbalances, as the wealth effects of such depreciation run counter to the relative price effects (United Nations, 2005, ch. I).

On the negative side, the current account deficit that the US has to incur to provide a net supply of dollar assets to the rest of the world implies that some of the stimulus generated by the expansionary policies of the major reserve issuing country must benefit the rest of the world (Stiglitz, 2006, ch. 9). To the extent that cyclical upswings are also characterized by the appreciation of the US dollar, other countries also gain during theses phases through the increased real value (in terms of their domestic currencies) of assets held in the US.

As we have seen, among the three phases of balance of payments imbalances that the US has experienced under the fiduciary dollar standard, the most recent one has been larger in magnitude and has lasted longer. Some analysts have argued that deepening global financial integration has made current imbalances more sustainable. In particular, orthodox analysis has always claimed that in a world of perfect capital markets, current account imbalances merely reflect private decisions to allocate savings to the places where it is optimal to invest them. This would imply that current account imbalances are, as such, irrelevant.

Still other analysts have argued that current account imbalances can be sustained for a long time, as the system has evolved into a "Second Bretton Woods" (see Dooley et al., 2003). This school of thought contends that the "mercantilist" decision of the Asian countries to avoid exchange rate appreciation to sustain their export-led growth models implies that they are willing to continue financing US current account deficits. According to this point of view, the economic benefits of stable and weak exchange rates exceed, for those countries, the costs of reserve accumulation (see below).

In contrast to the former views, an increasing number of observers has indicated in recent years that the risks associated with the accumulation of a net US debtor position imply that official and private agents may be unwilling to continue to accumulate dollar assets, due to the possible losses associated with further dollar depreciation (see, for instance, Williamson, 2004). Indeed, the US current account deficits in recent years have been problematic, as they have been financing domestic consumption rather than investment, US investment has been shifting towards non-tradable sectors, and the deficit has been increasingly funded by short-term flows rather than direct investment (Summers, 2004). Curiously, these are the same issues that have been raised many times in relation to external imbalances of developing countries, most notably in Latin America.

As the defenders of the Second Bretton Woods hypothesis have recently argued (Dooley et al., 2009), the current crisis has not been accompanied by a run on the dollar. The basic reasons, as we have seen, have been the lack of a large alternative supply of safe assets and the demand for dollars generated by de-leveraging. However, this does not imply that the US is safe from a classical balance of payments crisis—that is, a run on dollar assets (including Treasury bills) which will force *both* dollar depreciation and an increase in US interest rates. The sharp rise in the public sector debt of the United States and the expansion in the balance sheet of the Federal Reserve under way add up to the accumulated net external liabilities of the United States, and generate risks in that direction.

As we will see below, the desire to run a truly independent monetary and fiscal policy during the current crisis without having to take into account these global implications could actually be a reason why it may be in the interest of the US to move to a non-dollar based reserve system. But even if a classical balance of payments crisis does not take place in the US, this does not eliminate the basic deficiencies of the fiduciary dollar standard, which go beyond that specific risk.

The growing inequities of the global reserve system

The volatility and contagion that characterize financial markets have been demonstrated by a long history of successive phases of "appetite for risk" (or, more accurately, underestimation of risks) followed by periods of "flight to quality" (risk aversion) (Kindleberger, 1978). These boom–bust cycles follow the endogenous unstable dynamics analyzed by Minsky (1982), who argued that financial booms generate excessive risk taking by market agents, which eventually leads to crises. A similar explanation was suggested more recently by White (2005), who underscored how the "search for yield" characteristic of low interest rate environments generates incentives for credit creation, carry trade, and leverage that easily build up asset bubbles. The recent boom–bust cycle in the US and several other countries is a dramatic demonstration of the validity of this view, as are the sharp cycles of financing experienced by the developing world in recent decades. The transmission of shocks, positive and negative, has been enhanced by the liberalization of cross-border capital flows and deregulation of domestic financial markets.

An important feature of contagion is the tendency of markets to cluster countries and firms in certain risk categories. Independently of their objective basis, this clustering becomes a "self-fulfilling prophecy": events that take place in one country or firm tend to be seen as "representative" of an asset class, and therefore tend to generate reactions that affect other members of the cluster. Thus, as the experience of emerging markets indicates, even countries with weak "fundamentals" may be drawn into a financial boom; again, with some independence from their fundamentals, they will be later drawn into "sudden stops" of external financing.

The volatility that is inherent in finance is reflected in varying ways in different segments of financial markets. Agents that are perceived to be risky borrowers are subject to the strongest swings in terms of both the availability and costs of financing. Riskier agents include both some domestic agents in industrial countries (e.g., small- and medium-sized enterprises, poorer households) and emerging markets and, more generally, developing country borrowers. In relation to developing countries, this segmentation of global financial markets is deeply rooted in basic asymmetries that characterize the world economy (Ocampo and Martin, 2003), which in the financial area involve: (i) constraints faced by most developing countries in issuing liabilities in international markets denominated in their own currencies, a phenomenon that has come to be called "original sin" (Eichengreen and Hausman, 2005); (ii) differences in the degree of domestic financial and capital market development, which lead to an under-supply of long-term financial instruments in domestic markets; and (iii) the small size of developing countries' domestic financial markets relative to the speculative pressures they potentially face.

The first two asymmetries imply that financial markets are more "incomplete" in developing countries and, as a result, portfolios of market agents are characterized by variable mixes of currency and maturity mismatches. It also implies that some financial intermediation must be conducted through international markets—to the extent, of course, that agents have access to such markets.[8] A major implication of currency mismatches is that exchange rate fluctuations induced by capital flows (real appreciation during capital account booms, depreciation during crises) generate pro-cyclical wealth effects. Maturity mismatches imply that domestic private and public sector agents finance long-term investment with short-term finance. This means that debtors face stronger interest rate risks, and that refinancing requirements associated with debt rotation are high and may lead to bankruptcy during crises.

It is important to note that, although the boom of local currency debt markets that has taken place in the developing world since the Asian crisis partly corrects the original sin, it may just substitute maturity mismatches for currency mismatches. Furthermore, the demand for local currency instruments depends on expectations of exchange rate appreciation, and may therefore lead to outflows when there are expectations of depreciation, as the 2008 crisis has demonstrated. This implies that a more precise definition of original sin should refer to the absence of a stable net demand, in international markets, for assets denominated in the currencies of developing countries. Obviously, domestic agents who do have a permanent demand for assets denominated in developing countries' currencies also respond in a speculative way to exchange rate expectations.

All of these factors imply that integration of developing countries into global financial markets is always a *segmented* integration—that is, integration into a market that is segmented by the risk category according to which borrowers are bundled, and one in which high-risk borrowers are subject to strong pro-cyclical swings (Frenkel, 2008). There is, indeed, overwhelming empirical evidence that capital flows to developing countries are pro-cyclical and thus exacerbate rather than dampen both booms and recessions (Prasad et al., 2003).

The volatility that developing countries face includes short-term fluctuations, such as the erratic behavior of short-term capital flows, or the very intense upward movement of spreads and the periods of total rationing of financing observed during the Mexican, Asian, and the Russian crises, as well as the recent world financial meltdown. Equally important, however, are the *medium-term* cycles in the availability and costs (spreads) of financing that these countries face. Since the mid-1970s, three full medium-term cycles were experienced: a boom of external financing in the 1970s, followed by a major debt crisis in the 1980s; a new boom in the 1990s, followed by a sharp reduction in net flows after the succession of the Asian and Russian crises of 1997–8; and a new boom from 2002–3, which had already come to a close in mid-2008, prior to the global financial meltdown of September 2008.

Financial asymmetries also generate important macroeconomic asymmetries. In particular, whereas major industrial countries have large room to maneuver to adopt counter-cyclical macroeconomic policies, developing countries face significant constraints to do so (Stiglitz et al., 2006; Ocampo, 2008). There is indeed ample evidence that macroeconomic policies in developing countries are pro-cyclical (Kaminsky et al., 2004) and that this pro-cyclical behavior has adverse effects on growth (Ocampo and Vos, 2008, ch. IV).

However, within the limited maneuvering room that these countries have, there is a strong rationale for the adoption of the counter-cyclical macroeconomic policies that are available, aiming either at correcting the direct source of the disturbance, capital account volatility (through capital account regulations), or its macroeconomic effects. Although there have been movements in several policy directions, the most common one during the recent boom was the accumulation of foreign exchange reserves.

The basic rationale for foreign reserve accumulation during booms is to smooth out the effects of pro-cyclical capital flows on exchange rates. If adequately sterilized, such policy makes it possible to target both the exchange rate and the interest rate, thus avoiding (within some limits) the "trilemma" of open economies (Frenkel, 2007). A similar logic applies to primary commodity exporting countries facing terms of trade shocks. Indeed, saving some of the exceptional export revenues and associated fiscal revenues has long been accepted as a good practice. More generally, to the extent that international trade is pro-cyclical, export booms always have a transitory component. It makes sense therefore to respond to cyclical swings in export revenues by accumulating the excess supply of foreign exchange during booms to be used during the succeeding crises. It is interesting to emphasize, however, that this had not been the practice in the past. Rather, the tendency to overspend capital account as well as trade booms had been the rule rather than the exception.

The very costly crises that developing countries faced in the 1980s and late 1990s finally led them to use reserve accumulation in an active and, in some cases, aggressive way. As Figure 16.2 indicates, until the 1980s, the demand for reserves by developing countries was not very different from that of the industrial countries, around 3 per cent of GDP. Since the 1990s, however, the demand for reserves by developing countries—both middle and low income countries alike—started to diverge radically from that of the industrial world (Japan was the only exception in this regard, as it also joined the reserve boom from the mid-1990s). China was the most aggressive, of course, and had accumulated by 2007 non-gold reserves equivalent to 46.7 per cent of its GDP. But in 2007, middle income countries, excluding China, and low income countries also held foreign exchange reserves equivalent to 20.6 and 16.2 per cent of GDP respectively. In contrast, industrial countries excluding Japan only held reserves equivalent to 2.6 per cent of GDP, a similar level to that of the 1970s and 1980s. As a result of this trend, the annual additional demand for reserves, which had already increased in the 1990s, skyrocketed during the recent boom: from an annual average of $111.6 billion in 1991–7 to $776.9 billion in 2003–7, or from $75.3 to $430.8 billion excluding China and Japan (see Table 16.1).

Although reserve accumulation had started after the Latin American crisis of the 1980s, the Asian crisis was the most important turning point. This turning point indicates that the succession of crises, particularly those since 1997, revealed the lack of adequate institutions to manage crises that originated in

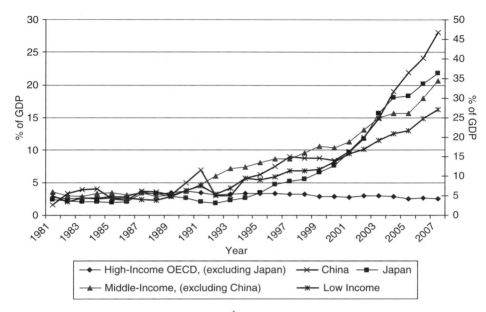

Figure 16.2 Reserves minus gold (% of GDP)[1]

[1]The left-hand scale is used for all countries except China, which is measured against the left-hand scale.

Source: World Bank, *World Development Indicators*; International Monetary Fund.

the capital account, as well as the excessive conditionalities attached to those that are available—i.e., emergency IMF financing. The radical increase in the demand for reserves since the 1990s is, of course, a paradox for those who believe that exchange rate flexibility reduces the demand for reserves. Actually, in the developing world, greater flexibility was accompanied by a higher demand for reserves. This made flexible but highly intervened exchange rate regimes quite common in the developing world.

The mercantilist motives of such accumulation have been emphasized by the Second Bretton Woods literature. A reinforcing factor may be the lack of appropriate mechanisms for exchange rate coordination in export-led economies, which generate incentives to keep exchange rates competitive. The idea that weak exchange rates and strong current account balances tend to accelerate economic growth in developing countries has, of course, a respectable tradition in the development literature.[9]

However, the recent literature definitely favors self-protection against capital account volatility as the main motive for foreign exchange reserve accumulation in recent decades (see, for example, Aizenman and Lee, 2007; Ocampo

Table 16.1 Accumulation of foreign exchange reserves, 1981–2007

	$ million				% of GDP			
	1982–90	1991–7	1998–2002	2003–7	1990 vs 1981	1997 vs 1990	2002 vs 1997	2007 vs 2002
High income: OECD	42,805	30,889	59,358	140,715	0.80	0.08	0.83	0.39
Japan	5,588	20,164	48,307	98,320	0.18	2.56	6.61	10.00
Others	37,217	10,725	11,051	42,395	0.94	−0.46	−0.15	−0.47
High income: non-OECD		21,833	28,554	69,822				
Middle income	6,734	56,950	63,739	548,444	0.65	5.58	5.13	12.18
China	2,725	16,168	29,673	247,831	5.72	6.64	5.04	26.63
Excluding China	4,009	40,782	34,066	300,613	0.11	4.97	4.49	7.50
Low income	212	1,952	3,654	17,938	0.76	3.06	3.37	6.04
World	59,946	111,624	155,305	776,919	0.83	1.43	1.88	4.19
Excluding China and Japan	51,633	75,292	77,325	430,768				

Source: World Bank, *World Development Indicators*; International Monetary Fund.

et al., 2007, ch. 4). Indeed, one of the reasons why a strong current account is seen as one of the factors that has positive effects on growth is that it reduces the dependence on the volatility associated with capital flows. If this is the major reason, it would imply that the motivation is really self-protection rather than mercantilism.

The motive for self-protection against financial crises goes beyond the Guidotti-Greenspan rule, which argues that countries should keep foreign exchange reserves at least equivalent to short-term external liabilities. Indeed, if managing *medium-term* capital account fluctuations is the most challenging issue, there is a precautionary demand for international reserves that is proportional to *total* external liabilities, with the proportion actually increasing the more open the capital account is. The recent boom in commodity markets and, more generally, export revenues, also led developing countries to accumulate as foreign exchange reserves a proportion of the additional export revenues. Precautionary demands associated with the expectations that both capital inflows and export revenues had a strong temporary component were therefore behind the rapid rise in reserves in 2003–7.

The pattern of reserve accumulation differs across countries and regions (see also Chapter 12 by Akyüz and Chapter 15 by Carvalho). Three types of developing countries can be differentiated in this regard. A first group includes countries with current account deficits for which the only source of reserve accumulation was net capital flows. This is the largest group, and includes whole regions (Central and Eastern Europe, South Asia, and sub-Saharan Africa), including major developing countries such as India, Turkey, and Brazil (which ceased to run a current account surplus in the last quarter of 2007), but also a large number of smaller countries. The second group includes countries that mixed current account and capital account surpluses. The major case is China but the group also includes several mineral exporters of Latin America. The third group basically contains energy exporters with strong current account surplus that are net exporters of capital. In any case, the major peaks in reserve accumulation over the past two decades, such as 1993 and 2007, are clearly associated with booms in external financing, particularly when China and the Middle East are excluded (see Figure 16.3).[10] Of course, a significant difference with the previous boom is that, whereas the capital account inflows led to a deterioration in the current account in the 1990s, they did not do so during the recent boom (or did do so, but rather late).

A third explanation for heavy interventions in foreign exchange markets may be called the "financial stability" motive (Obstfeld et al., 2008). The major argument is that financially open economies must hold reserves against capital flight, particularly the desire to convert money balances (defined in a broad sense) into foreign exchange. However, it is difficult to separate this demand from that for self-protection. The fact that reserves tend to be accumulated when there are excess net inflows of capital is the best demonstration that self-protection is the dominant motive.

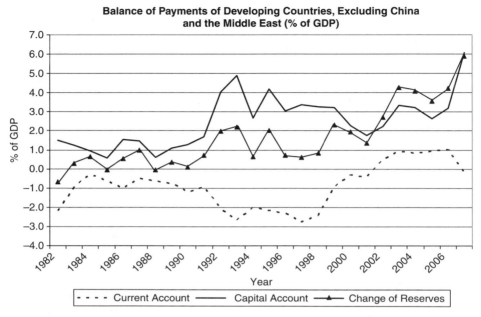

Figure 16.3 Balance of payments: developing countries (excluding China and the Middle East)

Source: World Bank, *World Development Indicators*; International Monetary Fund.

This behavior raises, of course, some interesting policy questions. From the point of view of the individual countries, the most important is that capital account liberalization forces developing countries to absorb net capital inflows in the form of additional foreign exchange reserves—that is, to deepen both sides of the national balance sheet. This is costly and, in a sense, destroys the rationale for capital inflows in the first place, which is to transfer resources from rich to poorer countries. It also implies that the additional rationale for capital account liberalization, to diversify risks, is clearly insufficient, as countries feel in any case that they need the additional self-protection in the form of larger foreign exchange reserves.

For the issue at hand in this paper, what matters, however, is the fact that this strong counter-cyclical rationale generates fallacy of composition effects that feed into global imbalances. Indeed, if a large group of developing countries follows this route, it generates a current account surplus and an additional demand for safe assets that has contractionary effects on the world economy unless it is matched by current account deficits and the supply of those assets by industrial countries.

Therefore, self-protection is not only a costly form of insurance for individual countries (Rodrik, 2006) but is also a source of instability to the global economy.

However, the problem cannot be solved simply by asking developing countries to appreciate their currencies to correct their balance of payments surpluses. It must first resolve the sources of demand for self-protection, which are strong pro-cyclical capital and trade flows and the lack of adequate supply of collective insurance against balance of payments crises. In the latter case, the problem has many similarities with the instability that a national banking system faced in the past in the absence of a lender of last resort. So, a mix of more active use of capital account regulations and better collective insurance against crises would be the only ways to reduce the strong prudential demand for foreign exchange reserves.

Reforming the system

The major conclusion of this paper is that the current global reserve system exhibits three fundamental flaws. First, it shows the deflationary bias associated with any system in which all the burden of adjustment falls on deficit countries (the anti-Keynesian bias). Second, it is inherently unstable due to two distinct features: the use of a national currency as the major reserve asset (the Triffin dilemma) and the high demand for self-protection that developing countries face (the inequity–instability link). The latter is related, in turn, to the mix of highly pro-cyclical capital flows and (until now) the absence of adequate supply of "collective insurance" to manage balance of payments crises, which generate a high demand for foreign exchange reserves by developing countries. This implies, third, that the system is inequitable (the inequity bias), and that such inequities have grown as developing countries have accumulated large quantities of foreign exchange reserves.

There could be several potential ways to reform the system, but as pointed out in the first section of this chapter, the easiest way would be to complete the expectations of the reforms of the 1960s, when SDRs were created. Obviously, the role of SDRs has changed, particularly in light of the fiduciary dollar standard that arose in the early 1970s. The issues of adequate provision of international liquidity that were at the center of early post-war debates, and were still much in fashion in the 1960s, are not important now, except during extraordinary conjunctures such as those generated during the severe shortage of liquidity created by the world financial collapse of September and October 2008. Actually, as we have seen, the fiduciary dollar standard may actually exhibit an inflationary bias during long periods. However, other problems that were also receiving attention in the 1960s continue to be paramount or are even more important today; in particular, this includes those associated with the composition of world reserves, the access to liquidity by developing countries and associated equity issues.[11]

Any reform effort must considerably increase the size of the IMF, which has lagged significantly behind the size of the world economy since the 1998 quota review and relative to world capital flows since the 1970s.[12] Note that, in this regard, the way the Fund is financed is essential. SDR allocations and quota increases are much better mechanisms than "arrangements to borrow" in their different modalities—the major option chosen in April 2009 by the G-20, as in the past, to make more resources available to the Fund during crises.[13] The quota system could be improved by making contributions exclusively in the currencies of the member countries, thus eliminating the obligation of developing countries to make a fourth of their contribution in SDRs or hard currencies; this would make quotas equivalent to a generalized swap arrangement among central banks. However, the best alternative is to move into a fully SDR-based IMF. As Polak (2005, Part II), and Keynes suggested during the debates leading to the creation of the IMF, one advantage of a system based on a truly global reserve currency is that it would eliminate the need for the IMF to manage a multiplicity of currencies, only a small fraction of which (30 per cent according to Polak) can be used for IMF lending.

No allocations of SDRs had been made since 1981, up until 2009. The IMF Board of Governors agreed in 1997 on a special one-time allocation, but the associated reform of the IMF Articles of Agreement was only approved by US Congress in June 2009. The G-20 made a call in April 2009 to finish this process and make an additional issue of SDRs equivalent to $250 billion. Both allocations are now underway. The cessation of SDR allocations over more than a quarter century had negative effects for developing countries and the world economy, as it actually coincided with their growing demand for foreign exchange reserves.

Several proposals to renew SDR allocations have been made in recent years, following two different models. The first is issuing SDRs in a counter-cyclical way, concentrating them essentially in periods of world financial stress and possibly destroying them partly once financial conditions normalize (United Nations, 1999; Camdessus, 2000; Ocampo, 2002; Akyüz, 2005). This would develop a counter-cyclical element in world liquidity management, along the lines suggested below. The second model proposes regular allocations of SDRs similar to the additional world demand for reserves, which according to Table 16.1 is at least $100–150 billion a year, if we leave aside the exceptional recent period of reserve accumulation. This is also the magnitude of SDRs that must be issued in the long term under a counter-cyclical rule.

Moving into a fully SDR-based IMF with a clear counter-cyclical focus would involve two dimensions. The first would be to make counter-cyclical *allocations* of SDRs, which would represent, in the traditional terminology, "unconditional" liquidity. The second would involve financing *all IMF lending* with SDRs. One alternative in this regard is that proposed by Polak (2005, chs. 7–8), according to which IMF lending during crises would actually create new SDRs, similar to how domestic credit by national central banks creates money. SDRs in circulation would in turn be automatically destroyed once such loans are paid for.[14] The other alternative would be to tie the counter-cyclical issues of SDRs with IMF financing during crises, by treating SDRs that are not used by countries as deposits in (or lending to) the IMF that can be used by the institution to lend to countries in need.[15] In either of the two options, SDR-funded IMF financing would improve the provision of collective insurance.

For this to work, it is of course essential that IMF credit lines, their conditionality and the stigma associated with borrowing from this institution be overcome, so that countries would actually prefer collective insurance over self-protection. Although there have been recent efforts to improve IMF lending facilities, particularly the March 2009 reforms, it remains to be seen whether they solve these problems. In particular, we still have to see whether the new Flexible Credit Line for crisis prevention purposes would meet the purpose that its predecessors (the Contingency Credit Line and the Short-Term Liquidity Facility) failed to do. This credit line has, as its predecessors, the problem that it unduly divides developing countries into two categories, those with good policies and those with bad policies, which is not only a very unclear division to draw but also generates significant additional risks for the latter. So, it is perhaps time to adopt at least one part of Keynes' original plan for a post-war arrangement: the creation of generous overdraft (or, in the terminology of the Fund, drawing) facilities that can be used *unconditionally* by *all* IMF members up to a certain cap and for a pre-established time period. Collective insurance would provide both unconditional and conditional lending.

A major problem that this reform faces is that current IMF quota allocations and borrowing limits, which are also the basis for SDR issues, do not reflect the realities of the world economy today. Aside from the issues that have been discussed in the recent debates on IMF quotas, which have led to some marginal improvements, an even more important issue is the huge disparity in the demand for reserves by developing versus industrial economies, which are at the center of both the inequities of the current reserve system and the inequity–instability links highlighted in this chapter. This problem can be corrected only with either one or a mix of three types of reforms (since they are not mutually exclusive). They should be combined, anyway, with the previous proposals on SDR allocations and SDR-funded collective insurance, which represents the hard core of the reform proposal.

The first proposal is an asymmetric issuance of SDRs, which would imply that all or a larger proportion of allocations would be given to those countries with the highest demand for reserves—i.e., essentially developing countries.

The second would be to create a clear development link in SDR allocations. One of the proposals on the table is the use of allocation to industrial countries to finance additional aid for the poorest countries and the provision of global public goods (Stiglitz 2006, ch. 9). This proposal has many virtues but poses the problem that such transfers are fiscal in character, and may thus require in every case the approval of national parliaments. The alternative would be a scheme similar to that proposed by the Group of Experts convened by UNCTAD in the 1960s (UNCTAD, 1965), which would allow the IMF to buy bonds from multi-lateral development banks with the SDRs that are not utilized by member states, which would then finance the demands for long-term resources by developing countries.

The third is encouraging the creation of *regional* reserve arrangements among developing countries—such as the Latin American Reserve Fund and the Chiang Mai Agreement—that provide a complementary form of collective insurance. A major incentive to the formation of such regional arrangements would be a provision that allocations of SDRs would be proportional not only to IMF quotas but also to reserves that developing countries have placed in com-mon reserve funds—thus making pooled reserves equivalent to IMF quotas for this purpose (United Nations, 1999; Ocampo, 2002).

An active use of SDRs with some mix of these features would go a long way to correct the major problems that the current system has, with perhaps one exception: the anti-Keynesian bias. The proposal to put in place Keynes' over-draft facility is perhaps the best recommendation in that regard. An additional step would be to force all countries to keep a minimum proportion of (or even all) their foreign exchange beyond a certain level in the IMF, again in the form of SDRs. Allocations of SDRs could also be denied to those countries with "excessive reserves." The definition of excessive reserves would have to take into account, of course, the exceptional demand by developing countries for such reserves due to the pro-cyclicality of finance and trade (particularly, but not only, terms of trade) volatility.

The current environment could actually be a good time to introduce these reforms. First, the inflationary risks associated with SDR issues are minimal.[16] Second, the United States has embarked on a large fiscal deficit and an aggres-sive monetary strategy. This has potential implications for the stability of the current reserve system, as some countries (particularly China) have already indicated. Under the current circumstances, the US might actually find its role at the center of the global monetary system quite uncomfortable, as it could eventually constrain its policy freedom. Also, as indicated above, by giving up its dominant reserve currency status, the US would also free itself from the need to generate current account deficits to provide world liquidity, which have adverse aggregate demand effect on its economy.

In any case, it must be emphasized that giving up the role of the dollar as the major *reserve* currency would still keep its role as the major international *means of payment,* unless the SDRs are used in broader financial transactions, as some have suggested in the past (Kenen, 1983; Polak, 2005, Part II). Although this is a possibility for the future of the SDRs or an alternative global reserve asset, it is preferable to concentrate current reforms on enhancing its capacity to serve as a reserve asset, thus limiting its holding to central banks and a few other institutions. The use of the dollar as a means of payments increases the demands for the services of the US financial system, and have other implications for the US that have been explored by other authors (see, for example, Cooper, 1987, ch. 7). It remains to be seen, of course, whether the ongoing financial crisis will have permanent effects on the role of the US as the world's major banker.

The reform of the global reserve system is obviously only part of the reform of the global financial architecture. There are several complementary reforms that can help alleviate some of the problems of the system and strengthen, in particular, the counter-cyclical dimensions of the global financial architecture. As argued by Ocampo and Griffith-Jones (2008), this should be the essential framework for redesigning such architecture from the perspective of developing countries, and should include a particular emphasis on increasing the "policy space" that these countries have to adopt counter-cyclical macroeconomic and financial policies.

The first reform is the more active use of capital account regulations, particularly to restrict excessive capital inflows during booms. So, the Fund should be encouraged not only to tolerate but actually advise countries on what regulations to impose under given circumstances. In this regard, the global regulatory structure that would emerge from the crisis should include provisions that apply to cross-border capital movements, such as: generalized reserve requirements on cross-border flows, minimum stay periods, and prohibitions to lend in foreign currencies to economic agents that do not have revenues in those currencies. The second are instruments aimed at better distributing the risk faced by developing countries through the business cycle (GDP-linked or commodity-indexed bonds) or that encourage more stable private flows (such as counter-cyclical guarantees). Third, and very importantly, to avoid the moral hazard issues associated with strengthened IMF emergency financing facilities, a good international debt workout mechanism should be put in place (see, in this regard, Akyüz, 2005, and Herman et al., 2009).

Finally, the reform of the global reserve system should be viewed as part of a broader reform aimed at placing the IMF at the center of world macroeconomic policy management. Indeed, such an approach would allow the Fund to go beyond its function as an "emergency financier" of balance of payments crises in the developing world, the essential role that it has played since the mid-1970s. Such reinforcement of the IMF would require strengthening the surveillance of major economies as well as its role as an honest broker in macroeconomic policy coordination, which has been managed through ad hoc mechanisms since the 1980s (the G-5, then the G-7 and now perhaps the G-20). The multilateral surveillance on global imbalances launched by the Fund in 2006 was an interesting step in that direction, but it lacked binding commitment by the parties and an accountability mechanism.

It must also be emphasized that, despite the problems of representation that the IMF has, which must continue to be addressed, it is the only institution where *all* member developing countries have a voice, through their constituencies, on global macroeconomic policy issues.

Notes

1. The views expressed in this chapter have been enriched by debates that have taken place in the Commission of Experts of the UN General Assembly on Reforms of the International Monetary and Financial System, led by Joseph E. Stiglitz, of which the author is a member (see also in this regard Chapter 17). I am also grateful to Jomo K. S., Thomas Palley, Lance Taylor, Eduardo Wiesner, and John Williamson for detailed comments on a previous draft. The chapter also draws in part from Ocampo (2007/8), with permission from M. E. Sharp. Support from the Ford Foundation is kindly acknowledged.
2. Professor and Co-President of the Initiative for Policy Dialogue at Columbia University. Former Under-Secretary General of the United Nations for Economic and Social Affairs and Executive Secretary of the Economic Commission for Latin America and the Caribbean, and former Minister of Finance of Colombia.
3. I will follow the convention of referring to the biases or risks as "deflationary" or "inflationary," although they may affect the level of economic activity rather than the price level, and therefore could rather be called "contractionary" or "expansionary."
4. See also the interesting proposal made in the 1960s to design a commodity-based reserve system, which has interesting counter-cyclical features (Hart et al., 1964). I put aside a discussion of a return to a gold standard, which collapsed on its own right and would be unviable under the "embedded liberalism" of the post-Second World War arrangements, as emphasized by Eichengreen (1996).
5. See Frankel (1994) for a detailed account of these development and efforts at international policy coordination during the 1980s.
6. The preference of China for an orderly appreciation since 2005 seems to be grounded in similar concerns.
7. This assumes that these countries (particularly developing countries) have net liabilities denominated in foreign currencies. Of course, there are agents that profit from depreciation (those with net assets in foreign currencies) as well as agents that lose (those with net liabilities in foreign currencies). If the country has positive net assets (a characteristic that more developing countries have as the result of the large foreign exchange reserves accumulated in recent years), the real balance effect would be positive, but there will still be distributive effects.
8. This generates an additional set of asymmetries that I will not analyze here. I refer to the fact that poorer countries as well as small firms in all developing countries have very limited or no access to international financial markets. Countries with a poor track record will also have more limited access to these markets.
9. See a survey of this literature in Chapter 14.
10. For this group of countries, whereas the correlation of variation of reserves with net capital flows (both as a proportion of GDP) is 0.715 for the period 1982–2007 as a

whole, that between the current account and reserve accumulation is actually negative and not statistically significant (−0.165).

11. See good summaries of the debates of the 1960s in Solomon (1977) and Triffin (1968) and an interesting contrast between the role of SDRs then and now in Clark and Polak (2004).

12. See IMF (2009) and an analysis of different financing options in Truman (2008).

13. On the deficiencies of arrangements to borrow, see Kenen (2001).

14. There would of course be limits on total lending—the total "quotas" of member states, which would now have a fairly notional sense, except that they would be the basis for SDR allocations and perhaps to determine who bears the costs of running the Fund.

15. Any of these proposals would involve eliminating the division between what are called the General Resource the SDR Accounts. See Polak (2005, part II) and Cooper (1987, ch. 12).

16. They are probably minimal even in normal times, as the $100–150 billion represents less than 0.2 and 0.3 per cent of world GDP, respectively.

References

Aizenman, J. and Lee, J. (2007) 'International Reserves: Mercantilist vs. Precautionary View, Theory and Evidence.' *Open Economies Review*, 18(2), pp. 191–214.

Akyüz, Y. (2005) 'Reforming the IMF: Back to the Drawing Board.' Third World Network, Global Economy Series, No. 7.

Camdessus, M. (2000) 'An Agenda for the IMF at the Start of the 21st Century,' Remarks at the Council on Foreign Relations, New York (February).

Clark, P. B. and Polak, J. J. (2004) 'International Liquidity and the Role of the SDR in the International Monetary System.' *IMF Staff Papers*, 51(1), pp. 49–71. Reproduced in Polak (2005, ch. 9).

Cooper, R. (1987) *The International Monetary System: Essays in World Economics.* Cambridge, Mass.: MIT Press.

D'Arista, J. (1999) 'Reforming the Privatized International Monetary and Financial Architecture.' *Financial Markets and Society* (November).

Dooley, M. P., Folkerts-Landau, D., and Garber, P. (2003) 'An Essay on the Revived Bretton Woods System.' NBER Working Paper, No. 9971 (September).

—— (2009) 'Bretton Woods II Still Defines the International Monetary System.' NBER Working Paper, No. 14731 (February).

Eichengreen, B. (1996) *Globalizing Capital: A History of the International Monetary System.* Princeton, NJ: Princeton University Press.

—— (2007) *Global Imbalances and the Lessons of Bretton Woods.* Cambridge, Mass.: MIT Press.

—— and Hausmann, R. (eds.) (2005) *Other People's Money: Debt Denomination and Financial Instability in Emerging Market Economies.* Chicago: University of Chicago Press.

Frankel, J. (1994) 'Exchange Rate Policy.' In Martin Feldstein (ed.), *American Economic Policy in the 1980s.* Chicago: University of Chicago Press, pp. 293–341.

Frenkel, R. (2007) 'The Sustainability of Monetary Sterilization Policies.' *CEPAL Review*, No. 93 (December).

—— (2008) 'From the Boom in Capital Inflows to Financial Traps.' In J. A. Ocampo and J. E. Stiglitz (eds.), *Capital Market Liberalization and Development*. New York: Oxford University Press.

Hart, A. G., Kaldor, N., and Tinbergen, J. (1964) 'The Case for an International Commodity Reserve Currency.' UNCTAD. Geneva, Reproduced in Nicholas Kaldor (1980) *Essays on Economic Policy II: Vol. IV of Collected Economic Essays*. New York: Holmes and Meier, ch. 18.

Herman, B., Ocampo, J. A., and Spiegel, S. (eds.) (2009) *Overcoming Developing Country Debt Crises*. New York: Oxford University Press.

International Monetary Fund (2009) 'Review of the Adequacy of and Options for Supplementing Fund Resources' (January 12).

Kaminsky, G. L., Reinhart, C. M., and Végh, C. A. (2004) 'When It Rains, It Pours: Procyclical Capital Flows and Macroeconomic Policies.' NBER Working Paper, No. 10780 (September).

Kenen, P. B. (1983) 'Use of SDR to Supplement or Substitute for Other Means of Finance.' In George M. von Furstenberg (ed.), *International Money and Credit: The Policy Roles*. Washington, DC: International Monetary Fund, ch. 7.

—— (2001) *The International Financial Architecture: What's New? What's Missing?*' Washington, DC: Institute for International Economics.

Keynes, J. M. (1942–43) 'The Keynes Plan.' Reproduced in J. Keith Horsefield (ed.) (1969), *The International Monetary Fund 1945–1965: Twenty Years of International Monetary Cooperation*, Vol. III: Documents. Washington, DC: International Monetary Fund, pp. 3–36.

Kindleberger, C. P. (1978) *Maniacs, Panics, and Crashes: A History of Financial Crises*. New York: John Wiley and Sons.

Minsky, H. P. (1982) 'The Financial Instability Hypothesis: A Restatement.' In *Can 'It' Happen Again? Essays on Instability and Finance*. Armonk, NY: M. E. Sharpe, ch. 5.

Obstfeld, M., Shambaugh, J. C., and Taylor, A. M. (2008) 'Financial Stability, The Trilemma, and International Reserves.' NBER Working Paper, 14217 (August).

Ocampo, J. A. (2002) 'Recasting the International Financial Agenda.' In John Eatwell and Lance Taylor (eds.), *International Capital Markets: Systems in Transition*. New York: Oxford University Press, pp. 41–73.

—— (2007/8) 'The Instability and Inequities of the Global Reserve System.' *International Journal of Political Economy*, 36(4).

—— (2008) 'A Broad View of Macroeconomic Stability.' In Narcis Serra and J. E. Stiglitz (eds.), *The Washington Consensus Reconsidered: Towards a New Global Governance*. New York: Oxford University Press.

—— and Martin, J. (2003) *Globalization and Development: A Latin American and Caribbean Perspective*. Palo Alto: Stanford University Press, Economic Commission for Latin America and the Caribbean and World Bank.

—— Kregel, J. and Griffith-Jones, S. (2007) *International Finance and Development*. London: Zed Books.

—— and Griffith-Jones, S. (2008) 'A Counter-cyclical Framework for a Development-friendly International Financial Architecture.' In José María Fanelli (ed.), *Macroeconomic Volatility, Institutions and Financial Architecture: The Developing World Experience*. Houndmills: Palgrave/Macmillan.

—— and Vos, R. (2008) *Uneven Economic Development*. Hyderabad, London, and Penang: Orient Longman, Zed Books, and Third World Network.

Polak, Jacques J. (2005), *Economic Theory and Financial Policy: Selected Essays of Jacques J. Polak 1994–2004*, ed. James M. Boughton. Armonk, NY: M. E. Sharpe.

Prasad, E. S., Rogoff, K., Wei, S. J., and Rose, M. A. (2003) 'Effects of Financial Globalization on Developing Countries: Some Empirical Evidence.' *Occasional Paper* 220. Washington, DC: International Monetary Fund.

Rodrik, D. (2006) 'The Social Costs of Foreign Exchange Reserves.' *International Economic Journal*, 20(3).

Solomon, R. (1977) *The International Monetary System 1945–1976: An Insider's View*. New York: Harper & Row.

Stiglitz, J. E. (2006) *Making Globalization Work*. New York: WW Norton.

—— Ocampo, J. A., Spiegel, S., Ffrench-Davis, R., and Nayyar, D. (2006) *Stability with Growth: Macroeconomics, Liberalization, and Development*. New York: Oxford University Press.

Summers, L. H. (2004) 'The US Current Account Deficit and the Global Economy.' Per Jacobson Lecture, Washington, DC.

Triffin, R. (1961) *Gold and the Dollar Crisis* (Revised edition). New Haven: Yale University Press.

—— (1968) *Our International Monetary System: Yesterday, Today and Tomorrow*. New York: Random House.

Truman, E. M. (2008) 'On What Terms Is the IMF Worth Funding?' Working Paper 08–11. Washington, DC: Peterson Institute for International Economics.

UNCTAD (1965) *International Monetary Issues and the Developing Countries: Report of the Group of Experts*. New York: United Nations.

United Nations (1999) 'Towards a New International Financial Architecture: Report of the Task Force of the Executive Committee on Economic and Social Affairs of the United Nations' <http://www.un.org/esa/coordination/ecesa/ecesa-1.pdf>.

—— (2001) *Report of the High-level Panel on Financing for Development* (Zedillo Report) <http://www.un.org/reports/financing>.

—— (2005) *World Economic Situation and Prospects 2005*.

White, W. R. (2005) 'Procyclicality in the Financial System: Do We Need a New Macro-financial Stabilization Framework?' *Kiel Economic Policy Papers*. Kiel: Kiel Institute for Economic Policy (September).

Williamson, J. (2004) 'The Future of the Global Financial System.' *Journal of Post-Keynesian Economics*, 26(4).

17

A Modest Proposal for International Monetary Reform[1]

Bruce Greenwald[2] and Joseph E. Stiglitz[3]

An ideal system of international payments should be characterized by stability and balance: stability in exchange rates and the absence of sudden crises, and balance in the sense that individual national economies should suffer neither from the deflationary effects of chronic external deficits nor the distorting consequences of chronic external surpluses. Both requirements are essential to the efficient international movement of capital. Yet neither requirement appears to have been met by the current dollar-based reserve currency system. Recurrent crises in Asia, Latin America, and Eastern Europe, and chronic and growing US payments deficits (with their associated deflationary impact) are longstanding characteristics of the current system.

This chapter argues that the problems just described are fundamental aspects of the present system and that, without reform, they will continue to plague the global economy. However, a simple set of institutional reforms would go a long way toward alleviating these difficulties. In order to understand the need for and nature of these reforms, we begin by analyzing the dynamics of the current system using a simple global macroeconomics framework. Within this context, we examine a number of proposed explanations for current imbalances and ultimately focus on a small number of potentially responsible factors. They bear a striking similarity to those which Keynes cited in connection with the failure of the pre-Bretton Woods system. The chapter then lays out reforms designed to alleviate these problems. Finally, it ends with a broader analysis of the costs and benefits of such a reformed system.

Issues of reform of the global reserve system have achieved increasing attention, especially since the UN Commission on the Reform of the Global Monetary and Financial System, chaired by Stiglitz, suggested that this was the most important item on the longer-term agenda for ensuring a more stable global financial system. China's Central Bank governor has added his voice to those suggesting a need for a reform.[4]

We argue that a key explanation for the massive global imbalances that prevailed in the years prior to the crisis—and whose disorderly unwinding has been a recurrent subject of concern—is the large increase in the demand for reserves, partially explained in turn by the need for self-insurance against global instability. This has been a persistent problem in recent years, but the crisis has given immediacy to the demands for reform for two reasons. First, those holding large amounts of dollars have suddenly become aware of the riskiness of their reserve holdings; the dollar has become a poor store of value, as its value has decreased and become volatile. But worse, the massive debt and massive lending by the Fed have stoked worries about the risk of a decrease in the value of the dollar as a result of inflation. Compounding the problem is that the return on Treasury bills has fallen to near-zero. Countries holding dollars in reserves are bearing risk without reward, and quite naturally, the citizens of these countries have become worried that the assets which they view as having resulted from their hard work and thrift will quickly dissipate. These concerns have been reinforced by the large losses by China's sovereign wealth funds on its investment in Blackstone. (China's premier's stern warning to the US, to maintain the value of what China has invested in the US, needs to be seen in this light.)

International dynamics within the current international monetary system

An analysis of the macrodynamics of the global economy must begin with an analysis of the macroeconomic balances within each of its constituent economies. Those balances, in turn, rest on the equality of savings and investment. Formally, in any national economy, domestic investments (I) plus the net foreign surplus (NFS), which corresponds to net overseas investment, must equal the sum of net private savings (NPS) by households and firms and net government savings (NGS), the surplus in aggregate government budgets. For ease of future reference we will designate this as

$$I + NFS \equiv NPS + NGS$$

or, in terms of external balance,

$$NFS \equiv NPS + NGS - I \qquad (1)$$

This formulation presupposes nothing about whether the economies in question are fully classical, with interest rates adjusting to ensure satisfaction of equation (1) at full employment, or subject to Keynesian unemployment, with the level of output being an important equilibrating variable whose distance from full employment depends on the efficacy of monetary and fiscal policy.

The fundamental discipline imposed by any international monetary system is embodied in the fact that the sum over all countries of net foreign surplus must be zero, namely

$$\Sigma NFS_i = \Sigma NPS_i + \Sigma NGS_i - \Sigma I_i \equiv 0 \qquad (2)$$

where the summations are taken over all individual national economies.[5] Equations (1) and (2), together with the behavioral regularities determining their individual components, govern the dynamics of the international monetary system. Equations (1) and (2) are identities and are always true. It will be useful to look at that system from the perspective of these two equations.

The twin deficits theory

The standard analysis of trade deficits is based on *the theory of the twin deficits*, which holds that when a country has a fiscal deficit it is likely to have a current account deficit as well.

In a partial equilibrium setting the relationship is clear: *ceteris paribus*, any increase in the government deficit reduces domestic national saving.[6] In equilibrium, capital inflows have to equal the difference between domestic investment and domestic savings; but capital inflows also have to equal the difference between imports and exports. Hence, if domestic savings falls *and nothing else changes*, then capital inflows and the trade deficit *must* increase.

In terms of equation (1), the twin deficit theory assumes that I and NPS remain unchanged. Of course, in the real world, *ceteris paribus* does not hold. Some economists have argued that when fiscal deficits increase, taxpayers, realizing that there are future bills to be paid, increase their savings *in a fully offsetting way*. (This is called the Barro-Ricardo model.) If that were true, increased fiscal deficits would be accompanied by increased private savings, and national savings would be unaffected. Increases in fiscal deficits would not be accompanied by increases in trade deficits. There would be no such thing as the "twin deficits."

This is an example of a "theory" that, although widely taught, especially in graduate schools, makes little sense and has little empirical support.[7] Recent events in the US provide a dramatic illustration. Under President George W. Bush, fiscal deficits had risen, but household saving had actually declined (to zero, or even negative in some quarters). When one hears somebody say, "Economic theory says..." one must be cautious. Often such statements refer to a theory that assumes perfect markets, perfect information, and perfect risk sharing in an economy with identical individuals living infinitely long. The assumptions are suspect, at best, in the most advanced industrialized countries and certainly not true in the developing world.

The Barro-Ricardo model, though implausible, does make one important point: we are not living in a *ceteris paribus* world; there are lots of other things going on simultaneously. We have to be careful in analyzing what are endogenous and what are exogenous variables.

A (cyclical) increase in investment, for instance, may lead to an increase in GDP, a (cyclical) increase in government and private savings, and an increase in imports. Whether capital inflows decrease or increase depends on whether government and private savings increase to fully offset (or not quite offset) the increase in investment. In this case, both the government deficit and the trade deficit are endogenous variables.

Both cross sectional and time series data make clear that there is no simple relationship between fiscal and trade deficits. Figure 17.1 provides aggregate G-7 data on twin deficits (aggregate current account and government balances as a percentage of GDP). If one believed in the twin deficits argument, the data would be aligned along a 45 degree line through the origin; the two would increase in tandem. In fact, no real pattern is discernible in the data.

More interesting is the time series data, shown for each of the G-7 countries in the following figures. Again, "twin deficit theory" has an obvious prediction: an increase in the fiscal deficit should be quickly reflected in an increase in the current account deficit. We can evaluate this theory by examining time series data on the current account as a percentage of GDP (country_CA_PGDP) and the government balance as a percentage of GDP (country_GB_PGDP).

Figure 17.2 shows data for the US since 1980. What is striking is that the trade deficit has been steadily increasing *regardless* of what happened with the fiscal deficit and regardless of who was in the White House. The pattern goes back

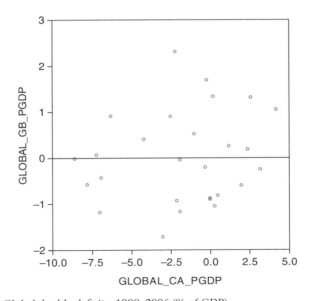

Figure 17.1 Global double deficits, 1980–2006 (% of GDP)

Source: International Monetary Fund, World Economic and Financial Surveys Series.

even earlier. The US government deficit rises steadily from the early 1970s to the late 1980s, begins to decline in the 1990s and moves into surplus in 1998, and finally rises sharply post-2000. In contrast, the current account deficit grows steadily throughout the period. Thus, in the 1990s the trade deficit increased, even as the fiscal deficit decreased. (The good thing about the 1990s was that it was linked to an increase in investment. In the present decade, under President Bush, money was to a large extent going into a consumption binge, with household savings approaching zero. From a balance sheet perspective it did make a big difference; borrowing to finance consumption rather than to finance an asset leaves the balance sheet obviously much worse off.)

It is clear from the data that there is no systematic relationship between the trade deficit and the fiscal deficit; in other words, there is no such thing as "twin deficits." Actually, if one looks at the other G-7 countries, it is also apparent that there is no systematic relationship, except for in one country, Canada (see Figure 17.8).[8]

In the case of Canada there is a systematic relationship, but it is not the fiscal deficits that are giving rise to the trade deficits. Rather, if we do a Granger causality test,[9] it appears that the fiscal deficit is endogenous and is being driven

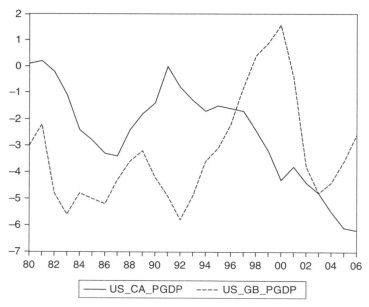

Figure 17.2 Current account and government balances: United States, 1980–2006 (% of GDP)

Source: International Monetary Fund, World Economic and Financial Surveys Series.

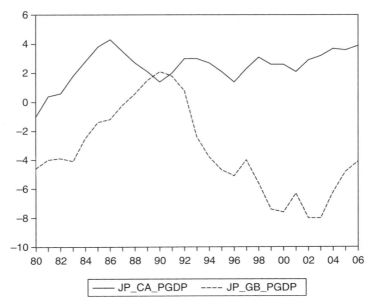

Figure 17.3 Current account and government balances: Japan, 1980–2006 (% of GDP)
Source: International Monetary Fund, World Economic and Financial Surveys Series.

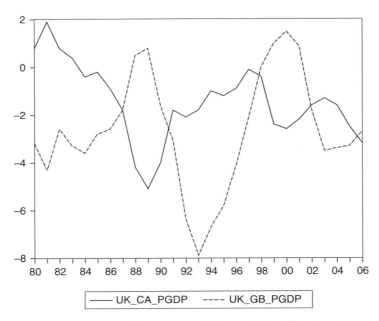

Figure 17.4 Current account and government balances: United Kingdom, 1980–2006 (% of GDP)
Source: International Monetary Fund, World Economic and Financial Surveys Series.

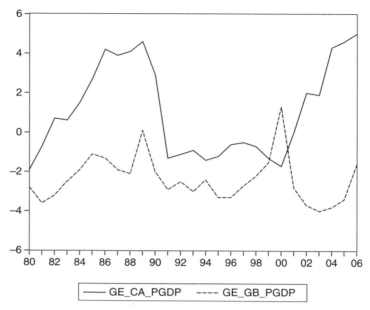

Figure 17.5 Current account and government balances: Germany,[1] 1980–2006 (% of GDP)
[1] Pre-1990 data are for West Germany; post-1990 data are for unified Germany.
Source: International Monetary Fund, World Economic and Financial Surveys Series.

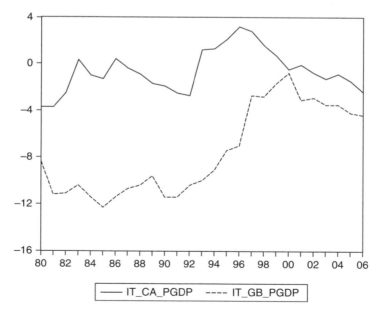

Figure 17.6 Current account and government balances: Italy, 1980–2006 (% of GDP)
Source: International Monetary Fund, World Economic and Financial Surveys Series.

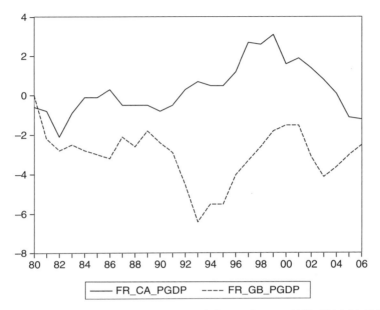

Figure 17.7 Current account and government balances: France, 1980–2006 (% of GDP)
Source: International Monetary Fund, World Economic and Financial Surveys Series.

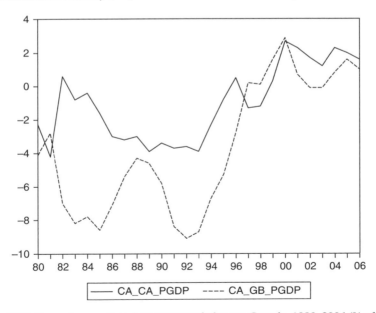

Figure 17.8 Current account and government balances: Canada, 1980–2006 (% of GDP)
Source: International Monetary Fund, World Economic and Financial Surveys Series.

Table 17.1 Pairwise Granger causality tests

Sample: 1960–2007

Lags: 1

Null hypothesis:	Observations	F-Statistic	Probability[1]
CA_GB_PGDP does not Granger Cause CA_CA_PGDP	26	6.54829	0.0175
CA_CA_PGDP does not Granger Cause CA_GB_PGDP		1.12550	0.2998

[1] Probability of rejecting the Null hypothesis.

by the trade deficit. It is actually easy to understand what is going on, on the basis of standard Keynesian economics.

Fiscal deficits help maintain the economy at full employment. For a country like Canada, at least in the very short run, the trade deficit (capital inflows) is exogenous. A downturn in the US economy reduces, for instance, Canada's exports to the US and increases the trade deficit. But as external circumstances affect the economy (e.g. exports decrease), the government has to respond. It typically uses fiscal policy to stimulate the economy to offset a potential threat of recession. Thus, it is the fiscal deficit that follows the trade deficit.[10]

While the notion that trade deficits drive fiscal deficits seems plausible for a small country like Canada, we want to examine the view that, at least in part, capital flows should be treated as exogenous for the United States and increasingly so for Europe.

The demand for reserves and trade deficits

The problem with the twin deficit theory (at least for the US) is not just that it assumes that I and NPS are exogenous but that it views the entire world from a US centric perspective. Hidden behind all the behavioral equations are relative prices (i.e., exchange rates), and these are determined by the behavior of other countries as much as by the US, including their demands for holding US dollar-denominated assets. Any theory attempting to explain the US trade deficit must be based on a global general equilibrium model. In this section, we present the simplest such model.

In our current dollar-based reserve currency world a further specialization of equation (2) is useful:

$$\Sigma NFS \equiv NFS_R + NFS_N \equiv 0$$

and thus:

$$NFS_R \equiv NPS_R + NGS_R - I_R \equiv -NFS_N = -[NPS_N + NGS_N - I_N]$$

where the subscript R denotes the reserve currency country and the subscript N, the sum of balances for the non-reserve currency countries.

The different causes put forward to account for the chronic US international deficit are readily identifiable within this context. The basic "twin deficits" view that the imbalance is driven by US government deficits and low savings rates amounts to assuming that the exogenous variables in this relationship are NPS_R (relatively small[11]), NGS_R (large and negative) and I_R (relatively large and positive) which together determine a level of NFS_R that is large and negative (i.e. a large net foreign deficit). In turn, this deficit *drives* surpluses in the rest of the non-US world. This view is more broadly characteristic of a policy consensus which attributes international imbalances of individual countries to their management of variables on the right-hand side of equation (1). The focus is on national behavior rather than the global constraints embodied in equation (2).

While the twin deficit explanation of the trade deficit focuses on the US, and the misdeeds of the Bush Administration, others seek to shift the "blame" abroad. For instance, the US has consistently blamed China's undervalued exchange rate. A quick look at the numbers suggests what is wrong with such a claim: the United States' trade deficit in 2006 was more than $850 billion, whereas China's multilateral trade surplus was only about $150 billion; when the US started talking about China's trade imbalances, it was actually close to zero. China has been growing very rapidly, but even if China were to eliminate its current $150 billion trade surplus with the US, and even if this reduction in the bilateral trade deficit were translated dollar for dollar into a reduction in the US multilateral trade deficit, the US deficit would still stand at some $700 billion, or just under $2 billion per day. In fact, the likely outcome of China eliminating its trade surplus would be a very small change in the US multilateral trade deficit. The United States would quite simply start buying textiles and apparel from Cambodia, Bangladesh, or some other country rather than from China.

There is a real risk that global instability might actually be increased, because while China may be willing to finance the US deficit, it is not clear whether Cambodia or Bangladesh would. It is plausible that these countries will think it better to invest their money into their own country; and if they do lend their money abroad, they are more likely to put it into euros or yen rather than just financing the US deficits by holding dollars, which are a depreciating asset. While it is true that even if China did not buy US bonds another country would, to induce those purchases may require large changes in asset prices. There is a high likelihood of what has come to be called a disorderly adjustment, and such adjustments are likely to be painful.

While attempts to *blame* China for the US capital inflow/trade deficit seem misplaced, the discussion highlights the role of the behavior of foreigners in determining the US trade deficit.

In terms of our framework, this means that NFS_N, the net foreign surplus for non-reserve countries, is treated as the exogenous variable. It is strongly positive. The resulting net domestic savings must be deployed abroad, so that the strongly positive NSF_N drives the offsetting US position (NSF_R) to be strongly negative. The capital inflow into the United States, combined with weak aggregate demand from high imports, "forces" the government to have a large trade deficit (not unlike the earlier story for Canada.) While the United States may be larger than any other country, it is still far smaller than the rest of the world put together.

Savings glut as an explanation

This explanation for chronic US international imbalances is, at least in recent years, related to the view of a global "saving glut" (see Bernanke, 2004).[12] There are many reasons that "the rest of the world" might have an imbalance of savings and investment. From a taxonomic perspective, a high value of NFS_N, in turn, occurs because high private savings (NPS_N) and low government deficits (NGS_N) are not offset by comparably high rates of investment (I_N).

There are two complementary versions of this argument. The first is classical in spirit. At full employment, local interest rates, determined by local capital market conditions, foreign investment opportunities (ultimately in the United States) are relatively attractive. This drives down exchange rates and creates surpluses in the external current accounts to offset the desired level of external investment. These surpluses then translate into US deficits. The second explanation is Keynesian in spirit. Excess local savings relative to investment lead to local aggregate demand shortfalls. If local constraints on monetary and fiscal policy mean that they cannot compensate for this deficiency in aggregate demand, then full employment may still be pursued by manipulating exchange rates to produce offsetting current account surpluses (namely by selling local currency to drive down exchange rates). The net result is to export the excess savings (aggregate demand shortfalls) to the United States. Again US deficits are created by local current account surpluses.

These explanations may have some relevance for the past half decade: high oil prices have increased income in the oil exporting countries faster than they can invest the proceeds; and while governments (which, in most of the world, receive a large fraction of the increased value of oil sales) have used some of the proceeds to increase consumption, they prudently realize that these high oil prices may not last and so have wanted to save substantial fractions of the income. (Real returns in the United States may have not been as large as market participants believed; they were attracted to the US by its bubbles, and the high *apparent* returns. The fact that so much of the investment was going into housing—combined with the indicia of a bubble and widespread financial shenanigans—should, perhaps, have been a warning.)

However, while perhaps a partial explanation for the recent imbalance, both evidence and theory argue against this as an explanation for what has been going on for the past three decades. Empirically, it is difficult to believe that a global "savings glut" has been a constantly increasing fact of international economic life for the past thirty years. Yet this is what the history of the US current account deficit—i.e. almost constant growth—requires. Theoretically, it is not clear why over the long run a structural imbalance between global (non-US) savings and investment should exist and why, if it does, the gap should not be offset on a country-by-country basis by appropriate local fiscal and monetary policies. The fact that so much of the rest of the world is developing, with a capital scarcity, would suggest not a global savings glut but a global savings dearth. Over this period, the US, with the impending retirement of the baby boomers, should have been having a net savings surplus.

One thing that both explanations (twin deficits and global savings glut) have in common is that they focus primarily on the right-hand side of equation (1) on a country-by-country basis, although the global savings view does at least recognize the constraint embodied in equation (2). An alternative is to focus on the left-hand side of equation (1) and the requirement of international balance (equation (2)), looking directly at the determinants of external balances and then examining the consequences of international balance for domestic macroeconomic circumstances. This generates dynamic behavior that appears to be far more consistent with the relevant history. It also captures more effectively the full range of potential national behaviors in a world where there are policy variables that can be used to manage external balances (notably exchange rates) independently of local domestic macroeconomic goals.

A simple global general equilibrium model

A natural starting point of this alternative perspective is to examine national demands for reserves. Just as individual households and firms hold cash to offset temporary imbalances between income and expenditures, so do national governments presumably hold reserves to offset temporary imbalances between the supply of and demand for their currencies (i.e. foreign capital outflows and inflows). Like cash holdings, the demand for reserves should grow with the volume of international transactions. As international transactions volume grows over time, nations should seek to add to their currency reserve positions. If the growth in transactions is proportional, then the size of these desired additions to reserves should also grow over time. Since reserves can only be accumulated by running official balance of payment surpluses, the demand for reserve additions translates immediately into a demand for official surpluses. As the level of desired additions to reserves grows, the level of these desired official surpluses grows as well.

Especially since the 1997 global financial crisis, foreign governments have wanted to increase their currency reserves. Reserves increased from 6–8 per cent of GDP to 30 per cent of GDP by 2004.[13] Developing countries do not want to have to call upon the International Monetary Fund (IMF) for a bail-out, in the event of a crisis. There is a high price to accumulating reserves—the money could have been spent, say, to increase investment and hence growth—but there is an even higher price to pay if they do not have sufficient reserves and have to call upon the IMF.[14] It is not just that the policies the IMF has imposed put the repayment of creditors above all else (even at the cost of countries sinking into recessions or depressions); borrowers also must worry about the loss of sovereignty entailed by IMF conditionality. Figure 17.9 shows the holdings of total reserves minus gold for both the industrialized and the emerging/developing countries. Figure 17.10 shows the evolution of the spread in reserves between the industrialized and developing countries. Figure 17.11 shows the gold holdings of the two groups. Note that the industrialized countries have been reducing their gold holdings just as the price of gold has reached record highs. Meanwhile, the emerging markets have been slowly and steadily accumulating gold.

There is another reason, not unrelated, why matters may have become "worse" in recent years. In the past, countries offset the savings represented

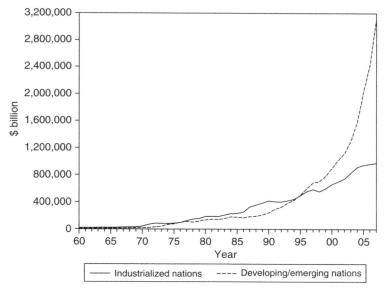

Figure 17.9 Total reserves minus gold

Source: International Monetary Fund, International Financial Statistics.

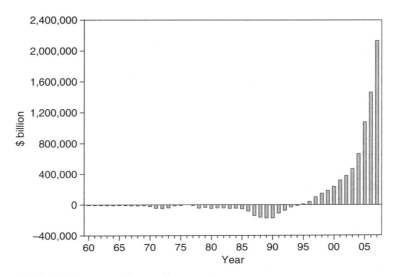

Figure 17.10 Total reserves minus gold spread
Source: International Monetary Fund, International Financial Statistics.

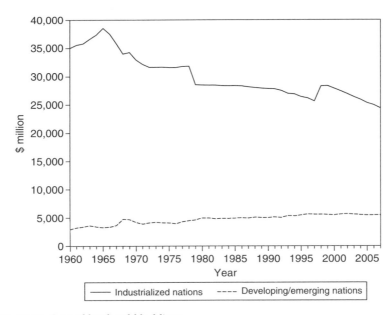

Figure 17.11 Central bank gold holdings
Source: International Monetary Fund, International Financial Statistics.

by reserve accumulations by profligate fiscal policies and loose monetary policies; or perhaps more accurately, some developing countries offset the savings of other developing countries. But in recent years, as the religion of sound fiscal and monetary policy has been adopted, there has been nothing to offset this saving of non-reserve countries.

Of course, from the global perspective, a savings glut is nothing more than an insufficiency of aggregate demand. Unless there is an excess of investment over savings in the US, *at full employment,* to make up for the excess of savings in the rest of the world, there will be a problem of global insufficiency of demand. The money put into reserves is part of global output (= income) that is not being spent. The United States has become the *consumer of last resort*—making up for the deficiency in aggregate demand elsewhere—a problem which has become worse as other countries have learned to follow prudent monetary and fiscal policies. At the same time, as other countries strive to make sure that they do not have large trade deficits (harbinger of a crisis to come), the United States has also become the *deficit of last resort*—as identity (2) makes clear that it must.

At times, US government officials have been explicit about this role of the United States' "imbalances." They have argued that the rest of the world should thank the US for keeping up global demand and growth. Yet, as we comment below, there is something peculiar about a global economic order which depends on the richest country of the world consuming beyond its means in order to maintain global full employment. We can summarize these identities and behavioral relations in the following simple, global general equilibrium model:

$$\text{NFS}_R \equiv -\text{NFS}_N \tag{3a}$$

$$\text{NFS}_R \equiv \text{NPS}_R(p_R, v_R, e) + \text{NGS}_R(p_R, v_R, e) - I_R(p_R, v_R, e) \tag{3b}$$

$$\text{NFS}_N \equiv \text{NPS}_N(p_N, v_N, e) + \text{NGS}_N(p_N, v_N, e) - I_N(p_N, v_N, e) \tag{3c}$$

where p_i is a vector of policy variables in the reserve (non-reserve) countries, v_i is a vector of exogenous variables (preferences, technology, etc.), and e is the exchange rate. There are, of course, a large number of endogenous variables (prices, interest rates, etc.) within each country that we assume have been solved.[15]

We deconstruct government savings into the demand for reserves and the fiscal deficit (FD); the former we treat as exogenous, the latter as a function of policies (e.g. expenditure policies), the exchange rate, and exogenous variables.

$$\text{NGS}_N = \text{NDR}_N + \text{FD}(p_N, v_N, e) \tag{3d}$$

where NDR_N denotes the aggregate demand for addition to reserves.

Equations (3a–d) are identities—they are always true. In the old, fixed exchange rate system, we can think of e as exogenous and of equations (3a–d) as determining NGS_N—the value of increases (decreases) in reserves that will, at the fixed exchange rate, ensure that equations (3a–d) hold. But in the era of flexible exchange rate that has prevailed for the past 35 years, e is endogenous, and reserves are exogenous.[16] If foreigners wish to hold more reserves, then there has to be a capital outflow from the non-reserve countries, a capital inflow into the US, i.e. imports *must* exceed exports, so the exchange rate has to rise to accommodate the capital inflow.[17]

In this interpretation, the longstanding US trade deficit is the result of the high demand for dollars as a reserve currency. With growth of the non-reserve countries, they are holding more and more reserves. In effect, the US is exporting Treasury bills to be held in reserves—partly at the expense of automobiles. And, except when the US is experiencing an investment boom—as in the 1990s—this means that the government *must* run a fiscal deficit to keep the economy at full employment. In a sense, the US story is much like that of Canada—though the complexity of the dynamics is such that the interaction between the trade deficit and the fiscal deficit is not as apparent.

The model presented here is, of course, a gross simplification. A more complete model would have similar equations for each date, a set of state variables, and a set of dynamic equations that describe the evolution of those state variables. Yet, these dynamic equations would complicate the analysis, without affecting the basic points which we wish to make.[18]

We should emphasize that there are a host of policy variables that can affect the exchange rate: anything that might affect the demand or supply of a country's currency today or in the future. Hence, an increase in the fiscal deficit could increase national income, increasing imports at each exchange rate, and thereby increase the equilibrium exchange rate.[19]

Allegations of exchange rate manipulation seem to be about intent: presumably, the policies of the US government which have led to a low exchange rate (or have they led to a higher exchange rate than otherwise would be the case?) were undertaken for other reasons. But, of course, the same point can be made about interventions by those the US accuses of exchange rate manipulation, and there are other instruments that they could make use of which would have much the same effect. China could, for instance, allow more Chinese to invest abroad. There are good public policy reasons for doing this, but the effect would be to lower the exchange rate.

A special case

Analytically, the relationship between the demand for reserves and trade deficits can be seen most easily in the special case where there are no net private capital flows. The total NFS for any single country consists of the official surplus

plus the private surplus. In terms of target levels, the NFS for a country will be the sum of the desired official surplus plus the desired private surplus. The desired private foreign surplus consists of the difference between desired overseas investment by private domestic agents and desired foreign private investment in the country.

As capital flows equalize returns (adjusted for risk) across national economies, private investment inflows and outflows should balance out over time. However, desired official surplus will always be positive, reflecting the continuing demand for additions to reserves as international transactions grow. Assuming for convenience that desired private capital flows across non-reserve countries are zero,[20] the aggregate desired level of net foreign surplus for the non-reserve countries is equal to the sum of the desired official surplus or, equivalently, to the aggregate demand for additional reserves. Symbolically,

$$\text{NFS}_N = \text{NFS}_N(\text{official}) = \text{NDR}_N$$

where NDR_N denotes the aggregate demand for addition to reserves. This figure is positive, as long as international transactions volume grows and keeps growing, since growth in transaction volume is proportional. Thus, as long as non-reserve countries attain their desired levels of reserve accumulations, the reserve money currency country (i.e. the US) will be faced with chronic growing deficits (as the United States has).[21]

The methods by which non-reserve currencies might attain these goals are fairly straight forward. Favorable tax and regulatory treatment of export industries and impediments to imports and exchange rate management are the obvious ways to do so. However, if the reserve currency country is not content to run the required deficits, then these methods might be insufficient as each non-reserve nation struggles to acquire its desired share of a supply of reserves that overall is inadequate. If all countries, including the reserve currency country, simultaneously seek to devalue their currencies, then none will succeed. The further result may, therefore, be increasing barriers to trade, which will also be mutually defeating, or worse still, competing domestic deflations, designed to reduce import demand.

An example of this kind of situation in practice is the experience of crisis and contagion in the middle and late 1990s. In the struggle to run net foreign surpluses, some countries will inevitably lose out, either because their policy options are inadequate to the task or, what amounts to almost the same thing, because they are unwilling to make the domestic economic sacrifices necessary to succeed. South Korea, Indonesia, Thailand, and Malaysia appear to have been in this situation in the early to middle 1990s. Despite various degrees of government fiscal restraint and rapid economic growth, they all experienced large deficits in the current account. (In the case of Thailand, the government tried the standard procedure of raising interest rates to dampen demand; but this simply attracted more capital, strengthening the baht and increasing the foreign trade deficit. Ironically, Korea's crisis happened just after it had managed to reduce its current account deficit.) Ultimately, these deficits undermined confidence in their currencies, leading to capital flight, rapidly falling exchange rates, rising foreign debt burdens (in local currency terms) and severe economic contraction. The combination of lower exchange rates and reduced economic activity (through reduced import demand) moved all these economies into net foreign surplus positions but at great economic cost. More importantly, as they moved into surplus, other countries necessarily had to move into greater deficit, since the aggregate zero constraint on ΣNFS (equation (2)) is always binding. Deficits are like hot potatoes—so long as some countries are in surpluses, the sum of the deficits of the other countries must add up to the value of their surpluses. If the US did not absorb these new surpluses they would migrate to other relatively weak economies like Russia, Mexico, and Brazil (as they did). *In the absence of sufficiently high deficits by the reserve currency country, the whole reserve currency payments system is inherently unstable with a deflationary bias.*

Reserve accumulation represents a subtraction from global purchasing power. If the United States were to fail to offset this subtraction by aggressive consumption and government deficit spending, the consequences might well be a serious prolonged global recession. Yet as the United States does this, US consumers, who are among the richest in the world, benefit at the expense of those (often much poorer) nations accumulating dollar reserves.

Thus, chronic and growing US deficits are an essential feature of the current system. This basic imbalance may be exacerbated by a number of factors. For idiosyncratic reasons, individual national economies may be committed to producing net foreign surpluses beyond their need for reserves. One example already cited is that of countries like China that turn to foreign demand as an engine of output growth since they lack sufficient monetary and fiscal controls to manage their macroeconomies locally.[22]

Whatever the explanation, China has run large persistent net foreign surpluses as an adjunct to its domestic macro policy, and these must be absorbed by other nations in the global system.[23] Japan has also been in persistent surplus despite the advent of flexible exchange rates in 1971. It appears to regard itself as a resource-poor, highly vulnerable economy, the security of which depends on a powerful ability to sell its manufacturers to the world at large. The result has been a range of policies that through all domestic economic conditions has continued to produce net foreign surpluses, and again, these must be absorbed by the rest of the world. In other countries, most notably in Europe, powerfully entrenched interest groups in manufacturing (unions and management) and agriculture have been protected over many years in ways that have generated persistent net foreign surpluses. In agriculture this has been achieved by restricting import competition. In manufacturing, since domestic demand has been inadequate to support these large establishments, foreign demand has been an important target. To cite two examples, Germany and France (until very recently undermined by the rise in the euro) have had long-lasting foreign surpluses on current account.

These structural surpluses exacerbate the basic imbalance at the heart of the reserve currency system. As Keynes noted, deficits are self-limiting, as non-reserve countries run out of reserves. Surplus countries as long as they neutralize the domestic inflationary pressure of surpluses can go on forever. This is especially true in a flexible exchange rate world since surplus countries can always counteract the adverse consequences of rising pressure on exchange rates by selling their own currencies, which they possess in unlimited supply.

We have already noted another source of excess global demand for surpluses is the experience of countries like Korea, Thailand, and Indonesia—and those who have learned from their experiences. Having suffered the consequences of persistent deficits, these nations are likely to embrace policies (e.g. low exchange rates) that engender persistent surplus as a precautionary matter. By doing so, they exacerbate the problem of global balance and, in particular, of US deficits.

Having looked at the equilibrium system described by equations (1) and (2) from the perspective of net foreign surplus (NFS), it is relatively straightforward to examine the domestic macroeconomic consequences of global interactions. In the reserve currency country, the result is chronic deflationary pressure which must be offset by aggressive monetary and fiscal policy, except when, by coincidence, the country otherwise would have been confronted with a period of excess demand. That was the situation confronting the US in the 1990s. Irrational exuberance, then based on the internet bubble, was so great that in spite of the trade deficit, the economy could maintain itself at full employment. (It benefited, too, from the deflation in China, combined with its stable exchange rate, which enabled the US to have low manufacturing prices even with low levels of unemployment. It was not the careful conduct of monetary policy in the US that led to the benign confluence of high growth and low inflation, but the overinvestment in competitive manufacturing in China.)

In non-reserve currency countries, sudden changes in $\{v_i, p_i\}$—at home or abroad—can lead to sudden changes in exchange rates or reserves, with the potential of Asia-type crises.

What we have ignored, of course, is the mutual interaction of domestic and international policies. They can be summarized as follows:

1. The efficacy and stability of the present system depends on continuing and growing US foreign payment deficits.

2. These foreign payments deficits exert a powerful deflationary effect on the US domestic economy, which can only be offset by aggressive US government fiscal and monetary policy.

3. These difficulties are exacerbated by chronic surplus countries whose behavior is difficult to control within the context of the current system.

4. These surplus countries tend to export deflationary tendencies not only to the United States but also to other industrial economies.

This list elucidates many of the shortcomings of the current dollar reserve currency system. One final shortcoming of the present system should be noted. As the US increasingly becomes the deficit country of last resort, the world becomes increasingly awash with dollars. This is an unavoidable consequence of the present system and the economic behaviors of powerful participating nations.[24] Nevertheless, the flood of dollars inevitably undermines confidence in the value of the dollar which, in turn, contributes to exchange rate instability and concern in national economies about the value of their increasing level of dollar holdings. The result is an increased level of concern and potential instability that it would be useful to alleviate.

Equity[25]

While the global reserve system has contributed to weaknesses in the global economy and to its instability, it is a system that is particularly unfair to developing countries. They suffer particularly from the instability—especially given the failure of international financial markets in shifting risk to the rich. But while they pay a high cost from the failure of the system to produce stability, they also pay a high dollar cost directly in the way the system is run.

In effect, the system allows the US to have access to a ready supply of cheap credit. This has resulted in the most peculiar situation noted earlier where the world's richest country is living well beyond its means, borrowing from countries far poorer. Just as risk should move from the poor to the rich, but is not, so too capital should flow from the rich to the poor—but in fact is moving in the opposite direction.[26]

There is essentially a net transfer from developing countries to the richest country in the world, as the poor countries make low interest loans to the United States (often reborrowing some of the money at much higher interest rates.)[27] Obviously, these net transfers—which exceed the value of the aid many of the poor countries receive from the US—have adverse consequences for the countries' growth.[28]

The cost to developing countries of holding dollar reserves in recent years has been very high. China, for instance, has earned (in terms of its own currency) a return, which must be close to zero, or even negative, with the interest not compensating for the depreciation of the value of the dollar. Surely, there are investments in their own country that would yield a higher return. Developing countries maintain such large holdings in part at least because the cost of not having these holdings is even greater—the risk of a crisis, with the attendant possibility of the loss of national economic sovereignty.

The weakening of the dollar has had a profound effect in changing mindsets about reserves. The dollar is increasingly no longer viewed as a good store of value. It has heightened a focus on reserve management, and this in turn shifts attention towards portfolio diversification. Concern about low returns from holding Treasury bills has motivated the formation of sovereign wealth funds, which, while they might rectify the inequities associated with differential returns, have in turned heightened protectionist sentiments.

But as the example of China makes clear, there are multiple motivations for large reserve holdings. The reserve holdings may be the result of a foreign exchange rate policy, with growth benefits identified earlier. In estimating the *net* cost of reserve holdings, one has to subtract out the ancillary benefits.

A simple reform proposal

The primary goals of any international monetary reform should be to alleviate these problems by: (i) decoupling reserve accumulation from the deficit positions of any reserve currency countries; (ii) providing some means of disciplining surplus countries; and (iii) providing a more stable store of international value than the dollar or any other reserve currency. In addition, an international monetary reform should be equitable—with the benefits of any seignorage arising from reserves shared equitably.

One way to do this would be to issue special drawing rights (SDRs) on a substantial and regular basis as a non-reserve currency source of international reserves. Current international reserves are about $3,000 billion. Assuming the demand for reserves increases at the average rate of world trade (about 7 per cent), an annual issue of $200 billion in SDRs would satisfy any demand for reserve accumulation without a US payments deficit. The reserves could be simply credited to the IMF accounts of current member countries in proposition to their current IMF fund positions.

Since SDRs are valued as a weighted average of all convertible currencies, their value is largely stable in the face of changing exchange rates. Thus, as SDRs become more widely available as a source of reserves, they might ultimately serve as a stable international unit of account for pricing international commodities such as oil.

Finally, SDR allocations could serve as a basis for partially offsetting the externalities generated by chronic surplus countries. SDR allocations could be taxed at a rate of 50 per cent (or some other appropriate fraction) per unit of current account surplus up to the full amount of a country's allocation. The resulting SDR taxes could then be used as a source of global financial aid to be distributed among developing countries (which might then be required to subscribe to a set of "good government" principles—e.g. nuclear non-proliferation—to qualify for such distributions).

One could view the new reserve system as a form of cooperative mutual help. The international community would be providing entitlements to automatic "help" in times of crisis, allowing the country to spend beyond its means and beyond what international financial markets are willing to lend, as each country guarantees that the new reserve currency could be converted into their own currency.

Political economy of reform: incentive compatibility

In the limited space available here, we cannot discuss the political economy of reform. Suffice it to say that since the gains to all—including the United States—are significant (described more fully in the next section), there should be widespread support. But as an alternative, the reform could be implemented in a piecemeal manner, as a group of countries agreed to the new system, and agreed that those who join the system would gradually move toward holding only the new reserve currency and the currencies of other members of the "club," as reserves. If enough countries joined the "club" there would be an incentive for any country that currently is a reserve currency (and believes that it gains from being a reserve currency) to join the club too.

Here is how the club might work. Every year, each of the members of the "club" would contribute a stipulated amount to the GRF (global reserve fund), and at the same time, the GRF would issue "global greenbacks" of equivalent value to the country, which they would hold in their reserves. There is no change in the net worth of any country; it has acquired an asset (a claim on others) and issued a claim on itself. Something real has happened, however: it has obtained an asset, which it can use in times of an emergency. (And at the same time, it has agreed to let others call upon its resources in times of emergency.)

Normally, of course, except for the cost of holding reserves, these exchanges of pieces of paper make no difference. Each country goes about its business in the same way as it did before. It conducts monetary and fiscal policy much as it did before. Even in times of emergency, life looks much as it did before. Consider, for instance, an attack on the currency. Before, the country would have sold dollars (buying up its own currency) to support the value of its currency. (Whether such intervention makes sense is not a question we address here.) And it can continue to do that so long as it has dollars in its reserves (or it can obtain dollars from the IMF). Now, it exchanges the global greenbacks for conventional hard currencies to support its currency.[29, 30]

Because each country is holding global greenbacks, each no longer has to hold dollars or euros as reserves, and for the global economy, this has enormous consequences, both for the (former) reserve currency countries and for global economic stability. The deflationary pressure noted earlier would no longer be present, because each country would no longer have to "bury in the ground" some of its purchasing power. Reserve currency countries, whose "exports" of IOUs are matched by a current account trade deficit, would no longer face the systematic deflationary bias of net imports.

For a country like the United States, which has been tempted to have large fiscal deficits because of the low cost of financing these deficits, the enhanced discipline would contribute to long-term fiscal probity. If it ran huge deficits year after year, it almost surely would face higher and higher real interest rates.

Cost and benefits of a revised system

Such a system appears likely to benefit all participants in the global financial system. Superficially, the greatest "loser" would be the United States, which would at least partially forego its monopoly on issuing paper claims for real goods and services. However, the UK enjoyed such a partial monopoly prior to Bretton Woods, and Keynes rightly recognized that it represented a very mixed blessing. The benefits of seignorage were perhaps more than offset by the adverse consequences of chronic net foreign deficits through their deflationary effect on the domestic UK macroeconomy. The United States has avoided many of these effects by running large, persistent government deficits to sustain full employment, but that policy too has potential adverse consequences. Keynes' immediate solution for the UK's situation was to offload the dubious benefits of reserve currency status on the United States. However, he ultimately envisioned a system similar to that outlined above (including discipline imposed on chronic surplus countries).

The euro community, to the extent that it too envisaged becoming a reserve currency, might also be said to suffer. However, its recently ambiguous experience with the rise of the euro appears to have qualified its enthusiasm for the chronic deficit position associated with reserve currency status.

Foreign central banks concerned with the stability of the value of their dollar holdings would benefit in three ways. First, the creation of SDR reserves would provide an alternative store of value, which would at a minimum diversify their reserve holdings. At best SDRs would provide a far more stable store of value than any individual currency. Second, the issue of SDRs would reduce the demand for dollar reserves and reduce the US current account deficit. This would reduce the continuing downward pressure on the value of dollar holdings (although there might be a significant interim adjustment in the value of the dollar). Third, an external source of liquidity should alleviate some of the pressure of competition to acquire reserves, which should help stabilize international payment and exchange rate dynamics.

With the annual issuance of these new reserves, the adverse consequences of the fact that the sum of deficits equals the sum of surpluses would be broken: any country could run a deficit equal to its receipts of new reserves without worrying about a crisis.[31] The "hot potato" problem would be reduced, if not fully solved.[32]

The fact that each country receives an annual emission of global greenbacks means that it can import more than it exports without facing an imminent crisis. So long as imports do not exceed exports by more than the emissions, its reserves are actually increasing, and so there would be little anxiety of a crisis occurring.[33] Because of the fact that under this system the cost of holding reserves appears lower,[34] reserves may be higher (especially for developing countries), so that even when imports exceed exports by more than the value of the emissions, crises may be less frequent.

The greater financial stability of developing countries would enhance their ability to issue debt in their own currency—thereby reducing at least exchange rate risks (one of the major sources of problems in developing countries).

All economies, not just the United States, should benefit from the reduction in the deflationary bias of the current system.[35] And clearly the way the deflationary bias is addressed is far more equitable than under the current system.

Finally, having a significant source of automatic purchasing power transferable to well-functioning developing economies would support economic development far more effectively than the current patchwork of national and multinational aid programs.

The evolving reserve system

The essential requirement of a reserve currency is that it be a good store of value. This is why inflation has always been viewed so negatively by central bankers. But the credibility of a currency as a reserve currency depends also on exchange rates. For foreign holders of dollars, a weakening of the exchange rate is as bad as an increase in inflation. This is, in a sense, even true for domestic wealth holders; because of opportunity costs, even citizens of a country with a stable exchange rate may want to diversify out of holding assets denominated in that country's currency if there is high instability.

For most of the last part of the twentieth century, US dollars have been used as the world's de facto reserve currency. But the current system is under threat from negative dynamics: confidence in the dollar erodes, causing people to move out of the currency, and as they do so, the currency is further weakened. While the huge fiscal and trade deficits of the Bush Administration have contributed to this weakening, the problem for the US dollar is partly inherent; the Bush Administration simply accelerated what would have eventually happened in any case. The reserve currency country naturally becomes increasingly indebted, because the ease of selling debt entices over-borrowing. Others want to hold Treasury bills; it is tempting to respond to the demand with an increase in supply. But eventually, debt levels get so high that credibility starts to be questioned.

This may well be happening today. Certainly there has been a major shift in thinking among central banks. Over the years, they have gone from thinking that a currency needs gold as backing to thinking that sterling is required to back their currency, to thinking that dollars should back their currency. But now, they realize what matters is wealth. They no longer rely solely on the dollar for their reserves, as they have realized that the dollar is not a good store of value, and are beginning to manage their reserves as a more diversified portfolio, which is sensitive to risk and return. With multiple hard currencies to choose from, central banks may find it prudent to hold reserves in multiple currencies—or even in other assets. And as the US dollar appears more risky, they will naturally continue to shift out of dollars—a process which is already well under way.[36]

But this shift out of the dollar reserve system is not necessarily a smooth one. Now, investors have to think not only about how other investors are thinking, but also about how central banks are changing their perceptions of risk and reserve policy.[37]

A multiple reserve currency system?

Having a two-reserve currency system is *not* a solution. Some in Europe had hoped that the euro would take on this role as a reserve currency. This has happened, at least to some extent, but it has not been good for Europe or the world.

As the euro becomes a reserve currency, Europe too then faces a deflationary bias. Given its institutional structure, a central bank focusing exclusively on inflation and a growth and stability pact restricting the use of expansionary fiscal policy, there are doubts about whether Europe is able to respond effectively to the consequences of having a reserve currency. If it does not, Europe, and the world, may face strong contractionary pressures.

Moreover, just as the bimetallic system was viewed as more unstable than the gold standard, a multiple reserve currency system may be more unstable—with rapid shifts from one reserve currency to another with changing perceptions.

Europe—and the world—should hope that it does not get its wish, to become a global reserve currency; but rather, that the world move to a new global reserve system, along the lines we have proposed.

Concluding remarks

It should be clear that the current global reserve system is not working well, that it is contributing to the current high level of exchange rate volatility, and that this volatility has adverse effects on the global economic system. It is essential for the functioning of the global economic system that the global financial system functions well. The global financial system and the global reserve system are changing rapidly, but one should question whether they are changing in ways which will enhance global economic stability.

Certainly events of the last decades give us reason to pause and reflect on the weaknesses of the existing financial system. We have witnessed repeated crises and high levels of global financial instability—in spite of the fact that we have (supposedly) increased our understanding of how financial markets work, created new financial instruments to manage risk, and strengthened markets from an institutional perspective to help them perform better. The developing countries in particular have experienced enormous instability, which has come at great cost to the people in those regions. Some of that instability is a result of instabilities in the global financial system and of the failure of markets to effectively shift risk to the developed countries, which could, on a relative basis, bear it better.

There has been a great debate about allocating blame—the relative role of structural versus macroeconomic factors. Here, we have highlighted one aspect of the global economic system, which we believe has received too little attention—the global reserve system. We have suggested a simple reform to the global reserve system, which holds out the promises of greater stability, higher output, and enhanced equity. It is, in some ways, an old idea—but perhaps an idea whose time has finally come.

Notes

1. An earlier version of this chapter was presented as a keynote address to the International Economic Association in Istanbul, Turkey, June 25–29, 2008. The authors are indebted to the Ford, Macarthur, and Hewlett Foundations for financial support. The authors are grateful to Giselle Guzmán for research assistance. All equations have been estimated and graphs generated with Eviews by Quantitative Micro Software, LLC.
2. Columbia University.
3. Columbia University, Co-President of the Initiative for Policy Dialogue and Visiting Professor at University of Manchester.
4. See the Commission of Experts of the President of the UN General Assembly on Reforms of the International Monetary and Financial System website for more information <http://www.un.org/ga/president/63/commission/background.shtml>.
5. The term "net savings" is used to note that some individuals may be dissaving, some individuals may save part of the year and dissave other parts of the year, and still others may be saving. What matters for the national income accounts is the net savings of the private sector. Conceptually, we should have a parallel analysis for the public sector, in which case investment would include both private and public investment. Later, however, we interpret the model using standard data, in which there is no distinction between government consumption and investment. The fiscal

deficit is the difference between government expenditures (whether investment or not) and government revenue.

6. There are other partial equilibrium stories that one can tell. We discuss one in the next section. Another, discussed in Ocampo et al. (2009), focuses on movements in private and public sector deficits.

7. Empirical research rejects Ricardian equivalence in its pure form, although some studies have found Ricardian effects in saving behavior. For a technical review of the literature, see Briotti (2005).

8. Note that in Figure 17.5, the pre-1990 figures are for West Germany while the post figures are for unified Germany.

9. A variable X is said to Granger cause another variable Y if lagged values of X provide statistically significant information about future values of Y.

10. In the case of the other countries, even though there is no strong relationship, we can still ask the (obviously weak) direction of causation. In the case of the US and all other countries, except Italy, we cannot reject the hypothesis that the trade deficit is causing the fiscal deficit. See Appendix 17.1.

11. NPS includes corporate as well as household savings. While household savings was zero, corporate savings was moderate—though far less than aggregate investment. (Investment includes housing.)

12. A savings glut reflects a gap between savings and investment—which can arise either because of high savings or low investment. The current problem seems generated more by the latter—what Ocampo has called investment anemia.

13. International Monetary Fund, International Financial Statistics; Rodrik (forthcoming).

14. In fact, the price paid for accumulating reserves may be less than seems apparent. The accumulation of reserves helps depress exchange rates, which increases exports and growth. See Greenwald and Stiglitz (2006).

15. Behavior may depend in important ways on other important variables, most notably on expectations of changes in the exchange rate.

16. In fact, some countries may determine their exchange rate accumulations to target an exchange rate, even under a flexible exchange rate system.

17. It is natural to use this general equilibrium approach to ask: what accounts for the deteriorating value of the dollar? It appears that to accommodate the *same* trade deficit, the dollar has to be weaker; this suggests a weakening of the demand for US exports *at a given exchange rate*. Since inflation in the US and most of its competitors has been relatively low and differences in inflation rates small, while US growth has been slower than that of the global economy, this suggests a shift downward for the demand for US exports. As we argue below, we can expect a reduced demand for dollars as a reserve currency, and this would suggest a further deterioration of the exchange rate.

18. As an example of the complexity introduced by dynamics, consider the impact of lowering interest rates in the US (the reserve country). This increases income (in the standard Keynesian model, if the economy is not at full employment); and while income in the non-reserve country also increases, it increases by less. For the US trade deficit to remain at the same level (to fulfill foreign demand for reserves) requires a fall in the exchange rate. There is an intertemporal arbitrage equation—the difference in reserve and non-reserve interest rates must be equal to the expected rate of appreciation. But to determine the latter, we have to

specify expectations about the values of all the relevant variables in future periods.

19. A dynamic model would emphasize another effect: the increased deficit may lead to lower confidence in the country's currency. The expectation of inflation may lead to a decrease in demand for the currency (at the current exchange rate), thereby leading to a lower exchange rate.

20. This is a much weaker assumption than assuming approximate long-term balance in national private capital accounts. It effectively requires only that the US not be the target of global foreign investment over the long term. Moreover, allowing for net private capital flows would complicate the analysis without altering its basic implications. See endnote 14.

21. These results highlight the role that the simplification that net private flows are zero plays in the analysis. A country could increase its reserves by borrowing abroad, with the immediate implication that the change in the demand for foreign reserves results in no change in the value of NFS_N. If the borrowing is done by the government, the transaction is a wash, and any appearance of an increase in reserves is simply an accounting deception. Presumably, private flows are determined by values of relevant variables (incomes, exchange rates, expectations of these variables, etc.) but *not* by government demand for reserves. It is possible that changes in government demands for reserves induce changes in these variables in ways which affect net private flows that partially offset the official flows, thus mitigating to some extent the magnitude of the effects to which this paper calls attention. In recent years, some have argued that developing countries should have reserve policies which make reserves endogenous: as short-term private sector flows increase, then government reserves should increase in tandem. It is clear that while a few low income countries follow this policy, most of the increase in reserves in recent years is related to an increase in the demand for reserves (e.g. by the East Asian countries), and that the increase in the demand for reserves has (in total) not been fully offset by an increase in private flows. Some of the reserves may be viewed as "borrowed," but not all. Of course, even when reserves are borrowed, there are important implications for the stability of the system (the nature of the obligations mean that though the net flows may be zero, what is going on is not a wash.)

22. An alternative interpretation is that by distorting their economy towards exports and manufacturing, they increase their capacity to "learn," to absorb technology from more advanced industrial countries. While these benefits first touch the export sectors, they quickly diffuse throughout the economy. Elsewhere, we have referred to this as the "infant economy" argument for protection, and we have argued that maintaining an "undervalued" exchange rate may be an efficient way of implementing such policies. See Greenwald and Stiglitz (2006).

23. The data may, however, exaggerate the magnitude of these surpluses because of over-invoicing of exports and under-invoicing of imports.

24. See also Triffin (1960).

25. Concerns about the equity (as well as instability) of the global reserve system have, of course, been raised by many from the developing world. See, for instance, Ocampo (2007) and the references cited there. See also Stiglitz (2006) and the references cited there.

26. Some have argued that being a reserve currency facilitates its ability to borrow in its own currency and to have more independence in the conduct of macro policy. While it is true that the fact that the United States borrows in its own currency allows it more freedom of action, many non-reserve currencies have long borrowed in their own currencies.

27. In a sense, the inequities are even more transparent in the case of "borrowed reserves" noted earlier—for instance, in poor countries that have to increase their reserves to offset increases in short-term private liabilities.

28. The inequities are increased further by the way that the international financial system has been run, with pro-cyclical monetary and fiscal policies being forced on developing countries (e.g. by IMF/World Bank conditionality), while the developed countries pursue counter-cyclical monetary and fiscal policies. This increases the riskiness of the periphery relative to the center, reinforces the pro-cyclical patterns of private capital flows that simultaneously are used to justify the differential treatment and exacerbate fluctuations in developing countries, and increase interest rate differentials. See, for example, Soros (2009).

29. There is an important detail: the exchange rate between global greenbacks and various currencies. In a world of fixed exchange rates (the kind of world for which the SDR proposal was first devised) this would not, of course, be a problem; in a world of variable exchange rates, matters are more problematic. So long as global greenbacks are held only by central banks, there is no real problem of speculation, so that the "official" exchange rate could differ from market exchange rates. One could use current market rates; alternatively, the official exchange rate, for instance, could be set as the average of the exchange rates over the preceding three years. In such a case, to avoid central banks taking advantage of discrepancies between current market rates and the official exchange rate, restrictions could be imposed on conversions (for instance, such conversions could only occur in the event of a crisis, defined by a major change in the country's exchange rate, output, or unemployment rate).

30. We envision global greenbacks only being held by central banks, but a more ambitious version of this proposal would allow global greenbacks to be held by individuals, in which case there would be a market price for global greenbacks, and the government could simply treat the global greenbacks as any other "hard" currency.

31. Of course, the sum of deficits would still have to equal the sum of surpluses: this is an identity.

32. Clearly, our proposal does not solve all of the problems leading to global instability of the financial system. We have already called attention to the important asymmetries in policy responses (pro-cyclical in developing countries, counter-cyclical in developed countries). Countries with fully open capital accounts will still be afflicted with pro-cyclical private capital flows. Our proposal would reduce (though not necessarily eliminate) the necessity of developing countries creating offsetting reserves, with the associated costs already noted. One could go further, as Ocampo (2007) and Ocampo et al. (2009) have done, in developing counter-cyclical allocations of global greenbacks.

33. Crises can also be precipitated by short-term dollar denominated liabilities exceeding reserves (see Furman and Stiglitz, 1998, and the references cited there); but again,

because countries are likely to hold more reserves, it is less likely that this too will occur.

34. In some sense, there is still an opportunity cost: if there were no restriction of the kind set forth in the previous footnote, then the country could have converted the global greenbacks into dollars and used the dollars to purchase productive assets.

35. By the same token, the annual issuance of SDRs would not be inflationary— it would just undo the existing deflationary bias of the current system.

36. To the extent that motivation of holding reserves was to keep the exchange rate with the dollar low, countries may have limited scope for reallocating portfolios. They have to keep in dollar-denominated assets. Even as they began to shift out of dollars, the emphasis on portfolio management to which we drew attention earlier has led them to move out of Treasury bills into other dollar-denominated assets. This, in turn, has raised other concerns, most forcefully in the context of the debate over sovereign wealth funds.

37. Changes in central bank holdings, or market perceptions of central bank holdings, may contribute to instability; but in fact, central bankers are likely to be less volatile in their behavior than private market participants.

Bibliography

Briotti, G. (2005) 'Economic Reactions to Public Finance Consolidation: A Survey of the Literature.' European Central Bank Occasional Paper No. 38 (October).

Furman, J. and Stiglitz, J. E. (1998) 'Economic Crises: Evidence and Insights from East Asia.' *Brookings Papers on Economic Activity*, 1998(2), pp. 1–114.

Greenwald, B. and Stiglitz, J. E. (2006) 'Helping Infant Economies Grow: Foundations of Trade Policies for Developing Countries.' *American Economic Review: AEA Papers and Proceedings*, 96(2), pp. 141–6.

International Monetary Fund (various) *International Financial Statistics*.

Ocampo, J. A. (2007) 'The Instability and Inequities of the Global Reserve System.' *International Journal of Political Economy*, 36(4), pp. 71–96.

—— Rada, C., and Taylor, L. (2009) *Growth and Policy in Developing Countries: A Structuralist Approach*. New York: Columbia University Press.

Rodrik, D. (2000) 'The Social Cost of Foreign Exchange Reserves.' *International Economic Journal*, 20(3), pp. 253–66.

Stiglitz, J. E. (2006) *Making Globalization Work*. New York: WW Norton.

Soros, G. (2009) 'Testimony before the Senate Foreign Relations Committee Hearing on "Foreign Policy and the Global Financial Crisis."' March 25, 2009.

Triffin, R. (1960) *Gold and the Dollar Crisis*. New Haven: Yale University Press.

A Modest Proposal

Appendix 17.1 Relationships between current account balances and government balances

	Observations	F-Statistic	Probability[1]
FR_GB_PGDP does not Granger Cause FR_CA_PGDP	26	0.97237	0.3343
FR_CA_PGDP does not Granger Cause FR_GB_PGDP		0.80137	0.3800
GE_GB_PGDP does not Granger Cause GE_CA_PGDP	26	0.39029	0.5383
GE_CA_PGDP does not Granger Cause GE_GB_PGDP		0.69059	0.4145
IT_GB_PGDP does not Granger Cause IT_CA_PGDP	26	1.57813	0.2216
IT_CA_PGDP does not Granger Cause IT_GB_PGDP		12.7867	0.0016
JP_GB_PGDP does not Granger Cause JP_CA_PGDP	26	0.47538	0.4974
JP_CA_PGDP does not Granger Cause JP_GB_PGDP		0.02899	0.8663
UK_GB_PGDP does not Granger Cause UK_CA_PGDP	26	1.42696	0.2444
UK_CA_PGDP does not Granger Cause UK_GB_PGDP		2.12446	0.1585
US_GB_PGDP does not Granger Cause US_CA_PGDP	26	0.01131	0.9162
US_CA_PGDP does not Granger Cause US_GB_PGDP		0.16075	0.6922

[1] Probability of rejecting the Null hypothesis.

Index

Index

Emerging Markets Bond Index 256
junk bonds 71

Kaldor-Verdoorn law 262
Kalekian-structuralist model 261
Kane, Ed 57
Keynes, John Maynard, *The General Theory of Employment, Interest and Money* 101, 270
Kindleberger, Charles 52
King, Mervyn 173
Kohn, Donald 197
Kongwa Groundnut scheme 52, 60
Korea 233
  non-resident equity holdings 224
  property price increases 225
Kupiec, Paul 179

last resort
  consumer of 327
  deficit of 327
  lender of 54, 78, 104, 127, 201
Latin America
  capital flows 222
  current account balance 222
  debt crisis 23, 292, 300
  reserves 222
  US lending to 1
Latin American Reserve Fund 308
legal action 59
Lehman Brothers 25, 76, 77, 104, 118, 187, 256
lender of first resort 78
lender of last resort 54, 78, 104, 127, 201
lending 106
  against assets with credit risk 121
  predatory 21
lending rate 78
leverage 158
  excessive 3
leveraged capital flows 130–2
LIBOR 107, 119, 181, 188
liquidity 129–30, 143–6
  creation of 71
  and credit default swaps 196–7
  cross-border provision 117–20

demand 270–2
excess 20
funding of 157
global management 214
increased 77
international 270–4
in market-based system 144–6
regulation by central banks 113–15
liquidity crisis
  central bank assistance 104–8
  government involvement 103–4
  origins of 101–3
  role of central bank 103–4
  role of regulators 103–4
  stages of 104
liquidity policies
  acceptance of illiquid paper as collateral 120
  CGFS recommendations 108–9
  counterparties 120–1
  drawbacks of 109–13
    avoidance of credit losses 111
    central bank replacing market 112
    central bank taking government responsibilities 110
    contamination of monetary policy 110
    inadvertent aid to failing banks 111–12
    moral hazard 112–13
  lending against assets with credit risk 121
  outright purchase of government bonds 121–2
  outright purchase of private sector assets 121
  permanent measures 115–20
    cross-border liquidity provision 117–20
    increased term financing 115–16
    wider deposit arrangements for banks 116–17
liquidity principle 73
loans
  Alt-A 71
  direct vs bail-outs 89

353

transparency (*cont.*)
  lack of 92
Treasury bill rate 78
Triffin dilemma 272, 290, 305
Triffin, Robert 272, 290
Troubled Asset Relief Program
  (TARP) 93–4, 188
twin deficits theory 316–23

unemployment insurance 79
unified banking systems 72
United Kingdom
  Association of Corporate Treasurers 166
  current account/government
    balances 319
  Financial Services Authority 114,
    137, 162
United Nations
  Commission on the Reform of the
    Global Monetary and Financial
    System 314
  Conference on Trade and
    Development 258
Universal Banking Systems 5, 55
US monetary crisis 3–6, 19–49
  failure of financial systems 31–3
  financial reforms 33–43
    improving incentives 34–7
    information, accounting and capital
      adequacy frameworks 37–9
    regulatory structures 39–43
  incentive problems 21–8
    Bernanki-Greenspan put 24–5
    credit freeze 25–6
    executive compensation systems 21
    fraud 26–7
    incentives for accounting firms 21–2
    rating agency incentives 23
    repeal of Glass-Steagall 24
    securitization 22–3
    transparency and complexity 26
  modeling problems 28–31
    diversification 28

intellectual incoherence 30–1
Ponzi schemes 29–30
systemic risk 28–9
source of 20–33
USA
  current account deficit 293–5
  current account/government
    balances 318
  economic stimulus 80–1
  Employee Retirement Income Security
    Act (ERISA) 132
  Federal Reserve *see* Federal Reserve
  Federal Reserve Act (1913) 145
  independent monetary policy 290
  Latin American loans 1
  monetary crisis *see* US monetary
    crisis
  national banking system 4
  New Deal legislation 4
  prudential regulation 62–3
  real exchange rate 293–4
  Securities and Exchange
    Commission 165
  trade deficit 329
  Treasury Blueprint for Financial
    Regulatory Reform 136–7
  unemployment insurance 5

value-accounting 8
Vietnam, property price increases 225
vulnerability 42

wealth distribution 92–3
White Plan 282, 285
White, William 128
wholesale markets 101
Williamson, John 262
Wolf, Martin 136
World Bank 39
  'Private Capital Flows to Developing
    Countries: The Road to Financial
    Integration' 48
WorldCom 24, 32, 37